Violence and Crime in
Cross-National Perspective

VIOLENCE AND CRIME IN CROSS-NATIONAL PERSPECTIVE

Dane Archer and Rosemary Gartner

YALE UNIVERSITY PRESS
New Haven and London

*For the future and, in particular,
for Zachary, Nathaniel, and Cameron*

Published with assistance from the foundation established in memory of Henry Weldon Barnes of the Class of 1882, Yale College.

Designed by Nancy Ovedovitz and set in Baskerville type. Printed in the United States of America by Edwards Brothers, Inc., Ann Arbor, Michigan.

Library of Congress Cataloging in Publication Data

Archer, Dane.
　Violence and crime in cross-national perspective.
　Bibliography: p.
　Includes index.
　1. Crime and criminals—History—20th century—Cross-cultural studies.
　2. Violent crimes—History—20th century—Cross-cultural studies.
　I. Gartner, Rosemary.　II. Title.
HV6030.A73　1984　　　364'.042　　　83–21700
ISBN 0–300–03149–1

The paper in this book meets the guidelines for permanence and durability of the Committee on Production Guidelines for Book Longevity of the Council on Library Resources.

10　9　8　7　6　5　4　3　2　1

Contents

v

Tables and Figures

TABLES

FIGURES

Acknowledgments

Any attempt to assemble and examine cross-national crime data would be impossible without the support and kind assistance of many people. Our effort to collect and compare nearly a century of records from 110 societies has taken us roughly a decade. During these ten years, the project has been made possible by a variety of sources. One of the most precious qualities of academic life is time, and fellowships provided to the first author by the Guggenheim Foundation and the German Marshall Fund were indispensable to our success. Some early work with the Comparative Crime Data File was also supported by an award from the Center for Studies of Crime and Delinquency at the National Institutes of Mental Health (grant no. MH 27427).

In addition to these sources of support, our project depended on the much-appreciated but entirely uncompensated assistance of a very large number of individuals in the nations and cities for which we sought to assemble data. These individuals, too numerous to thank individually, were extremely generous in their contribution of both information and time. Within the United States, a number of people have contributed significant assistance to our work, including Mark Beittel, Marc Lieberman, Tom Phelan, Tim Lockwood, and Robin Akert. A number of distinguished and thoughtful scholars have commented on the project and individual studies using the CCDF. While the number of these contributions has been large, we are particularly grateful for suggestions made by Marvin E. Wolfgang, Thorsten Sellin, John I. Kitsuse, Donald R. Cressey, Wesley Skogan, Daniel Glaser, and Thomas Pettigrew. We are also extremely grateful for the contributions Mary Frances Archer has made to this project. Finally, we would like to thank Gladys Topkis and Elizabeth Casey for their uncommon patience and fine editorial vision.

I

COMPARATIVE EVIDENCE ON PATTERNS AND CAUSES OF CRIME

O N E

The Need for a Comparative Approach

This book is about crime and violence. What makes it unlike the very large number of studies of crime and violence already in existence is that it seeks to place these subjects in a cross-national perspective. The analyses and comparisons presented in this volume are based upon recorded patterns of crime and violence in 110 nations and 44 major international cities, covering the period from approximately 1900 to 1970. We call the data set upon which this project is based the Comparative Crime Data File (CCDF).

The plan of this work is straightforward. The creation and contents of the data archive are described in the first part of the book. In order to establish a context for later substantive chapters, these first chapters present a theoretical and methodological rationale for a cross-national approach to the study of crime and violence.

Chapters in part 2 attempt to use the CCDF to furnish some comparative insight into a series of specific questions about the pattern and etiology of violent crime. Some of these analyses center on questions which have lingered at the center of several social sciences for a considerable period. Others treat matters that have been untestable in the past. The final part presents the data set itself.

In preparing this work, we have attempted to serve four related ends: (1) to use our cross-national data to identify recurrent patterns in and some of the "causes" of violent crime; (2) to provide illustrative case studies of the kinds of investigation made possible by comparative research on violence; (3) to furnish a large data set of potential interest and value to investigators pursuing a wide range of emerging hypotheses; and (4) to present a series of admittedly rough guidelines intended to maximize the validity of future research designs in which these (and similar) comparative data can be employed.

THE NEED FOR A COMPARATIVE APPROACH

Research on crime and its causes has been lamentably insular. Systematic research on homicide, for example, has been limited to a handful of societies—chiefly the United States and Britain. The reason for this cultural bias has not been a lack of interest. The need for a truly comparative approach to the study of crime and violence has been recognized at least since the Belgian statistician Adolphe Quetelet pioneered the collection of crime data in the 1830s.

Although comparative research on crime has been impeded by several analytic problems, described in a later chapter, the principal obstacle has not been methodological. The field has suffered from a spectacular lack of international information. Social scientists simply have not had access to adequate historical (or "time series") data on rates of homicide and other offenses in a large sample of societies. What has been missing, in short, is information from many nations over many years. Without such a cross-national data base, rigorous comparative research necessarily has been in short supply. As a result, our understanding of the nature and causes of homicide and other offenses remains provincial at best and, at worst, simply wrong.

Without knowledge of the experiences of other societies, we are greatly limited in our ability to anticipate the effects of changes within our own society. In the absence of a comparative record against which to evaluate specific policies, our own efforts to deal with crime and violence are guided by intuition, untested theories, and political expediency. A medical analogy may be appropriate: it is as if physicians in our society were attempting to prevent polio by means of a vitamin treatment while physicians in other societies had long before identified and used an effective vaccine.

The need for cross-national comparisons seems particularly acute for research on crime and violence since national differences on these phenomena are of a remarkable magnitude. In some societies, homicide is an hourly, highly visible, and therefore somewhat unexceptional cause of death. In other nations, homicides are so infrequent that, when they do occur, they receive national attention and lasting notoriety. The size of these differences invites examination and efforts at explanation. In most contemporary industrial nations, similarities outweigh differences on many dimensions: life expectancy, family size, literacy rates, and so forth. This is clearly not the case with violent crime. These differences also may have implications for efforts to influence offense rates. Since some societies appear to have escaped or minimized the costs of crime and violence, they may contain the answers to dilemmas which other societies are confronting with methods that are ineffective or even counterproductive.

Cross-national comparisons of crime and violence also can provide the empirical foundation for tests of theories about crime, law, demography, and social change. Tests using comparative records can add to our knowledge about the social origins of crime and violence. Although explanations must exist for the dramatically high rates of violence in some societies and its near absence in others, these explanations are at present undeveloped and largely untestable. Despite some pioneering comparative efforts, our knowledge about the nature and causes of crime and violence remains disconcertingly provincial. It is possible, of course, that some of our conceptions about crime and violence will turn out to be well founded. Without rigorous cross-national comparisons, however, the generality of many propositions about crime and violence simply cannot be known.

An undesirably large part of existing research on crime and violence is grounded in the single case of the United States. In addition, research done outside the United States has frequently been done within the boundaries of a single society. The effects of these tendencies upon scientific rigor have been predictably limiting. The absence of comparative and longitudinal data on crime and violence has caused a proliferation of methods which are *known* to be of low analytic power and poor resistance to error. As an example, the field has been dominated by "cross-sectional" (i.e., nonlongitudinal) analyses. (The constraints inherent in this approach are described in some detail in chapter 3.) The empirical poverty and provincialism of the field has produced these formidable problems:

Generalization. It has been impossible to test the generality of a finding based on single-society research by means of replication in a sample of several societies. This has produced a scatter of single-nation observations, with little coherent notion of the degree to which they can be generalized.

Controlled Comparison. The absence of a sufficient number of cases (e.g., nations or cities) has hindered rigorous comparisons between those cases affected by some social change and "control" cases unaffected by the same change. Other types of controls are also of great potential importance—for instance, death penalty studies in which changes in homicide rates are compared to a control group of nonhomicide offenses. In general, adequate data for meaningful controls simply have not existed. This has precluded controlled or "quasi-experimental" comparisons, and researchers have had to settle for less powerful research designs.

Causal Inference. With longitudinal data unavailable, researchers have not been able to satisfy one of the classic requirements for making causal inferences: a temporal relationship among the variables under study. In the absence of continuous records on homicide and other offenses over time, it has not been possible to identify the factors which may precede changes in the rates of these offenses. This data scarcity has dictated the widespread use of cross-sectional designs, and these comparisons can be misleading or meaningless.

Mediation and Intervening Variables. Without a reasonably large sample of nations, it is impossible to discover whether certain variables may mediate the effects of a social change. For example, worsening unemployment might increase homicide rates in one type of economic system but not in another. As a result, individual case studies may appear (perhaps incorrectly) to contradict one another. Without a large sample of societies, a general pattern that explains or orders these different outcomes will never be seen.

Methodological Uncertainty. Finally, without an archive of broadly comparative and longitudinal crime data, some key methodological issues have been largely uninvestigable. For example, it has not been possible to assess the reliability of different crime indicators like the number of "offenses known" or the number of "arrests" using data from a number of societies. While different indicators of the same offense almost certainly bear some relationship to one another, and to the actual incidence of the offense, these relationships have been the subject of much conjecture but inadequate scrutiny. Uncertainties of this kind have prompted a number of running debates about what types of research designs are justifiable given the nature of crime data. In the absence of appropriate test data, these debates have remained largely theoretical.

In summary, the absence of a versatile, reasonably general record of cross-national data on crime and violence has impoverished both policy and science. In the arena of policy, we appear unable to discern the "causes" of crime and incapable of predicting the effects of specific policies. The absence of comparative data has also created a ceiling on the scientific progress of the disciplines which address crime and violence, including sociology, economics, political science, psychology, anthropology, and of course criminology.

Specific illustrations of these problems are, unfortunately, not difficult to find. For example, it has been suspected for centuries that wars might somehow produce a postwar increase in violent crime. As will be seen in chapter 4, this hypothesis dates back at least to the time of Erasmus, More, and Machiavelli. In the absence of cross-national and historical records on rates of homicide and other crimes, however, investigations of this hypothesis have been limited to isolated case studies such as the experience of a single nation after a single war. For example, the eminent criminologist Hermann Mannheim in 1941 published an entire book on the effects of war. Solely on the basis of the English experience after World War I, Mannheim concluded that wars did not produce postwar "waves" of homicide.

This conclusion, which appears to have been premature, provides an excellent illustration of the need for a comparative approach. Mannheim was evidently misled by generalizing from a single nation's experience—an experience which, unknown to him, was idiosyncratic. In most of the social sciences, a sample size as small as a single case is regarded as highly problematic. In research on crime and its causes, however, a sample size of one has been the rule rather than the exception. Without a larger sample of societies, it has not been possible to test the limits of generalization—just as Mannheim could not have known that the English case was atypical.

As a second example, consider the well-known but still curious phenomenon of urban crime rates. Using comparisons of large and small U.S. cities in a single year, researchers have established that larger cities have dramatically higher homicide rates. This conclusion has become one of the most generally accepted "findings" about violent crime. Virtually every criminology textbook dutifully reports that a city's absolute size is an excellent predictor of its homicide rate. Whether or not this assertion is generally true, it is a rather remarkable instance of ethno-. centrism in that it rests almost exclusively on American data; the effect of city size on homicide rates in other societies remains largely uninvestigated. Chapter 5 addresses this matter in some detail.

The subject of urban crime rates also contains an intriguing paradox. Even if it proves to be the case that larger cities *always* have higher homicide rates than smaller cities, can this difference be attributed to the absolute size of the larger cities? There is little conclusive historical evidence that urban homicide rates have increased as the cities have grown in size. This suggests the following paradox: How can the allegedly high homicide rates of large cities be explained if *not* by the growth of these cities from small to large size? The reason for our continuing ignorance on this question is again the frustrating absence of rich historical data on homicide in a broad cross-section of societies. What one would like to have in order to explore this paradox of urban crime is a cross-national file of historical data for large cities in many societies.

A third example is the "deterrence hypothesis"—the idea that specific qualities of criminal penalties (such as the certainty or severity of punishment) will affect whether or not an offense is committed. A classic instance concerns the deterrent value, if any, of the death penalty and this question is the focus of chapter 6. Many studies of this question have been severely flawed in design or limited in scope and, as a result, the effects of capital punishment remain disputed. Some researchers have made direct comparisons of the homicide rates of two states, one with the death penalty and one without it. Such cross-sectional comparisons cannot inform us about the longitudinal effects of imposing or abolishing the death penalty. Similarly, most deterrence studies have been confined to a single society. There are several complex issues inherent in any test of criminal deterrence but, as indicated in chapter 6, the presence of homicide data from a sample of societies can enable a researcher to construct previously impossible comparisons as a test of this important question.

There are many other areas in which our knowledge about homicide and crime generally is both deficient and culture-bound. Some of these areas are of fundamental importance both to scholars and to public policy makers. Here are a few examples of such unanswered or unexamined questions:

1. How do fluctuations in unemployment affect rates of homicide and other offenses?
2. How do major economic events such as recessions and depressions influence the incidence of specific offenses? If economic events do appear to affect crime rates, are the effects the same in capitalist and noncapitalist societies?
3. Are major social changes such as revolutions or coups d'état foreshadowed or followed by increases in acts of "private" violence?
4. The argument is sometimes made that all industrial societies have undergone dramatic crime rate increases. Are there any nations with *declining* rates of homicide and other crimes in the twentieth century?
5. What is the relationship between judicial or legislative change and crime rates? For instance, have changes in rules regarding admissible testimony resulted in changes in the reported incidence of rape?
6. Can cross-national data help us to gauge, or even predict, the likely consequences of specific changes in policy or law? For example, what crime rate changes, if any, have occurred in societies which have abolished (or reinstated) the death penalty for capital offenses?
7. Despite much speculation about the "causes" of crime, one suspects that different crimes may have quite different causes. Are crime "waves" uniform across all types of offenses, or do the rates of some offenses consistently increase at the same time that others decline?
8. Do changes in the extent of gun ownership in a society have an effect upon the rates of violent crimes? Do changes in the laws relating to weapons ownership have a discernible effect upon crime rates?
9. Since societies presumably vary in their incidence of violent crime, what are the patterns of this variation? For example, do "frontier" societies have high rates of violent crime? Do societies with relatively egalitarian distributions of wealth have low rates of property crime?

10. What are the effects of major demographic events? For example, what happens to a society's crime rates as the shape of its demographic "pyramid" changes—for example, as a "baby boom" population enters (or passes out of) young adulthood?

THE COMPARATIVE CRIME DATA FILE (CCDF)

Having charted a brief overview of this volume, it may be appropriate to confess that the scope and nature of this project have evolved in ways that were entirely unanticipated. At the outset, it was not our intent to create a cross-national data set like the CCDF. Instead, we had planned to locate and use an existing comparative data file to test a specific hypothesis concerning the effect of wars upon domestic violent crime rates in postwar societies. We then discovered that a comprehensive cross-national data file on rates of homicide and other offenses did not exist. With some trepidation, we decided to see if one could be created.

In 1972, we set out to assemble a cross-national file of longitudinal data on rates of homicide and four other offenses. The resulting archive, which we have called the Comparative Crime Data File (CCDF), now contains data on up to five offenses for 110 nations and 44 major international cities between the years 1900 and approximately 1970.

It soon became clear that the data archive we had assembled had research potential much greater than the particular question which had prompted its creation. The historical depth and comparative breadth of the CCDF exceeded even our most optimistic expectations. In the past few years, we have tried to use the records in the CCDF to address a number of classic and contemporary questions about the patterns and antecedents of violent crime. The results of these inquiries are presented in this volume.

Apart from the unique substantive concerns of these individual studies, it has been our hope that they could provide illustrations of the potential analytic power of the comparative approach which data like those in the CCDF can make possible. Although our own analyses are certain to contain limits of their own, we have attempted to illustrate the relative advantages of a data-rich, comparative approach to the study of crime and violence. As we conceive it, this approach seeks to combine distinctive features of the *scientific method* (controlled comparison, longitudinal analysis, replication, data quality control, etc.) with the principal objectives of *comparative analysis* (the search for cross-national consistencies, sensitivity to both patterns and exceptional cases, and an effort to explain cross-national differences).

Having outlined a project of such sweeping scope, it is perhaps prudent to add a few cautious qualifications. Some of these have to do with the nature and contents of the CCDF. First, although our cross-national data file begins in 1900, many of the records are discontinuous, and others exist only for more recent periods. Second, as a great many scholars have learned (sometimes to their considerable chagrin), societies vary—sometimes incommensurably—in the ways in which they define, act upon, and record the different behaviors included under the same crime label. For the unwary researcher, these differences pose a veritable methodological quicksand, and one must try to understand the limits of different types of comparison or lapse into serious error. For example, although simple comparisons across nations are extremely tempting, they are often of questionable value and murky methodological rigor.

Each of these concerns poses formidable problems which will be discussed in later chapters. With appropriate caution, some of these problems are readily solvable while others defy solution by all imaginable means. Throughout this project, one of our most important premises has been that while some cross-national comparisons clearly have meaning, there are some that do not.

The data file reproduced in part 3 can assist researchers in testing an almost infinite variety of hypotheses about crime and violence. With the file, we have included a parsimonious guide that lists the contents (years of data, time period covered, and specific offense categories) of each national and urban entry in the CCDF. One of our objectives has been to try to identify optimal research designs in terms of their resistance or immunity to various methodological problems. These issues and some pragmatic cautions to guide users of the CCDF are discussed in detail in chapter 3.

Some of the topics treated in this volume, such as the questions examined in chapter 3, are devoted to basic findings about the CCDF itself. These issues are internal to the data set and concern the methodological properties of rates of homicide and other offenses, matters of central interest to researchers of crime and violence. Other chapters reflect preliminary efforts to use the CCDF to examine more general questions—for example, the effect of various types of social change on a nation's rate of homicide. These studies are partly external to the CCDF, since they attempt to relate other variables to the crime data, but none could have been undertaken without the CCDF.

In each study, we have tried to be guided by a kind of "methodological parsimony." In each case, we have tried to answer a research question using the most widely understood, least esoteric method available. We believe that this strategy imposes the fewest restrictions on potential readers and users of the CCDF. This may be of particular importance since the problems of crime and violence are of interest to individuals in a large number of disciplines and professions who, presumably, vary in their taste for quantitative research.

Since this chapter argues the need for a comparative approach to the study of crime and violence, it seems appropriate to close with our own objectives in publishing the studies and the CCDF archive. In our less guarded moments, we sometimes imagine that publication of this volume in some finite way will help the study of crime and violence to come of age as a science. In addition, we hope that it will provide an antidote to the insular, ethnocentric, and predominantly nationalistic way in which our beliefs about crime and violence have been generated. Finally, it is our hope that this book will be the catalyst for a new, vigorous, and ground-breaking line of previously impossible investigations.

T W O

The Comparative Crime Data File (CCDF):
A History and Description

In assembling the Comparative Crime Data File, we sought to create an archive with both comparative breadth and historical depth. Although the CCDF eventually grew to include 110 national and 44 urban entries, with data for roughly 1900–70, we undertook the project with no idea that the archive would reach this size. Data collection occurred over approximately five years. We pursued several methods of obtaining information, particularly early in this period. While some methods proved generally more effective than others, certain approaches were appropriate for certain societies. Given the great variety of nations and cities for which we hoped to assemble data, it was perhaps inevitable that no single technique would prove adequate in all cases.

The principal sources from which the homicide data were collected were (1) correspondence with national and metropolitan government sources in virtually all nations in the world; (2) a painstaking search through annual statistical reports and other official documents of those nations which have (at least at some time) published annual crime data; and (3) secondary examination of the records kept by various national and international agencies.

Although all three methods generated entries for the CCDF, the first strategy was the most productive and also the most interesting. Our initial procedure was to contact the consulates and embassies that most nations maintain in the United States. Personnel in some of these offices were able to refer us to authorities or specific agencies in their home nations. When references of this kind were not obtainable, our next procedure was to send "blind" (i.e., not addressed to named individuals) letters to various ministries in each country. In general, we invented the names of specific government agencies (e.g., "the Department of Justice") without knowing whether they existed. Each letter explained that we were interested in studying changing levels of five specific offenses in several nations during the twentieth century. Our inquiry asked whether the recipient of the letter could provide or direct us to annual data on the offenses of homicide, assault, robbery, theft, and rape or other sex offenses between 1900 and 1970.

Our inquiry stressed that the offenses we listed might be American or Western categories and that their own records might well be organized under different headings. We emphasized that we were interested in seeing their recording categories in their original form. In addition to national data, the letter requested parallel data for a specific major city in the same country. The letter expressed our appreciation for any help the recipient could provide and offered to pay any photocopying costs incurred by our request.

In many cases, our initial inquiry produced a reply directing us to another agency; we then sent our request letter to the suggested source. In some cases, the initial letter failed to produce a response, even after several months. In these instances, we invented the name of a different agency and sent our request letter again. Because of this need for a second (and in many cases a third or fourth) letter, we sent out many successive waves of requests, totaling perhaps five hundred letters.[1] In most nations, the individuals we managed to contact were extremely cooperative and generous with their time, resources, and information. Many of them responded promptly with the information we had requested, and several sent more than we had asked for. Because our first contact rarely had information for both the nation and the large city, additional inquiries were usually necessary to obtain the urban data. In some cases, months passed without word, and then, unexpectedly, the information arrived. Agencies in a few nations placed us on the mailing list for their government's statistical annuals, and some of these publications continued to arrive years after our initial request for information.

Over a period of five years, the responses to our letters arrived from around the world in a seemingly limitless variety of shapes, sizes, languages, alphabets, letterheads, envelopes, and stamps. The data themselves took equally varied forms—booklets, penciled charts, entire volumes of national yearbooks, photocopies of published or unpublished lists, and massive typed or handwritten tables which unfolded like roadmaps. The variety reflected in the data was impressive, and the project quickly taught us how little we knew about political geography. We wrote to and received data from nations whose existence had been unknown to us prior to the project. In other cases, our ignorance about the situations of individual societies was underlined—when, for example, our correspondent referred to a set of data as for the "mainland" only. Without the aid of a political atlas, many of these comments would have been incomprehensible.

In some cases, the requested information arrived paired with a provocative national or political sentiment. For example, the Philippines Department of Justice letterhead read: "An orderly people make an enduring nation." Swaziland's envelope bore the legend: "Umhlaba

Uyimpilo Yetfhu—Wonge!" This was accompanied, fortunately, by the translation: "The soil is our greatest asset—help conserve it!" Many of the agencies responding to our inquiry furnished, in addition to the requested data, clarifications of their reporting procedures, informational pamphlets about their institutions and systems of justice, and various cautions about aspects of the data and their appropriate interpretation. Finally, almost all of our correspondents expressed great interest in our undertaking, and many asked to be informed of our results.

For many societies, there were indications that the information we received was not only unpublished but also untabulated prior to our request. The data we received from these societies were in the form of individually typed or even handwritten tables. Many correspondents were kind enough to construct their replies in English, and we began to appreciate just how difficult this must have been for some of them when we began receiving a flood of replies in a bewildering array of languages. In many of the letters we received, the only thing we could read was our own address at the top of the letter.

For the more frequently encountered languages, we were able to benefit from translations provided by helpful colleagues at the University of California. Less familiar languages posed greater problems; there were cases in which we could not recognize a single character in the entire correspondence. In these instances, we asked for and generally received assistance from appropriate embassy and consulate officials in the United States. Even after translation had been completed, some terminological problems remained. For example, it was often necessary to group the unique categories used by a nation under a more general rubric—for instance, a society might have as many as twelve distinct recording categories for homicides. Obviously, classifications of this kind can be difficult even when the literal meaning of a nation's recording categories has been translated.

Our primary goal, of course, was to assemble an orderly file of quantitative data on crime and violence to facilitate previously impossible comparative research. It is our expectation that much of the research which the CCDF makes possible will use the data in some form of aggregate analysis—that is, in a relatively dispassionate manner which emphasizes the data themselves more than the special characteristics of the historical period in which they were generated. This approach is, of course, an indispensable feature of most empirical research.

It seems vital to remember, however, that these comparative crime data were recorded across the moving history of changing societies. In some cases, this history spanned gradual changes in the political and social conditions of a nation. In other cases, it encompassed transformations so acute that it seems arguable whether the same nation existed before and after. When these historical events have been extremely dramatic or abrupt, it seems appropriate to consider whether and how the relatively fragile process of producing social indicators like crime data has been perturbed.

The letters and information we received with the requested crime records were an unanticipated but fascinating dividend of the data collection process. These documents provide an intriguing window on the histories of individual nations. Our correspondents sometimes volunteered information and opinions about the ways in which various national crises and changes could have altered the data they sent us. Some of these comments about dramatic events were made in a manner which seemed, to us, curiously understated. For example, our correspondent in Brunei wrote that some gaps in that nation's data were "due to various factors including a rebellion in 1962." Our correspondent in Denmark wrote, almost as an aside, a single sentence about what must have been one of the most desperate periods in his nation's long history: "We wish to add that the Danish police statistics date back to 1921 but are missing as far as the years 1944 and 1945, 'the policeless years,' are concerned." Similarly, our correspondent from West Germany noted that although other types of crime statistics had been maintained for an extended period, the police began making their own record of crimes for the first time under the German Reich in 1936.

Correspondents in other societies also commented on long-term changes which had affected or even transformed their nations. Some of this information was indispensable to understanding the data they sent us. Our Hungarian correspondent, for example, drew our attention to the Treaty of Trianon, which in 1920 stripped his nation of two-thirds of its area and population. Officials in other nations commented on the impact of chronic political conflict on records of crime. For example, the commander of Israel's Criminal Investigation Department commented on the periodic wars and guerrilla actions that his nation had experienced: "Even if a record had been kept of all incidents of murder, manslaughter, assault, robbery, etc., during the relevant [wartime] period, it is still extremely doubtful whether it would be possible to differentiate between incidents of a political or criminal motivation." Similarly, the crime data from Belfast and Northern Ireland arrived with an "x" noted before several years in the table and the following legend: "An 'x' denotes years in which subversive elements were to the fore in the Province."

The comments of a few correspondents also revealed, perhaps unwittingly, the potential interplay between political changes and a nation's recorded rates of crime. In one Asian nation, for example, our correspondent commented that his nation had a "stormy history full of ups and downs" and gave the following account of its recent experience:

> In our nation, violence is apt to be exercised by groups or with the back-up of some groups. From 1968 to 1970, prosecution intensified control of these villain groups and tried to reform them by organizing the national land construction corps to work on the irrigation and reclamation projects. However, these projects could not last so long because they were financed by the government. New minor gangsters sprang up like mushrooms both in the capital and in the countryside.

The case of another nation, whose civil liberties practices are a matter of current debate, provides a more chilling illustration of the ways in which crime data can sometimes be brazenly conscripted to serve political ends.[2] Our correspondent commented on recent trends in his nation's crime rates, asserting—without any apparent foundation in the data he himself sent us—that these rates had recently returned to the level of the 1950s after a long and steady increase. It is his analysis of this alleged change, however, that is of greatest interest:

> This drastic reduction in the crime volume is due to various improvements in police service instituted by our government to improve peace and order which is one of the notable achievements in the new order in our country that have helped evolve a new concept in police work since the imposition of martial law in [date]. As a result, other syndicated crimes like smuggling, counterfeiting, and trafficking in illicit drugs have also been greatly reduced not only in [the major city] but throughout [the nation].

A European correspondent also commented on his nation's recent trends in various offenses and loyally attributed what he saw as improvements to the successes of the current regime. These three correspondents were the only ones, out of all those we contacted, who attempted to extract partisan political meanings from the data they sent us.

It is possible, of course, that many other nations also try to use crime rate fluctuations for domestic political purposes—to use "good" trends to justify the current administration or "bad" trends to provide a mandate for the next. Our work does not indicate how frequently crime data are politicized; we do know that letters from only three of our correspondents openly reflected this tendency. Naturally, to the degree that the data in a given society have direct political consequences, researchers must be concerned about possible pressures and temptations to create fraudulent records. This is true of any potentially political social indicator—housing conditions, infant mortality, life expectancy, median income, and so forth—and is not unique to crime data.

In summary, almost all the agencies and officials who responded to our request did so generously. Indeed, since the only reward for providing information was the altruistic satisfaction one might conceivably feel at assisting the halting progress of knowledge, the spirited cooperation we received was particularly impressive. Even when a correspondent reported that he did not possess the requested data, he generally expressed interest in our project and tried to suggest alternate sources.

In a project of this scale, some exceptions to this general pattern of remarkable cooperation were perhaps inevitable. In the case of a small number of countries, none of our letters was ever returned or answered, even after repeated requests. These nations, unfortunately, included the U.S.S.R. and several other Eastern European societies. Other nations usually thought of as Soviet bloc states—such as Hungary and Poland—readily provided data in response to our request. All our letters to the People's Republic of China were returned unopened, although various postmarks indicated that the letters had in fact reached Peking.

There were also a number of curious responses. In a few nations, for example, our first correspondents asserted that the data we requested had never been collected or had been lost—only to have other agencies in the same society send us these very data in response to a follow-up letter. In one industrialized society, this contradiction occurred between two agencies located in the same city. In these cases, it was only our persistence in sending additional letters to new addresses that secured the data for these nations.

We interpret these cases as additional evidence that, in some nations, historical crime records have not been the sole responsibility of any single agency. This kind of administrative diffusion poses the obvious danger that irreplaceable data can be lost—indeed, we assume that this has already happened for some of the nations missing from the CCDF. The obvious fragility of historical records of this kind seemed to us to lend added urgency to our efforts at collection and preservation.

As we have noted, direct correspondence with multiple agencies in other countries was by far the most successful of the various methods we used in assembling the CCDF. Correspondence produced data series which were longer, more complete, and more annotated than the series obtained in any other way. However, we also obtained information for some nations in two other ways.

One of these involved perusing hundreds of national statistical annuals. In general, these were of limited usefulness. Many nations do not include crime data in their statistical publications—although information on the nation's annual output of "pork bellies" or any other monetized commodity is abundantly available. This selective accounting may say something about the aspects of national life which individual societies regard as worth recording. Statistical annuals are problematic for technical reasons as well. They tend, quite reasonably, to be printed exclusively in the nation's primary language, and they also present data without explanation or annotation. This makes it difficult to know which offenses are classified under various categories and also whether changes in law or recording practices have occurred. Despite these obstacles, we did obtain data for quite a number of societies from statistical annuals.

The third and final method we used was by far the least satisfactory. The International Criminal Police Organization (Interpol) maintains some crime records on member nations, and we examined all the annual volumes it had published through 1970. The most glaring disadvantage of this source for our purposes is that Interpol began assembling and publishing crime data only in 1953—and this makes the analysis of long-term trends impossible using these data. In addition, Interpol records begin with only 40 nations and do not report separate data for cities. Despite these problems, we included these data in the CCDF when all other methods failed to provide alternative records.

There are several other Interpol practices which further reduce the usefulness of its data, and these should be kept in mind in any analysis relying on Interpol statistics. For one thing, since Interpol depends on annual submissions of data by member nations, its records are frequently discontinuous. Interpol records are also virtually unannotated, leaving the reader completely uninformed about national changes in practice, law, reporting, or definition. Interpol also reports a summary index of the "total number of offenses." This index is apparently modeled on the kind of aggregate index favored by the U.S. Federal Bureau of Investigation's *Uniform Crime Reports*; this index sums across all offenses and is therefore analytically meaningless.

The most serious problem with Interpol data, in our view, is both simple and insurmountable. The data are collected using a standardized form of Interpol's own invention. This form includes six offense categories intended to "cover certain broad categories of ordinary law crimes which are recognized and punished in the criminal laws of almost all countries."[3] These are murder, sex offenses, larceny, fraud, counterfeit currency offenses, and drug offenses. However, the scope of these categories appears to have changed slightly even during the short period in which Interpol has collected data. The murder category excludes "accidental manslaughter" in 1953, but by 1969 it excludes all "manslaughter." In addition, the adjective "illicit" was added to the drug offense description sometime between 1953 and 1969.

The use of a rigid, inflexible set of recording categories seems to us highly problematic because these offense types are rather arbitrary impositions on Interpol's member nations. These allegedly universal categories seem certain to obscure each nation's actual experience of crime and violence. Interpol deliberately redefines the "native" terms, categories, and classifications used by individual nations. For example, the 1969–70 volume notes:

The General Secretariat simply reproduces the information given on [the standard Interpol] forms from each country. It is not possible to extract data from official statistics compiled by countries on the basis of criteria other than those of the I.C.P.O.-Interpol international form. The information contained in the report is unsophisticated but uniform.

The motive behind Interpol's interest in uniformity is understandable but, we feel, ill conceived. The probable goal of uniform categories was to facilitate direct cross-sectional comparisons—for example, does nation A have more of a specific crime than nation B? The problem with this approach is that direct comparisons of this kind may be justified for the offense of homicide but are almost certainly unwarranted in the case of other offenses (this issue is discussed in detail in the next chapter).

Even if these crude comparisons were Interpol's goal, its own instructions to member nations seem more likely to produce erratic changes than uniform reporting. As just one example, Interpol's many instructions to member nations include the following (emphasis added): "If a case includes several offenses which are *not directly connected with one another,* each offense should be counted separately; if the offenses are *directly related,* only the most serious one should be counted." Since these distinctions are surely a matter of some judgment, they introduce a new source of systematic error—different nations seem certain to implement this and other Interpol directives differently.

A simpler and much superior procedure, in our opinion, would be to record "native" categories as they occur. This is in general the method we have followed in assembling our own Comparative Crime Data File. Instead of insisting on its own set of invariant categories, Interpol could have collated crime records exactly as the reporting nations recorded them, along with any necessary details on each nation's definitions and changes in law and practice. This would have minimized the errors which are inevitably produced when external categories are imposed on a nation's necessarily idiosyncratic experience.

This approach also seems more appropriate scientifically since, as discussed in the next chapter, longitudinal analyses within nations are more valid than the kinds of direct cross-sectional comparisons for which Interpol data have typically been used. For longitudinal analyses, the most important quality of a data set is the consistency with which it has been generated over time—and Interpol's arbitrary modifications of each nation's data seem certain to have reduced this consistency in unknown ways. Finally, it is also surprising that *none* of the international agencies we contacted either referred us to Interpol's publications or acknowledged their existence. This omission seems especially striking since, presumably, Interpol must interact with these same international agencies to obtain the records it publishes.

Having indicated the ways in which the data were collected, it is also appropriate to note some of the data collection strategies that proved fruitless. For one thing, some international agencies and institutions which might be expected to record and furnish crime data have not done so. For example, the United Nations publishes an impressive quantity of social indicators which enable a researcher to study a wide range of national characteristics, from the number of physicians per 100,000 population to the number of radios. The United Nations does not, however, furnish any detailed, longitudinal data on crime rates, although it once made an effort in this direction. For example, in the late 1940s, the United Nations did report an index of the number of offenses known to the police for a small number of member nations. This index did not refer to specific types of crimes and was only a summary of "major" and "minor" offenses. Various U.N. publications also reported juvenile court conviction data intermittently during the period 1946–56.

In general, however, data on crime and violence have been omitted from the United Nations' published interest in its member nations. This is somewhat surprising in view of the exhaustive detail which U.N. publications present for other indicators of far less apparent significance. There are indirect indications, however, that the U.N. does not publish crime data at least in part because it regards these data as potentially embarrassing to member nations—perhaps because the publication of comparative data would expose those nations with unusually high rates of crime and violence.

This interpretation was given additional credibility by the United Nations' curious and seemingly contradictory responses to our inquiries about whether it maintained crime data. Our first inquiry prompted a response from the assistant director of the "Crime Prevention and Criminal Justice Section," which said simply, "I am afraid that we are not in a position to provide you with the material you require." Since we assumed that this was a reference to the time and effort involved, we offered to go to New York to examine the records ourselves. We also offered to reciprocate by providing the United Nations with the considerable archive of data we had collected on our own. The reply we received informed us that "any information available here is for member states." We wrote again asking whether or not the United Nations in fact had the data we were seeking and, if so, whether these data were considered classified information. In reply, we received the following single sentence: "The answer to your questions is that information here is not available to the public or to individual researchers." This curious and rather secretive episode lent support to our belief that the U.N. does not publish crime data because they are regarded as politically sensitive. At any rate, the United Nations' secrecy was ultimately unimportant since our own methods of data collection proved successful.

A number of scholarly collections of "world indicators" have also omitted data on crime and violence. The two best-known collections of these indicators are the works of the World Data Analysis Program at Yale University (Russett, Alker, Deutsch, and Lasswell, 1964; Taylor and Hudson, 1972). Neither of these handbooks of social indicators has any information on crime. The omission of crime data in these social indicator volumes is perhaps understandable since both works depend heavily on U.N. publications. In any case, these two handbooks of world social indicators are only cross-sectional, so that longitudinal research designs are impossible with these data. Even if it is unpreventable, the absence of data on crime and violence from social indicator collections remains somewhat ironic, as Jouvenal (1966) observed:

> The indisputable pioneer of social indicators is Quetelet. A large part of his work deals with the frequency of crimes of violence which he tried to correlate with various social characteristics. It is strange that [the authors of the social indicator volumes] who pay homage to Quetelet do not give us this measurement which he considered so important.

In summary, international agencies and previous scholarly efforts have failed to provide historical records on the rates of crime for a large sample of societies. The uncharted character of international crime rates made our own program of research seem well worth the effort required.

PREPARING THE CCDF

The finished array of data in the completed Comparative Crime Data File exhibits an orderliness which the original records obviously did not possess. Since the information arrived in a great variety of forms, it was necessary for us to make a series of procedural decisions before entering each nation's data set in the archive. In all these decisions, our general goal was to understand and, as much as possible, preserve the unique or "native" meaning the data sets carried within the society in which they were generated. We felt that this approach would minimize the risk of arbitrary interference with the data, and we wanted to avoid imposing a specific viewpoint, methodological fashion, or perspective. At the same time, we tried to be zealous about detecting any potential problems with each data set. Our approach, in short, was to try to maximize the external intelligibility of each nation's data without compromising their original meaning.

Since many data sets arrived in need of an English translation, this was our first priority. In many cases, idiosyncratic terminology was a problem—and this was generally unaffected by translation. We ran across a great many terms which were completely mysterious to us. In these cases, we wrote to our international correspondents asking for clarification. The distinction between problems of translation and those posed by obscure terms can be illustrated with the specific cases of Hungary and India. Language, not terminology, was the problem in the Hungarian case, while terminology, not language, was the problem in the Indian data. The Hungarian information arrived in six large (11″ × 16″) hand-typed tables accompanied by a four-page letter. Not one word was in English, but, with the aid of a native speaker, we learned the difference between *emberoles* (murder) and *testi sertes* (assault).

The Indian data, by contrast, arrived in English. There were a number of terms, however, which were both unknown to us and unexplained. For example, all the offenses were listed in terms of the "volume of crime per one *lakh* of population," and listed next to robbery was the crime of *dacoity*. In search of an explanation, we wrote to the director of the Bureau of Police Research and Development in India, who informed us that a lakh was equal to 100,000 people. He quoted the definiton of dacoity from the Indian Penal Code:

> When five or more persons conjointly commit or attempt to commit a robbery, or where the whole number of persons conjointly committing or attempting to commit a robbery, and persons present and aiding such commission or attempt, amount to five or more, every person so committing, attempting or aiding, is said to commit "dacoity."

Translation and repeated correspondence were, therefore, the tools with which we tried to understand the internal meaning of the data sets. Although preserving the original qualities of the national data sets was our guiding principle, preparing these data for analysis made it necessary to establish and follow a series of conventions to maximize the validity and usefulness of this diverse archive. These conventions were as follows:

I. Offense Categories

National data were recorded in their original offense categories. For this purpose, we established three distinct categories of homicide data: murder, manslaughter, and homicide. Each nation's data were tabled under the label with which they arrived. Some nations record data in more than one of these categories, and other nations record only a single combined category such as "murder and manslaughter." A few nations recorded one series (e.g., "murder") only until a given year, and then a different series (e.g., "homicide") after that time. In all cases, we constructed footnotes to indicate our best understanding of the exact nature of each nation's indicators.

2. Multiple Indicators

In some cases, more than a single indicator was identified for the same offense for the same period—for instance, homicide "offenses known" and also homicide "convictions." Parallel indicators of this kind were sometimes received from relatively independent sources, such as a Bureau of Police Statistics and a Department of Justice. The three distinct homicide categories in the CCDF made it possible for us to include more than one homicide series. We recorded these indicators in separate categories even though the same case could conceivably be present in both series—as an offense known and, later, as a conviction. The existence of these potentially redundant homicide series made it possible for us to address a classic methodological question about the reliability and validity of crime indicators, and this analysis is described in the next chapter. In cases where multiple indicators were available for the same offense, we again used footnotes to indicate the precise nature of each indicator.

3. Unique Indicators

In some cases, the original category labels used by individual nations were not identical to any of the general CCDF categories. In these cases, we used the closest equivalent and recorded the original offense name in a footnote. For example, Scotland's "culpable homicide" was tabled under homicide; Caracas's undifferentiated "violent crimes" was listed in place of homicide; and India's "dacoity" was included with conventional robberies.

4. Aggregate Indicators

In a few cases, space considerations made it necessary to collapse some of the detailed distinctions preserved in the original data. In these cases, we tabled the resulting aggregate under a single CCDF category. In the case of France, for example, we combined *meurtre, assassinat, parricide,* and *empoisonnement* into the single offense category of murder. Aggregations of this kind were, again, explained in footnotes.

5. Raw and Rate Data

We decided to present data on both the raw number of offenses *and* the offense rate per 100,000 population. For any systematic analysis, of course, data in raw form are useless, and virtually all the research reported in this volume is based on rates. In some societies, however, a change as small as a single offense can produce a misleadingly dramatic change in the offense rate. In New Zealand, for example, the homicide rate doubled from 1946 to 1947—but the raw number of homicides increased from only two to four! We decided to present both raw and rate data in the CCDF to provide the kind of context and perspective that may be invisible with rate data alone.

6. National Populations

The data from some nations arrived in both raw and rate form. For many societies, however, we received only raw data. In these cases, it was necessary to obtain annual data on the population of these nations. We did this by consulting a variety of secondary statistical publications, including the *U.N. Demographic Yearbook,* using these population figures to generate the offense rates per 100,000 persons.

Even when a nation's data were received in both raw and rate form, we compared the same secondary population sources to the population figures the nations themselves had used in their own rate calculations. When differences were found, we preferred the secondary data and used them to recalculate the rates the nations had reported. The rationale for this preference was simple: the calculation of rates in non-census years requires the use of population estimates based only on the single most recent census, while retrospective population series are based on interpolations between two known census figures. For this reason, we believe that we have used the best population estimates available. Since the CCDF presents both raw and rate data, however, future users of the file will be able to recalculate a nation's rates using any population data the researcher prefers.

7. Measure Changes

For each nation and city in the CCDF, we sought to determine whether the series contained any discontinuities which could not meaningfully be crossed. This was of obvious importance, since certain types of changes would render the before-and-after data incomparable. This could present major problems for longitudinal designs.[4] It should be mentioned that only the data from some nations in the CCDF have problematic change points of this kind. Some of these changes, ironically, were produced when nations improved their statistical practices. The most frequent improvement of this kind involved a nation's decision to report the number of "offenses known" rather than another indicator from later in the "career" of an offense—for instance, arrests, indictments, convictions, incarcerations, or even prison populations.

The number of offenses known has been regarded as the optimal indicator for several decades although, as will be seen in the next chapter, we have discovered that several other indicators are equally valid indices of offense trends. At different points in this century, however, a number of nations have discarded a less optimal indicator in favor of the number of offenses known. Although these changes were obviously well intended, they have sometimes done a disservice to researchers since some nations have abandoned their old indicator entirely instead of recording both the old and the new together.

The single most common indicator change in the CCDF has been from data on convictions to statistics on the number of offenses known. Finland made this change in 1927, Indonesia in 1929, and Australia as late as 1963. The effect of these measure changes on a nation's data is, not surprisingly, dramatic. Since the number of convictions is generally no more than a fraction of the number of known offenses, this change in indicators produces an enormous paper "increase" in the data—although this increase is of course an artifact. For example, after Australia changed from convictions to offenses known, in 1963, the homicide data almost tripled and the assault data increased more than tenfold. Most of our correspondents in individual nations were quick to draw our attention to these indicator changes when they had occurred.

Other measure changes were more subtle. For example, our Hungarian correspondent informed us that his nation began including cases of intent to commit murder in its murder data after 1962. We felt it was imperative to include cautions about all such measure changes, whether or not they appeared to have any discernible effect on the series. In Hungary, for example, no effect is apparent. In the case of all measure changes, then, we have tried to alert potential users of the CCDF to the danger of crossing—at least unwittingly—these change points. In the CCDF data set, all measure changes are explained in the data for each nation or city.

Finally, some data sets show interruptions because of wars, coups d'état, national emergencies, or bureaucratic lapses. When these interruptions produce a gap in the data for a particular nation, the effect is to produce more than one series of data for a given offense.

8. Political Changes

A few of our correspondents drew our attention to political changes which had altered the borders and populations of their nations. These changes reflect history and the vagaries of national fortunes. For example, the CCDF contains data for "Germany" from 1900 to 1930, but only data for West Germany after 1953. Similar political changes are reflected in the offense data of a few other nations: the partition of Hungary in 1920, the carving of Northern Ireland out of a formerly undivided state in the same year, and so on.

The net effect of changes of this kind is to create more than one independent series within a single entry in the CCDF. For example, the file contains a series for an undivided Ireland from 1900 to 1912 and then, after an interruption, data for only the smaller Republic of Ireland beginning in 1923. A separate listing of data for Northern Ireland begins in 1922. Political changes of this nature are also explained in footnotes in the CCDF.

9. Data Quality

In any undertaking of this scale, when the original statistics are generated by hundreds of different agencies around the world, it seems necessary to assume that the quality of the data is variable. Because the issue of data quality in crime indicators is rather complex, a detailed discussion of these issues is presented in the next chapter rather than here. Since these concerns did affect the way in which we assembled the CCDF, however, their impact on our procedures deserves a brief explanation.

Some of these issues reflect differences among various offenses. As discussed in the next chapter, we restricted most of our attention to homicide because there is evidence that homicide data are more valid than data on other offenses. This difference explains our decision to record up to three different indicators of homicide offenses but only a single indicator of each other offense.

Other concerns about data quality refer to variation across different indicators of the same offense. As noted earlier, the indicator of offenses known has been preferred in the past over data on arrests, convictions, sentencings, or prison populations. It should again be emphasized that this classic concern about differences among indicators appears to be much less important for longitudinal analyses. The CCDF does contain a fairly wide range of indicator types. In the "C" section alone, Cameroon records "number of offenses reported," Canada records "convictions," and Colombia records "number arrested." Because of this diversity, the entries in the CCDF label the specific indicators which individual nations and cities have reported. This information is potentially useful for researchers who decide to limit their analyses to only those cases with the offenses known indicator, on the assumption that this restriction will maximize the validity of a given analysis.

The indicator label in the CCDF files also makes it possible for a researcher to test a hypothesis using progressive "waves" of data—that is, first using nations with the "best" indicator, then using nations with other indicators. A data quality control procedure of this kind allows a researcher to learn what effect, if any, data presumed to differ in quality have upon the conclusion one would draw from a given analysis.[5] This procedure is ideally suited to cross-national research with large numbers of cases. In addition, data quality control is easily incorporated into most research designs and can greatly increase rigor and precision. The usefulness of data quality control for the CCDF is illustrated in chapter 4, on the effects of war. In summary, since indicator quality is a recurring concern in cross-national research, each entry in the CCDF carries an indicator label. Individual researchers can use this label in sampling and research designs of their choice.

10. National Qualifications

As noted earlier, a number of our correspondents sent us certain cautions along with their nations' data. Some of these referred to specific gaps in the crime data, unusual time periods, or even a specific year. We recorded these qualifications in footnotes in the CCDF. In addition, we received cautions of a more general nature from a few correspondents. For example, some of them appeared to be concerned, rightfully, about the appropriateness of direct international comparisons of the absolute "amount" of a given crime. Thus, our New Zealand correspondent asked whether national differences in crime definition and reporting made exact international comparisons possible. These national differences are indeed problematic in direct cross-sectional comparisons, but they are controlled for in the longitudinal designs which constitute the largest part of our work.

Similarly, our correspondent in Scotland felt confident that his nation's data for both murder and culpable homicide were solidly comparable across the entire period from 1900 to 1973, but he wondered whether less serious offenses had been affected over this long period as much by variations in recording practices as by variations in the actual incidence of crime. We had also anticipated this concern, and it is reflected in our decision to focus primarily on homicide rather than less grievous offenses. In most cases, then, we had anticipated these general concerns in our choice of research designs.

Even nonhomicide offenses can be useful in a variety of longitudinal designs. For example, one could use the data on rape rates to identify the years in which *reported* rape appears to have increased in each of a sample of nations. This increase can be of considerable interest—perhaps in a study of the ways in which increased societal concern or police cooperation can affect offense reporting, even if one flatly assumes that no actual increase in the "real" rate has occurred. One might study changes in the willingness to report rape as an index of emergent concern about women's rights, as a measure of the effectiveness of reforms in police practice and jurisprudence, or as a reflection of other social changes. In addition, changes in the reported incidence of rape might occur in an interesting temporal order in various societies.

An understanding of these and other methodological issues is obviously of pivotal importance to an informed use of the data in the CCDF. For this reason, any researcher interested in using this archive to answer a question of his or her own is strongly urged to become familiar with the discussion and caveats presented in the following chapter.

THE CCDF: AN OVERVIEW

Once the data for a nation or city had been prepared for analysis according to the ten conventions listed above, we used them to construct an entry for the CCDF. These entries were computerized and the complete file was printed in the format shown in the last part of this volume. A total of 110 nations and 44 international cities are listed in the archive. An overview of the contents of the CCDF is given in tables just prior to the entries themselves. This information can be used to select individual cases according to the needs of a given researcher. The tables indicate the total number of years for each entry in the CCDF and the approximate time period for each. Entries marked by one, two, or three asterisks contain a minimum of ten, twenty, or thirty years of continuous coverage independent of measure changes and gaps. Abbreviations are used to show which specific offenses are included for each nation and city.

NOTES

1. Since we asked the recipients to go to considerable lengths on our behalf, we felt that an individually typed letter would be more effective than a form solicitation, despite the large number of requests involved. Our solution to this problem was to use word processing. A general form of our request letter (in English or Spanish) was programmed, and each individual request letter was generated by adding the name of an individual agency, city, and nation. The resulting letters were indistinguishable from a manually typed letter.
2. In this and the preceding example, we have not identified the nation so as to protect our correspondent from possible reprisals. In at least one case, our correspondent wrote that he had tried for over a month to obtain his Director's approval to send the letter to us—without success. Despite this, our correspondent decided on his own to send us the letter and data.
3. *International Crime Statistics* (Saint-Cloud, France: Interpol, 1969–70), p. ix.
4. Even in the case of shifts and discontinuities, approximate longitudinal analyses are in some cases possible. If two series overlap for at least some period, it is possible to test for a relationship between the two series. If a strong relationship exists, the researcher can generate estimated values for the interrupted series. Even when the change is from one homicide indicator (convictions) to another (offenses known), we have found that the two indicators are highly colinear, as discussed in the next chapter. In theory, this would allow a researcher to project estimates for the missing values in either series when one has terminated. This kind of analysis is common in econometrics but until recently has been infrequently used in the other social sciences.
5. Data quality control was pioneered by Raoul Naroll. The concept and procedure are described in his book *Data Quality Control: A New Research Technique* (New York: Free Press, 1962) and in later work (Naroll, Michik, and Naroll, 1980).

T H R E E

Problems and Prospects in Comparative Crime Research

INTRODUCTION TO THE ISSUES

Over the past two decades, researchers have raised important questions about possible sources of inaccuracy, incompleteness, and bias in official crime statistics. Although these critics have focused on a wide range of potential problems, the net effect of this close scrutiny has been to impugn the validity and usefulness of these records (Kitsuse and Cicourel, 1963; Wolfgang, 1963; Nettler, 1974; and Skogan, 1977). In the case of American statistics, the most frequent criticism is that these records reflect only a proportion of all crime because they fail to include unreported offenses. This problem has been given various names but is most frequently called *underreporting*.

While most research on underreporting has examined American crime data, the issue is presumably generic to official crime statistics from any society. The specter of missing or inaccurate data is of obvious significance for a data archive such as the CCDF. If massive underreporting is a factor in international crime statistics, the resulting ambiguities could be fatal to certain types of comparisons. Underreporting could hopelessly confound "real" changes in crime with "paper" changes—meaningless differences reflecting only variation or changes in reporting practices. Because this potential artifact clearly threatens some uses of international crime statistics, it is important to understand the precise nature and implications of underreporting.

A second problem concerns definitions and procedures. In the case of international statistics, it is said that cross-national comparisons are not tenable because different societies often use different *indicators* of crime—for example, offenses known, arrests, court cases, convictions, incarcerations, or even prison populations. If two societies maintain different indicators of the same offense, it is obvious that direct comparisons of the volume of the offense are problematic or impossible. While there may be other questions about crime data quality, the problems of underreporting and different indicators have caused the greatest methodological concern.

IMPLICATIONS FOR COMPARATIVE RESEARCH

In this chapter, an effort is made to assess the implications for comparative research of these two sources of potential invalidity or incomparability in official crime statistics. Our central goal is to identify (1) what kinds of research designs are jeopardized or even invalidated by these data quality problems, and (2) what research designs are valid despite them. By means of this analysis, we hope to provide potential comparative researchers with a highly practical guide to the relative validity of a range of research designs. Our basic theoretical approach is to treat various methodological concerns as hypotheses and subject them to empirical test or, if an empirical test is not possible, to try to identify what design types are most immune to the error and invalidity which would be produced *if* a critical hypothesis of this kind was, in fact, correct.

In our view, a sophisticated approach requires that one eschew *both* a blanket indictment of the usefulness of crime statistics and a naive or unthinking faith in their direct interpretability. Both of these approaches, we believe, are equally reckless and unwarranted. In addition, as this chapter makes clear, neither approach is supported by the existing evidence. Our intent is to try to identify the precise implications of several potential problems, and our approach is, wherever possible, empirical. We assume that official crime statistics may well contain sources of error but, in addition, we assume that these types of error pose a unique and variable jeopardy for different research designs.

For these reasons, it is our view that one of the best models for these methodological issues is a typology which examines the unique impact each potential problem poses for different research designs. Recent evidence on the problems of underreporting and nonstandardized indicators suggests that the degree to which they are problematic is a function of the specific comparisons one wishes to make. These two problems will be considered separately. Some recent evidence, particularly on the problem of underreporting, uses surveys of crime victims to generate unofficial estimates of crime rates. These "victimization" crime rates are then compared with official police statistics to estimate the "hidden figure" of unreported crime. Other research, particularly on the problem of different indicators, is now possible for the first time because of the CCDF. On the basis of this analysis, four different comparative research designs are compared in a summary typology which appraises the vulnerability of each design to these two data quality problems.

PROBLEM I: UNDERREPORTING

Few criticisms of official crime statistics have received more attention than underreporting, and few have been seen as potentially more important. The interest in this issue is scarcely surprising. It is difficult to think of any area of research on crime and violence—with the possible exception of ethnographic, descriptive, or case study approaches—in which the numerical *incidence* of crime is not of central concern. Studies of trends in crime, ecological differences, offender and victim populations, and virtually all other topics in the study of crime and violence depend at least in part on knowledge of the frequency and extent of the offense under study. The keen interest with which underreporting research has been greeted is due to the fact that measurement of the incidence of offenses is indispensable to empirical research on crime and violence.

Perhaps because empirical, quantitative research on crime statistics has been pursued with more enthusiasm in the United States than in many other nations, research on underreporting has centered upon American crime data. In addition, the crime records of other societies may be of higher quality than American data and, as a consequence, underreporting may be more of a problem in American crime statistics than in international data. This argument has been made by several scholars (e.g., Mulvihill and Tumin, 1969; Skogan, 1976) and also by a U.S. Presidential Task Force which concluded:

> The United States is today, in the era of the high speed computer, trying to keep track of crime and criminals with a system that was less than adequate in the days of the horse and buggy. . . . In some respects the present system is not as good as that used in some European countries 100 years ago. (*Task Force Report: Crime and Its Impact—An Assessment,* President's Commission on Law Enforcement and the Administration of Justice, 1967: 123)

The principal reason for this criticism, at least in the United States, is that for approximately a half century this nation's official crime statistics have been drawn from police records, reflecting the number of complaints to and arrests made by individual police departments. The data from these departments are then forwarded to the Federal Bureau of Investigation which aggregates the data and publishes them as the *Uniform Crime Reports* (UCR). It may be that every system of recording crime statistics has a weakness, but the weakness of this particular system is particularly disquieting. Unless one is willing to assume that citizens are never reluctant or unmotivated to report crimes, it seems clear that these official police statistics are diminished by underreporting. As a consequence, it seems reasonable to be concerned that what appear to be characteristics of crime (e.g., an increase in rape) are in fact characteristics of underreporting (e.g., an increase in citizen willingness to report rape).

Underreporting has drawn attention to the "dark" or "hidden" figure of crime—that is, the unknown volume of offenses which never appear in official American crime statistics. The sources and dangers of underreporting have been addressed by Wolfgang (1963) and Skogan (1976, 1977, and 1981) among other scholars. The hidden figure of crime is in many ways an empirical question, and the past fifteen years have seen a bewildering number of "victimization" surveys designed to estimate the magnitude and characteristics of the underreporting problem (Biderman, 1967; Biderman and Reiss, 1967; Ennis, 1967; Santarelli, Work, and Velde, 1974; Hindelang, 1976; Skogan, 1977 and 1981). Victimization surveys have even captured the imagination of the federal government; the United States conducts a periodic *National Crime Survey* to provide survey-based estimates of national crime rates.

The basic paradigm of victimization surveys involves the use of classical sample survey methods to produce estimates of the incidence of a variety of offenses. In a typical victimization survey, the respondent is asked whether he or she or anyone else in the household was the victim of a given crime within a specified time period, usually the previous twelve months. Depending on the sampling method used, the marginal incidence of the offense is then used to project a national rate for this particular crime. When these survey-based rates are compared to the rates based on the FBI's police statistics, the survey-based rates generally produce much higher estimates of crime rates.

The size of the hidden figure of crime appears to vary from offense to offense. In one study, for example, it was estimated that police statistics had recorded about one-third of all the burglaries and about half of the robberies, aggravated assaults, and rapes (Hindelang, 1976). Victimization surveys generally find that roughly half the respondents who mention an offense to the interviewer admit that they did not report it to the police, generally out of fear of reprisal, general cynicism, unwillingness to get the offender in trouble, or distrust of the police and judicial system. Underreporting also stems from the failure of the police to detect some crimes, to make arrests in some of the crimes they do detect, or to record some of the crimes that are reported to them—for instance, police "unfounding" procedures dismiss some reported offenses as false. Still other offenses may be lost if, in cases where an individual commits multiple offenses, only the most serious is recorded.

It has been suggested that underreporting may be an important social process in its own right, not merely a source of methodological contamination for crime statistics. Kitsuse and Cicourel (1963) have drawn attention to the role social definition plays in the reporting process, suggesting that crime statistics can be interpreted as indicators of official concern rather than as objective measures of the true volume of illegal acts. One researcher (Wheeler, 1967) has proposed that researchers examine the ways in which offenders, victims, and police interact to produce official crime statistics. A number of researchers have, in fact, approached the phenomenon of underreporting by direct observation of the differences between police records and the actual behaviors of delinquents, gang members, and young men generally (Murphy et al., 1946; McCord and McCord, 1959; Piliavin and Briar, 1964; Miller, 1967). In general, these observational or "field" studies concur with the general conclusion of victimization surveys that significant numbers of offenses are never recorded in official police statistics.

Most research on underreporting has, however, been undertaken to provide estimates of the "true" incidence of an offense and the magnitude of the underreporting proportion—the ratio of officially recorded offenses to the total number of offenses reported in victimization surveys. Direct comparisons between survey-based crime rates and official crime statistics are sometimes difficult because of differences in coverage, and a number of researchers have argued against direct comparison (e.g., Velde, Work, and Holtzman, 1975). Many surveys limit the age of their sample (e.g., to those over 12) while police statistics nominally include individuals of all ages; many surveys do not include homicide, white collar crimes, shoplifting, and other offenses included in police statistics.

It should be mentioned that victimization surveys are not without problems of their own if one's objective is an unbiased estimate of the "real" volume of crime. For example, just as police statistics may be diminished by underreporting, victimization surveys may also miss those offenses which respondents are reluctant to reveal to an interviewer. Certain offenses, such as rape by an acquaintance or a family member, are perhaps as unlikely to be reported in a survey as they are unlikely to reach police statistics (Skogan, 1976: 139). This problem has led to the suggestion that, at least for certain offenses, there is a "doubly dark" figure of crime—that is, offenses which are not reported to the police *or* to an interviewer in a victimization survey (Skogan, 1977b: 45).

Victimization surveys are also subject to a number of specific methodological problems. One of these has been called "telescoping"—the tendency of some respondents to report crimes that actually occurred before the time period covered in the survey. There may also be certain social class differences in the tendency to recall or report crime during an interview. This has been called the problem of "differential productivity of respondents" (Skogan, 1981).

In addition, problems intrinsic to survey research may also affect victimization studies. For example, Maltz (1977) reports that some of the National Crime Panel survey data show disquieting variance across interviewers—that is, some interviewers produce high rates of reported criminal victimization while other interviewers produce low rates. It is difficult to know the precise reasons for this differential response, although it suggests that respondents are encouraged by or willing to confide in some interviewers more than others. Finally, there is some evidence that the structure of the victimization interview may also affect the likelihood that crimes will be recalled or remembered. In one study, respondents were more likely to recall a crime if they were first asked about their attitudes toward crime and the police; they were less likely to recall an offense if these attitude items were omitted (Maltz, 1977).

Despite these problems, it seems clear that the method of victimization research can produce useful information about crime and official statistics. This method also allows us to investigate the phenomenon of admitted underreporting—that is, the circumstances which characterize a victim's decision not to report an offense to the police. At least three variables in the offense itself appear to play a role in the decision to report the offense to the police: (1) in the case of thefts, the higher the value of the stolen items, the more likely the victim is to report the loss; (2) in the case of assaultive crimes, the victim is more likely to report the offense if a weapon is present; and (3) if the victim and offenders are strangers, the offense is more likely to be reported to police (Skogan, 1977). Existing research suggests that many victim characteristics, such as race, do not affect underreporting. Age, however, appears to be an important variable. Victimization surveys indicate that people under the age of twenty are much less likely than older people to report crimes to the police.

The seriousness of the offense is by far the most important determinant of whether or not it is reported. This has led to a tempering of what appeared to be, early in victimization research, somewhat revolutionary expectations. The finding in early victimization surveys that large *numbers* of offenses were missing from police statistics led some to assume that the "crime problem"—which already seemed grievous when judged from police statistics—was in fact a great deal worse than had been imagined. If only a third or a half of the crimes committed were being reported, according to this reasoning, then the actual rates of crime were in fact many times higher than the (already high) official crime rates.

New evidence suggests that this concern was exaggerated. While it is true that large *numbers* of crimes never reach police statistics, the *importance* of these unreported offenses is highly debatable. It is now recognized that most unreported crime consists of minor property offenses (Skogan, 1977b: 49). This finding has changed our understanding of the hidden figure of crime:

> The reservoir of unreported crime contains a disproportionate number of less serious incidents involving small financial loss, little serious injury, and (infrequent) use of weapons. (Skogan, 1977b: 41.)

Contrary to considerable speculation about the portentous implications of unreported crime, these data indicate that the vast pool of incidents which do not come to the attention of the police does not conceal a large amount of serious crime. (Skogan, 1977b: 46)

It now appears, therefore, that while official American crime statistics do underenumerate, the degree of underenumeration varies inversely with the seriousness of the offense. With the possible exception of certain offenses such as rape, in which reporting could embarrass or stigmatize the victim, it seems reasonable to assume that the official data provide a reasonably accurate record of *serious* offenses. This new evidence restores to official crime statistics some important forms of usefulness.

The finding that serious offenses are relatively immune to underreporting has particular significance for the offense of homicide. At this time, there is no evidence that homicide data suffer from underreporting; in fact, there are strong reasons to believe that this particular violent crime is fully enumerated in official crime statistics. For example, a presidential crime commission concluded that, compared to other offenses, homicide was an especially valid indicator because it appeared to be invulnerable to police misclassification (Mulvihill and Tumin, 1969). Historians of crime and violence also have urged attention to this offense precisely because it appears to have been relatively invariant in definition and tabulation. Crime historians have been particularly sensitive to the risk of confusing mere definition or measurement changes with actual crime rate changes and, in general, they have concluded that this risk

is more serious for certain kinds of crimes than for others. For example, it is unlikely that there has been significant change over the last hundred years in the way in which murder has been defined or murderers apprehended. (Ferdinand, 1967: 86)

There is other evidence on this question as well. Researchers on homicide have concluded that the overwhelming majority of homicides are cleared by arrest and that, as a result, police statistics fully enumerate this offense. Other researchers have concluded that the FBI's *Uniform Crime Report* is accurate for the offenses of murder and non-negligent manslaughter (Hindelang, 1974). In most victimization surveys, including the National Crime Panel Survey, the offense of homicide is not even included because it is believed to be fully enumerated (Skogan, 1977b: 45).

In the victimization survey by Ennis (1967), however, respondents were asked to note any homicides of which they were aware. In this study, the data indicated that official crime statistics on this offense were accurate and valid. Thus, evidence on this question appears to be consistent and persuasive: homicide is the most valid of offense indicators in that official statistics on this offense are immune to underreporting.[1]

Since the majority of victimization surveys have been done in the United States, the effect of underreporting on international crime data is less well understood. As indicated earlier, there is a widespread belief that the official crime statistics of the United States are in many ways inferior to those of other industrial nations. At the same time, the few cross-national victimization surveys that have been done suggest that underreporting also occurs in other societies and that the pattern of decreasing underreporting with the increasing severity of an offense is similar to that in the United States (e.g., Sparks, 1976; Sparks, Genn, and Dodd, 1977).

In cross-national records on homicide, it appears to be the case—as in the United States—that underreporting is simply not an issue. Existing evidence suggests that homicides are fully enumerated (Phillipson, 1974; Verkko, 1953 and 1956). These findings indicate, again, that data on homicide are superior to other offense data in terms of their resistance to underreporting. As a result, as will be discussed below, homicide data can be presumed to be valid for a wide range of research designs—only *some* of which are appropriate for data on less serious offenses.

Underreporting and Levels of Crime

These findings that not all offenses are reflected in official crime statistics and, at the same time, that the most serious offenses—particularly homicides—are fully enumerated have nontrivial implications for the validity of research on crime and violence. These implications, clearly, vary depending upon the specific offense examined and the uses to which official crime data are applied.

The research designs most vulnerable to the problem of underreporting are those which address the absolute volume or *level* of an offense. The basic problem with this sort of analysis is that one cannot assume a priori that the "underreporting proportion"—the ratio of reported offenses to total offenses—is invariant. For example, a study using official crime statistics to compare the levels of burglary in two cities (or two nations) will be jeopardized or even invalidated if the underreporting proportions in these two units differ. Similarly, a study comparing the level of burglary in a city (or nation) in 1960 and 1970 will produce spurious results if the underreporting proportion has changed during this decade. This problem is not limited to comparisons: it also affects one-sample studies—for example, a simple estimate of the probability that a home in a given city or nation will be burglarized in a given year will be inaccurate if the underreporting proportion for this offense is low.

The generic problem in such research designs is that the "real" crime rate and the underreporting proportion are hopelessly confounded. If official statistics show that city A has a higher rate of burglary than city B, we can conclude *either* that city A really has a higher burglary rate or that city A does not have a higher burglary rate but merely a more complete enumeration of this offense. This uncertainty is irreducible for certain uses of official crime statistics. In some cases, of course, one could do victimization surveys to answer these questions—but, quite apart from the different set of problems which characterize victimization surveys, the expense and time required would severely restrict the number and range of possible investigations.

There are a number of possible solutions to this problem of the confounding of offense levels and underreporting proportions. Each of these solutions carries a different form of threat to the validity of the inferences a researcher might hope to draw. The most conservative solution is to renounce all comparisons of the levels of various offenses. One might argue that the confounding effects of underreporting proportions make the "real" level or volume of an offense fatally ambiguous and, therefore, useless to the investigator.

While we are not unsympathetic with this conclusion, our own inclinations are to take a somewhat less conservative approach. This purist argument is highly persuasive, in our view, for a particular combination of indicators and designs which we believe may well be generally invalidated by underreporting: *analyses of the absolute level of nonhomicide offenses.* Instances of this research design abound in both American and cross-national research—for example, contrasting the robbery rate in California and New York, estimating the frequency of assault in Chicago, calculating the "clearance rate" (arrests/number of offenses) for burglary in the United States, and comparing rape rates in the United States and Britain. Such studies require us to believe that official statistics provide valid estimate of the real level of these offenses—and the evidence from underreporting research makes this belief generally untenable.

In some cases, these questions may have empirical answers. For example, before making the comparisons of crime levels mentioned above, one could examine victimization survey data from the affected jurisdictions to determine whether the underreporting proportions differ in the jurisdictions to be compared. If the underreporting proportions do not differ, the evidence from the victimization research could be reported as empirical justification for using offical crime statistics in a direct comparison of crime levels.

On the other hand, if the underreporting proportions *do* differ in the jurisdictions one wishes to compare, a weighting procedure might be appropriate. This procedure can be illustrated using one of the hypothetical comparisons listed above—a design which contrasts the robbery rate in California and New York. Suppose that official statistics show the robbery rates of these two states to be, respectively, 100 and 65 offenses per 100,000 population. Suppose further that victimization surveys have shown the respective underreporting proportions to be .80 to .50—i.e., that 80% of all robberies are reported to the police in California but only 50% of all robberies are reported to the police in New York.

One can use this information to produce new estimates of the robbery rates in the two jurisdictions. In this example, the "corrected" or "adjusted" robbery rates (i.e., the official rate divided by the underreporting proportion) are 125 and 130. Contrary to the impression produced by official statistics, therefore, New York would have a *higher* robbery rate than California when the official statistics are corrected for underreporting.

In summary, research on the *levels* of one or more crimes requires that certain assumptions be made about the underreporting proportions which characterize the offenses under study. Two reporting units (cities, states, or nations) can be compared on the level of an offense only if one or more of the following conditions are met: (1) underreporting is not a problem for this offense; (2) underreporting proportions for this crime are known and are essentially equal for both reporting units; or (3) underreporting proportions for this crime are unequal but can be used as weights to correct the official rates for this offense.

These conditions are clearly stringent. At present, there is only a single offense for which underreporting can be assumed to be no problem: homicide.[2] For this reason, comparisons of the *level* of homicide in different jurisdictions can reasonably be assumed to be immune to underreporting and therefore valid. There are, of course, other considerations which affect cross-national comparisons—for instance, statutory differences between nations in the way this offense is defined, an example being the distinction between homicide and manslaughter.

In general, however, homicide is an offense which appears valid for virtually all comparative research designs because all existing evidence suggests that this offense is fully enumerated. Research designs on the levels of nonhomicide offenses must therefore meet at least one of the remaining two conditions, both of which require estimates of the underreporting proportions for the jursidictional units in the research design. For cross-national comparisons of the *levels* of an offense, these two conditions cannot be met at present since little or no empirical research has been done on underreporting proportions in other societies. Although the prevailing belief among many social scientists is that underreporting is not a problem in many other nations, this assumption has not been widely documented with victimization research in a large sample of nations.

With the exception of the fully reported offense of homicide, therefore, simple cross-national comparisons of the levels of a crime are at present imprudent or even unwarranted. In the absence of empirical estimates of underreporting proportions in the societies under study, such comparisons would require the seemingly indefensible assumption that the two unknown proportions are equal.

The prospects for the comparisons of crime levels *within* the United States may be somewhat brighter, if only because more victimization surveys have been done. If one examines a number of victimization surveys, it appears that—even though underreporting certainly exists— the underreporting proportions are fairly stable across different jurisdictions. A number of such surveys are listed in table 3.1, and the underreporting proportions uncovered in these surveys are indicated. For the offense of robbery, for example, table 3.1 indicates that the mean

Table 3.1. Comparison of Independent Estimates of Underreporting Proportions for Five Offenses

Offense	Five-city study[a]		Eight-city study[b]		Thirteen-city study[c]		UCR/ Ennis[d]
	Mean proportion	Range	Mean proportion	Range	Mean proportion	Range	
Robbery	.51	(.47–.60)	.52	(.44–.57)	.53	(.44–.65)	.65
Simple Assault	.33	(.28–.37)	.33	(.27–.39)	.33	(.29–.45)	—[e]
Aggravated Assault	.53	(.51–.57)	.51	(.46–.60)	.48	(.41–.55)	.49
Aggravated Assault with Injury	.66	(.57–.73)	.58	(.52–.63)	.58	(.46–.77)	—[e]
Rape	.54	(.46–.61)	.50	(.35–.58)	.49	(.34–.65)	.27
Burglary	.54	(.52–.57)	.54	(.50–.57)	.53	(.46–.58)	.31
Household Larceny	.24	(.22–.26)	.27	(.20–.32)	.25	(.19–.32)	.44

NOTES: The underreporting proportions in the five-, eight- and thirteen-city studies are the ratio of two self-report figures: (1) the number of crimes respondents said they reported to police and (2) the total number of crimes respondents said they experienced. The UCR/Ennis proportion, however, compares self-report data to the actual police statistics compiled in the FBI's *Uniform Crime Report.*
[a] Means calculated from Table 8 of Santarelli et al. (1974b).
[b] Means calculated from Table 8 of Santarelli et al. (1974a).
[c] Means calculated from the thirteen different Table 6's of Velde et al. (1975).
[d] Underreporting proportion calculated from Table 1 of Ennis (1967), using the UCR rates for individuals and residencies.
[e] The Ennis survey did not report rates for these assault categories.

underreporting proportion was .51 in a five-city survey, .52 in an eight-city survey, and .53 in a thirteen-city survey. Table 3.1 also presents the range of underreporting proportions—for example, in the five-city survey, the robbery underreporting proportion varied from .47 to .60.[3]

It is apparent from table 3.1 that underreporting varies from offense to offense—for instance, household larcenies appear to be reported relatively infrequently while robbery and aggravated assault with injury appear to be enumerated much more fully. Despite the variation *across* offenses, the range of the underreporting proportions *within* each offense category appears to be narrow, at least for some offenses. Since sampling errors occur in any survey, it may not be unreasonable to assume that ranges of this magnitude could be accounted for merely by the standard error of the mean. At any rate, it does not appear to be the case—at least for some offenses—that the underreporting proportions vary widely from city to city. This stability is perhaps particularly impressive since the twenty-six cities included in this comparison vary greatly in size and other characteristics.

For these twenty-six cities, then, valid comparisons of the absolute level of certain crimes, particularly the more serious offenses of aggravated assault and robbery, may be possible. The jurisdictional stability of underreporting in this analysis supports the conclusion that underreporting may be due to the nature of the offense rather than to a wide range of variables which vary unpredictably from city to city. This information could be used in diverse ways. If underreporting proportions appear highly stable across jurisdictions—as they do for the offense of robbery—then one would feel encouraged to compare directly official statistics on the robbery rates in these cities.

For other offenses, one could even compute how different the underreporting proportions would have to be to produce spurious offense rate differences of an observed size. For example, suppose city A reports an aggravated assault rate of 200 (per 100,000 persons), while city B reports an aggravated assault rate of 400. For this difference to be spurious (i.e., due to inter-city variation in underreporting), the underreporting proportions in the two cities would have to differ by a factor of at least 2:1. For example, the underreporting proportions would have to be something like .40 in city A and .80 in city B. An examination of table 3.1 shows that, across all twenty-six cities in the comparison, the offense of aggravated assault varied only from .41 to .60. This suggests that a 2:1 ratio between the underreporting proportions of city A and city B is extremely unlikely and that the observed higher assault rate in city B is real rather than spurious.

This analysis can be stated in more general form. The relative stability of the underreporting proportion can be used to determine how likely

it is that an observed difference in the official offense rates of two jurisdictions is only an artifact of differential reporting. The general form
of this informal "spuriousness test" might be stated as follows:

> If two jurisdictions have rates of the same offense which have a ratio of x/y,
> this difference in offense rates is (other things being equal) genuine unless
> one is willing to assume that the underreporting proportions in the two
> jurisdictions have a ratio which is as large as or larger than y/x.

This spuriousness test has the obvious implication that large differences are affected less by underreporting artifacts than are small differences. For example, if two cities have burglary rates of 3000 and 1000
(per 100,000 population), these rates make a ratio of 3:1. The underreporting proportion in the city with the apparently higher burglary rate
would have to be *three* times higher (e.g., .31 vs .93) for this crime rate
difference to be an artifact due to underreporting. As the data for burglary in table 3.1 indicate, differences of this magnitude in underreporting proportions seem extremely unlikely.

A smaller difference in observed offense rates would, of course, be
more vulnerable to underreporting. If two jurisdictions had reported
rape rates of 20 and 30 (per 100,000 population), for example, this
difference could be an artifact if the underreporting proportions in the
two jurisdictions had a ratio of 3:2—e.g., .60 and .40. As can be seen
from table 3.1, this difference is—unlike previous examples—within the
apparent range of underreporting for the offense of rape. As a result,
it might be judicious in this instance to conclude that the comparison is
indeterminate. The difference between the two jurisdictions could be
genuine, but it could as easily be an artifact of differential underreporting in the two jurisdictions.

In summary, studies of the *level* of an offense are vulnerable to underreporting. In particular, the following conclusions appear warranted:
(1) in the case of homicide, underreporting appears to be negligible or
nonexistent, and studies of the levels of this offense are therefore not
problematic; (2) for other offenses, it appears that the most serious
offenses are well enumerated—that is, most are reported; (3) less serious
offenses are more often underreported; (4) in cases where the magnitude
of the underreporting of an offense can be estimated, this estimate can
be used to produce weighted or corrected estimates of the offense rate;
(5) even for the less serious offenses, underreporting proportions appear
to be fairly stable, at least in the United States; and (6) in comparisons
of crime rates in two jurisdictions, one can determine whether observed
differences in crime rates are likely to be genuine or an artifact of differential underreporting in the two jurisdictions. Some of these conclusions, while warranted in terms of available evidence from U.S. crime

statistics, have not been examined using cross-national data. For this reason, some caution seems appropriate before assuming that these conclusions also apply to the data of other nations.

From the above analysis, it appears that underreporting proportions are reasonably stable across different jurisdictions. This stability provides indirect encouragement for comparisons of offense levels in the same jurisdiction at two or more points in time. Longitudinal research designs examine changes in an offense rate over time. This type of design seems warranted on theoretical grounds, since most of the factors which produce underreporting seem likely to be relatively enduring in nature.[4] This assumption about the temporal stability of underreporting proportions is addressed in the next section of this chapter.

Underreporting and Trends of Crime

In the previous section, we examined the implications of underreporting for studies of the level of an offense. For reasons which will be indicated in this section, studies of *trends* of an offense are almost certainly less vulnerable to underreporting. This is because many of the idiosyncratic ways in which a nation generates offense rates—definition, record keeping, social or cultural attitudes about the seriousness of different offenses, etc.—are relatively durable over time. Studies of offense trends therefore hold these idiosyncrasies—and the underreporting proportions they produce—constant.

A comparison of how German and American assault rates changed after World War I would, for example, be unaffected by national differences in underreporting proportions as long as the proportions remained consistent. This comparison would not require that the underreporting proportions be the same in both countries, only that they be stable within each country. As an extreme example, one could make this comparison even if 80%·of all assaults were reported to the police in Germany (i.e., an underreporting proportion of .80) but only 20% of the American assaults were reported. This very large difference would have no effect on the study of assault rate changes after World War I—as long as these proportions were stable within both societies. Similarly, a comparison of the relationship between unemployment fluctuations and trends in robbery in the United States and England would be unaffected by different underreporting proportions in these nations, as long as the proportions remained internally consistent.

While studies of offense levels are strongly affected by underreporting, studies of offense trends are relatively unaffected because trend research does not require the assumption that underreporting proportions are the same in the jurisdictions to be compared. The importance of this distinction between studies of offense levels and studies of offense trends has been recognized for some time, although its implications for the problem of underreporting have not been generally recognized. More than forty years ago, however, the difference between offense levels and offense trends was noted by the celebrated historian of crime Leon Radzinowicz:

> The impossibility of determining numerically the static aspect of criminality need not be any bar to a determination of its dynamic aspect—i.e., the changes taking place in the course of time. (1939: 275)

Trend designs are relatively invulnerable to underreporting because, unlike studies of offense levels, they require only a single condition or assumption: that reported offenses are related to the real number of offenses by some constant, which can be known or unknown. For example, if roughly 50% of a nation's robberies are consistently reported to the police, then official statistics on this offense are a perfectly valid index of *trends* in robbery—even though the official statistics greatly underestimate the actual incidence of this offense.[5]

In trend designs, it is unnecessary to use weighting to correct for underreporting proportions or even to know what these proportions are—as long as a researcher is willing to assume that these proportions are stable over time. Trend designs are even valid if some types of variation occur in the underreporting proportion over time. If this proportion fluctuates randomly around some mean value, then trend designs would suffer only from random (or "benign") error and not biased (or "malignant") error (Naroll, 1962). Random error has been called "benign" because it generally affects a research design only in a conservative direction—that is, it can decrease a researcher's chance of discovering a relationship in a data set, but is unlikely to produce a spurious finding. In the case of crime trend research, this is because random errors inflate the nonmeaningful variance or "noise" in the offense rate. The effect of this "noise" upon research is called "attenuation," a reduction in the researcher's chance of identifying an important change or a relationship between two variables.

Spurious findings, by contrast, occur in cases of biased or malignant error—e.g., cases in which the error in the underreporting proportion over time is correlated, directly or indirectly, with an independent variable in a research design. For example, an urban police department's announced "crackdown" on street robberies could have the paradoxical effect of increasing the *official* robbery rate if the announcement somehow increases the likelihood that victims will report robberies, thus changing the underreporting proportion. The research designs in greatest jeopardy of spurious findings of this kind are, of course, studies designed to evaluate some intervention or policy change.

In general, trend designs require only the minimal assumption that underreporting proportions are stable over time, or at least stable with only random fluctuations. In theory, at least, this is an eminently testable assumption. In the case of American offense data, for example, one could test the temporal stability of underreporting proportions by means of consecutive replications of victimization surveys in the same jurisdictions—for example, by replicating in serial fashion the surveys of Santarelli et al. (1974a and 1974b) and Velde et al. (1975). Longitudinal victimization surveys of this kind could indicate whether underreporting proportions are stable over time. At the present time, however, definitive evidence on this question does not exist. For example, Skogan (1977b: 50) concluded that there were no data upon which to estimate the temporal relationship between reported and unreported offenses. At the same time, the existence of a National Crime Panel presupposes serial victimization surveys and, from a purely methodological perspective, this would be one of the most important contributions victimization research could make.

Lacking victimization surveys which are comparable over long periods of time, a number of less satisfactory approximations are available. For example, one of the reports of the National Crime Panel survey (Velde, McQuade, Wormeli, Bratt, and Renshaw, 1976) compared underreporting proportions in the 1973 and 1974 surveys; another (Velde, Wormeli, Bratt, and Renshaw, 1977) compared underreporting in the 1974 and 1975 victimization surveys. These comparisons do not provide ideal tests because they compare data from consecutive years rather than from longer intervals. But we have examined these data to see whether there are any changes in reporting over time and, if there are, whether these changes are any greater than the random fluctuations one would expect from sampling error alone in any survey.

In the study comparing the 1973 and 1974 data, the median percent change in reporting (offenses victims say they reported to police/all offenses victims say occurred) was +2.8% over 33 different offense categories. This figure was roughly half the median standard error (5.7%) for these 33 offense categories—that is, this 2.8% change in reporting appears to be due to sampling differences alone. In the comparison of the 1974 and 1975 data, the median change in reporting was +1.9% over 33 offense categories. This figure was, again, much smaller than the median standard error in these surveys (5.3%). In these two studies, therefore, the reporting proportions appear to be impressively stable, with no evidence of overall changes in underreporting.[6]

There is also some indirect evidence which offers grounds for considerable optimism on this point. The underreporting proportions for the twenty-six cities in table 3.1, for example, show generally impressive consistency within a given crime category. This cross-sectional evidence suggests that the magnitude of underreporting may be firmly linked to the nature of specific offenses rather than to the (presumably changing) conditions of individual cities.

In summary, the study of offense trends is notably less problematic than research on offense levels. Although much research remains to be done, existing evidence suggests that underreporting proportions are reasonably stable over time, at least for the more serious offenses. This relative stability may be because underreporting is a function primarily of the seriousness of an offense rather than of other, more transitory factors. As discussed earlier, data on homicide are immune to the effects of underreporting and therefore are a valid basis for comparative analyses of both levels of and trends in this offense.

PROBLEM 2: DIFFERENT INDICATORS

A persistent concern of researchers on crime and violence has been the relative merits of different indicators of the "real" level or rate of various offenses. There is a variety of potential indicators inherent in any criminal justice system: (1) the number of criminal acts known to the police ("offenses known"); (2) the number of suspected offenders detained ("arrests"); (3) the number of persons brought to trial ("indictments"); (4) the number of individuals found guilty of an offense ("convictions"); (5) the number of people sent to prison or some other institution ("incarcerations"); and even (6) the total number of persons incarcerated at any one time ("prison population").

Each of these indicators can provide a reflection of how much of a given offense is occurring in a society although, obviously, not all these reflections would be of equal size or accuracy. Various indicators occur at different distances from the offense itself, so that one would expect to observe roughly declining sums at successive points in the justice system: fewer arrests than offenses, fewer indictments than arrests, fewer convictions than indictments, and so on. This pattern of diminishing numbers has been called "criminal case mortality" (Van Vechten, 1942). One of the most famous dicta in the study of crime concerns this issue: "The value of a crime for index purposes decreases as the distance from the crime itself in terms of procedure increases" (Sellin, 1931: 346).

It is for this reason that the number of offenses known is considered to be the most accurate official measure of actual criminal behavior. It can be argued, of course, that victimization surveys are even closer to the offense than *any* of these official indicators (Maltz, 1977: 35). As a result, some researchers have concluded that, except for the fully enumerated offense of homicide, no official statistic will correspond directly to the number of criminal acts in society (Nettler, 1974: 44). At the same time, it is certainly the case that not all official statistics are equally accurate, and the number of known offenses is considered highly preferable to other indicators (Clinard and Abbott, 1973: 22).

Although less desirable as measures of the volume of crime, other indicators still have potential uses. For example, one could use the indicator of the prison population to see whether conviction and sentencing patterns are affected by crowding or vacancies in a society's prisons. It might be that judicial discretion in sentencing (e.g., suspended vs. served sentences) is highly sensitive to the prison space available. If so, one would expect to find that the severity of judicial sentencing would correlate with, but lag behind, fluctuations in indicators of the prison population.

For research designs in which the incidence of an offense is theoretically important, however, many researchers have assumed that valid analyses are impossible with measures other than the number of offenses known. This is a methodologically rather "purist" position and, although it appears to be widely held, an analysis presented later in this chapter suggests that this position greatly understates the validity and usefulness of other types of indicators. Whether or not the offenses-known indicator is available, however, it seems clear that many types of direct comparisons are not meaningful unless one has at least the *same* indicator in the jurisdictions one wishes to compare.

Different Indicators and Levels of Crimes

The problems posed by different indicators are particularly important for comparisons of the absolute level of an offense in a number of jurisdictions. These difficulties become acute in cross-national research because it cannot be assumed that the magnitudes of "case mortality" (e.g., attrition from the number of known offenses to the number of convictions) are similar across nations. Direct comparison using different indicators is vulnerable to potentially gross differences in the efficiency of national systems of criminal justice. It might be the case that 80% of all robberies are cleared by arrest in one society but only 25% in another nation. In this instance, national differences in the incidence of the offense would be hopelessly confounded with national differences in the clearance rate for this offense.

The hazards posed by this indicator problem are easy to illustrate concretely. Suppose, for example, that one wished to make a comparison of the absolute level of the homicide rates in the United States and Canada in 1970. This comparison would be impossible if only convictions data were available for the United States and only offenses known data for Canada. In some cases, the availability of additional data can solve this problem. If *both* indicators can be obtained for a sample jurisdiction or sample time period in one of these societies, one can determine the ratio of the two indicators and, on this basis, generate an estimate of the value of the missing indicator.

For example, if sample data show that homicide convictions in the United States are consistently .8 (4/5) times the number of known offenses, the convictions data could be weighted by 1.25 (5/4) to estimate the number of known offenses. This estimated number of known offenses in the United States in 1970 can then be compared with the reported number of known offenses in Canada in 1970. In the absence of a sample of simultaneous indicators for at least one society, however, a simple comparison across two different indicators would produce a spurious elevation in the estimate of the homicide rate in Canada.

The problem of different indicators has implications for research with the CCDF since our data file includes a variety of indicators. For most nations in the file, the preferred indicator of known offenses is available. For a few nations in the file, only a less desirable indicator, such as convictions, is available. For some of the nations in the CCDF, two indicators are available for the same years. Nations with multiple indicators can be used to assess the value of even poor indicators for certain research designs, and this analysis is presented below.

Different Indicators and Trends of Crime

As discussed above, different types of indicators are of variable quality for estimating the "true" incidence of an offense.[7] However, even imperfect indicators of the volume of an offense can still be useful indices of the *trends* in an offense if they can be assumed or shown to be related to the number of known offenses over time by some constant function. If this can be demonstrated, then fluctuations in these imperfect indicators (arrests, convictions, etc.) can still be used as indices of fluctuations in the incidence of known offenses. If indicators of different quality were found to bear a linear relationship to the number of known offenses, in short, it would be possible to use imperfect indicators to estimate trends in a good indicator which is not available.

Thus the critical empirical question concerns the relationship between good and imperfect indicators. Using data from the CCDF, we were able to assess the degree to which several different indicators manifest the same trends over time. The results of this analysis, using sixteen cases in the CCDF for which two indicators are available, are presented in table 3.2.

The evidence in table 3.2 strongly suggests that even poor indicators can serve as valid indicators of offense trends. This finding has nontrivial

Table 3.2. Correlations between Good and Imperfect Indicators of the Same Offense

Nation	Years	Indicators	Correlation between two indicators for each offense	
Australia	1964–1972	(1) Crimes known (2) Crimes cleared	Murder and manslaughter	1.00[a]
			Assault	1.00[a]
			Rape	.98
			Robbery	.96
Canada	1919–1943	(1) Offenses known (2) Convictions	Offenses against the person; murder, manslaughter and assault	.90
			Offenses against property with violence; robbery and burglary	.93
			Offenses against property without violence; theft	.94
Canada	1952–1967	(1) Charges (2) Convictions	Homicide	.82
			Assault	.96
			Robbery	1.00[a]
			Theft	.93
			Offenses against women	.98
Denmark	1933–1947	(1) Crimes known (2) Crimes cleared	Homicide	.95
			Assault	.96
			Rape	.90
			Robbery	.91
			Theft	.97
Denmark	1948–1959	(1) Crimes known (2) Crimes cleared	Homicide	.92
			Assault	.92
			Robbery	.91
			Theft	.87
			Rape	.81
Finland	1913–1924	(1) Offenses reported (2) Prosecutions	Homicide	.84
		(1) Offenses reported (2) Convictions	Homicide	.74

Table 3.2. (continued)

Nation	Years	Indicators	Correlation between two indicators for each offense	
Ireland	1961–1964	(1) Crimes known	Murder	.85
		(2) Court cases	Manslaughter	1.00[a]
			Assault	1.00[a]
			Indecent assaults against females	.99
			Robbery	1.00[a]
			Burglary and housebreaking	.99
			Offenses against property without violence	.41
Kenya	1964–1968	(1) Crimes known	Homicide	.79
		(2) Arrests	Robbery	.11
			Theft	.93
		(1) Crimes known	Homicide	.94
		(2) Convictions	Robbery	−.59
			Theft	.85
Mexico	1966–1972	(1) Cases presented	Homicide	.73
			Assault	.81
		(2) Convictions	Rape	.65
			Robbery	.89
Netherlands	1949–1972	(1) Final sentences	Murder and manslaughter; crimes against life	.77
		(2) Crimes known	Assault	.79
			Robbery, theft and housebreaking	.41
New Zealand	1920–1954 1956–1971	(1) Offenses known	All offenses	.96
		(2) Offenses cleared	All offenses	.98
Norway	1957–1970	(1) Offenses known	Homicide	.42
			Assault	.92
		(2) Persons proceeded against	Robbery–theft	.97
			Rape	.42

Table 3.2. (continued)

Nation	Years	Indicators	Correlation between two indicators for each offense	
Sweden	1959–1966	(1) Offenses	Homicide	.89
		reported	Robbery	.86
		(2) Offenses	Burglary	.48
		cleared	Rape	.82
Tanzania	1962–1972	(1) Crimes known	Murder and	
		(2) Convictions	manslaughter	−.60
			Assault	−.52
			Robbery	.74
			Theft	−.39
Thailand	1945–1962	(1) Crimes known	All offenses	1.00[a]
		(2) Convictions		
U.S.	1933–1971	(1) UCR murder and non-negligent manslaughter	Homicide	.85
		(2) Rates of death caused by homicides— vital statistics of U.S.[b]		

Median correlation across all cases:

Homicide, murder and manslaughter	.85
Rape	.86
Assault	.92
Robbery, property offenses with violence	.90
Theft	.90
All offenses (3 cases)	.98

[a] Correlation is .995 or greater
[b] Vital statistics section of U.S. Statistical Abstract

implications for cross-national research because of the inevitable heterogeneity in the criminal justice systems of different nations. The analyses summarized in table 3.2 substantially expand the number of comparative research designs which appear warranted. The general conclusion which emerges is that offense indicators from various stages of criminal justice processing "covary" over time—that is, they appear to trace similar trends over time. This finding suggests that while the notion of "criminal case mortality" is well founded, this "mortality" appears to be crudely linear—e.g., the proportionate reduction from crimes reported to police to convictions in a given society is approximately constant.

The correlational analysis in table 3.2 indicates that good and imperfect indicators of an offense provide a consistent picture of the trends in the incidence of this offense. For the offense of homicide, for example, the median correlation between good and poor indicators for the sixteen cases is .85. This suggests the existence of an extremely strong relationship, over time, between a good indicator—know offenses—and less optimal indicators such as offenses cleared, prosecutions, convictions, etc. Although there is some variation across various societies, in general, the pattern of the relationships is both clear and strong. If one is interested in the *trend* of an offense, it appears that many different indicators—not merely the "best" indicator of known offenses—provide a valid index.

The pattern appears to be equally encouraging for offenses other than homicide, to judge by the median correlations between good and poor indicators in table 3.2: rape (.86), assault (.92), robbery (.90), theft (.87), and "all offenses" (.98). By the standards of measurement reliability in the social sciences, these values are extremely high. For example, intelligence tests and other measures in wide use in psychology tend to have reliabilities in the range of .60–.75. Attitude scales commonly have reliabilities which are lower still. Purely from the perspective of social science measurement, therefore, the fact that imperfect indicators are correlated with the best measure in the range of .85–.95 is impressive.[8]

This analysis suggests that, at least for some types of research designs, the widespread belief that indicators other than offenses known are unusable is unwarranted. Criminal case mortality has clear implications for studies of offense *levels*—some indicators are suitable for research on offense levels while others are not. But for *trend* designs, in which one seeks to characterize the direction and degree of change in an offense, it seems clear that a variety of indicators can provide a valid measure. In addition, trend estimates from imperfect indicators appear to be equally valid for homicide and less serious offenses.

On the basis of this analysis, we have concluded that data which cannot support certain research designs are entirely valid for other designs. If one has available only data on homicide convictions for Sri Lanka, for example, it is not possible to compare the absolute number of homicide offenses in Sri Lanka and another nation with only records on the number of known offenses. But the convictions indicator *is* valid if one wishes, for example, to (1) compare long-term trends in homicide in Sri Lanka and some other nation, (2) determine the effect of employment changes on homicide rates in Sri Lanka, or (3) test for the possible changes in the homicide rate if Sri Lanka abolishes capital punishment.

In our view, this analysis argues for a *design-specific methodology* which reconceives the potential validity of data on crime and violence in terms of the research design to which these data are to be applied. This *design specificity* is important since many of the research designs in greatest demand in the social sciences are, explicitly or not, trend designs in which an investigator is concerned with whether an offense rate goes up, remains stable, or goes down. In a great many cases, we believe it is possible to answer these questions about trends and changes with a high level of confidence even if the indicator available does not allow us to know the precise level of this offense at any one time.[9]

In summary, the problems of underreporting and different indicators clearly have *selective* effects rather than general effects. These problems jeopardize certain research designs while affecting other designs not at all. The analysis presented thus far can be summarized in typological form in table 3.3. This typology presents four generic comparative designs created from the combinations of two dichotomies: (1) offense levels vs. offense trends, and (2) homicide vs. other offenses. This typology subsumes a substantial proportion of all comparative research on crime and violence.

Because these four generic research designs are *differentially* susceptible to the problems of underreporting and different indicators, the typology provides a useful summary of the methodological issues addressed in this chapter. Because it provides a succinct summary of the relative vulnerability of these different designs, this typology is analogous to the comparisons which Campbell and Stanley (1966) published for nonexperimental research in general. Since table 3.3 addresses some of the unique problems inherent in comparative designs using crime data, it is intended to be both more concrete and directly applicable to this particular research domain.

It is clear from the table that not all designs are equally immune to methodological problems. Type IV designs—which involve comparisons of changes or trends in homicide rates—are unaffected by either underreporting or the problem of different indicators. For these reasons, they are preferable in terms of validity to all other research designs on crime and violence. At the other end of the validity spectrum, Type I designs—which seek to compare the levels of lesser offenses in different jurisdictions—are likely to be invalidated by *both* these serious methodological problems. For these reasons, it is difficult to imagine circumstances under which Type I research designs can be justified on the basis of official statistics alone.[10]

The other two research designs have methodological weaknesses which are complementary. Type II designs, which examine the levels of homicide in different jurisdictions, are invulnerable to underreporting but are problematic if different indicators (arrests vs. convictions, etc.) are used in these jurisdictions.[11] Type III designs, by contrast, are vulnerable to the possibility of different underreporting proportions in different jurisdictions. But if one is willing to make the assumption that underreporting proportions are comparable in two jurisdictions (or can use victimization surveys to produce corrected offense rates), then these designs are probably valid even if different indicators are reported for these jurisdictions.

As indicated by this typology, the four generic research designs vary greatly in terms of the degree to which they are methodologically vulnerable. For this reason, it does not appear to be meaningful to discuss, in general terms, whether "research on crime statistics" is valid. Instead, this discussion needs to be design-specific rather than global. While certain generic research designs are almost certainly insupportable (at least on the basis of official statistics alone), others are both valid and unproblematic.

Table 3.3. Comparative Research Design Typology: Implications of Two Data Problems in Each of Four Designs

Type of Comparison	Offense Type	
	Nonhomicide offenses	Homicide offenses
	Type I $(-,-)$	*Type II* $(+,-)$
Levels	*Underreporting* $(-)$: Comparisons of levels of lesser offenses cannot be made until the ratio (offenses reported/total offenses) has been estimated for each jurisdiction to be compared. *Different indicators* $(-)$: Comparisons of levels of lesser offenses are not possible if different indicators are present unless (1) underreporting proportions are known (above) and (2) the relationship between different indicators can be estimated.	*Underreporting* $(+)$: Not a problem in U.S. homicide data; probably not a problem in comparative data. *Different indicators* $(-)$: Comparisons of homicide rate levels in different jurisdictions cannot be made if different indicators are reported unless an indicator ratio (e.g., convictions/all homicides) can be estimated for one jurisdiction to produce a common indicator for comparison across jurisdictions.

Table 3.3. (continued)

	Offense Type	
Type of Comparison	Nonhomicide offenses	Homicide offenses
	Type III $(-,+)$	*Type IV* $(+,+)$
Trends	*Underreporting* $(-)$: Comparisons of trends of lesser offenses can only be made if one can assume or show that the ratio (offenses reported/total offenses) is a constant over time (with no more than random fluctuations) in each jurisdiction compared. *Different indicators* $(+)$: Comparisons of trends in lesser offenses are possible if one assumes a constant underreporting proportion (above) since different indicators of the same offense are strongly correlated over time.	*Underreporting* $(+)$: Not a problem in U.S. homicide data; probably not a problem in comparative data. *Different indicators* $(+)$: Not a problem in U.S. and comparative homicide data; different indicators of homicide are strongly correlated over time.

CONTROLLING DATA QUALITY

The evidence reviewed above suggests that considerable variation exists (1) between indicators of different crimes, with indicators of homicide having the greatest validity, and (2) between different indicators of the same crime, with the indicator of offenses known the best index of the actual volume of crime. If one's research design calls for a comparison of the levels of violent crime in several jurisdictions, therefore, one might try to include these known differences in data quality in the research design. This might be done, for example, by limiting comparisons to those cases with data on the number of homicide offenses known.

It has been recognized for some time that it should be possible to include in a research design information about the *variable* quality of different data. The idea of "data quality control" was first suggested by Naroll (1962; Naroll and Cohen, 1970) as a method for dealing with large data archives in which some of the data can be assumed to be of higher quality than others. The basic principle of data quality control is a simple one: one should include in comparative research known data quality differences as a *variable* in the analysis.

There are a number of ways in which this might be done, but perhaps the simplest involves analyzing the data in sequential waves—the first wave would include only the data sets of highest quality, the second wave cases of average quality, and the third wave cases of the most doubtful quality. In this way, an investigator can estimate a result or test a hypothesis *within* each level of data quality. This procedure eliminates the possibility that spurious findings could be produced by comparing indicators of different quality.

For some uses of the data in the CCDF, data quality control may be appropriate and useful. In chapter 4, we present a study of the effects of wars upon violent crime rates in postwar societies. Using the CCDF, it was possible to identify for this analysis a large number of "nation-wars" (one nation in one war) and a number of control societies uninvolved in war. As a test of the effect of wars upon violent crime, the homicide rates of combatant and noncombatant nations were compared before and after the war years. As a part of the analysis, a data quality control procedure was used. In the first analysis, *all* the cases for which any homicide indicator could be obtained were included in the analysis. The second analysis, however, included *only* those cases for which the best homicide indicator (offenses known) was available. In this instance, both analyses pointed to the same conclusion about the effect of wars.

By making variations in data quality an explicit part of the analysis, data quality control excludes the possibility of spurious results due to complex interactions between the antecedent or causal variable and the type of indicator used in the analysis. In our study of the effect of wars, for example, data quality control eliminates the methodological danger that wars could produce increases in the actual level of homicide (offenses known) but decreases in the willingness of judges and juries to sentence offenders to prison (convictions and incarcerations). If this were the case, one might observe homicide increases in nations with the indicator of known offenses but apparent "decreases" in nations with the indicator of convictions.[12] In a large data set, complex interactions like this simple example would be invisible to the researcher without a data quality control procedure.

Whether or not a data quality control procedure should be used in a given study is largely a matter of the researcher's judgment. Most of the CCDF entries have a good indicator for homicide, for example, and studies of this offense may therefore not require data quality controls. The general attraction of a data quality control procedure, however, is that this simple method allows the researcher to examine a relationship or test a hypothesis while holding constant known or presumed variation in the validity of various data sets.

SUMMARY AND CONCLUSIONS

The premise guiding the methodological discussions in this chapter has been that the validity of research on crime and violence is *design-specific*. As a result of a number of specific methodological problems, some research designs are not defensible on the basis of official statistics alone, while others are demonstrably unaffected by these same problems. As a result of this analysis, we believe that an undifferentiated approach to crime statistics is methodologically unjustifiable. It cannot be argued persuasively that these data are either suitable or unsuitable for all purposes. It should be emphasized that we are not arguing that the validity of research with crime statistics is in any way indeterminate. Instead, the analysis presented in this chapter demonstrates that great variation exists across different research designs. Some research designs are perhaps fatally flawed, while others can be presumed to be valid.

In addition to the general finding that these methodological problems are design-specific in their implications, a number of specific conclusions appear warranted on the basis of existing research and additional analyses of data from the CCDF:

1. Homicide Data in All Designs. There is no evidence that official statistics on homicides underenumerate the actual incidence of this offense. As a result, homicide data constitute a valid basis for comparative research on both the levels and trends of this violent crime.

2. Nonhomicide Offenses in Level Designs.. Research on the level of nonhomicide offenses involves some threats to validity because official statistics on these crimes are subject to underreporting. While the magnitude and consistency of the underreporting proportions for these offenses are not known for all jurisdictions and time periods, it appears that offense seriousness and underreporting are inversely related—that is, most serious offenses are reported. In addition, one can use information presented in this chapter to test for the likelihood that an observed difference in offense levels between two jurisdictions could be an artifact of differential underreporting.

3. Nonhomicide Offenses in Trend Designs. Research on trends in nonhomicide offenses is somewhat less problematic than research on offense levels. In these designs, it is not necessary to know the real level of an offense. The only methodological assumption necessary is that the underreporting proportion remains constant with no more than random fluctuations. In addition, one can use information presented in this chapter to test for the likelihood that an apparent change in an offense rate could be an artifact of differential reporting.

4. *Different Indicators in Level Designs.* In attempting direct comparisons of offense levels in two jurisdictions, it is obviously essential that both jurisdictions report the same indicator. If each jurisdiction reports a different indicator, comparisons of levels of an offense are possible only if one has a sample of two overlapping indicators for the same period for at least one of the two jurisdictions.

5. *Different Indicators in Trend Designs.* While it is true that the indicator of known offenses is preferable to other indicators as a measure of the level of a given offense, a wide variety of indicators appear to be equally valid in research on trends or changes in an offense. As shown in this chapter, good and imperfect indicators are strongly correlated over time and may be considered substitutive in research on offense trends. This finding expands considerably the number of comparisons of offense rate trends and changes which are possible.

6. *Data Quality Control.* In a data set like the CCDF, considerable variation exists across individual cases. This variation includes differences in the indicator used, in the type of offense reported (e.g., "violent crimes" or different violent crimes listed separately), and almost certainly in the quality of the data themselves. These differences can be included in a research design by using a data quality control procedure described in this chapter.

One of the conclusions of the design-specific model is that some research designs are more conservative than others. Since the offense of homicide is fully enumerated, the most conservative comparative research design is to limit comparisons to levels and trends in this offense. In addition, the indicator of offenses known is widely regarded as the most valid offense indicator, so an even more conservative design would be to limit comparisons only to those nations with this particular homicide indicator.

While this research design is certainly unimpeachable, it is our view that nonhomicide data and other indicators are still useful and valid in certain types of research designs. In general, our approach in this chapter has been to examine the strengths and limits of these designs. In many cases, there appears to be strong empirical support for certain less conservative research designs. For example, evidence indicates that a large number of indicators provide an index of crime trends as valid as that provided by the offenses-known indicator. This finding provides strong support for the essentially substitutive nature of different indicators in trend designs.

In other cases, the appropriateness of the less conservative research designs is more a matter of indirect evidence. For example, comparisons of nonhomicide offenses can *include* the likelihood that differences in underreporting could explain an observed difference in offense rates. In this instance, one may want to approach less conservative research designs in a probabilistic manner. Using information like that presented in this chapter, it is possible in some cases to assess the relative likelihood that an observed difference could be spuriously produced by artifacts like reporting differences or, alternately, that the observed difference is genuine.

In the final analysis, of course, the researcher is best served by all possible efforts to assess the validity of the data in any given analysis. As indicated in this chapter, however, a great many research designs are viable. Certain designs are immune to serious methodologial problems while others are less conservative but still valid for specific comparative purposes. While this chapter has attempted to indicate the nature of major methodological pitfalls, the prospect for many forms of comparative research is clearly auspicious.

NOTES

1. While this conclusion appears to be true, it should not be taken to mean that there are no *unknown* homicides. There are cases, for example, in which a homicide is discovered only long after the fact—for example, when the bodies of long-dead victims are unearthed. Prior to discovery, these victims may have been classified as "missing persons," "runaways," etc. One suspects that hidden homicides of this kind are more common in societies like the United States in which homicides are unusually common.
2. Traditional lore among crime researchers has held that the offense of auto theft is also fully enumerated because most insurance policies require that a loss be reported as a prerequisite to compensation. Some victimization surveys have found that this offense is fully enumerated (e.g., Ennis, 1967), while other surveys suggest that the underreporting proportion is at least .90, though less than 1.00 (Velde, Work, and Holtzman, 1975: 61; Skogan, 1977).
3. The underreporting proportion can be estimated in different ways. In the city surveys summarized in table 3.1, the underreporting proportions are the ratio of two *self-report* figures: (1) the number of crimes respondents said they reported to police, and (2) the total number of crimes respondents said they experienced. The UCR/Ennis proportion, however, compares self-report data to the actual police statistics compiled in the FBI's *Uniform Crime Report*.
4. There are some circumstances, however, which can produce a "paper" crime wave merely by sudden increases in the underreporting proportion. An example might be a wave of prostitution or gambling arrests just prior to an election. A celebrated case of changing underreporting proportions involved New York City crime statistics in 1950 (Leonard, 1952; Wolfgang, 1963: 715; President's Commission on Law Enforcement and the Administration of Justice, 1967: 22–23). Before 1950, New York's statistics for several offenses were suspiciously low—for example, the city reported an absolute number of robberies smaller than that for the city of Chicago, yet Chicago's population was half the size of New York's. Under pressure from the FBI's *Uniform*

Crime Reports, New York initiated a centralized reporting system. This innovation radically changed the city's underreporting proportion and produced a "paper" crime wave—reported robberies rose about 400% and burglaries increased 1300%.

5. The importance of this issue was first recognized by researchers in the early nineteenth century (Wolfgang, 1963: 713; President's Commission on Law Enforcement and the Administration of Justice, 1967: 21). The assumption that reported offenses bear a constant relation to actual offenses has been an expressed part of the rationale for the interpretability of the records on serious offenses maintained in the FBI's *Uniform Crime Reports* (Wolfgang, 1963: 709). Most researchers interested in comparative research also have concluded that underreporting proportions in other nations are stable over time (Verkko, 1953; Wolf, 1971).

6. Naturally, these comparisons assume that similar questions, question sequences, and interview formats are used. Surveys that used different descriptions of what constitutes "assault" would, of course, produce different levels of self-reported victimization. For this reason, a standardization of victimization survey methods is of obvious importance.

7. It should be emphasized that the "true" incidence of an offense, by definition, can never be known. As discussed earlier, even victimization surveys may omit offenses, particularly those which are either trivial or highly sensitive. In addition, victimization surveys are merely another *estimate* of the offense rate, and the absence of a palpable, perfect record of offense incidence makes it impossible to know precisely how accurate this estimate is. As a result, except in the case of the fully enumerated offense of homicide, all research on crime deals in estimates rather than the *real* incidence of an offense.

8. The obtained correlations in the range of .85–.95 can be seen either as measures of *reliability* (in the test-retest sense where the true volume of an offense is unknown) or as measures of *validity* (if one assumes that the good measure is a reasonably error-free index of the true volume of an offense).

9. The essential argument in this analysis is that one indicator can serve as a proxy for another indicator which happens to be unavailable. In this case, the evidence suggests that an imperfect indicator like convictions can be used as a proxy for the missing indicator of offenses known in a trend design. As will be discussed in a later chapter, other types of proxy indicators are possible—e.g., using trends in urban homicide data to estimate national trends in cases where the national data are unavailable. The use of proxy variables is not recommended, of course, unless one has empirical evidence that the proxy variables are likely to bear a strong relationship to the missing variable. In addition, although most social science research is concerned with trends, some studies involve an interest in residuals, short-term fluctuations which remain when time-series data have been "detrended." It is our view that this issue is less central to research on crime and violence, and we have not attempted it here. This question could be addressed using CCDF data, of course, simply by "detrending" a good and a poor indicator and then correlating the residuals (Kendall, 1973; Johnston, 1972).

10. Type I designs are possible, however, if one has available certain types of additional information. One would need estimates of the underreporting proportions for each jurisdiction to be compared and, in cases where different indicators are also involved, one would also need to be able to estimate the relationships among these different indicators (e.g., convictions/offenses known). While this additional information is not impossible to obtain, it cannot be estimated from official statistics alone.

11. This comparison is possible, of course, if one can estimate the relationship, within one of the societies, between the given indicator and the missing indicator. In the case of a society which reports only homicide convictions, for example, analysis of official archives might make it possible to learn for a sample of years how many homicide cases had produced the number of convictions reported. This would allow one to

estimate the convictions/known offenses ratio, and this ratio could be used to transform convictions data into estimates of the number of known offenses.

12. It should be noted that the mathematical possibility of interactions of this nature varies inversely with the degree to which different indicators of the same offense are correlated over time. The evidence reviewed earlier in this chapter suggests that different indicators (offenses known, convictions, etc.) are in fact *highly* correlated over time. As a result, it is improbable that homicide offenses and homicide convictions would show contradictory trends. For this reason, the risk of "indicator interactions" in trend designs may not be great in most cases.

II.

VIOLENCE IN CROSS-NATIONAL PERSPECTIVE

FOUR

Violent Acts and Violent Times: The Effect of Wars on Postwar Homicide Rates

The term *violence* conjures up the image of dangerous individuals. We tend to think of violent acts and violent actors in concrete, personalized form. This individualistic bias obscures the very real violence committed by authorities in the pursuit of domestic social control, or by governments in the pursuit of foreign war. Serious violence, including homicide, is produced routinely in the course of law enforcement, criminal punishment and executions, crowd and riot control, political subversion and assassination and, of course, war.

While these mortal acts are sometimes politically controversial, they clearly benefit from unique auspices. The private acts of destructive individuals are treated as illegal violence, while official acts of violence are granted the mantle of state authority, and thus shielded from criticism and criminal sanctions. The privileged nature of official violence cannot be explained by its consequences, since these can be extremely grave. Perhaps the most conspicuous example, war—in any era, but particularly in the nuclear age—consists of mass homicides on a scale that greatly overshadows the individual acts of even the bloodiest murderers.

The privileged status enjoyed by official violence instead appears to lie in the nature of authority itself. Official violence and killing are legitimated by a variety of justifications—to deter potential criminals, stem the spread of an alien ideology, defend private property, control government opponents, or secure national defense. Unlike the excuses of violent individuals, these justifications compel widespread support precisely because they are associated with authority. As a result, the state exercises an effective monopoly on legitimate violence.

Examples of the privileged status of official violence are not difficult to find. Surveys of public opinion in the United States indicate that, for many citizens, official violence is regarded as inherently unproblematic. These surveys show extremely widespread public support for violence committed by police—for shooting looters during riots, and for shooting political protesters in general (Gamson and McEvoy, 1972: 336; Kahn, 1972: 48). The privileged status of official force and killing affects even the meaning of the word *violence* itself. For example, one might imagine that all serious assaults and shooting would be regarded as acts of violence. In a 1969 survey, however, 30% of those questioned said that "police beating students" was not an act of violence, and an astonishing 57% said that "police shooting looters" was not an act of violence (Blumenthal, Kahn, Andrews, and Head, 1972: 73). The very label of violence, therefore, clearly reflects the perceived legitimacy of the actor and not merely the seriousness or mortality of the act itself.

A similar pattern has characterized many scholarly discussions. There are, to be sure, researchers whose work has focused on official violence. For example, Couch (1968) and Marx (1970) have drawn attention to the extensive and lethal violence often produced by authorities during riots, protests, and civil disorders; Singer and Small (1972) have inventoried the mortality of wars. Most textbooks on violence and aggression, however, rarely treat police homicides, capital punishment, crowd and riot control, or war. In part, this may be because governments often play an important role in defining the "problem" of violence and, in many instances, these definitions omit the acts of government itself (Archer and Gartner, 1978, 1981b, 1983). It is of course not surprising that scholars and governments find criminal homicides and illegal violence worthy of study. What is curious, however, is that this concern with violent individuals has all too often eclipsed the study of violent authorities.

An important instance of this definitional omission is contained in an account, written by the commission's codirector, of the prestigious President's Commission on the Causes and Prevention of Violence (Short, 1975). This commission initially adopted a neutral definition of violence, one that emphasized the nature of violent acts themselves: "[Violence is] the threat or use of force that results, or is intended to result, in the injury or forcible restraint or intimidation of persons, or the destruction or forcible seizure of property" (Short, 1975: 68). Early in the life of the commission, this definition prompted staff researchers to cast a wide net. The commission's *Progress Report* stressed this point:

> There is no implicit value judgment in this definition. The maintenance of law and order falls within it, for a policeman may find it necessary in the course of duty to threaten or use force, even to injure or kill an individual. Wars are included within this definition, as is some punishment of children. It also includes police brutality, the violence of the Nazis, and the physical abuse of a child. (Short, 1975: 68)

Even though official violence was therefore prominent in the commission's initial agenda, this emphasis all but disappeared in its subsequent research. For example, by the time its final report was issued, the commission was concentrating on "all illegal violence" (Short, 1975: 69).

The insertion of the adjective *illegal* excluded official violence, since the acts of government are seldom regarded as illegal, and shifted attention instead to violent felons, members of rioting mobs, assassins, and other "deviant" individuals. The exclusion of official violence is particularly striking since the commission performed its work at the height of the Vietnam War. Although some commission members had suggested creating a special task force on war, the idea was abandoned because of the "potentially explosive nature of such a direct focus on war in general and on the conflict in Indochina in particular" (Short, 1975: 71).

Because of their unrivaled scale, wars and wartime homicides are clearly the ultimate form of official violence. The governments in whose name wartime killings are done are likely to refer to these deaths using neutral terms like "casualties," "body counts," or simply "losses," just as civil authorities use the term "executions." These euphemisms for violent death are preferred by authorities because the terms *killing* or *murder* connote the kinds of illegal violence for which punishment is generally administered. Opponents of wars, or of capital punishment, are the only ones who challenge the euphemisms, claiming that these acts too are "killings" and "murders." The definitional boundary between official violence and illegal violence sometimes blurs, as in the intense controversies that sometimes surround alleged "war crimes" (Kelman and Lawrence, 1972). For many citizens, the concept of war crimes is unimaginable because, by definition, even the deadliest acts of governments are never conceived of or labeled as violence.

The widespread deference to war and other forms of official violence seems problematic, or at least curious, since acts of illegal violence appear to be universally abhorred and strongly condemned. This chapter examines one aspect of the boundary separating official violence from individual violence and, in particular, explores the possibility that legal killings may increase the probability that illegal killings will follow.

CONSEQUENCES OF VIOLENCE BY THE STATE

For the past several years, we have been interested in the consequences of violence by the state. Specifically, we wondered whether participation in a war tends to increase the level of violence in a society after the war is over. There are rather compelling theoretical reasons to suspect that wars might produce a legacy of postwar violence. For example, there is now powerful evidence that social learning or "modeling" mediates many forms of aggression and violence (Bandura, 1973).

Although most research in this area has used either experiments or causal regression techniques to assess the effects of watching violence on various media, "modeling" theory also appears to provide the best explanation of the apparently contagious patterning of specific murder methods, airplane hijackings, and terrorism (Bandura, 1973: 101–07). The basic tenet of social learning theory is that acts of violence, whether real and immediate or shown on the media, can provide a model or script, increasing the likelihood of imitative violence. In addition, research indicates that aggressive models appear to be most influential when they appear to be rewarded (Bandura, 1973).

If the violent acts of real or fictional individuals can compel imitation, it seemed to us possible that official violence like war could also provide a script for the postwar acts of individuals. Wars, after all, carry the full authority and prestige of the state, and wars also reward killing in the sense that some war "heroes" are decorated and lionized, often in direct proportion to the number of homicides they have committed. Wars also, of course, carry objectives and rationalizations unique to each war— securing the Crimea, humbling the Boers, stopping fascism, deterring Communism, and so on. But what all wars have in common is the unmistakable moral lesson that homicide is an acceptable, even praiseworthy, means to certain ends. It seems likely that this lesson will not be lost on at least some of the citizens in a warring nation. Wars, therefore, contain in particularly potent form all the ingredients necessary to produce imitative violence: great numbers of violent homicides under official auspices and legitimation, with conspicuous praise and rewards for killing and the killers.

This idea that wars might foster violence has a long history in both public discussions and scholarly forums. Erasmus, Sir Thomas More, and Machiavelli each claimed that wars left a legacy of increased crime and lawlessness (Abbott, 1918, 1927; Hamon, 1918). Such speculation has sometimes been supported by later research; thus Hanawalt (1979) found a sharp rise in violent crime in England in the mid-1300s that she attributes to various civil and foreign wars of that period.

Using records from France during and after the Franco-Prussian War, Durkheim postulated a somewhat complex relationship between war and various types of crime (1957: 117–18). He noted that while most crimes against property decreased during the war, a considerable increase occurred in 1871, at the close of the conflict. Of greater interest to him, however, was the relatively steady rate of homicide during the war, followed by a sharp rise (45% in his estimation) in the postwar period. To explain this pattern, Durkheim argued that war reinforces sentiments "alien to humanity and the individual":

[War] reduces societies, even the most cultivated, to a moral condition that recalls that of lower societies. The individual is obscured; he ceases to count; it is the mass which becomes the supreme social factor; a rigid authoritarian discipline is imposed on all volitions. (1957:117)

Just as Durkheim's interest in the influence of wars on criminal activity was sparked by his own nation's experiences in a contemporary war, much of the recent scholarly and popular writing on this topic has appeared during or immediately following the wars of the twentieth century. Shortly after World War I ended, for example, several public figures suggested that the war had increased criminality and lawlessness. Among these were Winston Churchill, Clarence Darrow, and President Abbott Lawrence Lowell of Harvard University (Abbott, 1927: 213; Darrow, 1922: 218; Lowell, 1926: 299).

The end of the First World War also saw the appearance of a number of scholarly works which focused on eighteenth- and nineteenth-century wars. Thus, Tarde (1912), Bonger (1916), and Roux (1917) examined changes in various crimes in France following the Revolution of 1848 and in both France and Germany after the Franco-Prussian War of 1870. On the basis of a review of six nineteenth-century wars, Sorokin (1928: 340–44) concluded that whether a war increased crime in a country depended upon such factors as the war's outcome, its popularity, and whether it was fought at home or abroad.

Using contemporary legislation and published accounts of the era, Nevins (1924) argued that the American Revolution produced an upsurge in horse-stealing and highway robbery in many states. Abbott's (1927) review of prison records from eleven states led her to conclude that the Civil War led to a great increase in the number of men sent to prison, many of them veterans. She quotes from a contemporary author:

> A man who has lost one arm in the defense of the nation working with the other at the convict's bench is not an agreeable spectacle nor do we like to see the comrades of Grant and Sherman, of Foote and Farragut, exchange the blue coat of victory for the prison jacket. (Abbott, 1927: 234)

Most research published in this period, however, was concerned with the impact of World War I itself. Studies were made in Austria (Exner, 1927), France (Calbairac, 1928), Italy (Levi, 1929), Czechoslovakia (Solnar, 1929), Germany (Leipman, 1930), the United States (Engelbrecht, 1937; Sutherland, 1943), and England (Mannheim, 1941, 1955). Among the most influential of these researchers were Exner (1927), who attributed crime increases to economic problems after wars, and Mannheim, who emphasized noneconomic factors, such as "the general cheapening of all values; loosening of family ties; [and] weakened respect for the law, human life, and property" (Mannheim, 1955: 112). In the most rigorous study of this period, Sellin (1926) compared postwar homicide changes in five belligerent nations in World War I with the changes in four nonbelligerent nations. He concluded that the warring nations did experience increases, although differences between the warring and noncombatant nations were not uniform.

World War II renewed interest in this question. A number of researchers dealt with crime changes during wartime years, including Sellin (1942), Reckless (1942), Glueck (1942), Bromberg (1943), and von Hentig (1947). Wartime changes in nine Allied and neutral nations were also surveyed by an international group of criminologists (Commission Internationale Pénale et Pénitentiaire, 1951). Post–World War II changes were examined for five countries by Lunden (1963, 1967), who compared the raw number of crimes committed after the war with the number committed during the single year prior to the outbreak of the war. Lunden reported finding increases after the war, which he attributed to social disorganization, increased mobility, and disruption of community life.

There have been few studies of crime changes during recent wars. As part of a study of American political turmoil during the Vietnam War, Tanter (1969) cited the increase in crimes of violence during the war years. This increase prompted him (1969: 436) to suggest that "as the war continues, it facilitates a state of 'normlessness' in which traditional strictures against criminal acts lose their effectiveness." In reviewing the historical waves of violent crime in the United States, Gurr (1981) noted that the third such wave commenced near the beginning of U.S. involvement in Vietnam. Indeed, during the Vietnam War, the murder and non-negligent manslaughter rate in the United States more than doubled, from 4.5 per 100,000 population in 1963 to 9.3 in 1973 (FBI *Uniform Crime Reports,* 1963–73). This rapid increase was especially striking because it followed a period of almost monotonic decline in the rate since record keeping began in 1933. The rising homicide rate served as only the most recent evidence for Gurr's (1981) conclusion that the greatest peaks in violent crime in England and the United States have consistently been associated with these nations' involvements in various wars.

This body of research is difficult to evaluate critically, partly because of differences in focus. Some studies are concerned with crime rate changes during wars; others, with postwar changes. There are studies of homicide, theft, violent crime, or crime in general, undifferentiated by type. There are studies of the direct effects of wars upon the behavior of returned veterans, and others focusing on more general effects upon the civilian populations of combatant nations. These differences have had important implications. Although individual reserachers have tended to generate hypotheses appropriate to only one possible effect of war— for example, postwar homicides committed by returned veterans—comparison of their findings is a formidable task, since they have frequently been discussing quite different phenomena.

For several reasons, some aspects of the study of war and crime are more problematic than others. For example, the interpretation of crime rates during major wars is severely complicated by the large number of simultaneous social changes. During major wars, crime rates are likely to be depressed by many social changes, including:

1. the massive removal of young men from the civilian population through conscription and enlistment. For example, von Hentig (1947) reported that New York City's population shrank by 750,000 people, mostly young males, during World War II, and Bennett (1953) estimated that during World War II, more than 80% of American men between 20 and 25 enlisted or were drafted.

2. the premature release of convicts on the condition that they enter the armed forces. This greatly reduces the number of offenders released into civilian society. Abbott (1918) reported that this practice is at least as old as the Civil War, and Mannheim (1965) found that it occurred in other nations as well.

3. the tendency not to convict or imprison persons arrested during major wars. Such judicial leniency obviously reduces criminal statistics on convictions and prison populations. Abbott (1918), Mannheim (1941), and von Hentig (1947) reported evidence of a reduced willingness to prosecute offenders and a tendency for wartime employers to pay the fines of their workers rather than lose them to imprisonment.

4. greater opportunity for parolees to enter the job market. Parolees too old for the armed services, unlike their peacetime counterparts, can easily find employment as a result of labor shortages created by wars (von Hentig, 1947).

5. the wartime shortages of commodities often involved in crimes, particularly alcohol (Abbott, 1918; Exner, 1927; Mannheim, 1941).

6. changes in national systems of law enforcement, including reductions in police forces (Mannheim, 1965).

The impact of all these factors seems likely to vary directly with the level of wartime mobilization; that is, crime rates will be more depressed by these factors in large wars than in small wars. During some wars, there also may be social changes that *increase* crime rates, including (1) the disruption of families by conscription, long employment hours, and, sometimes, evacuation (Mannheim, 1941); (2) the existence of special crime opportunities, like blackouts, bombed-out houses, and other unguarded property (Mannheim, 1941: 131); and (3) the creation of new types of crimes by special wartime regulations such as rationing (Sutherland and Cressey, 1960: 208).

Finally, other factors that have limited the usefulness of wartime offense data are (1) the confusion of crimes and acts of resistance in occupied nations (Mannheim, 1965); (2) a persistent belief that "crime-prone" persons tend to enlist, as Tarde (1912) proposed; (3) changes in the boundaries of warring nations (Sutherland, 1943); and (4) the fact that record keeping is often interrupted during wartime. Because of these and other simultaneous social and economic changes during major wars, many researchers have concluded that the immediate effects of wars on offense rates are difficult or even impossible to discern (von Hentig, 1947; Sutherland and Cressey, 1960; Mannheim, 1965; Will-bach, 1948).

Although there are also a number of complexities in the interpretation of postwar rates, this topic is more promising methodologically because many of the special characteristics of wartime society diminish or disappear with the end of the war. For example, peace generally returns large numbers of young men to civilian society, reunites families, eliminates tremendous wartime labor needs, restores law enforcement agencies to normal manpower levels, and ends war-related commodity shortages. There may be some social and demographic changes, however, that could continue to affect offense levels in postwar periods, generally in a *conservative direction*—that is, reducing levels of various offenses.

One of the most important of these factors, particularly after major wars, involves changes in the age and sex structure of a nation's population due to the number of young men killed during the war. These losses sometimes have been of enormous magnitude. For example, out of every 1,000 of their compatriots aged 20 to 45 at the outbreak of World War I, 182 Frenchmen had died by the end of the war, 166 Austrians, 155 Germans, 101 Italians, and 88 Englishmen (von Hentig, 1947: 349). Since young men are universally overrepresented in many offense rates, particularly homicide (Wolfgang and Ferracuti, 1967), massive losses of young men remove from the population precisely those most likely to commit these offenses in the postwar years.

A second factor which would operate in a conservative direction involves the possibility that veterans arrested for or convicted of certain crimes would be treated with leniency because of their military service. Such a practice has existed for some time; for example, Abbott (1918) said that after the Civil War judges often pardoned first offenders who were veterans. Leniency toward arrested veterans also has been cited by researchers of the First World War, even in cases involving very serious offenses (Mannheim, 1941: 119).

Such leniency would affect some offense indicators more than others, with the indicators farthest removed from the offense itself—that is, data on convictions and prison population—most influenced. Data on the number of offenses known to the police, however, would be unaffected by judicial leniency. This difference between types of crime indicators was emphasized in a discussion of wartime crime by Sutherland (1956), who concluded that conviction rates were potentially misleading (i.e., too low) because of factors like judicial leniency. At any rate, judicial leniency (like the loss of young men) could operate only in a conservative direction, so that the observed rates of some offenses would understate the actual incidence of these crimes.

Although the data needed for studies of postwar changes are therefore relatively interpretable, available studies on this question have left important questions unanswered—for example, whether only warring nations experience postwar increases or whether all nations, combatant and noncombatant, experience comparable increases. With apparently a single exception (the 1926 study by Sellin cited earlier), case studies of postwar crime rate trends have not analyzed a control group of nations uninvolved in war. Without such a controlled comparison based on a large sample of nations, it is impossible to separate the direct effects of war from international crime rate trends which happen to include the warring nations.

One reason a strategy of controlled comparison has not been attempted is simply that historical and comparative crime data have been unavailable; the lack of data has limited researchers to one or at most a handful of nations. The problem has been aggravated by variation in the types of indicators kept by individual nations (Wolfgang, 1967). It has been recognized for some time (Sellin, 1931) that arrest and conviction data are more subject to judicial and police discretion than are data on the number of known offenses. Since these types of discretion could be important factors in postwar societies (particularly in the case of veterans suspected of some offense), the net effect of this variation in record keeping is to reduce the comparability of data kept by certain nations.

A second limitation of studies of postwar changes has been their inattention to differences in national war experiences, which are likely to produce dissimilar effects on crime rates (Sorokin, 1928; Mannheim, 1941; Sutherland, 1956). In part, this has been an inevitable consequence of the extremely small samples available. However, Sutherland (1956) concluded that an examination of the effects of different types of war participation was impossible at the time he wrote because variations in the experiences of individual nations in individual wars had not been quantified. Since Sutherland believed that these differences could be important, the absence of empirical bases for comparing national war participation led him to conclude that, "For these reasons, the effect of wars on crimes is not a good theoretical problem" (Sutherland, 1956: 120).

In summary, studies of wartime and postwar changes in crime rates have tended to be inconclusive. Studies of crime changes during wartime probably cannot go beyond simple description because of the large number of interdependent social changes which occur during most wars. Studies of crime changes in postwar years, while more promising, have been weakened in the past by: (1) extremely small sample sizes, often as small as a single nation during a single war; (2) the absence of a control group of nations uninvolved in the war studied; (3) different types of crime rate indicators that may be differentially susceptible to artifacts and therefore incomparable; and (4) the failure to operationalize characteristics of different types of national participation in wars.

THEORETICAL MODELS

A number of theoretical models have been advanced to explain crime rate changes during war years, during postwar years, or both. Some indication of the variety of competing explanations is contained in a comment by Sutherland:

> One theory states that war produces an increase in crimes because of the emotional instability of wartime, and another states that wars produce a decrease in crimes because of an upsurge of national feeling. One states that crimes of violence increase in wartime because of the contagion of violence, and another that they decrease because of the vicarious satisfaction of the need for violence. (1956: 120–21)

We have identified seven theoretical models which attempt to explain the effects of war on wartime and postwar rates of various offenses. We have also tried to derive expectations or predictions from each of these models. There is some agreement between the predictions implicit in two or more of the theoretical explanations. However, the seven models are sufficiently distinct theoretically to justify a separate discussion of each.

I. Artifacts Model

Some researchers have suggested that any changes in wartime or postwar crime rates are due to various artifacts (e.g., Reckless, 1942: 378). Two examples of demographic artifacts are the depression of wartime crime rates by the conscription of young men and the depression of postwar rates by the loss of men killed and maimed in the war. In addition, specific artifacts may operate in individual nations in a given war. For example, American crime rates in the 1960s were increased by the age-

1969   1971   1964
1974

structure changes produced by the "baby boom" of the post–World War II period (President's Commission on Law Enforcement and the Administration of Justice, 1967: 25).

It may be possible to control for some artifacts. For example, in the case of the effect of the baby boom, data on the age of persons arrested could be examined to see if age groups other than the baby boom cohort experienced changes. The artifacts model does not make any general predictions but suggests the need to inspect any observed crime changes to control for possible artifacts.

2. Social Solidarity Model

Several researchers have suggested that wars increase social solidarity and, as a result, reduce crime rates. For example, Sumner wrote in his classic *Folkways* (1906: 12) that wars increased discipline and the strength of law. It has even been suggested that habitual criminals are influenced by the exigencies of war. For example, Mannheim (1941: 108) quoted a 1914 article from *The Times* of London: "The criminal like the honest citizen is impressed by the War conditions which make it every man's duty to give as little trouble as possible."

The social solidarity model leads to the expectation that rates of crime will decline during wartime compared to the prewar period. This model also predicts that postwar crime rates should, with the passing of the temporary crisis, be comparable to prewar rates.

3. Social Disorganization Model

Because wars disrupt the established order of societies, some researchers have attributed crime increases to this disorganization. The concept of social disorganization has been used with considerable imprecision, and there are really two versions of this model. Some researchers use it to describe anomic changes which could occur in any warring nation, victorious or defeated: property losses, rapid industrialization, changes in the labor force, sudden population migrations, the break up of families, and so forth.

Most researchers, however, have used the concept to describe the social and psychological changes in a defeated nation (Mannheim, 1965: 595; Lunden, 1963; 1967: 77–97). Sutherland and Cressey (1960: 209) used this version of the social disorganization model: "Postwar crime waves are confined largely to countries which suffer rather complete disintegration of their economic, political and social systems as a result of the war."

As used by some researchers, then, the social disorganization model predicts that postwar crime increases would occur as a function of rapid social changes which any warring nation could experience. As used by other researchers, this model predicts that crime rate increases would be largely confined to defeated nations.

4. Economic Factors Model

Economic factors often have been cited as a cause of wartime and postwar crime rate changes. Commodity shortages and other economic changes were the main variables in Exner's (1927) theory concerning wartime property crime. Mannheim (1941: 205) also concluded that property offenses "invariably thrive during and after wars." The general relationship between economic changes and homicide is, however, much less clear (e.g., Henry and Short, 1954; Radzinowicz, 1971).

Discussions of war-related economic changes have reflected two quite different explanatory variables: (1) scarcities created by wars and (2) the general level of employment and other economic indicators. This second explanation reflects the fact that while wartime years frequently have brought full employment, postwar years often have not. If economic factors are related to violent crimes, different homicide rate changes would be expected as a result of the relative economic health of prewar and postwar society.

The economic factors model, then, predicts a decrease in postwar property crime rates in cases where the postwar economy is relatively better than prewar, and an increase in property crime where the postwar economy is relatively worse. The implications of the economic factors model for homicide rates are, however, unclear.

5. Catharsis Model

A persistent belief about wars has been the idea that they substitute public violence for private violence. Sorokin (1925: 146) claimed that revolutions temporarily abate "criminal murders" only to have them return to normal levels at the end of the conflict. Many other researchers suggest that wars provide an outlet for aggressive sentiments or "instincts" (e.g., Mannheim, 1941: 128), and therefore predict that crimes of violence will decrease during wartime. The implications of this model for postwar rates depend upon how long the cathartic effects are thought to last. However, a corollary of the catharsis model might be the prediction that societies whose experiences in war have been the most violent, and therefore the most cathartic, will experience postwar decreases in violent crimes.

6. Violent Veteran Model

At least since the American Revolution, people have wondered whether war veterans are more likely than others to commit crimes of violence.

In a famous charge to a Charleston, South Carolina, grand jury in 1783, Judge Aedanus Burke said that violent crime was being committed by men who had become accustomed to plundering and killing during the Revolutionary War and had since turned upon their neighbors (Wecter, 1944: 70). The essential idea of this model is that the experience of war resocializes soldiers to be more accepting of violence and more proficient at it.

It has been suggested, for example, that combat develops an "appetite for violence" (Hamon, 1918: 355) and the "habit" of violent solutions to problems (Abbott, 1918: 40). Attorney Clarence Darrow (1922: 218) attributed post–World War I crime increases to returned veterans who had been "innoculated with the universal madness." The idea of the homicide-prone veteran has also appeared as a frequent theme in fiction (e.g., Remarque's *The Road Back*, 1931).

A number of spectacular case studies appear to lend substance to the image of the violent veteran. For example, some soldiers who rode with Quantrill's guerrillas during the American Civil War became well known for their postwar lawlessness; they were Jesse and Frank James and the Younger brothers. There are also more recent examples. In 1949 a combat veteran named Howard Unruh, who had won marksman and sharpshooter ratings during World War II, went on a rampage in Camden, New Jersey, killing twelve people with a souvenir pistol. During the Vietnam War, a soldier named Dwight Johnson killed about twenty of the enemy and was awarded the Congressional Medal of Honor; several months after his return home to Detroit, he was shot and killed while trying to rob a grocery store. Case studies prove very little by themselves, of course. The more general question is whether the acts of violent veterans can explain any homicide increases observed in postwar societies.

This recurring idea has appeared with renewed strength in connection with American veterans of the Vietnam War. Their potential problems are the subject of several articles in a collection edited by Mantell and Pilisuk (1975). Psychiatrist Robert J. Lifton (1970: 32) makes the following prediction about these veterans: "Some are likely to seek continuing outlets to a pattern of violence to which they have become habituated, whether by indulging in antisocial or criminal behavior or by offering their services to the highest bidder." This model predicts that violent crimes will increase in the postwar societies of all nations participating in a war as a result of the violent acts of returning war veterans.

7. Legitimation of Violence Model

The central concept of this explanation is that civilian members of a warring society also are influenced by the "model" of officially approved wartime killing and destruction. During a war, a society reverses its customary prohibitions against killing and instead honors acts of violence which would be regarded as murderous in peacetime. Several researchers have suggested that this social approval or legitimation of violence produces a lasting reduction of inhibitions against taking human life (Sorokin, 1925: 139; Engelbrecht, 1937: 188–90). A quote from Reverend Charles Parsons around the time of World War I illustrates this model:

> When the rules of civilized society are suspended, when killing becomes a business and a sign of valor and heroism, when the wanton destruction of peaceable women and children becomes an act of virtue, and is praised as a service to God and country, then it seems almost useless to talk about crime in the ordinary sense. (1917: 267)

If wartime killing does legitimate homicidal violence in some lasting or general way, as this model suggests, then one would expect increases in violent crime in postwar societies. In addition, since civilians and soldiers alike could be influenced by the legitimation process, this model predicts that homicide increases will occur among both veterans and nonveterans.

Having listed these seven theoretical models and the predictions associated with each one, we should point out that an empirical test of their relative strengths contains serious pitfalls. As discussed earlier, predictions concerning wartime crime are probably not investigable. There also may be some difficulties in evaluating predictions concerning postwar crime. For example, it may be that more than one of the models operates after a given war. If so, their interaction could make a comparison of the models extremely difficult since the effects of one model could mask the effects of another.

It is also interesting to consider what kinds of evidence would constitute disconfirmation of each theoretical model. In some previous studies, crime rate changes in a single society have been treated as sufficient evidence upon which to ground or to discount certain explanations. For example, Mannheim (1941) based his major work on a single nation during a single war—England during World War I. He interpreted the fact that English homicide rates did not increase after that war to mean that violent crimes do not in general increase after wars. The same single case was used by Sutherland and Cressey (1960) as evidence for a refutation of the violent veteran model.

It is our belief that a fair test of the different predictions requires a large and heterogeneous sample of cases to minimize the idiosyncratic experiences of individual nations or individual wars. Inspection of a large number of cases would also maximize the chances of discovering

differential effects of various types of wars and various types of participation. In addition, we believe that only a strategy of controlled comparison between combatant and noncombatant societies can discount the
possibility that both experience the same crime rate changes.

RECORDS OF WARS

Our previous discussion of the possible effects of wars on crime has
considered various problems with the independent variable—the meaningful measurement of characteristics of different wars. For example,
one of the problems cited by Sutherland was variation among wars:

> Wars vary widely in many respects, and the constituent elements have not
> been standardized, nor have their comparative weights in the total complex
> of war been determined. Consequently, we do not know, even approxi-
> mately, how much more "war" is involved in one war than in another. (1956:
> 120)

Since Sutherland, efforts have been made to operationalize measures
of the kind he indicated had been lacking. The most comprehensive
analysis has been published by Singer and Small (1972), who reviewed
wars between 1816 and 1965 and, for each war, recorded the number
of war dead, the length of each nation's participation, the size of each
nation's standing army, and several other variables. Although the Singer
and Small study does not include all the variables of possible relevance
to our study, it does provide indices which can be used to compare some
of the ways different wars have affected individual nations.

PROCEDURES

Our analysis uses the Singer and Small (1972) data to compare postwar
homicide rates with prewar rates, but, for reasons discussed earlier, will
not discuss wartime rates.[1] The basic design involves a comparison of
the mean level of the rate of homicide during a fixed prewar period
with the mean level of the rate of homicide during a fixed postwar period.
Somewhat arbitrarily, the length of both periods has been set at five
years, although homicide data are available for fewer than five years in
a few cases. This length was preferred over shorter periods (e.g., one
year) to minimize the impact of special social forces in the single year
before and after a war and to reduce the effect of annual fluctuations.
The five-year interval was chosen instead of longer periods for pragmatic
reasons—the history of the twentieth century has not been characterized
by long intervals of peace.

Even using a five-year interval, some wars cannot be studied. For example, the Korean War is not included in this design because the five years preceding it include the years immediately following World War II. Use of the five-year interval also makes it impossible to interpret some smaller wars. For example, France was involved in overlapping and consecutive colonial wars for many years after World War II. For this reason, no peacetime prewar and postwar periods could be identified for France for discrete wars in this period.

Two indices of change have been constructed to compare prewar and postwar rates. The first is the ratio of the mean homicide rate of the five postwar years over the mean rate of the five prewar years. This index can be expressed as a percent comparing the postwar rate to the prewar level, and is perhaps the simplest measure of change.

The second index of change is a t-test between the mean prewar homicide rate and the mean postwar rate. This index is similar to the percent measure but also takes into account the variance of the prewar and postwar rates. The t-test corrects for the degree of fluctuation in the prewar and postwar periods. In the case of a country with wildly erratic fluctuations, the t would tend to diminish the importance of the change. In the case of a country with very stable rates, however, the index of a postwar increase would be enhanced. The t-test in this instance is best thought of as an effect size index rather than as a conventional test of statistical significance (Cohen, 1977). This is because a t-test based on ten observations (five prewar years and five postwar years) is a low-power test; differences have to be very large to reach significance with samples this small. In addition, significance levels are potentially misleading when large numbers of t-tests are calculated. For these reasons, the t-test is used here only as an effect size index which takes into account both the means and the variances of the prewar and postwar periods.[2]

The two indices of change provide different kinds of information. The percent measure provides an easily interpretable index of the overall magnitude and direction of change. The t provides a rough index of how unusual the change is in terms of the general variability of the nation's homicide rate. Although the direction (positive or negative) of the two measures is always identical, their magnitudes can be very different.

There were several steps involved in carrying out the actual analysis.

First, the tables in Singer and Small (1972) were used to determine the dates of entrance and withdrawal for each nation participating in each war. This information was used to identify the five prewar years and the five postwar years.

Second, comparison or control nations not participating in a given war were identified from the CCDF. For World Wars I and II, the control group consisted of all the nations in the file for those years which did not participate in these wars. The control nations for other wars were chosen using procedures discussed below.

Third, the two measures of change in homicide rates (percent and t) were calculated for both participating and control nations. The changes for individual nations then were grouped into three categories according to the magnitude of the percent change measure. Nations that changed downward more than 10% were categorized as decreasing, nations that changed upward more than 10% were categorized as increasing, and nations in which the changes had an absolute magnitude of 10% or less were categorized as unchanged. Then the numbers of combatant and control nations falling into each of these categories were compared.

Fourth, using only combatant nations, an effort was made to determine what types of war participation produce the greatest changes. Two of the variables examined were the number of men killed during the war as a proportion of the nation's total population and whether the nation was victorious or defeated.

Finally, other data in the comparative crime file were used to test specific predictions derived from the seven theoretical models discussed earlier.

RESULTS OF THE ANALYSIS

Effects of the Two World Wars

Our analysis indicates that combatant nations in the two world wars were more likely than control nations to experience homicide rate increases. The two measures (percent and t) of homicide rate change for combatant and control nations are shown in table 4.1.

For these two wars, homicide rate changes in control nations were evenly distributed, with some nations decreasing, some increasing, and some remaining unchanged. For the twenty-five "nation-wars," however, postwar increases outnumbered decreases by nineteen to six.[3] Combatant nations in these two wars, therefore, were more likely to undergo postwar increases than were control nations.[4]

The increases experienced by some combatant nations were very large. In Italy following World War II, for example, the homicide rate more than doubled (an increase of 133%). The large effect size index (t) associated with this change (3.07) indicates that this increase was very unusual with respect to Italy's general variability.[5]

There were also cases of modest increases that were still relatively large in terms of the general variability of the homicide rate. For example, the homicide rate in Belgium after World War I showed a 24%

Table 4.I. Homicide Rate Changes in Combatant and Control Nations After World War I and World War II

	Decrease	%	t	Unchanged (< |10%|)	%	t	Increase	%	t
Combatant nations	Australia (I)	-23	-2.42*	England (I)	-5	-0.67	Belgium (I)	24	5.36**
	Canada[a] (I)	-25	-2.41*	France (I)	4	0.37	Bulgaria[a] (I)	22	1.54
	Hungary (I)	-57	-10.70***	S. Africa[a] (I)	-1	-0.29	Germany (I)	98	5.19***
	Finland (II)	-15	-1.31	Canada[b] (II)	6	0.65	Italy (I)	52	3.06**
	N. Ireland (II)	-83	-1.57				Japan (I)	12	1.46
	U.S.[b] (II)	-12	-2.63*				Portugal (I)	47	4.93***
							Scotland (I)	50	3.02**
							U.S. (I)	13	3.03**
							Australia (II)	32	2.74**
							Denmark[c] (II)	169	7.08***
							England (II)	13	1.62
							France (II)	51	3.74**
							Italy (II)	133	3.07**
							Japan (II)	20	1.53
							Netherlands[b] (II)	13	0.93
							New Zealand (II)	313	3.15**
							Norway (II)	65	1.90*
							Scotland (II)	11	0.77
							S. Africa (II)	104	6.77***
Control nations	Norway (I)	-37	-1.34	Ceylon (I)	8	2.36*	Finland (I)	124	4.47**
	Ceylon (II)	-19	-1.91*	Chile (I)	-3	-0.92	Thailand (I)	112	2.02*
	Chile (II)	-67	-6.34***	Netherlands (I)	-2	-0.19	Colombia (II)	34	1.05
	El Salvador (II)	-20	-2.49*				Sweden (II)	14	0.60
	Ireland (II)	-22	-0.75				Turkey (II)	12	0.55
	Switzerland[a] (II)	-42	-13.41***						
	Thailand (II)	-17	-2.72*						

[a] Crimes against the person; homicide included. [b] Murder and manslaughter. [c] Denmark is included because it was occupied, although it never declared war.

* $p < .05$. ** $p < .01$. *** $p < .001$.

increase, but the t associated with this increase (5.36) suggests that the change was very large in terms of Belgium's general variability.

Finally, there was at least one case where the percent increase was comparatively larger than the corresponding t-test. For Norway following World War II, a fairly large increase in the homicide rate (65%) was tempered by an only moderate t (1.90). This indicates that Norwegian homicide rates were characterized by considerable variation during this period.

Even though the difference between combatant and control nations in table 4.1 is quite large, this comparison is a conservative test. The large numbers of young men killed in these wars dramatically changed the age and sex structures of the populations of many combatant nations. As a result, the postwar homicide rates for the combatant nations were based on populations depleted of young men—the group most likely to commit homicide. The analysis in table 4.1 may be conservative for a second reason as well: the birth of postwar babies in combatant nations (particularly after World War II) tends to reduce postwar homicide rates by inflating the population denominator on which they are based.

The net effect of these two demographic changes is to reduce postwar homicide rates in the combatant nations. If refined homicide rates were available based on only the population "at risk" for homicide (e.g., males over 15), the increases for combatant nations would be even larger than those shown in table 4.1 (Nettler, 1974: 59). The fact that combatant nations still showed increases greater than the control nations—despite the conservative effect of these two demographic changes—is therefore particularly striking.[6]

National Experiences After Twelve Other Wars

For smaller wars, the differences are in the same direction, although less pronounced. For the Vietnam War, since postwar data were unavailable in the CCDF, the measure of change is a comparison of wartime years with the prewar period. This war did not require total mobilization of the combatant societies (except for Vietnam itself), and therefore wartime rates are unlikely to have been distorted by major demographic changes. Data for six combatant nations in this war are included in table 4.2.

All six combatant nations in the Vietnam War experienced homicide rate increases, although three of these increases were less than 10%. The selection of control nations for this war posed some problems since the 1960s are a thickly covered period in the CCDF. The control nations shown in table 4.2 were matched with the six Vietnam combatants on the basis of geographic proximity. Three of the six control nations experienced increases, but the other three controls experienced decreases.

Table 4.2. Homicide Rate Changes in Combatant and Control Nations for the Vietnam War and 11 Other Wars

			Homicide rate change (%, t)						
	Decrease	%	t	Unchanged (<|10%|)	%	t	Increase	%	t
Combatant nations	India (1962 Sino-Ind)	−14	−2.23*	Australia (VN)	7	0.81	New Zealand (VN)	50	1.35
	Israel (1956 Sinai)	−58	−4.37**	Korea (VN)	6	0.31	Thailand (VN)	14	1.86*
	Italy (1896 Italo-Eth)	−15	−3.29**	Philippines (VN)	9	0.94	U.S.b (VN)	42	2.58*
	Italy (1935 Italo-Eth)	−44	−4.76***	Egypt (1956 Sinai)	−2	−2.57*	Hungary (1956 Russo-H)	13	0.80
				Egypt (1967 6-Day)	−4	−0.27	Israel (1967 6-Day)	14	0.64
				France (1884 Sino-Fr)	0	0.07	Japan (1894 Sino-Jap)	15	1.84
				India (1965 2nd Kash)	6	1.76	Jordan (1967 6-Day)	35	2.72*
				Japan (1904 Russo-Jap)	−9	−1.78	Pakistan (1965 2nd Kash)	13	2.52*
				Japan (1932 Manch)	−8	−1.31			

Control nations								
Burma (VN)	−17	−2.06*	Thailand (1932 Manch)	7	−0.71	Canada (VN)	11	1.41
Indonesia (VN)	−23	−0.93	Ceylon (1962 Sino-Ind)	−4	−0.49	England (VN)	23	2.50*
Japan (VN)	−23	−6.30**				Taiwan (VN)	37	3.72**
Austria (1956 Russo-H)	−13	−1.31				Ceylon (1965 2nd Kash)	11	2.41*
Burma (1965 2nd Kash)	−13	−1.30						
France (1896 Italo-Eth)	−13	−2.59*						
Switzerland[a] (1935 Italo-Eth)	−22	−3.05**						
Turkey[b] (1956 Sinai)	−33	−3.69**						
Turkey[b] (1967 6-Day)	−19	−1.17						

NOTE: For the Vietnam War only, the measure of change is between the prewar rate and the rate during the war. For the other 11 wars, the comparison is between prewar and postwar periods.

[a] Crimes against the person, homicide included.

[b] Murder and manslaughter.

* $p < .05$.

** $p < .01$.

*** $p < .001$.

Although the number of combatant and control nations for the Vietnam analysis is small, there is a tendency toward more consistent increases among the combatants. There is also reason to think that post–Vietnam War homicide rates may be even higher than the wartime rates used in table 4.2. In the United States, for example, the homicide rate continued to increase with each year of the Vietnam War. As a result, although the mean U.S. wartime rate was 42% higher than the prewar rate (as shown in table 4.2), the rate in the last years of the war was much higher—for instance, in 1973 the U.S. homicide rate was 107% higher than the mean prewar rate. The magnitude of the U.S. homicide rate increase during the Vietnam War was also quite substantial when judged by the t measure of change. The t associated with this war (2.58) indicates that the wartime increase was very large when compared to the general stability of the homicide rate.

A similar pattern occurs in the other small wars for which analysis is possible. The number of interpretable nation-wars is constrained by the need for control nations, the need for a prewar and postwar five-year period of peace, and the absence of homicide data for some nations for certain periods. Despite these constraints, the effects of an additional eleven small wars can be assessed. Because of the large number of possible control nations for some of these wars, the controls shown in table 4.2 were selected as the closest noncombatant neighbors of participating nations.

The results of this analysis are consistent with those for World Wars I and II. The nations participating in these twelve wars were somewhat more likely to experience increases than were the controls. For combatant nations in these small wars, those with increases outnumbered those with decreases by two to one. The data in tables 4.1 and 4.2 can be pooled for an overall test of significance. If the tables are superimposed, the differences between the fifty combatant nation-wars and the thirty controls are easily significant ($\chi^2 = 9.54$, $p = .0088$). The same result is obtained if the combatant and control nations are compared on the difference between their mean prewar homicide rate and their mean postwar rate (Mann-Whitney $U = 1006.5$, $z = 2.55$, $p = .0054$).

To control for the variable validity of different indicators, the analyses of tables 4.1 and 4.2 have been repeated using only nation-wars for which the optimal homicide indicator is available—the number of offenses known. This data quality control procedure, which removes nations with indicators like arrests and convictions, produces the comparison shown in table 4.3. The results again show that combatants were more likely than controls to have homicide increases. The difference between combatants and controls, therefore, remains even when only the best homicide indicator is used.

Table 4.3. Homicide Rate Changes in Combatant and Control Nations with the Most Valid Indicator

	Homicide rate changes		
	Decrease	Unchanged	Increase
Combatant nations	Finland (II) India (1962 Sino-Ind) Israel (1956 Sinai) Italy (1896 Italo-Eth) Italy (1935 Italo-Eth) N. Ireland (II)	Australia (VN) Egypt (1956 Sinai) Egypt (1967 6-Day) England (I) India (1965 2nd Kash) Japan (1904 Russo-Jap) Japan (1932 Manch) Philippines (VN)	Bulgaria[a] (I) Denmark (II) England (II) France (II) Israel (1967 6-Day) Italy (I) Italy (II) Japan (1894 Sino-Jap) Japan (I) Japan (II) Jordan (1967 6-Day) Pakistan (1965 2nd Kashmir) Scotland (I) Scotland (II) Thailand (VN)
Control nations	Austria (1956 Russo-H) Burma (VN) Burma (1965 2nd Kash) Ceylon (II) El Salvador (II) Indonesia (VN) Ireland (II) Japan (VN) Libya (1967 6-Day)	Ceylon (I) Ceylon (1962 Sino-Ind)	Ceylon (1965 2nd Kash) Finland (I) Hong Kong (VN)

NOTE: A data quality control procedure, using only data on the number of offenses known.
[a] Crimes against the person, homicide included.

Effects of Differences in Level of Wartime Involvement

There were some combatant nations, however, which did not experience postwar increases. This suggests that some types of participation are more likely to produce increases than others, as a number of researchers have speculated (e.g., Sorokin, 1928). In an effort to assess one dimension of involvement—the degree to which participation in a war was costly for a nation in terms of lives lost in battle—we divided the combatant nations into two groups: nation-wars with more than 500 battle deaths per million prewar population and those with fewer than 500 battle deaths per million prewar population (Singer and Small, 1972). If changes in the homicide rate are a function of the degree of a nation's war involvement, then one would expect homicide increases to be greatest for those nations with the greatest losses. A comparison of the changes in the two groups of nation-wars is shown in table 4.4.

The differences are in the expected direction. Nations with large combat losses showed homicide increases much more frequently than nations with less extensive losses. Moreover, this comparison no doubt understates the actual differences between the two groups. Nations with large combat losses had greatly reduced numbers of young men; thus, if rates were available for men over 15, the difference between the two groups would be even larger than that shown in table 4.4. We interpret these results as an internal validation since postwar homicide rates rose most consistently in precisely that group of nations from which war exacted the highest toll. The analysis in table 4.4 suggests an explanation for some of the anomalous cases in tables 4.1 and 4.2: nations with only limited participation and losses in war may not exhibit postwar homicide increases.

The effect of other dimensions of war participation also can be assessed. For example, nations can be compared on the outcome of the war. Combatant nations were classified as victorious or defeated using Singer and Small (1972) and other sources for more recent wars, with the results shown in table 4.5. Both victorious and defeated nations show homicide increases, although victorious nations were more likely than defeated nations to experience increases. This table confirms our finding that wars with heavy combat losses produce homicide increases and indicates that these increases occur more often for those nations that win the wars.

In summary, combatant nations experienced increases in homicide more often than control nations; nations with high battle deaths experienced homicide increases more often than nations with fewer battle deaths; and victorious nations experienced homicide increases more often than defeated nations.

Table 4.4. Postwar Homicide Rate Changes as a Function of the Level of Combat Deaths

	Homicide rate changes		
	Decrease	Unchanged	Increase
Greater than 500 battle deaths per million prewar population[a]	Finland (II) Hungary (I) U.S.[c] (II)	Canada[c] (II) England (I) France (I) Japan (1904 Russo-Jap)	Australia (II) Belgium (I) Bulgaria[b] (I) England (II) France (II) Germany (I) Hungary (1956 Russo-H) Italy (I) Italy (II) Japan (II) Jordan (1967 6-Day) Netherlands[c] (II) New Zealand (II) Norway (II) Portugal (I) S. Africa (II) U.S. (I)
Fewer than 500 battle deaths per million prewar population	India (1962 Sino-Ind) Israel (1956 Sinai) Italy (1896 Italo-Eth) Italy (1935 Italo-Eth)	Australia (VN) Egypt (1956 Sinai) France (1884 Sino-Fr) India (1965 2nd Kash) Japan (1932 Manch) Korea (VN) Philippines (VN)	Israel (1967 6-Day) Japan (1894 Sino-Jap) Japan (I) New Zealand (VN) Pakistan (1965 2nd Kash) Thailand (VN) U.S.[c] (VN)

[a] Eight of the nation-wars in tables 4.1 and 4.2 (Australia, Canada, Scotland and South Africa in WWI; Denmark, N. Ireland and Scotland in WWII; and Egypt in the 6-Day War) could not be included here because data on combat deaths were not available.
[b] Crimes against the person, homicide included.
[c] Murder and manslaughter.

PREDICTIONS VS. FINDINGS

Although a conclusive test of the predictions derived from the seven theoretical models discussed earlier is difficult, many of them can be inspected to see if they are consistent with or disconfirmed by our findings.

I. Artifacts Model

The major finding of our analysis runs counter to the effects of some artifacts. Combatant nations experienced postwar increases in homicide despite large losses of young men. The effect of this demographic artifact seems to be masked or overwhelmed by the size of the increases in homicide these nations experienced.

Another demographic artifact often cited as a factor in American crime increases during the 1960s (e.g., President's Commission on Law Enforcement and the Administration of Justice, 1967) involves the effects of the post–World War II "baby boom" on homicide rates a generation later. It is important to note that the "baby boom" argument could not explain increases following any wars in our analysis other than Vietnam. In addition, only three of the six Vietnam combatant nations

Table 4.5. Postwar Homicide Rate Changes as a Function of Both the Level of Combat Deaths and the Outcome of War

		Homicide rate change		
		Decrease	Unchanged	Increase
> 500 battle deaths per million prewar population	Victorious nations	U.S.[b] (II)	Canada[b] (II) England (I) France (I) Japan (1904 Russo-Jap)	Australia (II) Belgium (I) England (II) France (II) Italy (I) Netherlands[b] (II) New Zealand (II) Norway (II) Portugal (I) South Africa (II) U.S. (I)
	Defeated nations	Finland (II) Hungary (I)		Bulgaria[a] (I) Germany (I) Hungary (1956 Russo-H) Italy (II) Japan (II)
< 500 battle deaths per million prewar population	Victorious nations	Israel (1956 Sinai) Italy (1896 Italo-Eth) Italy (1935 Italo-Eth)	Japan (1932 Manch)	Israel (1967 6-Day) Japan (1894 Sino-Jap) Japan (I) Pakistan (1965 2nd Kash)
	Defeated nations	India (1962 Sino-Ind)	Egypt (1956 Sinai) India (1965 2nd Kash)	Jordan (1967 6-Day)

[a] Crimes against the person, homicide included.
[b] Murder and manslaughter.

were World War II combatants who could have experienced the maturation of a baby boom cohort during the Vietnam War: the United States, Australia, and New Zealand. The baby boom cannot explain homicide rate increases after the other forty-seven nation-wars in the study. But there is also evidence that this argument cannot sufficiently explain even these three increases.

As table 4.6 indicates, homicide arrest rates, when analyzed by the age of offenders, increased in all age groups, not just the baby boom cohort. For example, the age group of 25 or older could not have included the baby boom cohort until 1970. But, as shown in table 4.6, the homicide rate for this age group as well as for older groups increased throughout the Vietnam War. The baby boom clearly did have an effect on American homicide rates, as shown by the increase in the number of arrests for those under 25. However, older cohorts also experienced increases, indicating that the baby boom argument is not a sufficient explanation of U.S. homicide increases in this period.

Table 4.6. Age of Persons Arrested for Homicide in the United States Before and During the Vietnam War

	Age of person arrested for homicide						
	Raw <25	Rate[a]	Raw 25–34	Rate[a]	Raw 35–44	Rate[a]	Raw >45	Rate[a]
Prewar								
1960	1674	6.96	1615	7.08	1162	4.82	1083	2.06
1961	1868	7.41	1674	7.38	1143	4.69	1162	2.16
1962	1950	7.33	1660	7.38	1335	5.45	1123	2.06
Wartime								
1963	2041	7.37	1669	7.52	1234	5.07	1135	2.05
1964	2104	7.26	1870	8.42	1295	5.29	1143	2.03
1965	2594	8.56	2038	9.18	1444	5.94	1297	2.27
1966	2897	9.26	2148	9.63	1478	6.13	1258	2.17
1967	3415	10.57	2454	10.76	1721	7.23	1556	2.64
1968	4157	12.56	2856	12.05	1781	7.58	1598	2.67
1969	4182	12.23	2621	10.74	1527	6.58	1408	2.32
1970	5575	15.75	3399	13.65	1979	8.57	1883	3.04
1971	6415	16.93	3960	15.90	2134	9.32	2038	3.24
1972	6578	17.18	4354	15.90	2150	9.47	1957	3.08
1973	6426	16.52	4006	14.00	2089	9.16	1878	2.92
1960–62 mean	1831	7.23	1650	7.28	1213	4.99	1123	2.09
1963–73 mean	4217	12.2	2852	11.61	1712	7.30	1559	2.59
% increase	130%	69%	73%	60%	41%	46%	39%	24%

NOTE: Adapted from FBI *Uniform Crime Reports*, 1960–73.
[a] Rates calculated by dividing the number of arrests in each group by the population of that age, except in the case of the <25 age group where arrests are divided by the population aged 15–24. Population data obtained from the U.S. Statistical Abstract.

2. Social Solidarity Model

One of the predictions of this model was that homicide rates would decline during wartime and then, at or soon after the war's end, return to prewar levels. Although no analysis of wartime crime was attempted, the evidence presented above in tables 4.1 and 4.2 indicates that this explanation does not appear to be supported: postwar homicide rates were generally higher than prewar rates for combatant nations.

3. Social Disorganization Model

As discussed earlier, there are two versions of this model. One suggests that any crime increases would be due to disruptions that all warring societies would probably experience, such as rapid industrialization, population movements, and the breakup of families. Since these social changes apply to most or all wars, this version of the model is not testable using the present data set. The second version of the social disorganization model predicts that homicide increases would be largely confined to defeated nations. This prediction can be considered disconfirmed (see table 4.5 above); postwar increases were not limited to defeated nations and were actually more frequent among victorious nations than defeated nations.

4. Economic Factors Model

An explanation derived from this model was that postwar increases, if they occurred, would be a function of worsened economic conditions. As a rough test of this explanation, we compared homicide changes in two groups of nations: those with worsened postwar economies compared to the prewar period and those with improved postwar economies. We were able to collect prewar and postwar unemployment rates for only a portion of the nation-wars in tables 4.1 and 4.2. These nations were classified according to the direction of unemployment rate change between the five prewar years and the five postwar years. The homicide rate changes experienced by these nations are shown in table 4.7, along with the percent change in each nation's unemployment rate.

The results do not support an economic explanation of postwar homicide rate increases. Both those nations with worsened economies and those with improved economies experienced postwar homicide increases. In fact, nations with improved economies were slightly more prone to homicide increases than nations with worsened economies.

5. Catharsis Model

A prediction derived from this model was that societies whose wartime experiences had been the most violent would manifest the greatest postwar declines in violent crimes. This prediction appears to be discon-firmed by the results shown in table 4.4: nations with the most numerous fatalities in war were the *most* likely to show postwar homicide increases.

6. Violent Veteran Model

A prediction of this model was that postwar increases in homicide would be due to the acts of veterans. Since most nations, including the United States, do not maintain records on the military background of persons arrested for homicide, it is difficult to determine whether veterans are overrepresented in homicide statistics. Even if the number of homicides committed by veterans were known, it is not clear what rate we would compare this with, since veterans and nonveterans differ in many re-spects in addition to military service. An indirect approach to this ques-tion involves comparisons between two types of veterans, combat and noncombat. Recent research has not found unusually high rates of of-fenses or violence among combat veterans (Borus, 1975). In the absence of firm evidence, the image of the violent veteran may be more myth than reality (Archer and Gartner, 1976[a]).

Indeed, we have found evidence that the violent veteran model is insufficient as an explanation of the postwar homicide increases observed in warring nations. Central to this evidence are data which indicate that

Table 4.7. Homicide Rate Changes as a Function of Changes in National Employment

	Homicide rate change					
	Decrease		Unchanged		Increase	
Postwar economy worse— unemployment increased (%)	Australia (I) Finland (II)	44%[a] 193	England (I) Philippines (VN)	128 5	Belgium (I) Germany (I) Italy (II) U.S.[b] (VN)	201 128 96 25
Postwar economy better— unemployment decreased (%)	U.S.[b] (II)	−73	Canada[b] (II) Japan (1932 Manch)	−80 −28	Australia (II) Denmark (II) England (II) Israel (1967 6-Day) Japan (II)	−90 −56 −84 −5 −52

[a] The percent shown in this table indicates the difference between prewar and post-war levels of unemployment—i.e., a positive number indicates a postwar increase in un-employment and a negative number indicates a postwar decrease in unemployment.
[b] Murder and manslaughter.

postwar increases in violence have occurred among groups of people who could not have been combat veterans. During the ten-year period of the Vietnam War, for example, U.S. arrests for homicide increased dramatically for both men and women—101% and 59% respectively (FBI *Uniform Crime Reports,* 1963–73). Homicide arrests also increased for all age groups—including people over the age of 45. For the Vietnam War, therefore, the violent veteran model clearly is inadequate to explain the increases in the homicide rate.

Evidence on this question also can be obtained for other wars. Although sex-specific data for homicide are not available for all fifty nation-wars, they are available for several. Data on offenses by men and women in five nations after World War II were published by the Commission Internationale Pénale et Pénitentiaire (1951), and data on an additional six nation-wars were obtained from the CCDF. Postwar changes in offense rates are shown separately for men and women for eleven nation-wars in table 4.8.

As the table indicates, the postwar changes for women were comparable to those for men in these eleven nation-wars. Even if postwar increases do occur among veterans, therefore, these increases are not confined to this group but occur among both sexes. The model of the violent veteran, while difficult to disconfirm, cannot be a sufficient explanation of postwar increases.

7. Legitimation of Violence Model

Our findings are consistent with this explanation. This may mean either that the model has some validity—that wars do tend to legitimate the general use of violence in domestic society—or that we have not identified a compelling and testable prediction which can be derived from the model. Merely showing that rival explanations are disconfirmed or insufficient does not mean that the surviving theory is automatically the correct one. Although we have tried to formulate and test a variety of theoretical models suggested by classical and recent discussions of the possible effects of wars upon violent crimes, it is possible that an alternate explanation remains unexamined. However, the legitimation model is the only one of the seven presented here that is completely consistent with our finding of frequent and pervasive postwar homicide increases in combatant nations.

If wars do act to legitimate violence, it is interesting to speculate about the ways in which this effect could be mediated. Since this model suggests that the public acts of governments can influence the private acts of individuals, it might be possible to investigate potential links between the two. If panel survey data were available for each year during several different wars, for example, one might be able to see if public attitudes

Table 4.8. Sex Differences in Postwar Crime Rates in Combatant Nations

	Decrease		Unchanged (<|10%|)		Increase		
		%	t	%	t		%	t

	Homicide rate change (%, t)							
	Decrease	%	t	**Unchanged (<|10%|)**	%	t	**Increase**	%	t
Rates for men only	Belgium[a] (I)	−29	−11.43***	Netherlands[b,d] (II)	−4	−4.94**	Austria[d,f] (II)	211	1.68
	Belgium[b] (II)	−10	−1.66	Norway[b] (II)	4	0.54	Bulgaria[b] (I)	20	1.29
	Italy[a] (I)	−16	−1.65				Denmark[b,d] (II)	95	. . .[g]
							France[c] (II)	37	7.34**
							S. Africa[c] (II)	47	6.63***
							U.S.[d,e] (II)	33	4.88***
Rates for women only	Italy[a] (I)	−13	−4.09**	Belgium[a] (I)	−5	−0.91	Austria[d,f] (II)	123	1.72
				Belgium[b] (II)	5	0.98	Bulgaria[b] (I)	80	3.82**
							Denmark[b,d] (II)	140	. . .[g]
							France[c] (II)	153	11.25***
							Netherlands[b,d] (II)	37	4.95**
							Norway[b] (II)	20	0.96
							S. Africa[c] (II)	64	9.14***
							U.S.[d,e] (II)	86	9.34***

NOTE: For each war, two figures are shown, one for men and one for women. The figures shown are for all crimes—data on sex differences for homicide alone were unavailable.

[a] The direction of change for Belgium and Italy disagrees with the direction in table 4.1 because that table shows only homicide, while table 4.8 shows figures for all crimes. The ratio of homicide to all offenses is generally very small (e.g., approximately 1:1000 for Belgium).
[b] Convictions.
[c] Prosecutions.
[d] Percentages are calculated on actual numbers of offenses, not rates.
[e] Arrests.
[f] Prison population.
[g] Only one prewar and postwar year available; an estimation of variance is not possible.

* p < .05.
** p < .01.
*** p < .001.

become progressively more accepting or approving of violence with each year of a war. For example, one could measure attitudes toward shooting a burglar, toward using force during an argument, toward spanking a child, toward avenging an insult, toward the use of the death penalty.

In the absence of such surveys, other indices of the impact of wars might reveal potentially important links to individual behavior. As one example, Huggins and Straus (1975) have shown that fictional violence in children's literature reaches a maximum during war years. Wars also may produce changes in depictions of violence in movies, news stories, ads, and propaganda. Since most homicides grow out of disputes between relatives or close acquaintances, perhaps wars simply increase the probability that violence will be regarded as a justifiable means of resolving such disputes.

Wars are also inevitably accompanied by casualties, yet little is known about how the scale of wartime killing might affect members of warring societies. Wars could affect individual behavior simply through the awareness that violent homicides (in the form of soldiers killed in combat) are occurring—sometimes in staggeringly large numbers. This awareness could be communicated through a variety of media, not necessarily television, since we have found homicide increases after early twentieth-century wars as well as after more recent wars.

Homicides in war may be a potent influence on postwar domestic violence for another reason as well. Unlike other kinds of publicized killing (accidents, violent films and television, crime stories, etc.), war involves homicide legitimated by the highest auspices of the state. During many wars, the killing of enemy soldiers has been treated not merely as a regrettable and expedient measure but as praiseworthy and heroic. This legitimation is often explicit, in the form of official propaganda about the justice of the nation's cause, the inhumanity of the enemy, and the manly virtues of those who kill the most enemy soldiers. This legitimation is directed at both the nation's soldiers and the home front; but it may be more credible to civilians than to combat soldiers with direct experience of the realities of war.

Wars provide concrete evidence that homicide under some conditions is acceptable in the eyes of a nation's leaders. This wartime reversal of the customary peacetime prohibition against killing may somehow influence the threshold for using homicide as a means of settling conflict in everyday life.

Even though social scientists have in the past amassed impressive experimental evidence that violence can be produced through imitation or modeling, they have in general neglected the possibility that government—with its vast authority and resources—might turn out to be the most potent model of all. This powerful influence of governments on private behavior seems to be what Justice Louis Brandeis had in mind when he wrote in 1928: "Our government is the potent, the omnipresent teacher. For good or ill, it teaches the whole people by its example. Crime is contagious. If the government becomes a lawbreaker, it breeds contempt for the law."

The striking neglect of official violence in the social sciences has almost certainly resulted from the curious tendency of both citizens and scientists to avoid labeling the acts of governments—including even the extreme act of homicide—as violence. This deference to the legitimacy of governments has resulted in the near omission of wars and other forms of official homicide from discussions of violence. The new finding that wars cause a surge in postwar homicide rates suggests that this omission is lamentable and that the violent acts of individuals may in part be catalyzed by the violent times in which their governments cause them to live.

We believe that the scientific neglect of official violence needs to be remedied. First of all, acts of official violence can be particularly pernicious since they are the only forms of violence that carry the prestige and authority of the state. Second, many important questions about official violence await answers: What kinds of citizens support government violence most strongly? What kinds of government justifications for wars or executions are most effective in legitimating such violence? Do young children regard government violence, such as wartime killing, as "wrong"? At what developmental age are children socialized to accept government violence? Are people at various stages of "moral development" differentially supportive or critical of official violence? Do violent "criminals" support government violence more strongly than a matched group of noncriminals? How do the deputies who carry out official violence justify their behavior to themselves? What kinds of arguments are most persuasive to juries in death penalty cases? Are Americans more supportive or tolerant of official violence than are citizens of societies, like England, with little violent crime? This research agenda is clearly both rich and relatively unexplored.

SUMMARY AND CONCLUSIONS

The idea that war might increase the level of postwar homicide in combatant societies has occurred to many researchers. Speculation about the possible effects of wars on domestic violence has reflected seven theoretical models: (1) the *Artifacts Model*, which explains any postwar changes by demographic and other forces; (2) the *Social Solidarity Model*, which posits a wartime decrease in domestic homicide and a postwar return to normal levels; (3) the *Social Disorganization Model*, which predicts postwar increases but mainly for defeated nations; (4) the *Economic Factors Model,* which attributes any postwar increases to a worsened postwar economy; (5) the *Catharsis Model,* which predicts postwar decreases as a result of wartime killing; (6) the *Violent Veteran Model,* which attributes any postwar increases to combat veterans; and (7) the *Legitimation of Violence Model,* which predicts postwar increases as a result of the official sanction of killing in wartime.

Using homicide data from the CCDF, the homicide rates of fifty "nation-wars" were analyzed to learn (1) whether postwar homicide increases occurred and (2) whether the evidence was consistent with or disconfirmed any of the seven theoretical models.

Most of the combatant nations in the study experienced substantial postwar increases in their rates of homicide. These increases did not occur among a control group of noncombatant nations. The increases were pervasive and occurred after both large and small wars, with several types of homicide indicators, in victorious as well as defeated nations, in nations with improved postwar economies and nations with worsened economies, among both men and women offenders, and among several age groups. Postwar increases were most frequent among nations with large numbers of combat deaths.

These findings indicate (1) that postwar homicide increases occur consistently and (2) that several theoretical explanations are either disconfirmed by evidence on postwar changes or are insufficient to explain the changes. The one model that appears to be fully consistent with the evidence is the legitimation of violence model, which suggests that the presence of authorized or sanctioned killing during war has a residual effect on the level of homicide in peacetime society.

NOTES

1. Data from the Vietnam War are an exception to this general rule. For this war, the comparison will be between crime rates in the prewar period and those in the wartime years. This procedure was necessary for this war because postwar data were unavailable in the Comparative Crime Data File.
2. Indeed, since the number of prewar years and postwar years is the same (five), t bears a linear relation to d, an effect size index suggested for comparisons of two means (Cohen, 1977: 69). In general, $d = t \sqrt{2/n}$ and, in this case, $d = .63t$.
3. The unit of analysis is the "nation-war"—i.e., one nation in one war. The number of individual nations in table 4.1 is less than the number of units since some nations were involved in more than one war. In tables 4.1 and 4.2 combined, the total number of nation-wars is 50 and the total number of different combatant nations in these wars is 28.
4. Although most of the control nations in table 4.1 indicate no homicide increases or only small increases, there are two anomalous cases: Finland and Thailand after World War I. Both of these nations show large homicide increases after World War I; the size of these increases prompted us to investigate further the classification of these

nations as controls. A letter to the Finland Consulate revealed that Finland underwent an "internal" or civil war in 1918, and Thailand, according to the *Encyclopedia Britannica*, sent troops to the Allied cause during World War I. This information raises questions about the wisdom of classifying these two nations as controls for World War I. However, since neither nation was listed as a combatant by Singer and Small (1972), they are retained as controls in table 4.1.

5. The increase is even larger when judged only in terms of the prewar variation. We calculated a z-score measure of change which was the difference between the prewar mean and postwar mean, divided by the prewar standard deviation. For Italian homicide rate increases after World War II, this z-score measure was 11.62—larger than the corresponding t of 3.07. This indicates that the war not only increased the level of the homicide rate but also increased the instability or variance of the rate. For all the nation-wars in the study, however, this z-score index of change was significantly correlated with t ($r = .66$, $p < .001$).

6. The comparison is probably a conservative test for a third reason as well. That is, there may be some ways in which even control societies are affected by large wars like the two World Wars. The idea that the crime rates of even neutral nations might be influenced by massive wars has been suggested by Lunden (1963: 5). If changes did occur in neutral nations, of course, they would be reflected in inflated increases in the control nations in table 4.1.

FIVE

Cities and Homicide:
A New Look at an Old Paradox*

Cities have been regarded as centers of crime and violence since at least biblical times. For example, in Ezekiel 7:23, one of the explanations God is said to have given for his wrath is that "the land is full of bloody crimes and the city is full of violence."

Over the centuries, many writers have contrasted the immorality of cities with the innocence and purity of rural life. In some of these accounts, the city is described as seducing new arrivals into a life of crime. In the mid-eighteenth century, Adam Smith wrote that a man of "low moral character" could be constrained to behave properly in a village environment, "but as soon as he comes into a great city he is sunk in obscurity and darkness . . . and he is very likely to . . . abandon himself to every sort of low profligacy and vice" (quoted in Mannheim, 1965: 545).

This image of the city has been highly influential in the history of the social sciences and, with some refinement, constitutes one of the dominant theories about crime in cities. In sociology, this perspective is identified particularly with Emile Durkheim and Louis Wirth. In *The Division of Labor in Society,* Durkheim suggested that the "common conscience" is diluted as a city grows in size:

> Local opinion weighs less heavily upon each of us, and as the general opinion of society cannot replace its predecessor, not being able to watch closely the conduct of its citizens, the collective surveillance is irretrievably loosened, the common conscience loses its authority and individual variability grows. (1933: 300)

Wirth (1940) accepted this view of cities and discussed the mechanisms by which he believed cities dissolved traditional forms of social control. According to Wirth, the effects of urbanization included an increase in residential mobility, isolation, and anonymity as well as a breakdown of kinship ties and other informal sources of social control, all of which contributed to increases in pathological behavior.

*An earlier version of this chapter was coauthored with Robin Akert and Tim Lockwood.

98

In addition to the Durkheim-Wirth view of the city as a place where traditional social controls are minimized and anonymity is maximized, at least six theoretical explanations for higher rates of deviance have appeared in the literature on urban crime. These six hypotheses can be stated in abbreviated form as follows: (1) cities foster the development of criminal subcultures; (2) cities produce class, cultural, and racial conflict as a function of greater population heterogeneity; (3) cities increase criminal opportunities because of population size and the concentration of commercial establishments and consumer goods; (4) cities have relatively impersonal police-civilian relations, which leads to rigid law enforcement and arrest practices; (5) the age and sex composition of cities has been altered by the arrival of immigrants (from rural areas, other nations, etc.) who are predominantly young males, the population most likely to commit crimes; and (6) the greater population density and crowded living conditions in cities increase the likelihood of pathological behavior.

Despite these quite plausible theoretical explanations for the higher rate of violent crime in cities, the nature and origins of urban crime remain far from well understood. Much of this confusion is a function of the way in which different researchers have tried to answer the deceptively simple question, "*Do* cities have high rates of violent crime and, if so, *why?*" Like many other research questions, this topic has been clouded by a confusion between cross-sectional and longitudinal methods of addressing the issue.[1]

The difference between the cross-sectional and longitudinal approaches to this question can be illustrated easily. There are two ways in which cities and homicide could be related. There would be a cross-sectional relationship between the two if *city size* and homicide rates were related at any one time—if in a given year large cities had higher homicide rates than small cities. The cross-sectional effect of city size has been called "urbanism" (Lodhi and Tilly, 1973). By contrast, there would be a longitudinal relationship between cities and homicide if *city growth* and homicide rates were related over time—if, in a given period, a city's homicide rate rose as its population grew. The longitudinal effect of city growth is usually referred to as "urbanization."[2]

With few exceptions, almost all theories about urban violent crime rest on cross-sectional studies of city size—e.g., static comparisons of the homicide rates of cities of different size in a single year. For instance, Wolfgang (1968) reviewed U.S. crime statistics for cities of different size in 1965 and concluded that "the larger the city category, the higher the crime rate for all 'serious' crime combined"(p. 246). Using more recent data, Clinard (1974) also found a monotonic relationship between city size and homicide rates. This relationship appears to have held consistently in the United States over the past several decades (Ogburn, 1935; Boggs, 1966; President's Commission on Law Enforcement and the Administration of Justice, 1967; Glaser, 1970; McLennan, 1970; Sutherland and Cressey, 1970; Harries, 1974) and is also found in other societies (Szabo, 1960; Mannheim, 1965; Tarniquet, 1968).

The positive cross-sectional association between city size and homicide rates has become one of the most widely accepted maxims in the social sciences. Unfortunately, this finding has encouraged some researchers to infer that (1) rural areas have lower homicide rates than urban areas, and that (2) individual cities will undergo an increase in homicide rates as they grow in size.[3] Neither of these conclusions is logically warranted solely on the basis of the cross-sectional evidence discussed above. In fact, there is little empirical support for either conclusion.

Since rural areas are obviously less urban than even small cities, there has been a natural tendency to assume that their homicide rates are lower than the rates of small cities, an assumption that has been strengthened by the Durkheim-Wirth model, which tends to portray rural areas as more innocent, tranquil, and law-abiding than cities.[4] However, evidence on this question is mixed. For example, Wolfgang (1968) reported slightly higher homicide rates in 1965 for rural areas in the United States than for small cities—but he indicated that this pattern had been somewhat unstable over time. Several researchers have reported finding that rural homicide rates in some cases are higher than urban rates, both in the United States (Frankel, 1939; Vold, 1941; Sutherland and Cressey, 1970: 178) and in other countries (Dhanagare, 1969; Clinard and Abbott, 1973; Scherer, Abeles, and Fischer, 1975). Thus, even though it is theoretically reasonable to expect rural homicide rates to be lower than the rates of all cities, there is no robust evidence for this proposition.

The second inference, that cities experience rising homicide rates as they grow, also cannot be justified on the basis of cross-sectional studies. This question is clearly a longitudinal question about the effects of city growth and can be answered only by studying how homicide rates change over time as cities grow. Some longitudinal studies have been made, and the results of these investigations constitute the other half of the paradox of cities and homicide. These longitudinal studies are paradoxical because they have not found the expected result. Four studies have examined individual cities over a period of roughly one century: Powell (1966) studied Buffalo between 1854 and 1956; Ferdinand (1967) studied Boston from 1849 to 1951; and Lane (1969, 1979) studied both Boston and Philadelphia from the mid-nineteenth to the mid-twentieth century. These four studies of American city growth found a consistent decline in murder and other serious crimes over the century studied.

There have also been a number of longitudinal studies of crime and homicide rates for entire nations. Some of these have been limited to the twentieth century, such as Christiansen's (1960) analysis of Danish crime patterns from 1940 to 1955 and Venter's (1962) study of South Africa between 1913 and 1960. Relying on a variety of historical data sources, other researchers have covered periods beginning as far back as the 1700s, such as Tobias's (1967) study of English crime. Some of the most comprehensive historical research has focused on the experiences of France and Germany during the nineteenth and early twentieth centuries (Lodhi and Tilly, 1973; McHale and Johnson, 1977; Zehr, 1974, 1976). These studies present no evidence that increases in city size were related to increases in violent crimes. Finally, the results of Gurr's (1976) research on London, Stockholm, Sydney, and Calcutta over the period 1830–1930 provide added support for Zehr's conclusion that neither city size nor urban growth was associated with increases in violent crime.

This, then, is the paradox of cities and homicide rates: Why do large cities currently have higher homicide rates than small cities if there is no evidence of increasing homicide rates as a city grows? The cross-sectional evidence on city size and homicide seems to suggest that cities must grow to some absolute size (e.g., 100,000 persons) before having a high homicide rate. But this apparently reasonable proposition is contradicted by the longitudinal evidence, which shows that cities do not in fact show homicide rate increases as they grow. In short, if large cities have higher homicide rates than small cities, how did they get these high rates if *not* by growing in population size?

This chapter presents a new interpretation of this paradoxical relationship between cities and homicide rates. Both cross-sectional and longitudinal evidence will be examined in an effort to explain the apparent contradictions produced by these two approaches. Although American data will be examined briefly, the analysis will depend primarily upon homicide data from other societies. This comparative approach, which is intended to maximize the generalizable nature of the analysis, is made possible by the creation of the Comparative Crime Data File.

METHODS AND PROCEDURES

The cross-sectional effects of city size can be examined using both American and cross-national homicide data. The American data used in this analysis were obtained from the Federal Bureau of Investigation's annual *Uniform Crime Report*. This report provides aggregate homicide rates for the entire nation, rates for individual cities, and rates for cities in several categories of population size (e.g., 10,000–25,000, 25,000–50,000, etc.).

For this analysis, the rates of different categories of city size were averaged over a five-year period to smooth the effects of idiosyncratic annual fluctuations. These rates were examined to determine whether, as reported by previous researchers, (1) large American cities have consistently higher homicide rates than small cities; (2) the cross-sectional relationship between city size and homicide rates appears to be linear or follows some other form; and, finally, (3) whether rural U.S. homicide rates are higher than the rates of large cities, lower than the rates of small cities, or somewhere between these two extremes.

With the creation of the CCDF, it is also possible to examine some cross-sectional effects of city size in other societies. As described in chapter 2, in addition to aggregate data for entire nations, the CCDF includes offense data for forty-four "primary" cities—cities that are either the largest or one of the largest in a nation. This feature of the CCDF makes it possible to compare homicide rates in each primary city with the corresponding national homicide rate. If these two rates differ, it will be a conservative test of the relationship between city size and homicide rates for two reasons: (1) the national homicide rate obviously includes the primary-city rate, and this fact will diminish the observed difference between the two rates; and (2) the national homicide rate reflects both rural areas and other urban areas in addition to the primary city itself. Differences therefore will be observed only if the primary-city homicide rate differs from the aggregate homicide rate for all national sectors combined. This comparison will provide a cross-national answer to the cross-sectional question of whether large cities have homicide rates which are higher than the national averages.

The longitudinal issue of whether city growth is related to changes in homicide rates can be restated as two component questions: (1) Have the homicide rates of primary cities borne a *consistent* relationship to national homicide rates over time? (2) Have the homicide rates of the primary cities themselves increased over time as these cities have grown in population size? A separate analysis is necessary to answer each of these questions.

Because of the large volume of CCDF data needed to address the first of these longitudinal questions, a simple data-reduction strategy was adopted. For any given year, the median primary-city homicide rate was compared with the median national homicide rate. This is a controlled comparison strategy since each national rate acts as a "control" for each primary-city rate—that is, a primary city is included in the median for a given year only if its corresponding national rate is also available for that year. This controlled comparison prevents any bias due to the partial entry (e.g., only for cities) of homicide data from a society with unusually high or low homicide rates. The analysis will answer the question of whether primary-city homicide rates have differed in a consistent manner from national homicide rates over time.

The question of whether the rates of primary cities have increased with their population growth will be answered using a slightly different approach. The key concern here is whether the primary cities show a positive correlation over time between changes in their population size and changes in their homicide rate. This correlation can be calculated separately for each primary city. Since most cities show consistent population increases over time, this correlation will be very similar to the slope of the homicide rate for each city.

In summary, the relationship between cities and homicide will be examined using two cross-sectional analyses and two longitudinal analyses. These four steps will examine: (1) U.S. cross-sectional data on city size and homicide rates; (2) comparative cross-sectional data contrasting the homicide rates for primary cities and the rates for entire nations; (3) comparative longitudinal data on the relationship between primary-city homicide rates and national rates over time; and (4) comparative longitudinal data on the slope of primary-city homicide rates over time.

CROSS-SECTIONAL EVIDENCE

Cross-sectional data in the United States has the advantage that homicide rates are available for each of several city-size categories. In addition to general comparisons of urban and rural homicide rates, therefore, it is possible to speculate about the precise shape of the relationship between levels of city size and homicide rates. This cross-sectional relationship is shown for U.S. cities for the period 1971–1975 in table 5.1.

For cities alone, excluding suburban and rural areas, table 5.1 shows a strong and monotonic relationship between city size and homicide rate. Each category of city size has a higher homicide rate than all smaller city-size categories and a lower rate than all larger city-size categories. This analysis replicates earlier findings about homicide rate variations among U.S. cities of different sizes.

The suburban and rural areas, however, have homicide rates that are unexpectedly high. Even though these areas of the United States are less urban than all other categories of city size, they exceed the rates of some of these categories. For example, the rural U.S. homicide rate is higher than the rates for the three smallest city-size categories and as high as the rates for cities with populations between 50,000 and 100,000.

This interesting relationship between city size and homicide rates becomes even clearer when graphed, as in figure 5.1, which uses a logarithmic scale for city size because of the nonarithmetic nature of the population category intervals.

Table 5.1. City Size and Homicide Rates in the United States: 1971–1975

City size	Homicide rate (per 100,000)
Over 1,000,000	23.2
500,000 to 1,000,000	20.2
250,000 to 500,000	16.8
100,000 to 250,000	11.5
50,000 to 100,000	6.5
25,000 to 50,000	5.4
10,000 to 25,000	4.3
Under 10,000	3.6
Suburban Areas[a]	4.9
Rural Areas	6.4

NOTE: Adapted from the FBI's *Uniform Crime Reports*, 1971–75. To smooth the effects of annual fluctuations, the rates shown are the means of the murder and non-negligent manslaughter rates for five years 1971–75.
[a] Includes suburban, city, and county police agencies within metropolitan areas. Excludes core cities. Suburban cities are also included in other city groups.

Except for the rates of suburban and rural areas, figure 5.1 indicates that the categories of city size and homicide rates are logarithmically related—that is, when graphed on semi-logarithmic paper, the points approach a straight line. This shows that the most dramatic increases in homicide rates (rate increases per population increase) occur at the lower end of the city-size categories.[5] For more populous cities, much larger "increments" in city-size categories are required to produce homicide rate increases of the same size.

When suburban and rural homicide rates are included in figure 5.1, the relationship between city size and homicide rates is similar to a logarithmic J-curve.[6] This curve reaches a minimum for cities with fewer than 10,000 persons and increases for both rural areas and larger cities. At least in the United States, therefore, city size and homicide rates are related by the logarithmic J-curve shown in figure 5.1.

It would be fascinating, of course, to see if city size and homicide rates in other societies are also related by this logarithmic J-curve. However, since the CCDF does not include time-series homicide rates for more than one city in each society, it is not possible to use these data for this purpose.

As discussed earlier, however, it is possible to complete a somewhat different cross-sectional test for the effects of city size in other societies: the homicide rates of the primary cities in the CCDF can be contrasted with the corresponding national rates. A comparison of this kind is shown for twenty-four pairs of primary cities and nations in table 5.2. In order

Figure 5.1 City Size and Homicide Rates in the United States: 1971–1975

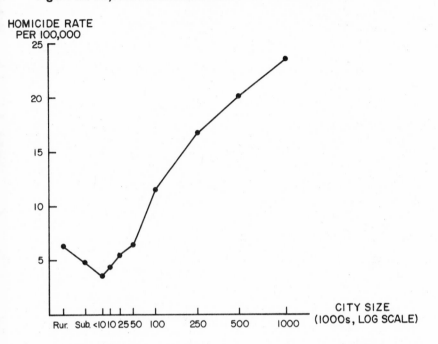

NOTE: Adapted from the FBI's *Uniform Crime Reports*. Rates shown are the means of the five-year period 1971–75.

to smooth the effects of erratic annual fluctuations, the rates shown in table 5.2 are the averages of (in general) the five-year period 1966– 1970—the most recent period in the CCDF.[7]

In general, the analysis indicates that the homicide rates of primary cities exceed the rates of nations as a whole. This was true for 75% (18 out of 24) of the pairs of cities and nations. As discussed earlier, it should be noted that the differences in table 5.2 understate the actual differences between large-city rates and nonurban rates because the national rate actually includes the primary-city rate and the rates of other cities as well as the rates of nonurban areas.

With some exceptions, the comparative evidence in table 5.2 parallels cross-sectional evidence for the United States; in both cases, large cities have homicide rates which are higher than their national averages. It is also interesting that although all of the cities in table 5.2 are large, there is obviously great variation among them in their homicide rates, just as there is great variation among the nations in their rates.[8] This indicates

Table 5.2. Primary-city and National Homicide Rates:
A Cross-sectional Comparison

City homicide rate lower than national rate ($n = 6$)	Homicide Rate[a]	City homicide rate higher than national rate ($n = 18$)	Homicide Rate
1. Guyana (1966–1970)	6.18	1. Australia (1966–1970)	1.28
Georgetown	5.21	Sydney	1.57
2. Japan (1966–1970)	2.23	2. Austria (1966–1970)	0.73
Tokyo	1.78	Vienna	0.89
3. Kenya (1964–1968)	5.67	3. Belgium (1965–1969)	0.29
Nairobi	5.27	Brussels	0.45
4. Panama (1966–1970)	11.07	4. Finland (1966–1970)	0.35
Panama City	4.96	Helsinki	0.65
5. Sri Lanka (1966–1970)	6.09	5. France (1966–1970)	0.45
Colombo City	5.59	Paris	0.61
6. Turkey (1966–1970)	9.65	6. India (1966–1970)	2.72
Istanbul	4.84	Bombay	2.85
		7. Ireland (1966–1970)	0.34
		Dublin	0.35
		8. Mexico (1962, 1966, 1967, 1972)	13.24
		Mexico City	13.34
		9. Netherlands (1966–1970)	0.50
		Amsterdam	1.23
		10. New Zealand (1966–1970)	0.16
		Wellington	2.32
		11. Northern Ireland (1964–1968)[b]	0.20
		Belfast	0.35
		12. Philippines (1966–1970)	7.98
		Manila	23.86
		13. Rhodesia (1966–1970)	5.33
		Salisbury	7.20
		14. Scotland (1966–1970)	0.78
		Glasgow	1.56
		15. Spain (1964–1968)	0.49
		Madrid	0.56
		16. Sudan (1961–1964, 1968)	5.67
		Khartoum	30.25
		17. Trinidad & Tobago (1966–1970)	14.00
		Port-of-Spain	15.31

Table 5.2. (continued)

City homicide rate lower than national rate ($n = 6$)		City homicide rate higher than national rate ($n = 18$)	
	Homicide Rate[a]		*Homicide Rate*
		18. United States (1966–1970)	6.62
		New York City	11.54
Median Country Rate:	6.14	Median Country Rate:	0.76
Median City Rate:	5.09	Median City Rate:	1.57

NOTE: Because of national idiosyncrasies in definition and reporting, the reader is cautioned against making direct cross-national comparisons of homicide rate levels. As explained in the text, this is not a problem for urban-national comparisons within the same society.

[a] Source for all data is the Comparative Crime Data File. Homicide rates are given in offenses per 100,000 population. In order to smooth the effect of annual fluctuations, the rates are the means of the years shown. The difference in rates between nations and cities is conservative for two reasons: (1) the national rate includes the urban rate, and (2) the national rate also includes other urban areas (i.e., the national rates aggregate both urban and rural areas).

[b] The period 1966–1970 also shows Belfast as having a higher homicide rate. This period was not used in this analysis, however, because Northern Ireland's most recent political violence began in 1969.

that absolute city size does not correspond in any direct way to the absolute magnitude of a city's homicide rate—that is, cities of 500,000 people do not necessarily have a homicide rate of, say, 17 per 100,000 people.

This finding suggests the intriguing possibility that large cities have homicide rates which are unusually high *only in terms of the overall homicide rates of their societies.* A primary city, therefore, can have a homicide rate which is remarkably low compared to that of large cities in other nations but which is high for its own society. This pattern can be convincingly illustrated using two of the cases in table 5.2. Both Paris and New York City had over 7,000,000 inhabitants in the period 1966–1970, but these cities had dramatically different homicide rates for these years. In both cases, however, the homicide rate of the primary city is higher than the rate of the entire society.

If this observation is generally correct, the relationship between city size and homicide rates is *relative* rather than absolute—that is, there is no formula relating specific homicide rates to specific city sizes. Researchers are unlikely, therefore, to identify a theoretical model which can predict an international city's homicide rate purely from the size of its population. On the basis of the evidence in table 5.2, it seems more promising to pursue theories which try to explain why large cities have homicide rates that are high only relative to the entire nation's homicide rate, whatever that rate is.

Finally, it is interesting to note that five of the six exceptions in table 5.2 are developing nations. This could mean that the factors which produce relatively higher rates in most primary cities do not operate in developing societies. It is not difficult to find hypothetical explanations for this difference. In terms of the Durkheim-Wirth hypothesis, it might be that primary cities weaken kinship and community ties in developed societies but not in developing societies. Perhaps developing societies have lower rates of mobility, or perhaps people moving to cities in developing societies move with their families rather than alone. Developed societies might also have greater controls over rural homicides—for example, decentralized law enforcement, which reduces blood feuds, marauding gangs, etc.

LONGITUDINAL EVIDENCE

Longitudinal evidence on cities and homicide can be examined to answer two related questions. The first is whether the pattern shown in table 5.2 has been consistent over time—i.e., have primary cities always had relatively high homicide rates?

This question was addressed using the method of controlled comparison described earlier. For each year, a median homicide rate was calculated for primary cities, and a second median rate was determined for the nations as a whole. In the computations for each year, therefore, the national homicide rate serves as a paired control for the primary-city rate. The longitudinal relationship between the homicide rates of primary cities and the rates of entire nations is shown in figure 5.2. Because of missing or incomparable homicide indicators, particularly in the early part of this century, only the period 1926–1970 is reflected in figure 5.2.

The most striking pattern in figure 5.2 is that primary cities consistently have had homicide rates higher than their national averages. The gap between the solid and broken lines in figure 5.2 is a conservative index of the effect of city size on homicide rates. It is conservative, again, because the dotted line actually includes the rate of the solid line, as well as the rates of other large and small cities.

The median homicide rates in figure 5.2 indicate that the main finding of table 5.2 (that primary cities have homicide rates higher than their national averages for 1966–1970) could be replicated for any period between 1926 and 1970. In fact, figure 5.2 suggests that the effect of

Figure 5.2 Primary-city and National Homicide Rates: A Longitudinal Comparison

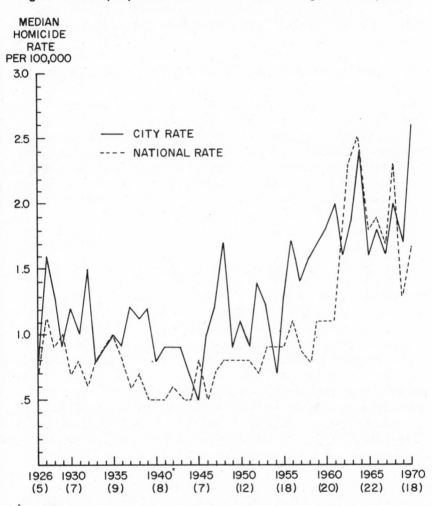

NOTES: The solid line shows the median homicide rate of primary cities for each year; the broken line shows the median rate of the corresponding nations. The number of pairs (each pair is one city and one nation) in the analysis is indicated at five-year intervals.

city size was even more pronounced earlier in this century than during the period 1966–1970.[9]

The consistent difference reflected in figure 5.2 is our most important longitudinal finding. Although we do not have homicide data which extend back into the eighteenth and nineteenth centuries, the consistently higher rates of the primary cities in figure 5.2 encourage us to make the following extrapolation: in general, large cities have always had homicide rates higher than their national averages, even when primary cities were much smaller than they are today. This inference suggests that the homicide rates of large cities are higher than national rates not because of the *absolute* population size of these cities but because of their *relative* size. Even when primary cities were much smaller than they are today, they were still relatively more urban and densely populated than their societies as a whole.

A final cautionary note should be mentioned concerning figure 5.2. Because different intervals reflect different cities (depending on the availability and comparability of city data), the slope of the solid line is not meaningful. Since different cities are included in this median line in various years, the line cannot provide an indication of how primary-city rates have changed in absolute terms over time.

The further question of whether primary cities have experienced any absolute increases in homicide rates over time cannot be answered from figure 5.2. The four longitudinal case studies of single American cities cited earlier (Powell, 1966; Ferdinand, 1967; Lane, 1969, 1979) found no homicide increases for these cities, nor did Gurr's (1976) analysis of four international cities reveal such trends. Similar conclusions were reached in the studies of nineteenth-century France and Germany.

In order to provide a rough answer to this question for each primary city in the CCDF, a simple zero-order correlation was calculated between the city's population and its homicide rate. Since almost all the cities increased continuously in population during this period,[10] this correlation provides a crude index of the homicide trend during the period. A positive correlation indicates homicide rate increases during this period; a zero correlation indicates essentially no change; a negative correlation indicates homicide rate decreases.

This analysis produced thirty-four correlations, each roughly analogous to the single-city studies of Buffalo, Boston, and Philadelphia discussed earlier. Since fewer than one hundred years were available for these thirty-four cities, however, our analysis is not as deep as the case studies. It is much broader, however, in that it examines thirty-four cities in twenty-eight countries.[11] The results of this analysis are shown in table 5.3.

As the table clearly indicates, there is no general relationship between city growth and changes in absolute homicide rates. The correlations range from a low of −0.66 to a high of 0.98, with the 34 cases evenly divided into 17 positive r's and 17 negative r's. This broad scatter is responsible for the essentially zero median correlation of −0.01.

The inconsistency of these longitudinal analyses suggests that there is no invariant tendency for the homicide rates of large cities to increase as these cities grow in size. In the period 1900–1970, homicide rates were as likely to decrease with city growth as they were to increase.

Even though the time periods reflected in table 5.3 are all shorter than the century-long studies of individual American cities cited earlier, four cities have data for more than fifty years. Comparison of these four cities still shows a median correlation of only − 0.46. Even for cities with a half-century or more of data, therefore, there is still no strong evidence that homicide rates increase with city growth.

It is possible, of course, that the near-zero median in table 5.3 conceals some orderly differences among different types of societies. For example, a casual reading of the table indicates that primary cities in developing societies seem to be overrepresented among the positive correlations—that is, primary cities in developing nations may be more likely than other cities to experience increasing homicide rates as they

Table 5.3. Homicide Rates and Population Size for Primary Cities: A Longitudinal Analysis

City	Correlation between city population and city homicide rate[a]	Number of years in the analysis	Significance
New York[b]	0.98	8	0.001
Istanbul	0.88	19	0.001
Manila	0.79	23	0.001
Quezon City[b, c]	0.64	8	0.090
Calcutta	0.51	16	0.044
New York[b]	0.47	12	0.121
Panama City	0.45	11	0.167
Salisbury[b, c]	0.41	22	0.058
Port-of-Spain	0.38	25	0.061
Johannesburg	0.33	10	0.360
Georgetown	0.27	18	0.273
Sydney	0.27	40	0.090
Quezon City[b]	0.26	11	0.437
Wellington	0.16	17	0.542
Colombo	0.15	74	0.198
Khartoum	0.13	13	0.683
Amsterdam	0.02	43	0.911
Port-of-Spain[c]	− 0.04	25	0.851
Mexico City	− 0.13	12	0.697
Dublin	− 0.15	47	0.315
Brussels	− 0.17	27	0.409

Table 5.3. (continued)

City	Correlation between city population and city homicide rate[a]	Number of years in the analysis	Significance
Oslo	-0.18	14	0.541
Salisbury[b]	-0.21	22	0.361
Munich	-0.26	28	0.181
Vienna	-0.32	21	0.155
Montevideo	-0.36	31	0.045
Glasgow	-0.38	72	0.001
Paris	-0.45	39	0.004
Nairobi	-0.50	21	0.022
Belfast	-0.54	52	0.001
Madrid	-0.57	16	0.021
Tokyo	-0.57	73	0.001
Helsinki	-0.58	43	0.001
Bombay	-0.66	16	0.005
Median r:	-0.01		

[a] Since most of these cities have grown consistently over time, the correlations are easily interpreted. A positive correlation means that the city's homicide rate has increased over time; a zero r indicates no consistent change in homicide rate; and a negative r means that the city's homicide rate has decreased over time.

[b] New York City, Salisbury, and Quezon City appear twice because records (or interruptions) produced two different homicide series.

[c] Indicates that a rate for "murder" was used for this city; other rates are homicide rates.

grow. This tendency is supported by Zehr's finding that higher rates of violent crime in nineteenth-century Germany and France were related to "the initial and/or most disruptive stages of the process [of urban growth]" (1976:128). This observation does not, of course, alter the general lack of a consistent pattern in table 5.3.

It is also interesting to speculate about the different conclusions that would have resulted from independent studies of different single cities in table 5.3. For example, a researcher examining twentieth-century data for Tokyo would have concluded that homicide rates declined with city growth; a different researcher studying data for Amsterdam would have found no relationship between the variables and would have concluded that previous researchers (e.g., Ferdinand, 1967) were correct; but a third researcher doing a case study of Manila would have found homicide rate increases associated with city growth and would have concluded that previous researchers were wrong. The unique strength of the CCDF for systematic research on homicide rates is that it can maximize a researcher's view of the range of possible outcomes across several societies and also indicate whether any general patterns exist. In this case, the CCDF data demonstrate that city growth can have a wide range of implications for homicide rates and that, in general, there is no evidence that cities and homicide rates grow together.

Seven of the primary cities in table 5.3 have essentially uninterrupted homicide data for the entire period 1926–1970. These seven cities are Amsterdam, Belfast, Colombo, Dublin, Glasgow, Helsinki, and Tokyo. The homicide rates of these cities can be represented by a median rate for each year. This median rate (unlike the solid line in figure 5.2) is not affected by the inclusion or exclusion from year to year of cities with unusually high or low homicide rates. When graphed, therefore, the median rate of these seven cities has an interpretable slope.

Figure 5.3 Trends in Homicide Rates for Seven Cities, 1926–1970

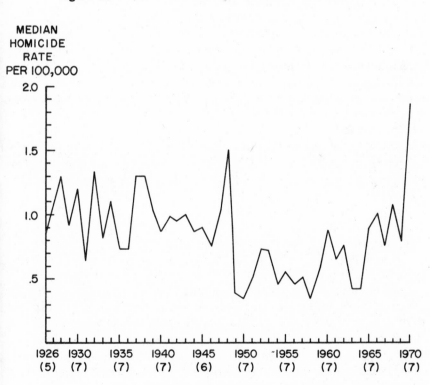

NOTE: The cities are Amsterdam, Belfast, Colombo, Dublin, Glasgow, Helsinki, and Tokyo. These cities have essentially uninterrupted homicide data for this entire period.

Just as table 5.3 provided evidence that urban homicide rates do not in general increase with city growth, figure 5.3 indicates that these seven primary cities do not show any consistent increase in homicide rates over time. The slope of the graph is essentially zero (-0.006)—that is, there is no evidence of progressively higher homicide rates over time. Since time and city growth are almost perfectly correlated (i.e., almost all cities in the file have grown consistently or even monotonically over time), these two analyses are in agreement: there is no evidence that city growth has any consistent implications for a city's homicide rate.

SUMMARY AND CONCLUSIONS

The scientific literature on urban homicide rates contains a paradox. Cross-sectional research on city size and homicide rates has found higher homicide rates in large cities than in small cities. The few longitudinal studies of city growth in individual cities, however, have not found increases in homicide rates as these cities grow. The paradox is this: If larger cities currently have high homicide rates, how did they acquire these high rates if not by growing in size?

Data from the CCDF, along with data on U.S. homicide rates, were used to investigate both the cross-sectional relationship between city size and homicide rates and the longitudinal relationship between city growth and homicide rates. These analyses produced the following conclusions:

1. Cross-sectional evidence for the United States indicates that city size and homicide rates are strongly related. The form of this relationship is a highly consistent logarithmic J-curve—the highest homicide rates are found in the largest cities and the lowest rates are found in cities with fewer than 10,000 people. Rates for each city size are higher than the rates for smaller cities and lower than the rates for larger cities. Homicide rates in suburban and rural areas, however, are higher than the rates of small cities—for instance, rural homicide rates in the United States are roughly equal to the rates of cities with populations between 50,000 and 100,000. For the United States in general, this analysis strongly supports the conclusion that city size and homicides are related.

2. Comparative cross-sectional evidence from the CCDF also indicates a relationship between city size and homicide rates. For the period 1966–1970, primary cities in twenty-four societies generally had homicide rates higher than their national averages. This analysis actually understates the relative magnitude of the primary-city homicide rates since the national rate includes data from the primary city and from other large and small cities as well.

3. The cross-sectional analysis also reveals wide variation among primary cities in terms of their absolute homicide rates. Variation in hom-

icide rates even occurs among primary cities with the same population size. The link between city size and homicide rate is, therefore, country-specific or relative, not absolute.

4. Comparative homicide data were also examined longitudinally. The median homicide rates of primary cities were compared to the rates of entire nations for each year between 1926 and 1970. This comparison reveals that the homicide rates of primary cities have consistently exceeded national rates over time. The observed difference in this analysis again understates the actual difference because the national rate includes the rates for the primary city and other large cities. The difference in rates is particularly impressive since the primary cities were much smaller in absolute terms at the beginning of this period. This suggests that urban homicide rates exceed national rates not because of the absolute population size of these cities but because of their *relative* size. Even when they were much smaller than they are now, these primary cities were highly "urban" compared to their societies as a whole.

5. Comparative longitudinal data were also used to test for a relationship over time between city growth and homicide rate changes in thirty-four international primary cities. Exactly half of these cities show homicide rate increases with city growth, and half show rate decreases with city growth. The median correlation between city population growth and homicide rates over time, therefore, is essentially zero. This analysis provides no evidence for the general proposition that city size and homicide rates increase together.

6. Finally, longitudinal data were used to examine the homicide rate trends of seven primary cities with uninterrupted homicide data from 1926–1970. The slope of the median homicide rates of these seven cities over time is essentially zero. This is further evidence that the absolute homicide rates of primary cities have not shown any consistent increases over time, despite the population increases of these cities.

Considered together, these findings provide the basis for a new interpretation of the paradox of how large cities acquired their high homicide rates. In part, our analyses provide broad comparative support for some earlier research on the two aspects of the paradox. Our cross-sectional analyses are consistent with earlier work in finding high homicide rates in large cities, not only in the United States but also in many other societies. However, we found that the rates of large cities were high only relative to the rates of their societies, not necessarily in any absolute or international sense. Our longitudinal analyses of thirty-four international primary cities also support earlier work in finding no evidence that city growth and homicide rates increase together.

We believe that a solution to this paradox lies in our longitudinal comparison of the homicide rates of primary cities with the rates of entire nations. This analysis showed that city rates have consistently exceeded national rates, even when the cities were much smaller in absolute terms. The determinant of a city's homicide rate is therefore not the absolute size of the city but its size *relative* to its contemporary society. We believe that this interpretation explains why homicide rates do not necessarily increase as a city grows. Large cities have always had relatively high homicide rates because they have always been more urban than their national environments.

This interpretation suggests that sociologists have been misled—undoubtedly by cross-sectional evidence—into the unwarranted assumption that absolute city sizes during a city's growth would correspond in some way to absolute homicide rates. Our analysis suggests that this assumption is invalid, despite its apparent reasonableness. On the basis of our evidence, we believe that a city's relative population size determines its relative homicide rate: any jurisdiction more urban than its national environment will have a homicide rate higher than the national average.

NOTES

1. For a discussion and examples of the differences between these two research designs, see Lieberson and Hansen (1974). Even when addressing the same question, these two methods are capable of producing different or even opposite results. In studies where both designs are possible, the longitudinal design is more powerful and more capable of identifying causal relationships.
2. We use the terms "city size" and "city growth" in place of "urbanism" and "urbanization" in the interest of terminological simplicity.
3. For example, Clinard (1942, 1964) found a cross-sectional relationship between criminal offenders and urban background and, from this finding alone, predicted a longitudinal increase in crime rates as urbanization occurred.
4. It should be noted that rural areas do appear to have a lower rate of most nonhomicide crimes, with the possible exception of rape (Wolfgang, 1968; Clinard and Abbott, 1973; Scherer, Abeles, and Fischer, 1975).
5. It should be emphasized, of course, that these are not genuine homicide "increases" (in the longitudinal sense) since this particular comparison is only cross-sectional.
6. Since suburban and rural areas are not associated with precise population sizes, they could not be included in any appropriate location on the logarithmic scale in figure 5.1. Instead, they are shown at an arbitrary distance from the smallest city category.
7. Even though the CCDF contains crime data for forty-four primary cities, several of these cities could not be included in table 5.2 for one of two reasons: (1) one (or both) of the city and nation time series were not available in the CCDF for the period 1966–70; or (2) even if both series were available for this period, the nation reported a different homicide indicator than was available for the primary city— e.g., homicide offenses known for the entire nation, but homicide convictions for the primary city. For example, in both Germany and South Africa, the primary-city rates exceeded the national rates—but these cases were excluded from table 5.2 because the city indicators differed in type from the national indicators in the CCDF.

8. Although it is tempting to try to make direct homicide rate comparisons across the primary cities or across the nations shown in table 5.2, such comparisons are hazardous without a careful inspection of the CCDF. Although the same indicator (e.g., offenses known) was used *within* each pair in table 5.2, not all pairs used the same indicator. In addition, national idiosyncrasies in homicide classification and definition make cross-national comparisons of absolute homicide rate levels far from uncomplicated.

9. A plausible interpretation for the narrowing of this gap after 1960 is suggested by the exceptional cases in table 5.2. After roughly 1960, developing nations are increasingly represented in the CCDF, and table 5.2 indicates that developing nations may not have the same relationship between city size and homicide as is found in developed nations.

10. Two of the cities in the CCDF that declined in population or showed discontinuous growth are Belfast and Glasgow.

11. Some of the forty-four primary cities in the CCDF have data points which are too few in number or too scattered to permit calculation of this correlation.

S I X

Homicide and the Death Penalty:
A Cross-National Test of a Deterrence
Hypothesis*

Debate over capital punishment has a long and extensive history. This debate has been complex and confused, partly because support for the death penalty has reflected no single theory but, instead, several different themes. These include a belief in the justice of retribution, the wish to avoid the economic costs of protracted imprisonment, disbelief in the possibility of rehabilitation and, finally, a conception that has come to be called "deterrence theory." While each argument for the death penalty can be considered on its merits, it is deterrence theory that has captured public imagination and scientific attention.

Briefly stated, deterrence theory holds that there is an effective relationship between specific *qualities* of punishment (for example, its certainty, celerity, or severity) and the likelihood that a punishable offense will be committed. A corollary of deterrence theory is that increasing the penalty for an offense will decrease its frequency, while decreasing the penalty will cause infractions to multiply. Deterrence theory therefore conceives of potential offenders as rational actors who weigh the qualities and probabilities of punishment before acting.

Although capital punishment is ancient, the genealogy of deterrence theory is much more recent. Until the past few centuries, the death penalty was imposed often and for many offenses, some of which seem trivial to the modern eye. For most of recorded history, the fate of the executed was regarded as deserved and morally unproblematic. Deterrence theory emerged only two or three centuries ago, when societies for the first time felt obliged to provide rational justifications for using the death penalty. This need reflected a number of historical developments, including a growing distaste for trial by torture, maiming, stoning, burning, and other forms of judicial violence (Archer, in press).

*An earlier version of this chapter was coauthored with Marc Beittel.

Unique aspects of the death penalty have contributed to abolitionist sentiment. The discovery of judicial errors in capital cases has emphasized the fallibility of determining criminal guilt. This recognition prompted Lafayette to remark, "I shall continue to demand the abolition of the death penalty until I have the infallibility of human judgments demonstrated to me" (Green, 1967). Similarly, violent retribution has become less palatable than it once was. If society's purpose in executions is to exact horrible suffering, it is not clear that contemporary executions maximize this purpose, as Clarence Darrow observed:

> But why not do a good job of it? . . . Why not boil them in oil, as they used to do? Why not burn them at the stake? Why not sew them in a bag with serpents and throw them out to sea? . . . Why not break every bone in their body on the rack, as has often been done for such serious offenses as heresy and witchcraft? (Green, 1967: 50).

At present, other justifications for the death penalty having become less tenable, deterrence theory occupies center stage in the debate over capital punishment. While deterrence theory may conceal elements of ancient themes (such as the desire for retribution), the theory's manifest justification involves *saving* lives: the killing of convicted offenders is alleged to preserve the lives of future victims of the convicted person and other potential offenders. In this sense, somewhat ironically, deterrence theory is itself a symptom of the increasing sanctity of life, since the theory argues that executions save lives.

While deterrence has been implicit in writings about punishment for centuries, the formal emergence of this theory is often identified with the eighteenth-century criminologist and jurist Cesare Beccaria. In his writings on the control and prevention of crime, Beccaria elaborated the general proposition that human behavior can be influenced by variations in punishments (Sellin, 1967). Deterrence theory also has been prominent in political and parliamentary debates, beginning with the French Constituent Assembly in 1791. It is interesting that the two sides of this 1791 debate over deterrence theory have resurfaced, with little modification, in virtually all subsequent debates:

> There is a class of people with whom the horror of crime counts a great deal less than the fear of punishment: their imagination needs to be shaken, that necessitates something which will resound in their soul, which will move it profoundly, so that the idea of punishment is inseparable from that of crime. . . . The wicked does not fear God, but he does have fear, i.e., the sentiment which the scoundrel feels at the sight of the scaffold. (Prugnon, 1791, cited in Hornum, 1967)

> It is not the fear of punishment which stops the sacrilegious hand of the assassin. . . . The scoundrel always flatters himself that he will escape the

law's surveillance.. . . . Also, one cannot believe that the man who is so bar-
baric that he can soak his hand in the blood of his fellow man will be held
back by the distant appearance of a cruel fate. (Villeneuve, 1791, cited in
Hornum, 1967)

The controversy has resurfaced recently in Western societies. In the
United States, changes in crime rates and public opinion have both
figured in this debate. Support for the death penalty has shown a pattern
of long-term decline and, more recently, resurgence. In the 1930s, surveys showed that roughly two-thirds of the American people supported
the death penalty, and as late as the 1950s, an average of seventy
executions a year were carried out in the United States. This number
fell precipitously during the 1960s. Surveys showed that fewer than half
the American people approved of the death penalty during the 1960s,
and from 1968 until January of 1977 there were no executions in the
United States.

Support for capital punishment has since revived. The engine driving
this reversal is almost certainly the crime rate. After a monotonic decline
since the 1930s, rates of homicide began to increase sharply in the mid-
1960s. As a single example, the rate for homicide and non-negligent
manslaughter in the United States doubled between 1963 and 1973.
Spurred by these increases, the death penalty once again enjoys the
support of a majority of the American people. While only a handful of
executions have been carried out since 1977, several states that had
previously abolished the death penalty have now restored it. As a result,
roughly a thousand convicts are now under sentence of death in the
United States, and the number grows with each passing week.

It should be noted that there is in this change an interesting non
sequitur. The momentary crime rate of course has no bearing on the
validity of deterrence theory—executions do not acquire more deterrent
value merely because a nation's crime rate has increased. Crime rates
and punishment instead have a *political* relationship in that crime rates
provide a context which may determine whether or not citizens and
politicians are willing to act *as if* the case for criminal deterrence was
clear and proven. For this reason, it should be stressed that scientific
evidence on the deterrence hypothesis is only one of several factors in
the dynamic processes of abolition and restoration.

Finally, the history of this issue is one of cycles; although recent support for the death penalty has mounted rapidly, it could as easily subside.
Apart from the seeming impermanence reflected in these changes, the
debate between abolitionists and restorationists has centered on a number of enduring questions, and it is to these more durable issues that
this chapter is devoted.

DIMENSIONS OF THE DETERRENCE HYPOTHESIS

he continuing debate over capital punishment has often been muddied
y fundamental confusion over the precise questions addressed. For this
eason, any attempt to summarize this debate should begin with a brief
escription of some of these issues and distinctions:

. *De Facto vs. De Jure.* Discussions of the effect of the death penalty
iffer in terms of whether they address the legal existence (de jure) of
apital punishment or its actual use in terms of the frequency of exe-
utions (de facto). This distinction is important for two reasons. First,
ome have argued that the mere existence of the death penalty can have
 deterrent effect, while others claim that only actual executions will be
 deterrent. Second, even when two jurisdictions share a de jure death
enalty, there may be great variation between them in its de facto
pplication.

. *Severity, Certainty, and Celerity of Punishment.* Various qualities of a
unishment might conceivably affect its deterrent effect. One of these
 severity—are severe punishments more of a deterrent than less severe
enalties? Severity has been a classic focus of attention since the death
enalty debate concerns the relative deterrence value of executions, on
ie one hand, and long prison sentences, on the other. A second and
ery differrent quality of punishment is its *certainty*—is a punishment
ess of a deterrent if it is only infrequently imposed? This distinction is
imilar to the de jure vs. de facto distinction noted above. Still another
uality of punishment is its *celerity*—does the length of time between an
rrest and the imposition of a punishment influence its deterrent value?

. *Public Knowledge of Legal Punishments.* Some researchers believe that
ie death penalty can be a deterrent even if its existence is only vaguely
erceived. Others argue that punishments are deterrents only if they
re well understood. This issue is of interest because surveys show that
oth the general public and convicted offenders tend not to know what
ffenses merit the death penalty, or even whether the state in which
iey live has capital punishment. Since deterrence theory implies that
otential offenders weigh the consequences of their actions, the question
f whether those consequences are known is of obvious importance.

. *Rationality of the Criminal Act.* There is disagreement about the degree
) which the commission of a violent crime is a rational act. For example,
hile an assassination may be highly purposive, there is overwhelming
vidence that most homicides are unplanned, impulsive acts against a
ictim who is an intimate or at least an acquaintance of the murderer.
iven the volatile nature of this offense, it seems improbable that the

participants are preoccupied with the gravity of likely punishment. Eve
if the penalties for capital crimes are intellectually known, therefore,
is not clear that violent crimes involve the kind of dispassionate calc\
lation implied by deterrence theory.

5. *Rationales for Punishment.* Societies can control or punish violent i\
dividuals by various means and with different purposes. For exampl
general deterrence involves the use of punishment to discourage crimin
behavior of individuals other than the person being punished. *Speci\
deterrence* refers to the effect of a punishment on the potential futu\
criminal activity of the punished offender. *Incapacitation* has the objecti\
of making offenders less of a threat through imprisonment or remov
from society. *Retribution* refers to the use of punishment to satisfy t\
wronged party (narrowly defined as the victim or, more broadly, \
citizens) by making the offender suffer for his or her wrongdoing. T\
objective most often given for the death penalty is general deterrenc
Incapacitation or specific deterrence could both be achieved by inca\
ceration, with or without rehabilitation. The principle of retribution h\
adherents but, as already indicated, seems less socially acceptable tha
the justification of deterrence.

6. *Simultaneous Effects of Crime and Punishment.* Any systematic test \
deterrence theory must consider possible feedback effects between crin
rates and punishments. For example, increasing crime rates may ove\
load the criminal justice system, reducing its efficiency. This could d
minish the likelihood or speed of the arrest, conviction, or execution \
a capital offender. The resulting decrease in deterrence, if any, wou\
be due as much to the escalating crime rate as to the nature of statuto\
punishments. While specific qualities of a punishment may influence \
effective deterrence, these qualities are not static but may vary with t\
crime rate and other dynamic features of the criminal justice system.

7. *Scientific vs. Philosophic Justifications.* Much of the death penalty deba
has centered on *scientific* efforts to assess the punishment's deterre\
effects. Another approach is, of course, a moral and philosophical on\
This second perspective is influenced not by scientific data but by fu\
damental support or opposition to the taking of human life as a for\
of punishment. For example, Gelles and Straus (1975) argue that suppo
for the death penalty increasingly reflects a retributive orientation—th\
is, some people favor the death penalty not because they believe that
deters crime but because they believe that offenders ought to suff\
extreme punishment. Similarly, the significance of moral sentiments c\
be seen in a survey which found that 75% of those who oppose cap
tal punishment would not change their position even in the face of co\

clusive proof that capital punishment deters homicide (Ellsworth and Ross, 1976).

GENERAL APPROACHES TO THE DETERRENCE QUESTION

As this list indicates, there are several issues in the death penalty debate which complicate efforts to summarize the deterrence literature. In addition, empirical studies of the deterrence hypothesis are characterized by substantial differences in the methods used, the scope of analysis, the quality of the data and research design, and, not surprisingly, the results. Over the past few years, several reviews of deterrence research have appeared (Bedau and Pierce, 1976; Blumstein, Cohen, and Nagin, 1978; Sellin, 1981). Rather than attempt another such review, this chapter selectively examines the issues most relevant to a comparative examination of the deterrence hypothesis.

Deterrence studies that use a cross-sectional design compare homicide rates at a single point in time. Such studies require a sample of at least two jurisdictions to provide a comparison. The de facto issue, for example, could be studied by comparisons of either (1) jurisdictions with a high "execution risk" (the probability of execution, given conviction for a capital offense) and those with a low execution risk, or (2) jurisdictions that have experienced a relatively large number of executions within a specified period of time and jurisdictions with few executions. Cross-sectional studies of the de jure question compare jurisdictions that have abolished (or never had) the death penalty with those that have retained (or restored) capital punishment. These de jure comparisons typically are made without regard to the actual imposition of the death penalty. In general, cross-sectional studies attempt to link higher execution risks, or retention of the death penalty, with observed differences in homicide rates.[1]

Cross-sectional designs are inherently weak and subject to invalidity on many grounds. For example, high or low crime rates could easily have led to changes in the severity of punishment rather than the other way around. These limitations have led most researchers to prefer longitudinal tests of the deterrence hypothesis. Examining changes in homicide rates over time makes it feasible to untangle the causal relationship between crimes and punishments. Longitudinal studies can involve one or more jurisdictions. Studying more than a single jurisdiction has advantages in terms of generalization and increased control over possibly unique factors in a single jurisdiction.

Like cross-sectional studies, longitudinal studies can examine either the de facto or the de jure question. De facto longitudinal studies compare changes in homicide rates before and after executions or as the general risk of execution changes over time. Most research on changes in execution probabilities have studied only a single jurisdiction. De jure longitudinal studies compare homicide rates in one or more jurisdictions before and after abolition (or restoration) of the death penalty.

Most tests of the deterrence hypothesis in this century have used one of the approaches just described. There have been changes in the methods used in deterrence research, but, with the exceptions indicated below, very little research has extended beyond national boundaries. A very large number of studies, in fact, have examined data only for individual American states or aggregate statistics for the United States. With the limitations of specific approaches and methods in mind, existing evidence on the deterrence hypothesis can be summarized briefly.

SELECTED EVIDENCE ON THE EFFECTS OF CAPITAL PUNISHMENT

Debate over capital punishment is anything but new. As early as the 1830s, the death penalty was under attack in several American state legislatures, and a moratorium on public executions was declared. A Massachusetts state legislator named Robert Rantoul, Jr., figured prominently in this debate. In various public meetings, Rantoul presented statistics he had assembled on the deterrence question. Rantoul's efforts were unusually sophisticated and were, in fact, more extensive and detailed than many studies done a century later.

Rantoul examined long-term trends in a number of European countries and found that nations with a low ratio of executions to convictions had recorded declining homicide rates over time—precisely the reverse of what deterrence theory would predict. Rantoul also examined short-term patterns and found that periods with unusually high numbers of executions were followed by increases in the incidence of homicide. Because of its sophistication and breadth, Rantoul's work (see Bowers and Pierce, 1980: 460–61) is a landmark in the history of deterrence research.

The beginning of systematic deterrence research by social scientists coincides with a second "reform" era in the United States early in this century. Over a period of fifty years, social scientists conducted a number of analyses focused primarily on the de jure issue. These studies include Bye (1919), Sutherland (1925), Vold (1932, 1952), Dann (1935), Schuessler (1952), Sellin (1961, 1967), and Reckless (1969). The general conclusion drawn from these studies is captured by Sellin's much-cited statement: "the presence of the death penalty—in law or practice—does not influence homicide death rates" (1967: 138). This body of de jure research has been criticized on several grounds, and

by the early 1970s the widely accepted conclusion that the death penalty
was not an effective deterrent was under increasing attack. Critics of de
jure research have pursued several arguments:

> They have complained (1) that gross homicide rates are not sensitive enough
> to pick up deterrent effects, specifically, that the proportion of capital to
> noncapital homicides could be varying even when the overall homicide rate
> remains unaffected by abolition; (2) that the use of contiguous jurisdictions
> and before and after comparisons does not fully control for all other factors
> which could conceivably be masking deterrent effects; and (3) that deterrent
> effects may not be "jurisdictionally specific" within a nation, that people
> may not be responsive to the presence of, or changes in, capital statutes in
> the particular state where they reside, as distinct from neighboring states.
> (Bowers, 1974)

These criticisms have prompted new research designs and different
approaches. Relying chiefly on the statistical use of multiple regression,
a number of studies have tried to control for differences across jurisdictions or over time which could conceivably influence homicide rates.
In this way, researchers attempt to determine how much of any observed
change in homicide rates is due to nonpunishment variables or, alter-
natively, to the existence of capital punishment statutes and actual
executions.

One of the first of these studies was conducted by Ehrlich (1975).
Using aggregate homicide data for the entire United States for the period
1933–1970, Ehrlich analyzed the effect of the probability of execution
(given a conviction for a capital offense) on homicide rates. He also
controlled for a variety of other factors including unemployment, age,
and per capita income. On the basis of this analysis, Ehrlich concluded
that executions did have a deterrent effect. Specifically, he claimed that
between seven and eight potential homicides were deterred by each
execution.

Although Ehrlich's work found an eager audience among many policy-
makers, his research has been extensively criticized by a number of
researchers using equally sophisticated methods, particularly Bowers and
Pierce (1975); Passell and Taylor (1976); Klein, Forst, and Filatov (1978);
Loftin (1980); and Brier and Fienberg (1980). Many of these criticisms
have been thoroughly summarized elsewhere (e.g., Blumstein, Cohen,
and Nagin, 1978) and need not be repeated here. Because Ehrlich's
work is one of very few studies to find support for the deterrence hypothesis, it is not surprising that this research garnered widespread popular and scientific interest.

Attempted replications of Ehrlich's work using similar techniques
(multivariate analyses and econometric methods) have failed, however,
to find a deterrence effect. For example, Loftin (1980) did an elaborate

ecological analysis of crime rates and social characteristics in the United States. When social and economic variables such as poverty, education, and family structure were controlled, this study found little or no evidence for the deterrence hypothesis. Similarly, Brier and Fienberg (1980) used econometric models to test for a deterrence effect and concluded that the claims made in Ehrlich's 1975 study were not supported by the evidence. Finally, some of the most interesting longitudinal evidence involves separate time-series analyses of data from five different states on the relationship between execution risk and homicide rates (Bailey, 1978a, 1978b, 1979a, 1979b, and 1979c). In these studies, the evidence ran contrary to deterrence theory in three of the five states examined.

In recent research, there is even some evidence for what might be called the "antideterrent" effect of capital punishment. A fine-grained study by Bowers and Pierce (1980) examined monthly homicide rates in New York State between 1907 and 1963 and found an average *increase* of two homicides in the month after an execution. This finding led the authors to postulate a "brutalizing" effect of the death penalty—that is, the possibility that executions might increase violent crimes rather than deter them.

In summary, recent studies of the *de facto* issue do not, as was initially thought, contradict the long-standing conclusion from *de jure* research that the death penalty has no consistent, demonstrable deterrent effect. A number of specific issues, some of which have already been mentioned, continue to bear on new research, *de jure* and *de facto,* on deterrence theory. Two of these are of generic importance, and recent evidence on each can be summarized briefly.

1. Are gross homicide rates sensitive enough to pick up deterrent effects? Over fifty years ago, Sutherland stated that "the ordinary practice of drawing conclusions regarding changes in murder rates from changes in homicide rates is logically invalid. But it is the only method that can be used, since we have no other statistics available" (1925: 522). Despite the introduction of the *Uniform Crime Reports* in 1933, the lack of specific, disaggregated statistics has remained a problem:

> In the United States, generally only one type of homicide—murder in the first degree—is punishable by death, with murder in the second degree and voluntary manslaughter usually being punished by imprisonment. Typically, however, investigations of the death penalty have operationally defined premeditated murder as homicide, a much more inclusive offense category. This practice has been necessitated by the fact that no alternative statistics are currently available on a nationwide basis that break down homicide by type and degree. As a result investigators have been forced to make a large and possibly erroneous assumption whether they use police or mortality statistics, that the proportion of first degree murders to total homicides

remains constant so that the statistics on the latter provide a reasonably adequate indicator of capital offenses. (Bailey, 1975: 418)

In order to test this crucial assumption, Bailey collected disaggregated data on first- and second-degree murder convictions from a number of state court systems. He then examined the relationship between capital punishment and murder rates in a manner similar to that used in earlier studies by Schuessler (1952) and Sellin (1959, 1967). Bailey's approach differed from these earlier analyses, however, in that "the murder data examined . . . permit a direct rather than indirect assessment of the relationship between capital homicides and the death penalty" Bailey, 1975: 418). Bailey found that there was no evidence for a deterrent effect whether one examined second-degree, first-degree, or all homicides combined. This research cast doubt on the claim that the deterrent effect has been obscured by the insensitivity of gross homicide rates.

2. *Does the use of contiguous jurisdictions and before and after comparisons fail to control for all factors that could mask deterrent effects?* Van den Haag, a strong critic of much deterrence research, has argued that "homicide rates do not depend exclusively on penalties any more than other crime rates [do]. A number of conditions which influence the propensity to crime (demographic, economic, or social) . . . may influence the homicide rate" (1969: 285). In order to control for these factors, some investigators have compared only similar retentionist and abolitionist jurisdictions such as contiguous states.

Because of differences between even contiguous jurisdictions, critics have claimed that this procedure provides inadequate controls. In response, Bailey (1975) compared states with and without the death penalty while controlling for two socioeconomic and five demographic variables. As an additional control, retentionist and abolitionist states with similar rates of aggravated assault were compared to hold constant potentially significant etiological factors. Regardless of which control variables were included, Bailey found that retentionist states had measurably higher homicide rates than abolitionist states. In this instance, again, the evidence runs contrary to the deterrence hypothesis. Therefore, while the inclusion of the suggested control variables would certainly have improved many studies that failed to find a deterrent effect, these controls would not have changed the conclusions these studies reached.

GENERAL AND SPECIFIC DETERRENCE HYPOTHESES

In its de jure form, the general deterrence hypothesis holds that, *ceteris paribus*, jurisdictions which abolish capital punishment will experience increased rates of homicide. As already indicated, there are other forms of the hypothesis, including the focus in de facto research on the fact of executions rather than their legal possibility. While de facto research has an incontestable importance, the de jure issue is inherently interesting and also central to policy decisions that are directly linked to the empirical question of whether and how abolition is likely to affect homicide rates. In addition to what is here called the *general* deterrence hypothesis, a number of more specific hypotheses can be derived.

Offense Deterrence

Criminal penalties, and therefore their hypothesized deterrent effects, are offense-specific. Where it exists, the death penalty is prescribed for a society's most grievous offenses, capital crimes. In terms of deterrence theory, the death penalty can be expected to have its most direct effects on the specific offenses for which this punishment can be imposed. A more precise hypothesis can therefore be derived from the theory of general deterrence.

This specific hypothesis, which might be called *offense deterrence*, holds that capital punishment will have its most perceptible effects on capital crimes, the offenses executions are imposed to deter. In terms of offense deterrence, the effect of capital punishment on lesser crimes is less predictable since these crimes (particularly theft, robbery, and other economic offenses) are not the object of this sanction. If the hypothesis of offense deterrence has merit, abolition of the death penalty should be followed by increases in the *specific* offenses (for example, homicides) putatively most affected by abolition. In addition, the increases in these capital offenses should be larger and more consistent than any other post-abolition crime rate changes.

Residual Deterrence

If the general deterrence hypothesis is correct, abolition should be followed by homicide rate increases. That this is a central expectation of deterrence theory is beyond dispute. There is disagreement, however, about the temporal qualities of this relationship, and this is a source of controversy in the interpretation of de jure case studies, the results of which can be summarized as follows:

> Comparative examinations of homicide rates before and after abolition [or] the restoration of the death penalty have .... questioned the efficacy of capital punishment. These investigations reveal that states that have abolished the death penalty have generally experienced no unusual increase in homicide. Moreover, the reintroduction of the death penalty (eleven states have abolished the death penalty but later restored it) has not been followed by a significant decrease in homicide. (Bailey, 1975: 417)

At least for the case studies that have been done, there is little disagreement about this empirical fact: abolition (or restoration) of the death penalty does *not* produce any sudden or dramatic changes in homicide rates. While this null result is frequently cited as evidence against the deterrence hypothesis, some have argued that it may reflect only public ignorance of changes in capital statutes. If citizens are uninformed about such changes, abolition might have no perceptible effect because individuals would continue to be deterred as if capital punishment still existed.

Research indicates that public ignorance of the law is widespread, and this issue is of obvious importance to an understanding of how deterrence does or does not work. In a survey of public awareness of recent increases in criminal penalties, half the respondents were unaware of the changes and could not even guess whether penalties had increased or decreased (Miller, Rosenthal, Miller, and Ruzek, 1971). Capital punishment statutes were not specifically examined in this study, yet it seems reasonable to assume that people would be better informed about these laws because of the extremity of the punishment, extensive media attention, and frequent controversy. Some deterrence theorists still believe, however, that genuine deterrence effects are masked by public ignorance:

> A constant homicide rate, despite abolition, may occur because of unawareness and not because of lack of deterrence: people remain deterred for a lengthy interval by the severity of the penalty in the past, or by the severity of penalties used in similar circumstances nearby. (Van den Haag, 1969: 286)

This hypothesis posits the existence of what might be called *residual deterrence*, an effect that lingers after the death penalty is abolished. Residual deterrence may complicate studies of the death penalty but does not, as some have implied, make systematic evaluation impossible. For example, even if residual deterrence exists, it should weaken over time as more people become aware that the law has changed. Thus residual deterrence should be strong in the first year after abolition, weaker five years later, and weaker still after many years. As a result, if it is true that potential murderers are deterred by the death penalty, one would expect to see progressive increases in homicide rates as residual deterrence erodes in the years following abolition.

Vicarious Deterrence

A parallel argument holds that citizens are deterred by the existence of the death penalty in adjacent jurisdictions. This might be called *vicarious deterrence*. If deterrence is not jurisdiction-specific, people living in a state without the death penalty might be deterred by an incorrect belief in the possibility of capital punishment. If vicarious deterrence does in fact occur, the existence of *any* capital statute could affect citizens in retentionist and abolitionist states alike (Van den Haag, 1969: 286). As a result, the effects of abolition might be invisible in de jure studies conducted in contiguous states.

The possibility of vicarious deterrence lends increased importance to cross-national research. If this hypothesis has substance, one would expect to find invisible or "masked" deterrence in certain de jure studies but not in others. Vicarious deterrence might produce misleading null results in studies of local jurisdictions such as states but should not affect studies of independent societies, since it seems unlikely that legislation in one nation would have any deterrent effects beyond its own boundaries. A cross-national study therefore provides a relatively pure test of the de jure hypothesis, unaffected by vicarious deterrence.

Despite their obvious importance, comparative studies of deterrence are relatively rare and large-sample comparisons are almost unknown. In the early 1930s the (British) Royal Commission on Capital Punishment heard extensive testimony from expert witnesses representing European and Commonwealth nations. On the basis of the available evidence, the Commission concluded, "Capital Punishment may be abolished in this country [Britain] without endangering life or property or impairing the security of society" (Calvert, 1931: 48). Almost two decades later, the Commission was reestablished for a more extensive, four-year examination of the question. The new Commission affirmed the earlier conclusion: "There is no clear evidence in any of the figures we have examined that the abolition of capital punishment has led to an increase in the homicide rate, or that its reintroduction has led to its fall" (1953: 23). This conclusion was supported, once again, by a separate study conducted by the 1962 European Committee on Crime Problems.

The trend toward abolition increased during the 1960s and, although it has since been reversed, there have been no systematic efforts during this period to collect and evaluate data from a large sample of abolitionist nations. The individual case studies that have been done vary greatly in their procedures and use of controlled comparisons. As a result, existing cross-national evidence suffers from a confusing patchwork of results. While a comparative test of the deterrence hypothesis is not without complications, the principal obstacle has been the absence of longitudinal offense data from a large sample of societies.

CROSS-NATIONAL DATA ON FOURTEEN CASES OF ABOLITION

A first step in any cross-national test involves identifying a sample of abolition cases. This task is more complicated than one might imagine.

Some societies have abolished capital punishment for mortal offenses generally but retain it for a small number of specific crimes, such as the murder of a prison guard by a prisoner serving a life term. Other nations have eliminated the death penalty but provided for its revival during civil emergencies or martial law. The de jure question is therefore complicated by the need for discrete classification of societies as abolitionist when, in fact, degrees of abolition may be present.

One solution to this classification problem employs a rough working definition: Jurisdictions are considered "abolitionist" if capital punishment is prohibited for civil offenses even if extraordinary crimes—such as murders committeed by individuals serving life sentences—are still punishable by death. It should be emphasized that this is a de jure classification. Nations in which no executions have occurred for long periods of time cannot be considered abolitionist under this definition if capital punishment remains in law. The dates of abolition also include potential ambiguities—for example, one could choose the date on which the penal code is changed or the date on which the change takes effect.

After examining various lists of abolitionist nations and dates, we adopted a modified form of the classifications made by Bowers (1974: 178) and Joyce (1961: 85). This consolidated list was juxtaposed with offense rate data from the Comparative Crime Data File to yield a total of fourteen sets of time-series data for twelve distinct cases of abolition. In two cases (Austria and Finland), separate records for the major cities, Vienna and Helsinki, provided the opportunity to "replicate" national cases with urban data.[2]

Before we present the results of these comparisons, it should be emphasized that most efforts to discern the independent effects of abolition err on the side of simplification. Offense rates are driven by many factors, and single-variable evaluations understate this complexity. For example, a number of abolitions occurred around wartime, and the data presented in chapter 4 indicate that wars frequently elevate postwar rates of violent crime. Similarly, vast demographic changes—such as the coming of age of the post–World War II "baby boom" cohort—can greatly inflate offense rates or otherwise complicate efforts to assess the effects of legal changes. In cross-national studies of deterrence, therefore, the effect of abolition is inevitably muddied somewhat by other changes.[3]

For reasons already discussed, a longitudinal design is preferable to crude cross-sectional comparisons. Because of the infinite number of idiosyncratic national characteristics, it makes little or no sense to compare abolitionist and retentionist countries at a single moment in time. The longitudinal approach, in which the individual experiences of a sample of countries are examined over time, provides a much stronger basis for inferences about the effect of abolition. As will be seen, the depth and breadth of data in the Comparative Crime Data File make possible longitudinal comparisons as well as a series of additional control procedures.

CROSS-NATIONAL TESTS OF SPECIFIC DETERRENCE HYPOTHESES

Data from this sample of fourteen cases can be examined in a number of ways. Some of these provide an overall test of the *general deterrence* theory prediction that abolition of the death penalty causes a perceptible increase in homicide rates. As indicated earlier, more specific deterrence hypotheses can be derived from the general theory. *Vicarious deterrence*, the alleged geographic spillover of deterrence from retentionist jurisdictions to abolitionist jurisdictions, is controlled in this design by the examination of sovereign nations. *Residual deterrence*, the alleged temporal spillover of deterrence from retentionist years to abolitionist years, can be tested directly by examining post-abolition time intervals of progressively greater lengths. If the hypothesis of residual deterrence has merit, homicide rate increases should become larger as longer intervals after abolition are examined. *Offense deterrence*, the prediction that post-abolition changes will be most conspicuous in rates of capital offenses, can be tested directly by a contrast between homicide and several non-capital crimes.

I. General Deterrence

An initial comparison of the short-term effects of abolition is presented in table 6.1. The percentages in this table indicate the increase or decrease in homicide rates from the year prior to abolition to the year following. The homicide rates on which the percentages are based are also included as a cautionary feature. In some cases, such as New Zealand, the homicide rate is so low in absolute terms that the addition of a single homicide can double the national offense rate. The precise indicators in this comparison (offenses known, convictions, etc.) are also shown since these differ for the fourteen cases.[4]

With these cautions in mind, the picture in table 6.1 is one of little change; in fact, eight of the fourteen cases (57%) show a homicide rate decrease in the year following abolition while only five (36%) show an increase. In this crude short-term comparison, therefore, there is no evidence for the deterrence hypothesis. De jure abolition appears to have had little effect. If anything, there appears to be a slight downturn in homicide rates.

Table 6.1. Homicide Rate Levels Before and After Abolition of the Death Penalty

Jurisdiction (date of abolition, indicator)	One year pre-abolition homicide rate	One year post-abolition homicide rate	% Change
Austria (1968, e)	.72	.71	−1
England and Wales (1965, a)	.36	.35	−3
Finland (1949, a)	1.05	.72	−31
Helsinki (1949, a)	1.96	1.90	−3
Israel (1954, a)	4.00	1.72	−57
Italy (1890, a)	13.30	12.94	−3
Sweden (1921, b)	.43	.15	−65
Switzerland (1942, d)	45.25	35.65	−21
Vienna (1968, e)	.93	.93	0
Canada (1967, a)	1.10	1.52	38
Denmark (1930, c)	33.89	35.68	5
Netherlands Antilles (1957, a)	13.19	20.32	54
New Zealand (1961, b)	.04	.08	100*
Norway (1905, b)	.35	.39	11

Key to offense indicators:
   a. homicide offenses known
   b. murder, manslaughter, or homicide convictions
   c. violent offenses known
   d. violent offenses convictions
   e. criminal statistics

*Because of an extremely low base rate, this 100% increase reflects a change from 1 to 2 cases.

2. Residual Deterrence

If one subscribes to the hypothesis of residual deterrence, however, the comparison in table 6.1 is inconclusive. The effects of deterrence could easily be masked by public ignorance of abolition, particularly in the first year following this change. For this reason, longer intervals are compared in table 6.2. It seems unlikely that residual deterrence could continue to affect behavior five years following abolition, and this hypothesis becomes even less plausible over longer intervals. The five-year statistics in table 6.2 compare the five years of homicide data before and after abolition. This comparison does not include all fourteen cases since some entries in the CCDF did not have data for all of these years. The "maximum possible" comparison in this table reflects the longest intervals before and after abolition for which homicide data were available.

This comparison again provides little evidence for the deterrence hypothesis in general or for residual deterrence in particular. In the five-year comparison, half of the ten cases for which the comparison can be made show homicide rate increases following abolition while half show decreases. There is even less support for the deterrence hypothesis when longer intervals are examined. When intervals of maximum possible length are compared, only five of the fourteen cases (36%) show homicide rate increases after abolition while eight (57%) show decreases. This finding runs directly counter to the hypothesis of residual deterrence. Since homicide rate decreases are found most consistently when long intervals are compared, the idea that deterrence progressively erodes in the years following abolition seems untenable.

3. Offense Deterrence

A final comparison addresses the question of whether capital punishment has any specific offense deterrence. The breadth of data in the CCDF makes it possible to contrast changes in capital offenses with changes in noncapital crimes. A deterrence theorist could conceivably argue that tables 6.1 and 6.2 conceal massive downward trends in crime generally and, consistent with the deterrence hypothesis, that homicide rates might be falling *relatively* more slowly than the rates of noncapital offenses. Even falling homicide rates after abolition might reflect deterrence if decreases were less precipitous than simultaneous decreases in noncapital offenses. The key test of offense deterrence, therefore, is whether homicide rate increases after abolition are greater (in absolute or relative terms) than any observed increases for noncapital crimes.

The offense deterrence hypothesis is examined in table 6.3. This table

Table 6.2. Homicide Rate Changes After Abolition: Longer Trends

Jurisdiction	One year	Five year means[a]	Maximum years possible[b]	
Austria	−1%	32%	9%	(15,5)
Canada	38	63	67	(5,6)
Denmark	5	—	4	(9,2)
England and Wales	−3	18	27	(14,7)
Finland	−31	−40	−59	(22,18)
Helsinki	−3	−27	−57	(22,18)
Israel	−57	−53	−65	(5,16)
Italy	−3	−5	−30	(10,24)
Netherlands Antilles	54	—	−4	(2,13)
New Zealand	100	117	0	(10,11)
Norway	−11	—	−24	(2,35)
Sweden	−65	—	−63	(1,28)
Switzerland	−21	−36	−46	(13,28)
Vienna	0	94	85	(15,5)

[a] Comparison of mean offense levels for five-year periods before and after abolition.
[b] Comparison of mean offense levels for maximum time periods before and after abolition for which data are available (years indicated in parentheses).

Table 6.3. Homicide Levels Before and After Abolition Using Other Offenses as Control Variables

Jurisdiction	One year						Five years						Maximum years possible*					
	Homicide	M†	R	A	Ro	T	Homicide	M†	R	A	Ro	T	Homicide	M†	R	A	Ro	T
Austria‡	-1%	+24	+12	-2	-9	+17	+32%	+57	+5	+8	+44	+55	+9%	+42	-3	+6	+72	+109
Canada	+38	+107	+32	+20	+42	—	+63	+11	+57	+76	+73	—	+67	+21	+68	+79	+78	—
Denmark	+5	—	0	+5	—	+8	—	—	—	—	—	—	+4	—	+25	—	—	+34
England	-3	+57	+23	+13	+44	+9	+18	+58	+56	+73	+102	+36	+27	+30	+86	+196	+248	—
Finland	-31	-27	+95	-10	-46	-43	-40	-44	+28	—	-80	-70	-59	-63	+102	—	-47	-9
Israel	-57	—	—	+40	-55	-6	-53	—	—	—	-75	+8	-65	—	—	—	-74	+60
Italy	-3	—	—	-10	+31	+4	-5	—	—	—	+32	—	-30	—	—	—	+35	—
Neth Antilles	+54	—	-50	—	+51	+13	—	—	—	—	—	—	-4	—	-20	—	+87	+18
New Zealand	+100	—	+11	+27	-43	-4	+117	—	+16	+46	-46	+7	0	—	—	—	-12	+46
Norway	+11	—	+36	-13	—	-10	—	—	—	—	—	—	-24	—	+100	-7	—	+10
Sweden	-65	—	-58	-33	-36	—	-36	—	—	—	—	—	-63	—	+123	-3	+19	—
Switzerland	-21	—	+12	+21	—	+7	-36	—	—	-36	—	-3	-46	—	—	—	—	-15
Helsinki	-3	-35	+1	+3	-52	-42	-27	-42	+23	—	-86	+79	-57	-55	+73	—	-71	-43
Vienna	0	+30	+32	-2	-11	+22	+94	+100	+6	+20	+49	+53	+85	+138	-3	+33	+100	+145
Median	-2%	+27	+12	-2	-11	+6	+7%	+34	+23	+33	+32	+22	-14%	+26	+71	+20	+35	+26

* For the number of years included in this comparison, see table 6.2.
† Crime types: M (Manslaughter), R (Rape), A (Assault), Ro (Robbery), T (Theft).
‡ Indicator type and year of abolition for each nation are given in table 6.1.

compares changes before and after abolition for three time periods (one year, five years, and the maximum interval possible) for homicide and five noncapital offenses. Median offense rate changes for all cases are shown at the bottom of the table. Missing percentages indicate that the comparison could not be made for this offense during this particular interval using the data in the CCDF.

In general, the data run strongly counter to the hypothesis of offense deterrence. While this hypothesis predicts that capital crimes will increase more rapidly after abolition than noncapital offenses, precisely the opposite pattern obtains. No matter which time interval is examined, noncapital offense rates show increases greater than the changes observed for homicide rates. While noncapital crime rates increased following abolition—perhaps as a result of demographic or other changes—rates of homicide were stationary or declined.

This difference between capital and noncapital rate changes is striking, and it is difficult to imagine a result more in contradiction with deterrence theory. Under this hypothesis, one would have expected absolute homicide rate increases, or at least increases relative to any changes in noncapital offenses. Yet these cross-national findings fail to support the offense deterrence hypothesis and, in fact, provide strategic evidence that the death penalty has no discernible effect on homicide rates.

SUMMARY AND CONCLUSIONS

If capital punishment is a more effective deterrent than the alternative punishment of long imprisonment, its abolition ought to be followed by homicide rate increases. The evidence examined here fails to support and, indeed, repeatedly contradicts this proposition. In this cross-national sample, abolition was followed more often than not by absolute *decreases* in homicide rates, not by the increases predicted by deterrence theory. Further, the homicide rates of these nations also decreased relative to the rates of noncapital offenses after abolition. Both of these findings hold true whether comparisons are made for short, medium, or the longest feasible time periods.

This cross-national research design controls for some possible defects in previous studies, including *vicarious deterrence,* the alleged jurisdictional nonspecificity of capital punishment. The results of this comparative analysis contradict general deterrence theory and also disconfirm specific hypotheses derived from this theory such as *residual deterrence* (the idea that deterrence continues for finite intervals after abolition) and *offense deterrence* (the idea that abolition inflates rates of homicide more than noncapital offenses). These findings lend new weight to the research literature running counter to deterrence theory:

In the face of the mounting evidence against any deterrent advantage of the death penalty, proponents increasingly find themselves affirming more idiosyncratic explanations for the effects they presume the death penalty has, but which research has yet to reveal . . . With each new set of findings their task becomes more arduous and their arguments become less plausible. (Bowers, 1974: 163)

As indicated early in this chapter, empirical evidence on the presence or absence of deterrent effects is only one participant in the debate over capital punishment. Public attitudes toward crime and criminals, moral sentiments, and changing intellectual fashions also play major roles. The function of scientific inquiry in this debate, while limited, is also unique. Research like that presented in this chapter addresses the most pervasive justification for capital punishment, the deterrence hypothesis.

Combined with previous research, evidence in this chapter confronts and consistently contradicts testable elements of deterrence theory. While there may be many persuasive reasons for capital punishment—including arguments based on retribution, economics, or other principles— the deterrence of potential offenders cannot be included among them. Other justifications for the death penalty can and presumably will be debated, but the deterrence hypothesis must be regarded at this time as scientifically unsupported.

A final note concerns future research and what constitutes a reasonable burden of proof. Although this chapter is focused on empirical research, the evidence presented complements a very different argument, one grounded in logic and philosophy rather than science. Unlike many topics in basic research, inquiry in this area addresses a question of literally life and death significance. At least in the United States, the populations of death rows continue to grow at a rapid pace and the debate over the death penalty is anything but abstract. In addition, the deterrence hypothesis currently is under discussion and review in many courts and state legislatures.

Clearly, the stakes in this debate are unusually high. Precisely for this reason, it seems fair to assume that the burden of proof is on the restorationists to show that a deterrent effect does exist—unless, of course, our society is prepared to shift from deterrence to retribution (or some other principle) as a justification for capital punishment. Given the extreme and irrevocable nature of capital punishment, the deterrent effect should be accepted as a sufficient basis for policy only if evidence shows this effect to be reliable, consistent, and large in magnitude. If the deterrent effect is anything less than this, executions cannot be expected to produce anything other than the deaths of the executed and the satisfaction of those who demand violent retribution. The exceptional nature of this burden of proof required of deterrence theory is cited in a study commissioned by the prestigious National Academy of Sciences:

In undertaking research on the deterrent effect of capital punishment . . . it should be recognized that the strong value content associated with decisions regarding capital punishment and the high risk associated with errors of commission make it likely that any policy use of scientific evidence on capital punishment will require *extremely severe standards of proof.* (Blumstein, Cohen, and Nagin, 1978: 63; emphasis added)

Empirical support for the deterrence hypothesis, including the evidence presented here, obviously cannot meet this exacting standard. The evidence runs strongly contrary to deterrence theory and, while more research can of course be done, the mere existence of this consistently contrary evidence demonstrates that the deterrent effect—if one exists at all—cannot by definition be reliable, consistent, or large in magnitude. If the deterrent effect had these robust qualities, the effect surely would have surfaced vividly and repeatedly in these investigations.

The available evidence suggests that no deterrent effect exists at all, and surely no deterrent effect exists whose strength and size could possibly serve as a sufficient justification for capital punishment. Although this analysis rests on comparative empirical evidence, its conclusion that restoration cannot be justified without overwhelming evidence for a deterrent effect is paralleled by some logical and philosophical considerations of the death penalty:

Capital punishment is certainly among the most extreme or severe deprivations that can be imposed as a punishment. . . . As a result the burden of justifiability falls in a correspondingly heavy fashion upon the defender of *that* kind of punishment. . . . As moral agents we ought, I believe, to require more convincing, if not decisive, reasons of a sort I am unable to bring to light before the decision to punish—especially by a deprivation as total and cataclysmic for the individual as death—can be the morally defensible one for us to make. (Wasserstrom, 1982: 478, 499)

The issue of the exceptional burden of proof facing restorationists therefore provides an intersection between logical arguments about the death penalty and scientific efforts to measure its deterrent effect. A humane and rational society should consider taking human life only if there is extremely strong and overwhelming evidence that this act will save lives by deterring other violence.

As this chapter and other studies make abundantly clear, there is no extremely strong and overwhelming evidence for deterrence, and the contrary conclusions of existing research suggest that such evidence for deterrence will not be forthcoming. In the absence of thoroughly persuasive evidence, it seems inconceivable that our society would be willing to take the extreme step of executing people in pursuit of what is almost certainly a hopeless objective.

NOTES

1. As discussed in chapter 3, direct cross-sectional comparisons of the *levels* of homicide across jurisdictions are of questionable validity if these jurisdictions do not share legal systems, definitions of crime, and practices of offense reporting and recording. Partly for these reasons, cross-sectional studies are almost always limited to comparisons of states within the United States. Even so, it has been argued that there is enough variation among states on these factors to warrant statistical control measures, an issue discussed later in this chapter.

2. Data for the 1890 Italian case predates the beginning of the CCDF and were obtained from source data for the CCDF. Data for Canada were supplemented by information from recent *Statistics Canada* publications.

3. Given sufficient data, it would be possible to introduce controls for these specific factors, although other unrecognized sources of variation would of course remain uncontrolled. In the absence of data for post hoc controls of this kind, it is important to have enough cases in the analysis to minimize the statistical probability of competing explanations for any observed offense rate changes.

4. Various indicators could conceivably be affected differentially before and after abolition. As before, the "offenses known" indicator is the preferred measure. Data on "convictions," however, almost certainly are biased in favor of the deterrence hypothesis. One would expect convictions indicators to *increase* after abolition simply because prosecutors would be more willing to bring charges for murder (rather than manslaughter), and judges and juries would be more likely to find defendants guilty, when not faced with the possible imposition of the death penalty. This type of increase in convictions data is not a true deterrent effect but is a potential artifact that works in the apparent favor of the deterrence hypothesis. If decreases are observed in convictions indicators, therefore, these decreases are particularly strong evidence contrary to the deterrence hypothesis.

SEVEN

Potential Applications and Future Imagination: A Diverse Research Agenda

INTRODUCTION

The preceding chapters illustrate only a few uses of comparative crime data; the potential applications are too numerous and diverse to anticipate fully. Comparative research on crime and violence is still a scarcely tapped field. The prospects for original research are propitious, and, as indicated by the list of potential studies in chapter 1, a large number of compelling questions await investigation.

In this final chapter, we present four fragmentary examples of additional applications of these comparative data. Unlike the more focused material provided in preceding chapters, these four brief examples offer a series of chance observations, unattempted questions, hypotheses yet to be developed, and modest suggestions that may be of assistance to future comparative researchers. The closing section describes five general research paradigms for which comparative data on crime and violence should prove valuable.

Example 1: Generating New Offense Rate Estimates from the CCDF

The records in the CCDF can be modified to generate an infinite number of new data sets. With different transformations, the data sets generated can be used to provide more precise estimates, to control for known sources of error, or for other analytic purposes. A single example involves the choice of appropriate population estimates to compute offense rates. The offense rates reproduced in this volume were generated using estimates of *total* populations. These rates reflect the number of offenses per 100,000 citizens; no effort has been made to disaggregate total populations. This approach is standard international practice. In addition, this rate is easily produced since data on total national populations are generally available.

Other rates can be generated, and it is for this reason that the number of *raw* offenses is included along with offense rates in the CCDF. For example, more fine-grained offense rates for violent crimes could be produced using specific age groups rather than the entire population.

Research on violent crimes consistently links a disproportionate share of these offenses to young men. The modal age of persons arrested for violent crimes in the United States tends to be in the late teens or early twenties: homicide (22), rape (18), robbery (17), aggravated assault (18) (U.S. Justice Department, *Sourcebook of Criminal Justice Statistics*, 1982).

The association between young adulthood and violent crime has the obvious consequence that, *ceteris paribus,* changes in national demography will be mirrored by changes in national offense rates. As a result, research can produce spurious results if one examines variables that happen to be correlated with demographic changes. In analyzing rates of violent crime in the United States during the 1960s and 1970s, for example, one would find that increased enrollments in universities correlated with increased crime rates—because both these variables reflect the maturation of the "baby boom" from the years following World War II.

Although this large cohort is one of the best-known demographic events, there are presumably others. Since these changes are certain to affect offense rates, it is desirable in some studies to control their effects. The question then becomes one of whether in a given period there are changes in offense rates apart from those due merely to known or unknown demographic changes. One solution to this problem is to generate new estimated offense rates using more finely grained population estimates. What one would like to have for this purpose, ideally, are international data on cohort-specific offense rates, such as the homicide rate among young men between the ages of 15 and 30.

Unfortunately, age-specific offense rates are generally unavailable in international data. In their absence, it is possible to use the raw offense data in the CCDF to produce new "age-adjusted" rates if one can obtain data on the changing size of the age group of interest. Given these population figures, new homicide rate variables can be created—for example, by dividing the total number of homicides by the size of the youthful population. It should be emphasized that this new variable is a "pseudo-rate" since it divides the number of homicides committed by citizens of all ages by the youthful population. This variable does not tell us what the youthful homicide rate is (since all homicides are included), but it does provide a means of controlling changes in homicide rates over time for increases or decreases in the youthful population.

This age-adjusted "pseudo-rate" has the advantage of straightforward calculation. Since the CCDF contains data on the aggregate number of offenses, a researcher needs to obtain only longitudinal data on the size of a nation's age cohorts. Even though most nations do not report genuine age-specific offense rates, the "pseudo-rate" is widely available since many nations report census data on the age of their populations. This generated rate can be used alone as a population-controlled estimate of the homicide rate or included along with the total offense rate as a data quality control procedure. In cases where both the total rate and the age-adjusted rate are available, it should be possible to identify "true" changes in offense rates—that is, changes that cannot be explained by demography alone.

The usefulness of generated offense rates can be illustrated using homicide rates in the United States between 1955 and 1972. This period witnessed a more than twofold increase in the absolute number of homicides. Since some of these increases undoubtedly reflect the maturation of the "baby boom" cohort, aggregate homicide rates cannot by themselves tell us whether "true" increases in homicide rates occurred during this period. The increased number of homicides might reflect no more than the increasing youthfulness of the population. As a test of whether "true" increases in homicide occurred, one can generate new homicide "pseudo-rates" to adjust for the growing number of young Americans; this has been done in two different ways in table 7.1.

Table 7.1 indicates the raw number of homicides in the United States between 1955 and 1972, and shows three rates that can be used to express the relative frequency of this offense. The first is the standard rate produced by dividing the raw number of homicides by the total population, and, in keeping with conventional practice, this rate is expressed per 100,000 citizens. As table 7.1 indicates, this standard rate suggests that the relative frequency of homicide nearly doubled (from 4.80 to 8.90) between 1955 and 1972. This conventional rate formula is, however, blind to the emergence of an unprecedentedly large population of young adults during this period.

The remaining two columns in table 7.1 contain new, generated offense rates obtained from readily available information on the size of the population at each age level (U.S. Bureau of the Census, *Current Population Reports*, Series P-25). One of these rates was produced by dividing the raw number of homicides by the population under the age of 30; the other, by dividing the raw number of homicides by the population aged 15–29. It should be emphasized that these are pseudo-rates since the numerator contains homicides committed by individuals of all ages.

In this case, age-adjusted rates present a somewhat different picture of changes in homicide between 1955 and 1972. While both pseudo-rates show large increases, these increases do not match the nearly two-fold change suggested by the conventional rate. On logical grounds, the second of the two pseudo-rates seems preferable to the first. This rate is relatively precise in that the age interval 15–29 captures youth and young adulthood and roughly straddles the modal homicide arrest age of 22. Unlike the other pseudo-rate in table 7.1. the 15–29 rate does not

Table 7.1. Raw and Age-adjusted U.S. Homicide Rates, 1955–1972

Year	Number of homicides	Rate per total population	Rate per population under 30[a]	Rate per population aged 15–29[b]
1955	7932	4.80	9.61	23.62
1956	8107	4.80	9.62	24.07
1957	8083	4.70	9.39	23.81
1958	8536	4.70	9.35	23.80
1959		4.80	9.51	24.36
1960	9034	5.00	9.86	25.44
1961	8637	4.70	9.22	23.92
1962	8586	4.60	8.97	22.73
1963	8524	4.50	8.73	21.75
1964	9414	4.90	9.45	23.14
1965	9909	5.10	9.78	23.53
1966	11007	5.60	10.69	25.20
1967	12121	6.10	11.62	26.76
1968	12644	6.30	11.98	26.97
1969	14796	7.30	13.86	30.49
1970	15980	7.80	14.78	31.82
1971	17599	8.50	16.10	33.99
1972	18587	8.90	16.90	34.88

[a]Rates derived from the total number of homicides (committed by individuals of all ages) divided by the population less than 30 years old.
[b]Rates derived from the total number of homicides (committed by individuals of all ages) divided by the population aged 15–29.

include infants and children, who of course figure in homicide little or not at all. Because the 15–29 pseudo-rate controls for the size of the youthful population, it offers a somewhat different account of changes in the homicide rate, as shown in figure 7.1.

In this figure, the base rate, represented by the horizontal dotted line, is calculated by the mean homicide rates during the period 1955–59. The points in the two curves express the homicide rates in each of the years 1960–72 as a ratio of the rates during the base years 1955–59. The two curves show that estimates of homicide rate changes differ depending on whether one uses the total population or only the youthful population as the basis for calculation.

The two estimates of the homicide rate are similar during the early 1960s but begin to diverge in mid-decade. By 1972, the last year shown in figure 7.1, the two offense rates provide quite different pictures of the magnitude of increase. The total homicide rate shows a nearly two-

Figure 7.1 Age-adjusted Homicide Rates in the United States

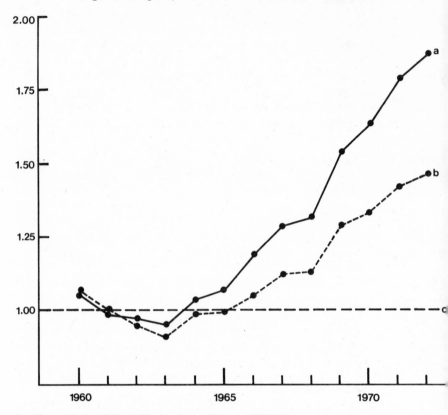

a. Change in (total homicides/total population), 1960–72.
b. Change in (total homicides/population aged 15–29), 1960–72.
c. Base rate = mean homicide rates for the period 1955–59.

fold increase while the age-adjusted rate shows a smaller growth of roughly 46% over the base years 1955–59. The increasing divergence between the two curves reflects the growing size and importance of the 15–29 age cohort during these years.[1]

The difference between the two rates in figure 7.1 prompts the following conclusions: first, the maturation of the baby boom cohort makes the total homicide rate somewhat misleading as a measure of changes in this offense; and, second, despite this demographic effect, there were homicide rate increases during this period that cannot be explained by demography alone. Other factors, including the postwar effects discussed in chapter 4, were presumably at work during this period. In summary, the age-adjusted pseudo-rate in figure 7.1 informs us that the increases in U.S. homicide rates between 1955 and 1972 were indeed large, but not as large as the untransformed, total population rate suggests.

An infinite number of new offense rates, such as the age-adjusted pseudo-rate described here, can be generated. In this instance, one might decide to use the age-adjusted rate instead of (or in addition to) the total population rate in any study of U.S. homicide rates during this period.[2] In general, the importance of this illustration is that a researcher can generate new estimates of crime rates using the raw data on offenses in the CCDF. While this file contains rates based on total populations, this convention is not restrictive. Depending on the specific problem under study, a researcher may prefer to use the raw data in the CCDF to generate new estimates that provide better controls or more accurately capture specific offense rate qualities.

Example 2: Proxy Variables for Missing Data

Like many archival records, data on criminal offenses are rarely available in as many areas and for as many years as a researcher might wish. Changes in recording practices, jurisdictional alterations, bureaucratic interruptions, and statistical innovations all reduce the breadth or depth of the researcher's potential vision. While these problems occur in American data, they become formidable obstacles when one attempts to gain a comparative perspective on the experience of several societies. In comparative research, the gaps in data from each individual society can accumulate to reduce greatly the effective sample size for which comparisons are possible. It may, however, be possible for a researcher to approximate certain missing data by using "proxy" variables.

As discussed in chapter 3, many comparative research designs focus on changes or relationships in each one of a sample of nations. In such designs, the researcher tests to see whether the same pattern replicates in a consistent manner. The concern here is with *intranational* trends and relationships, and static offense rates are of little concern. Examples of such research designs, called Type III and Type IV designs in chapter 3, are a hypothetical five-nation study of whether reported rape offenses increase after reforms in courtroom procedures for rape cases and a hypothetical ten-nation study of the effect of changes in firearms law on homicide rates. In these studies, what matters is whether and how offense rates change; the actual size of momentary rates is relatively inconsequential.

In these designs, one would of course like to have fully comparable indicators for each nation. In the absence of this ideal situation, however, Type III and Type IV comparisons are viable if a substitute or "proxy" for a missing indicator can be found. Since these designs focus on changes and trends, the obvious requirement for such a proxy variable is that it covary in an acceptable manner with the missing indicator. Stated in this form, this requirement is of course imprecise, and the degree of "acceptable" fit between a missing indicator and an available proxy is an area of potential, and quite legitimate, disagreement.[3] The principle, however, seems beyond dispute: use of a proxy for missing data is justified in longitudinal designs if it can be shown (or reasonably assumed) that the two variables have a strong relationship over time.

Since missing data are by definition unavailable, evidence for the suitability of a proxy variable can be only indirect. The question becomes one of whether there are sufficient grounds to assume that an available indicator bears a close relationship over time to the missing indicator. In some cases, the acceptability of proxy variables seems demonstrated. As shown in chapter 3, for example, different indicators (offenses known, convictions, etc.) of an offense such as homicide are strongly colinear over time. These different indicators therefore constitute acceptable proxy variables for longitudinal research—for example, one would probably not hesitate to use offenses-known data for France and arrest data for England in a two-country study of the effects of new laws on homicide rates.

Other suitable proxy variables almost certainly exist and, when used with appropriate caution, can extend the reach and sample size of comparative research. One obvious source of potential proxy variables is urban data. National data on offense rates require centralization of record keeping, effective methods of data collection and accumulation, and other systematic procedures. Urban data, however, are more easily gathered. For this reason, offense data for one or more large cities may be available even if national offense data are not. Since the CCDF contains data for forty-four international cities, it is possible to provide a general test of the relationship over time between urban and national data. This test, consisting of urban-national correlations for the same offenses in the same time periods, is shown in table 7.2.

This table contains a total of 129 urban-national correlations of which 85.3% are positive. If the apparently anomalous cases of India and the Philippines are excluded, 93.0% are positive. These relationships are partly tautological, since national offense rates include the urban data. While the two indicators are therefore not fully independent, they index very different jurisdictions. As discussed in chapter 5, urban offense rates are often unique, and this is one reason why the correlations in table 7.2 are not 1.0. While there are some negative correlations, the evidence in table 7.2 suggests that changes in urban offense rates generally approximate changes in national rates over time.

The magnitudes of the urban-national correlations vary, indicating that urban data provide a better proxy for national data in some societies

Table 7.2. Correlations between City and Country Data for
the Same Offenses and Time Period

City, Country	Years	Offenses	Correlation
Sydney, Australia	1938–1970	Murder (S)/Homicide (A)	.24
		Rape	.80
		Assault	.14
		Theft	.52
Vienna, Austria	1953–1973	Murder	.30
		Manslaughter	.71
		Rape	.55
		Assault	.42
		Robbery	.97
		Theft	.98
Brussels, Belgium	1946–1973	Murder (Br)/Homicide (Bel)	.65
		Rape	.22
		Theft	.56
Helsinki, Finland	1927–1970	Murder	.69
		Manslaughter	.83
		Rape	.75
		Assault	.78
		Robbery	.93
		Theft	.83
Paris, France	1931–1971	Murder	.73
	1956–1971	Manslaughter	.55
	1931–1971	Rape	.40
	"	Assault	.51
	"	Robbery	.69
	1956–1970	Theft	.44
Munich, Germany	1953–1972	Murder (M)/Homicide (G)	.76
	"	Rape	−.13
	1958–1972	Assault	.27
	1953–1972	Robbery	.94
	"	Theft	.97
Bombay, India	1953–1971	Murder	−.60
		Robbery	−.10
		Theft	.42
Calcutta, India	1956–1971	Murder	.78
		Robbery	.91
		Theft	−.19
Dublin, Ireland	1927–1973	Murder	.63
		Manslaughter	.71

Table 7.2. (continued)

City, Country	Years	Offenses	Correlation
Dublin, Ireland (continued)	1927–1973	Rape	.09
		Assault	.74
		Robbery	.99
		Theft	.96
Tokyo, Japan	1900–1970	Murder (T)/Homicide (J)	.61
		Robbery	.56
		Theft	.56
Nairobi, Kenya	1955–1968	Murder	.67
		Rape	.56
		Assault	.73
		Robbery	.90
		Theft	.54
Mexico City, Mexico	1952–1970	Murder (MC)/Homicide (M)	.60
		Rape	.75
		Assault	.93
		Robbery	.91
Amsterdam, Netherlands	1900–1970	Homicide	.27
		Rape	.76
		Assault	−.36
		Theft	.84
Wellington, New Zealand	1956–1973	Murder	.52
		Rape	.08
		Assault	.83
		Robbery	.76
		Theft	.85
Belfast, Northern Ireland	1922–1973	Homicide	1.00*
		Manslaughter	.68
		Assault	.91
		Rape	.75
		Robbery	1.00*
Panama City, Panama	1963–1973	Homicide	.06
		Rape	.54
		Assault	.97
Oslo, Norway	1923–1949	Murder	.20
		Manslaughter	.18
		Rape	.45
		Assault	.59
		Theft	.59

Table 7.2. (continued)

City, Country	Years	Offenses	Correlation
Manila, Philippines	1962–1972	Murder	−.36
	"	Homicide	−.20
	1962–1970	Rape	−.40
	1962–1972	Robbery	.26
	"	Theft	.29
Quezon City,	1962–1972	Murder	.03
Philippines		Homicide	−.68
		Rape	−.73
		Robbery	−.25
		Theft	−.13
Salisbury, Rhodesia	1950–1971	Murder	.16
		Murder (S)/Homicide (R)	−.08
		Homicide (S)/Murder (R)	−.04
		Homicide	.71
		Rape	.40
		Assault	.69
		Robbery	.80
		Theft	.61
Glasgow, Scotland	1902–1973	Murder	.92
	"	Murder (G)/Homicide (S)	.07
	1900–1973	Homicide (G)/Murder (S)	.13
	"	Homicide	.78
	"	Rape	.89
	"	Assault	.42
	"	Robbery	1.00*
	"	Theft	.89
Johannesburg,	1963–1971	Murder	.13
South Africa		Rape	.57
		Assault	.49
Madrid, Spain	1953–1968	Homicide	.70
		Rape	−.15
		Assault	.94
		Robbery	.85
		Theft	.67
Colombo City, Sri	1900–1973	Homicide	.46
Lanka	1938–1973	Robbery	.72
	"	Theft	.94
Port of Spain,	1950–1974	Murder	.63
Trinidad and		Murder(P)/Homicide (T)	−.19
Tobago			

Table 7.2. (continued)

City, Country	Years	Offenses	Correlation
Port of Spain,	1950–1974	Homicide (P)/Murder (T)	.10
Trinidad and		Homicide	.45
Tobago		Manslaughter	.89
(continued)		Rape	.89
		Robbery	.62
		Theft	.97
Istanbul, Turkey	1955–1973	Homicide	.70
	1955–1972	Rape	−.46
	1955–1973	Robbery	−.32
New York City,	1954–1965	Murder	.15
United States		Rape	−.16
		Assault	.98
		Robbery	.95
		Theft	.54

Median correlation across
all cases:

Homicide	.46
Manslaughter	.71
Rape	.45
Assault	.71
Robbery	.85
Theft	.60

*Correlation is .995 or greater

than others. In general, however, the magnitudes of these relationships, summarized at the end of table 7.2, are well within the tolerances of reliabilities encountered in social science research. At the same time, these correlations are lower than the very high correlations among different indicators (for example, arrests with offenses known) described in chapter 3. Given a choice, a researcher missing some national data should therefore prefer the proxy of a different indicator to the proxy of an urban offense rate.

In general, the evidence in chapter 3 and table 7.2 suggests that proxy variables can serve in many longitudinal studies as substitutes for missing national data. When proxy variables are used, of course, they need to be clearly labeled. In addition, in the interests of caution, a data quality control procedure can be used. In a study of the effect of changed firearms laws on homicide rates, for example, the researcher could examine the cases in waves—first those with national data on offenses known and then the cases with proxy indicators. This procedure allows the researcher to replicate the analysis at both levels of data quality. In summary, the evidence suggests that adequate substitute or proxy variables can be identified to repair some of the inevitable holes caused by missing data in longitudinal comparative research.

Example 3: The Factor Structure of Crime: A Meta-Analysis of Crime Rate Fluctuations

While many aspects of crime and violence compel attention, a persistent curiosity attaches to questions of etiology. These causal questions operate at two levels: the creation of individual criminals, on the one hand, and the fluctuations of aggregate crime rates, on the other. While the former preoccupies psychologists and other clinicians, the latter is the logical domain of social scientists. Previous chapters have illustrated some uses of aggregate offense rates in testing theories about the etiology of crime and violence.

Aggregate offense rates like those in the CCDF present both opportunities and obstacles for etiological research. The opportunities lie in the chance to fit patterns in offense rates to a series of presumed causal variables. This approach is comprehensive in that summary offense rates for samples of societies can be examined. At the same time, the very scale of the analysis makes individual actors invisible, and this creates an obvious potential for misattribution. For example, if one were to find a hypothetical link between fluctuations in national unemployment rates and changes in violent crime rates, one might be tempted to conclude that a causal relationship existed—that newly unemployed individuals were more likely to commit violent crimes.

However reasonable, this interpretation would be premature. When only aggregate data are examined, a researcher cannot know if they are linked at the level of the individual. In this hypothetical example, it is logically possible that *none* of the individuals contributing to the increased crime rate was recently unemployed. This is the well-known problem of the "ecological fallacy," in which aggregate data are falsely assumed to apply to specific individuals, and it continues to bedevil researchers using aggregate data. A number of studies report provocative statistical associations between aggregate indicators—for example, the unemployment rate and the total number of mental hospital admissions (Brenner, 1973). Without individual-level data, such as an employment history interview with persons newly arrested or institutionalized, causal explanations for such aggregate correlations remain elusive.

For this reason, researchers using aggregate data to illuminate the *causes* of crime (or of business failures, mental illness, divorce, and other conditions) are well advised to be cautious. The evidence for causal relationships in such studies is often more circumstantial than direct. In the absence of fine-grained evidence on the lives and characteristics of individual offenders, researchers using aggregate data must first uncover an interesting statistical association and then invent ways to examine as many plausible rival hypotheses as can be identified (Cook and Campbell, 1979). The challenge of aggregate data therefore lies in their large scale, and researchers scrutinizing aggregate indicators for causal relationships must be analytically inventive and intellectually circumspect.

In this section, we describe an investigation that exceeds even the large scale of most aggregate research and, for this reason, provides an unusually abstract approach to questions of etiology. In this analysis, fluctuations in offense rates are examined per se, rather than with respect to specific causal variables. These fluctuations can be inspected for underlying and unobvious patterns that, in turn, may reveal something about the social conditions that impact crime and violence. The method used is factor analysis, a multivariate technique sensitive to patterns of covariation among variables. This method is used to identify underlying components or "factors" which appear to affect several individual variables.

In the example described below, factor analysis is used to search for the possible existence of a "factor structure" of crime. Using individual societies as replicated cases, fluctuations in the rates of different offenses are examined for consistent and orderly patterns. One would like to find that offense rates are linked in a consistent manner to social changes— for example, that a specific social change, X_1, consistently produces an upward (or downward) change in the rates of offenses Y_1 and Y_2. Other social changes presumably affect other offenses, and this simplified etiological model can be summarized as follows:

$$X_1 \longrightarrow Y_1, Y_2$$
$$X_2 \longrightarrow Y_3, Y_4$$
$$X_3 \longrightarrow Y_5, Y_6$$
and in general
$$X_i \longrightarrow Y_j, Y_k$$

This etiological relationship, in which causal variables (X_i) impact specific offenses rates (Y_j, Y_k), can be consistent or inconsistent in two different ways: over time in the same society, and across nations. If consistencies exist, the prospects for etiological discovery are improved. Even in the absence of *identified* etiological variables, the existence of certain consistent patterns can provide circumstantial evidence that such etiological variables exist. If offenses Y_1 and Y_2 fluctuate in common over time, and this pattern is repeated in several societies, the orderly influence of one or more etiological forces is implied. Similarly, if offenses Y_3 and Y_4 fluctuate in common, the presence of a different set of causal forces is suggested. This circumstantial evidence can be informative, even if the responsible etiological variables $(X_1, X_2, X_3,$ etc.) are unidentified.

Even if specific causes are not unearthed, this approach can provide general evidence on a prior question: *Are there causes of crime, or do offense rates fluctuate in a random manner?* Etiological research on crime presupposes the existence of causes, although researchers generally address one or more specific causes rather than the more general question of whether causes exist. The random model, in which offense rates are hypothesized to fluctuate in mysterious and unpredictable ways, is of course much less inviting for rigorous research. Random fluctuations are, by definition, incapable of explication and of little theoretical interest.

Our approach to this abstract etiological question used factor analysis to identify patterns of covariation among different offenses. A series of factor analyses were completed, one within each appropriate national or urban data set from the CCDF. In some cases, more than a single factor analysis was performed for a single nation or city because of discontinuities in the data. Each analysis attempts to identify underlying dimensions that provide the best summary or statistical "explanation" of the changes in individual offense rates. A total of 55 two-factor solutions were identified, and table 7.3 presents several examples.[4]

This analysis illustrates again the advantage of a large comparative data set. Researchers with data for a single society seldom can distinguish idiosyncratic findings from general patterns. Given only one of the cases in table 7.3, the implications of this analysis are not obvious. Considered together, however, the five examples suggest the existence of an intriguing factor structure pattern. The most violent crimes, capital offenses, seem to be associated with one factor while the less violent property crimes, robbery and theft, are associated with the other. In the case of Finland, for example, one factor is strongly associated with murder (with a factor loading of .92) and manslaughter (.90), while the other factor is strongly associated with robbery (.87) and theft (.99). Table 7.3 suggests that other offenses are intermediate, loading sometimes on the "violent factor" and sometimes on the "nonviolent factor."

This pattern suggests an interesting "violent/nonviolent" hypothesis: *There may be two underlying dimensional causes of crime, one that affects violent offenses and one that affects property crimes and other nonviolent offenses.* If true, this would mean that two different social changes, or two different combinations of social changes, are causing increases and decreases in offense rates. Each of these causal factors could involve a single variable or a more complex formula of several changes, such as demographic changes (for example, the size of the population under 30) combined with industrialization.

While the variables in these two causal schemata are not specified, the violent/nonviolent hypothesis holds that the etiology of crime is twofold. The first hypothesized pattern of social changes constitutes the etiology

Table 7.3 Examples of Two-factor Solutions in International Crime Data

Country or city	Specific offense	Factor 1 loading	Factor 2 loading
England	Murder	.13	.91
(73 yrs.)	Manslaughter	−.10	.44
	Rape	.93	.08
	Assault	.99	−.02
	Robbery	.99	.03
	Theft	.96	−.28
United States	Murder	.26	.87
(73 yrs.)	Homicide	.02	.96
	Rape	.98	.08
	Assault	.99	.11
	Robbery	.79	.61
	Theft	.97	.21
Finland	Murder	.92	.22
(30 yrs.)	Manslaughter	.90	.37
	Rape	−.69	.33
	Assault	.73	.23
	Robbery	.48	.87
	Theft	.00	.99
Trinidad	Murder	−.10	−.18
(25 yrs.)	Manslaughter	.03	.99
	Homicide	.16	−.75
	Rape	.81	.04
	Robbery	.94	.10
	Theft	.88	−.04
Sydney	Murder	.10	.33
(40 yrs.)	Manslaughter	−.08	.69
	Rape	.85	.30
	Assault	.66	.75
	Theft	.98	−.09

of violent crimes; the second, the etiology of economic and nonviolent crimes. This hypothesis also implies that the two causal schemata are independent—for example, that one factor could cause major changes in violent crime while nonviolent offenses are unaffected.

If this hypothesis holds true, one might speak of *two different types of causes*, rather than of the "causes of crime" in general. This model could also be called the "violent/economic" hypothesis, since the economic offense of robbery is not necessarily nonviolent. The important point is that two *different* causal patterns appear to be operating: one for violent offenses and one for primarily nonviolent offenses that are economic or utilitarian in nature.

General evidence on the violent/nonviolent hypothesis derives from 55 two-factor solutions obtained using national and urban data from the CCDF. Each analysis was interpreted visually. An offense was considered to be associated with one factor if the loading exceeded .50 and if the offense was not also loaded on the opposite factor. In the example of U.S. data in table 7.3, murder is clearly loaded on one factor, Factor 2. In this same example, however, robbery is associated with both factors and therefore would not be classified with either.

This procedure provides a general test of the violent/nonviolent hypothesis, and the results of this analysis are presented in table 7.4. The figures in this table reflect the proportion of cases in which two offenses are loaded on the same factor. These values can be compared to 50.0%, the "chance" probability that any two offenses would be loaded on the same factor. Values above 50.0% indicate that two offenses covary, suggesting that they share common etiological factors. Values below 50.0% indicate that two offenses are relatively unrelated, suggesting the presence of different etiological factors. Values near 50.0% indicate that these two offenses do not show a general pattern of either association or independence.

Table 7.4 Proportion of Cases in Which Two Offenses Share the Same Factor

Offense	Mans.	Homi.	Rape	Assa.	Robb.	Thef.
Murder	58.8	42.9	50.0	44.0	50.0	31.2
	(17)	(7)	(26)	(25)	·(32)	(32)
Manslaughter		a	43.7	46.7	30.0	30.0
			(16)	(15)	(20)	(20)
Homicide			23.5	57.9	50.0	38.1
			(17)	(19)	(22)	(21)
Rape				40.0	48.6	44.4
				(25)	(35)	(36)
Assault					51.4	48.6
					(35)	(37)
Robbery						64.4
						(45)

NOTE: Each figure shows the percentage of cases in which these two offenses are associated with the same factor. The number of cases in each comparison is shown in parentheses. Although 55 factor analyses were performed, not all indicators are present for all societies, and some indicators were not clearly associated with either factor in some analyses.

a A figure is not included here because the percentage would be based on only two cases.

This result provides some support for the two-factor, violent/nonviolent etiological hypothesis. The violent offenses of murder, manslaughter, and homicide generally show factor loadings *opposite* to the loadings found for theft. In addition, there appear to be internal consistencies *within* violent offenses and *within* nonviolent offenses. Murder and manslaughter tend to be found on the same factor, and robbery and theft also share a common factor. Since this analysis of fifty-five cases subsumes great societal diversity, the emergence of a general violent/nonviolent factor structure is particularly intriguing.

Additional evidence can be obtained by examining more than two variables at a time. A three-variable outcome examines cases with one violent indicator (e.g., homicide) and two nonviolent indicators (robbery and theft).[5] Similarly, a four-variable outcome compares the factor location of two violent indicators (e.g., murder and manslaughter) with the location of two nonviolent indicators (robbery and theft).

In the three-variable case, outcomes such as ABB or BAA (violent indicator on one factor; nonviolent indicators both on opposite factor) indicate support for the general violent/nonviolent hypothesis. In the four-variable case, outcomes such as AABB or BBAA support the hypothesis. The observed results of the fifty-five factor analyses can be compared to the a priori or "chance" probability of such outcomes, and this comparison is presented in table 7.5.[6]

This analysis provides additional support for the two-factor hypothesis. The incidence of the violent/nonviolent outcome consistently exceeds the frequency predicted by chance alone. One proportion in table 7.5, the incidence of a violent/nonviolent outcome with only two variables (67.1%), is simply the weighted mean of three paired frequencies from table 7.4: murder–theft, manslaughter–theft, and homicide–theft. This indicates that capital offenses and theft are located on opposite factors in two-thirds of the cases.

Other comparisons also support the violent/nonviolent hypothesis. By chance alone, the four-variable outcome should show this pattern in only an eighth of the cases. As indicated in table 7.5, however, this outcome occurs in fully a third of the cases. As a data quality control procedure, table 7.5 also provides the same comparisons using only those cases with data for thirty-five years or more. As this comparison indicates, the violent/nonviolent hypothesis is supported even when one examines only the "best" data.

Although this evidence is admittedly circumstantial, it suggests that there are systematic causes of crime and, more specifically, that there are two distinct patterns of causes—one responsible for violent crime and the other for nonviolent offenses. This analysis, however, is blind to the specific composition of these underlying causal patterns; each of

Table 7.5 Proportion of Cases with a "Violent/Nonviolent" Factor Structure

Factor pattern[a]	Chance level	Observed (n): all cases	Observed (n): DQC sample[b]
Two variables: homicide indicator on one factor; theft on opposite factor	50.0%	67.1% (73)	66.7% (33)
Three variables: one homicide indicator on one factor; robbery and theft both on opposite factor	25.0%	31.8% (22)	33.3% (6)
Four variables: two homicide indicators on one factor; robbery and theft both on opposite factor	12.5%	36.4% (22)	37.5% (8)

[a] A total of 55 factor analyses produced two-factor solutions. Some cases included more than one homicide indicator, making the total number of possible comparisons greater than 55.
[b] This DQC (Data Quality Control) sample included only those cases with data for 35 years or more.

the two broad causal schemata could include a single social change or a combination of several changes.

It seems probable that one of these underlying causal patterns includes demographic changes such as the size of a society's youthful population and probably other factors such as industrialization, wartime participation, and economic conditions. In the present analysis, questions of etiology are approached abstractly, and concrete causal variables are not identified. In summary, this analysis suggests, first, that causes exist and, second, that the origins of violent crime lie in one combination of causes while those of nonviolent offenses lie in another.

Example 4: Unemployment and Violent Crime[7]

Researchers have long been curious about the impact of economic fluctuations on crime rates. This question reflects a long-standing suspicion that private "deviant" behavior has public roots in the economic condition of the wider society. Unemployment is one measure of economic well-being, although its impact falls heavily on a minority rather than on citizens generally. Economic events such as inflation, changes in per capita income, and changing interest rates are more general in their impact, although perhaps not as devastating for individuals as is unemployment.

The basic premise behind research in this area is that some economic changes greatly exacerbate the conditions of daily life. Increases in prices and a decline or disappearance of income involve obvious material consequences. Beyond these important material effects, economic changes presumably alter the attitudes and emotions of affected individuals and their families. It is conceivable that these material and nonmaterial changes accumulate to increase the probability of crime and violence.

Although this general hypothesis implies an empirical solution, the question could be approached in different ways and using various premises. For example, one researcher might assume that chronic economic hardship such as long-term unemployment is most conducive to crime. Another might assume that sudden economic deterioration such as recent unemployment is more devastating. A third might assume that widespread economic hardship is less "criminogenic" than conspicuous inequality.

Apart from these differences in theoretical premises, empirical efforts to test the effects of economic changes encounter additional obstacles. Measures of economic well-being remain in dispute, and conventional economic indicators may omit precisely those data one would most like to have. For example, unemployment figures may not include the chronic unemployed or those who despair of finding work. In addition, this question potentially contains a classic instance of the "ecological fallacy." Even if a researcher obtains a strong relationship between aggregate data on unemployment and aggregate data on offense rates, it cannot be assumed that the *individuals* involved in offenses are themselves unemployed.

For all these reasons, and although economic hypotheses about crime are of considerable interest, these hypotheses do not admit to simple resolution. The history of research in this area dates from pioneering work by Bonger (1916), who examined crime records during the 1800s and concluded that crimes of theft burgeoned during depressions. Other early and influential work on economic effects was done by Ogburn and Thomas (1922), Thomas (1927), Sellin (1937), and Henry and Short (1954). This literature is extremely diverse; the research on different facets of the general economic hypothesis is summarized by Braithwaite (1979). Even though many researchers have shared an interest in economic variables, individual studies frequently have examined dissimilar questions.

Some of this work has centered on industrialization and other aspects of national economic development. For example, Zehr (1976) examined the apparent effects of industrialization on offense rates in France and Germany between 1830 and 1920. Combined with other research on economic development (Wolf, 1971; Wellford, 1974; Shelley, 1981), this body of work suggests that violent crime is relatively unaffected by broad historical changes. Other researchers have used increasingly sophisticated techniques to examine the effects of fluctuations in indicators of national economic health. One of the best known of such efforts is the five-nation analysis by Brenner (1976a and 1976b), which examined the period 1900–1970. Unique in its effort to control for possible artifacts such as changes in the age structure of the population,[8] this work produced the interesting conclusion that relationships between offenses and economic conditions have changed *qualitatively* over time. In the case of violent crimes, Brenner found that the effects of economic fluctuations became more pronounced over time and that in recent decades these offenses have increased during periods of high unemployment.

A different perspective has focused not on national economic well-being as a whole but instead on the effects of inequality. Much of this research has examined measures of inequality—for example, the Gini Index or other measures of the degree to which income, wealth, or land is unequally distributed throughout a population. When these indicators are compared with national offense rates, an inverse relationship is generally found. Nations with the lowest rate of inequality also tend to have the lowest rates of violent crime (Krohn, 1976; Braithwaite, 1979). Some of this research has shared the general weaknesses of cross-sectional research in that the extraction of causal inferences about the observed relationship is problematic. Some longitudinal work on this question has been done, however, and this work supports the general conclusion that violent crime appears to be related to measures of economic inequality. One statement from this body of work summarizes the "inequality hypothesis":

> The most common progression of events that generates social violence is an unequal distribution of resources that creates asymmetric social relations that, in turn, create latent conflict that, if conditions are ripe, will become violent conflict. (Ball-Rokeach, 1980: 53)

It is not surprising that much research on the effects of economic conditions and changes has been limited in scope. Western societies, particularly the United States and England, have dominated empirical studies in this area. In the absence of longitudinal data for a large sample of societies, it has not been possible to investigate the possible effects of different types of economic systems. It seems to us that there are theoretical reasons to suspect that the effects of economic variables are mediated by the economic structure of individual societies.

It seems reasonable to hypothesize, for example, that the effects of increased unemployment will be mitigated in some economic systems more than in others. In societies with high chronic unemployment, losing a job may be seen as more serious and therefore desperate. Such societies tend to have marked inequality and conspicuous poverty, and the newly unemployed individual may therefore dread the prospect of imminent downward mobility. Similarly, unemployment may be less destructive in societies with high levels of social services and benefits for the unemployed.

This conception implies a contextual hypothesis: *the type of a nation's economic system may determine whether or not changing economic conditions will affect rates of violent crime.* As a preliminary and admittedly modest test of this contextual hypothesis, we have used a number of procedures to try to gauge the effect of unemployment on national homicide rates. Data on unemployment rates were obtained using national yearbooks, statistical annuals, labor and manpower statistics, and the *United Nations Statistical Yearbook.* Data on homicide rates were of course obtained from the CCDF. The overlap between these two sources of data produced sixteen cases for analysis, including two separate cases (because two independent homicide indicators were available) for the United States.

The relationship between unemployment rates and homicide rates can be approached in several different ways. The procedures in this analysis use lagged correlations to detect any evidence that these two variables are related. This procedure includes "forward" lags in which the homicide rate in year n is compared with unemployment rates in years $(n - 1)$ or $(n - 2)$. For example, the $(n - 1)$ lagged correlation would compare the homicide rates in 1960 and 1961 with, respectively, the unemployment rates in 1959 and 1960. This is a forward lag in that the hypothesized causal sequence calls for unemployment changes to occur first and then lead to homicide rate changes. This hypothesis seems plausible, and a number of researchers have speculated that the effects of economic changes would in fact occur after a year's delay or more (Radzinowicz, 1971: 433).

As a control procedure, we included a "backward" lag in the analysis. This correlation, which ran contrary to our hypothesis, compared homicide rates with subsequent unemployment rates. It seems unlikely that homicide is sufficiently widespread to make a serious dent in the number of the unemployed, and this backward lag therefore serves as a control procedure. If the causal sequence is as hypothesized—that is, if changes in unemployment do affect homicide rates—then the magnitude of the forward lagged correlations will be greater than that of the backward or control correlations. Because most existing studies have used unlagged correlations—that is, comparisons of two simultaneous indicators—these were included as well. In summary, the homicide rate in year n was correlated with the unemployment rate in year n (an unlagged correlation), year $n - 1$ (a one-year forward lag), year $n - 2$ (a two-year forward lag), and year $n + 1$ (a control, backward lag).[9]

The results of these comparisons are shown in table 7.6. In nations with positive correlations, homicide rates are relatively high in times of high unemployment. Conversely, nations with negative correlations have relatively low homicide rates in times of high unemployment. The data show that *both* outcomes occur, and the two groups of nations are listed separately in table 7.6.

In general, the unemployment–homicide relationship is stronger for the first group of nations, in which unemployment is positively associated with homicide rates. The effects of unemployment in the second group of nations are negative and of smaller magnitude, indicating that the

Table 7.6. Unemployment and Homicide Rates: Zero-order Lagged Correlations

Country	Homicide in year n, with unemployment in year $n-2$ −2	Homicide in year n, with unemployment in year $n-1$ −1	Same year (unlagged) 0	Homicide in year n, unemployment in year $n+1$ +1	Median
Positive Correlations					
Switzerland (19)[a]	.73	.79	.86	.91	.83
U.S.[b] (40)	.55	.66	.73	.81	.70
Italy (29)	.62	.57	.44	.32	.51
U.S.[c] (43)	.47	.48	.47	.51	.48
Austria (20)	.59	.48	.46	.44	.47
Japan (31)	.39	.37	.43	.26	.38
Germany (20)	.49	.40	.32	.23	.36
Netherlands (26)	−.23	−.01	.22	.27	.11
Ireland (34)	−.11	.02	.17	.19	.10
Median	.49	.48	.44	.32	
Negative Correlations					
Canada (36)	−.07	−.05	.04	.04	−.01
Norway (30)	.12	.19	−.28	−.37	−.05
Belgium (25)	−.33	−.25	−.02	.20	−.14
Australia (18)	−.53	−.33	−.14	.08	−.24
England (41)	−.27	−.24	−.26	−.25	−.26
Denmark (35)	−.58	−.53	−.49	−.45	−.52
Sweden (43)	−.62	−.59	−.56	−.53	−.58
Median	−.33	−.25	−.26	−.25	

[a] Number of years upon which correlation is based
[b] Homicide
[c] Murder

relationship between unemployment and homicide is not uniform, and suggesting that these nations are differentiated by one or more contextual variables that mediate the effects of unemployment.

This finding implies the existence of differences between these two groups of nations, although the nature of these differences remains speculative. For a variety of reasons, unemployment may be less devastating for citizens in the second group of nations in table 7.6. On a purely impressionistic basis, it seems that nations in the second group have more "redistributive" economic systems and more extensive policies designed to mitigate the effects of poverty and unemployment. Nations in the first group, on the other hand, may have more vivid inequalities, more extensive poverty, chronic unemployment, inadequate benefits for the jobless, or other policies and conditions that exacerbate the material and psychological costs of unemployment.

The lagged correlations in table 7.6 provide a crude test of the degree to which unemployment rates "lead" homicide rates, rather than the other way around. In general, this analysis suggests that the unemployment–homicide relationship is in the hypothesized direction. In several nations in the first group, particularly, the forward correlations (in which homicide rates lag behind unemployment rates) increase the size of the correlation while the control correlation (in which unemployment is lagged behind homicide) decreases the size of the correlation. The results of this analysis provide indirect support for the idea that the relationship between unemployment and homicide includes causal elements rather than correlation alone.[10]

Although far from a definitive analysis of economic effects on crime, this result illustrates one use of comparative research. While the reason for the differences in table 7.6 remains speculative, the existence of these differences suggests that national characteristics can determine whether or not an offense rate (Y) and its suspected cause (X) are related. In many comparative research designs, therefore, a researcher may wish to search both for general XY relationships and also for contextual differences. In some societies, XY may be found to be both positive and strong; in others, this relationship may be negative or absent.

FUTURE RESEARCH: AN INVITATION TO IMAGINATION

In these examples and in earlier chapters, we have tried to suggest the rich potential for systematic comparative research on crime and violence. The Comparative Crime Data File was assembled to test specific questions, but the file's possible applications seem boundless. Chapter 1 listed examples of specific hypotheses that could be investigated and there are at least five *general research paradigms* for which these comparative data should prove valuable.

Qualitative Case Studies

The analyses in this book emphasize quantitative tests of specific hypotheses. While this has been our method of choice, it is clearly not the only approach. There are many constraints inherent in the use of aggregate indicators, and some of these have been indicated in this chapter. Using such data, a researcher gains a global perspective but may feel that important qualities of individuals and their behavior are too often hidden from view. This perspectival limitation is a general problem of the "macroscope" of aggregate data. Analogously, from an airplane one has little difficulty spotting a nation's cities but, from 30,000 feet, qualities of urban life remain unknown.

Qualitative case studies offer a complementary perspective. In-depth research in one or a small number of societies can provide detailed descriptions of the social, cultural, and legal context in which crime and violence occur, as well as valuable information about the ways in which official records of crime are produced, defined, and recorded (e.g., Black and Reiss, 1970; Lundman, Sykes, and Clark, 1978). These concerns are central to "labeling" theorists and others interested in how individuals and their acts are "mapped" into the official categories of criminals and crime (Archer, in press). Official statistics, including the comparative data in this book, are the end product of complex processes that presumably include self-definition, reporting, societal reaction, and official classification. These elements clearly contribute to the "reality" of crime and violence, and their precise contributions deserve detailed investigation.

Qualitative research often combines the methods of anthropology, history, and qualitative sociology, and this approach can illuminate the links between violence and the unique conditions of individual societies. An early example was Bohannon's (1960) analysis of homicide in seven widely dispersed tribes in Africa. This analysis identified key points of cross-cultural variation, including the victim/offender relationship, the use of weapons, and types of motive. Such qualitative accounts can provide a detailed picture that cannot be gleaned from aggregate data.

Other case studies have used small-sample comparisons. Ross and Benson (1979) compared three industrialized democracies that differ greatly in their rates of violent crime: Japan, England, and the United States. These researchers attributed the variation to cultural differences in law enforcement training and practices, gun control laws, public involvement in law enforcement, and ethical education. An analogous study ascribed crime rate differences between Canada and the United States to greater individualism and tolerance for norm violation in the United States (Hagan and Leon, 1978).

The potential contributions of quantitative data to such qualitative undertakings are less obvious. The principal value of a quantitative archive for qualitative research lies in sampling. The CCDF can assist a qualitative researcher in choosing nations or cities to study. Whether one wishes to understand dissimilar offense rates in otherwise similar societies, or offense rate similarities in very different nations, the CCDF provides a continuum of cases. In addition, the archive can help the qualitative researcher identify trends, waves, or periods of particular interest within the sampled cases.

Policy Studies and Evaluation Research

Given a sufficiently large set of crime data, it is sometimes possible to discern the effects of "natural experiments"—changes in law, criminal justice procedures, or penalties. These reforms are often designed to affect offense rates, and historical crime records can provide a general verdict on whether a given change has succeeded. The importance of such natural experiments is twofold. After a change has been implemented, offense rates provide the basis for *evaluation research* on the effectiveness of the change. Comparative offense data can also be used in *prospective* research before a proposed change is implemented. The historical record of an innovation's effects in other societies can provide a prediction of the probable consequences if this same change is enacted in society Z.

An example of policy-relevant research is the description in chapter 6 of the search for deterrent effects of the death penalty. The data in the CCDF contain the potential for an almost infinite variety of other policy studies. All that is required is an interesting question—for example, what is the effect, if any, of nation Z's change in the penalty for armed robbery? As is true of any archive, the CCDF may not contain the precise data one would like to have for a specific policy evaluation. Using the methods described in this chapter and chapter 3, however, it is possible in many cases to use available indicators as proxies for absent data. In addition, specific features of the CCDF can contribute to policy research. For example, the urban data in the file can provide an important replication—for example, the effect of a penalty change for robbery can be assessed for Paris and for France generally.

Replication: General Tests of Specific Propositions

Upon close examination, "facts" about crime and violence frequently are found to rest on undesirably narrow evidence. In the absence of cross-

national data, there has been a tendency to assume that patterns uncovered in one society exist everywhere. This assumption is probably
unwarranted and certainly testable. One of the most important contributions of a broad data archive therefore lies in its potential for replication. If we are ever to have a rigorous understanding of crime and
violence, propositions derived from a single society need to be exposed
to the comparative light of other nations.

Cross-national replication provides an empirical edge that can distinguish the truly general from the merely local. While it may be interesting
to find a correlation between offense Y and cause X in a single society,
it is clearly more compelling if this same association recurs in a sample
of diverse societies. Widely replicable findings can increase our confidence that two phenomena are genuinely linked in a nontrivial and
nonspurious manner. This function of replication might be called *general
replication* since it involves the search for universals. An example, described in chapter 5, is the search for consistent effects of urbanism and
urbanization.

Replication also serves a second function if it identifies *orderly differences*. Finding consistent differences may be just as significant as finding
that an XY relationship is truly universal. For example, comparative
research may indicate that X and Y are strongly related in one type of
society but unrelated in other societies. This reflects the realistic possibility that the social and cultural context—in this case, the individual
nation—can determine whether or not X and Y are causally related.
This is one of the more subtle but potentially most important uses of
comparative research (Smelser, 1976: 162–95). This variety of cross-
national research might be called *contextual replication*, since the societal
context may determine whether or not a suspected cause and a specific
offense are related. The analysis of unemployment and homicide earlier
in this chapter illustrates the potential importance of contextual
differences.

Comparative data are indispensable to both types of replication. Recent studies have speculated about a wide variety of potential causes:
the historical transition toward a separation of the workplace and resi-
dence (Cohen and Felson, 1979), capital accumulation and subsequent
central city disadvantage (Humphries and Wallace, 1980), firearm availability (Cook, 1981), and many other variables. These hypotheses can
be examined by juxtaposing samples of data from the CCDF with indicators of the suspected causes. Almost certainly, instances of both *general* and *contextual* replication will be found. For example, the association
between the size of a nation's youth cohort and rates of violent crime is
likely to be generally replicable, while the effects of economic changes
may be only contextually replicable—that is, found in some economic
systems but not in others.

A final facet of replication concerns time. The examples mentioned thus far concern consistencies across space and, specifically, the question of whether an XY relationship found in one society will be found in all (or only some) other nations. It is also conceivable that an XY relationship operating in one time period will be absent in another. Time periods, like nations, therefore present opportunities for attempted replication.

There are increasing indications that the effects of specific time periods deserve close attention. For example, Skogan (1977a) examined a sample of American cities and found that the correlations between crime rates and population variables such as density, heterogeneity, and migration had changed over time. A similar conclusion was reached concerning the relationships between offense rates and economic variables (Brenner, 1976a and 1976b). The possibility that an XY relationship could exist in one era but not in another increases the importance and usefulness of longitudinal data. Just as replications search for causal relationships in several societies, so longitudinal data make it possible to seek these relationships in more than a single time period.

Empirical Research on Methodological Questions

Throughout this book we have indicated the nature and importance of recurring methodological questions. Some of these involve the scientific requirements for making supportable inferences. Crime and violence are the result of many causes. No matter how he or she cherishes a hypothesis, the investigator is obliged to consider plausible rival hypotheses for any outcome (Cook and Campbell, 1979; Webb, Campbell, Schwartz, Sechrest, and Grove, 1981). Some rival hypotheses imply a test for artifacts: demography is a case in point. As we have seen in this chapter, any hypothesis seeking to explain the increase in American homicide rates during the 1960s and early 1970s must consider the effects of the maturation of a very large youth cohort.

These methodological questions often have empirical implications in that they contain propositions which are testable. In some cases, these empirical implications are obvious; in others, they may need to be derived. Seen in this light, methodological issues can be regarded as investigable questions of considerable intellectual challenge. In many cases, it should be possible to identify an imaginative test of a suspected methodological problem. The ideal test would discover whether the hypothesized problem exists and, if it does, the extent and limits of its effects. In the case of a suspected demographic artifact, for example, a researcher might analyze data separately for several age groups. (This approach was used in the postwar violence study described in chapter 4.)

This book illustrates other applications of comparative data to specific methodological questions. In some cases, the evidence suggests that traditional conceptions of certain problems have overstated their seriousness. As discussed in chapter 3, for example, the long-standing debate about the validity of different offense indicators contains two separable questions. Cross-sectional comparisons clearly require the "best" (or at least the same) indicator for both jurisdictions. In longitudinal comparisons, however, different indicators are to a great extent interchangeable as valid indices of offense trends. This example illustrates the ways in which comparative data can provide concrete empirical tests of abstract methodological problems. This evidentiary approach to suspected problems is potentially important, first, because it goes beyond mere speculation and, second, because it may identify procedures that eliminate or minimize the effects of specific problems.

A final methodological use of comparative data involves opportunities for incorporating data quality controls in research designs. A researcher can use the records in the CCDF to generate new data series that control for suspected problems and artifacts. These new data can be included in a research design along with the original data to test for different outcomes. This chapter illustrates this approach in the example of "age-adjusted" homicide rates. Given an archive of cross-national data, a researcher can also decide to stratify the sample in terms of data quality—for example, by analyzing only cases with "offenses known" indicators.

As these examples indicate, our preference is to treat methodological problems as investigable empirical questions. This approach consists of two general strategies. First, the depth and breadth of data in the CCDF in many cases make possible direct tests of specific hypothesized problems. These direct tests can reveal evidence on the existence and magnitude of a suspected problem. On the basis of this information, a given research design can be discarded, modified, or judged defensible. Apart from such direct tests of methodological hypotheses, a second strategy involves the inclusion of specific controls and data quality procedures in research designs. In many instances, such design features can isolate the effect of a specific problem, or at least indicate whether a finding remains tenable even after this problem has been controlled.

Large-Sample Tests of the Effects of Social Structure and Social Change

We believe that the resources of the CCDF can make important contributions to each of the above genres of comparative research. The paradigm closest to our own work, however, involves large-sample tests of the effects of social structure and social change. The basic assumptions underlying this research paradigm are that there is a relationship between social structures, or changes in them, and rates of crime and violence and, further, that this relationship can be explored using aggregate data.

This paradigm has a strong tradition in the social sciences and dates at least from Durkheim's (1897) classic ecological study of suicide. Other pioneers of the comparative method, such as Bonger (1916), focused on the social effects of economic conditions. A more recent example is the excellent and extensive work by Gurr and his colleagues (1976, 1977, 1979, 1981) on explanations for historical patterns and changes in offense rates. This work combines a number of different comparative strategies in its use of both aggregate analysis and in-depth case studies.

The premise behind large-sample comparative research is that many relationships become visible and plausible only through a pattern of results that spans diverse cases. Given no more than a single case, an association between two variables is likely to go undetected and, even if detected, provides no evidence that the variables are causally linked. This point is obvious when the cases involve individuals—for example, the correlation between smoking and lung cancer become visible only when the health histories of a large sample of individuals are examined. In addition to their sheer number, the diversity of the cases compared can increase the plausibility of a hypothesized relationship—a researcher is more likely to believe that the correlation between smoking and lung disorder is causal if this relationship obtains repeatedly and across diverse samples.

Earlier chapters of this book describe large-sample comparative studies of the effects on violent crime of wars, urbanism and urbanization, and penal severity. This chapter presents other cross-national comparisons, including a large-sample factor analysis that suggests the presence of two general causal schema, one that "drives" violent crimes and a second that influences economic and other nonviolent offenses. This "violent/ nonviolent" hypothesis implies that many causally significant aspects of social change and social structure remain to be discovered. Judging from our subjective experience with the investigations described in this book, the agenda for future research is as challenging and provocative as it is largely untapped.

NOTES

1. It should be mentioned that the importance of this age group for homicide rates is implied rather than demonstrated by these data. The age-adjusted "pseudo-rate" in table 7.1 and figure 7.1 adjusts the total homicide rate for the size of the 15–29 cohort. Since these data do not by themselves show how many of these homicides were committed by individuals in this cohort, this is a potential instance of the ecological fallacy, which occurs frequently in the application of two sets of aggregate data. In this case,

we have abundant evidence from other sources (e.g., the *Sourcebook of Criminal Justice Statistics*) that young adults are in fact greatly overrepresented in the commission of violent offenses.

2. It may not be necessary to generate new rates if a researcher requires only statistical, post hoc controls. This is frequently the case, for example, in studies using regression techniques. In such studies, a researcher can simply include youthful cohort size as a covariate along with the other variables in the analysis. Whether or not new offense rates are formally generated, the principle remains the same.

3. Different scientific disciplines have evolved unique standards of "acceptable fit." These differences reflect epistemological dissimilarities in the data used in these sciences rather than simply differences in standards of evidence. Psychologists will use a short test with reliabilities in the .60–.75 range. Using "field" or interview data, sociologists often find that different measures of a concept like "social class" are less strongly related, with correlations in the .40–.65 range. Comparative political science indicators of national rankings on some characteristics (income inequality, literacy, etc.) show only modest reliability when estimated in two time periods, with agreements as low as .30–.45. Partly because they deal with several indicators of the same underlying variable, economists work with much larger correlations, as high as .80–.99, and this has led to an interest in "multi-colinearity"—the causal confusion resulting from essential inseparability of several variables. Because of these disciplinary differences, it is impossible to say precisely how high a bivariate relationship should be before one variable can be accepted as an empirical substitute for another.

4. Although the two-factor solution was the dominant outcome and is the one discussed here, there were exceptions. Four cases yielded three-factor outcomes. A number of other cases did not yield at least two eigenvalues of 1.0 or more, and no factor rotations were performed. The analytic model used principal factors with iteration and varimax rotations.

5. The other possible three-variable outcome, two homicide indicators and one nonviolent indicator, was not examined because both nonviolent indicators were present in most cases.

6. These chance probabilities reflect the relative likelihood of a violent/nonviolent factor solution compared to all other outcomes. In the three-variable case, the outcomes ABB and BAA support the hypothesis, while six other outcomes (AAA, AAB, ABA, BAB, BBA, and BBB) do not. The chance or probabilistic level for the violent/nonviolent outcome is therefore ⅜, or 25%. In the four-variable case, only the two outcomes AABB and BBAA support the hypothesis, while fourteen other outcomes (AAAA, AAAB, AABA, etc.) do not. The chance level for a violent/nonviolent solution with four variables is therefore 2/16, or 12.5%.

7. An earlier version of this section was coauthored with Tom Phelan.

8. A number of these studies apply regression, econometric methods, and statistical techniques like spectral analysis to longitudinal crime data. It should be noted that these methods require certain assumptions and, as a result, the most appropriate statistical procedures remain a matter of some disagreement (see, for example, Vigderhous, 1978).

9. It is clear that more complicated procedures can and should be used to explore this relationship. For example, the correlations reported here are all zero-order—that is, uncontrolled for third variables like age structure. This analysis is also simplified in that the data are used undetrended. An alternate approach, one we have not attempted, involves detrending the two time series and then correlating the residuals. Each of these approaches has merit and deserves further attention.

10. It should be emphasized that some other methodological problems are not eliminated by this comparison. This analysis does not eliminate the effects of secular trends,

periodicity, and other complicating features of time-series data. The use of lagged correlations does, however, provide some support for the hypothesized relationship between unemployment and homicide. Nevertheless, relationships between aggregate indicators cannot eliminate the possibility of an ecological fallacy. Even if unemployment rates precede and are strongly related to homicide rates, it is conceivable that no unemployed *individuals* commit a violent crime. This ecological problem is insoluble with aggregate data but could be addressed with individual-level data such as job history interviews with arrested suspects.

III

THE COMPARATIVE CRIME DATA FILE

Nations Included in the Comparative Crime Data File

Nation	Number of years in CCDF (one or more homicide indicators)[a]	Approximate period(s) covered	Offense categories[b]
1. Aden	6	1960–66	Mu, Ra, Ro, T
2. Argentina	2	1965–66	Mu, Ra, Ro, T
3. Australia[c]	67***	1903–72	Mu, Ma, H, Ra, A, Ro, T
4. Austria[c]	21**	1953–73	Mu, Ma, Ra, A, Ro, T
5. Bahrain	11*	1963–73	H, Ra, A, Ro, T
6. Belgium[c]	36**	1909–20, 41–69	Mu, H, Ra, A, T
7. Bermuda	32***	1941–74	Mu, Ma, Ra, A, Ro, T
8. Bolivia	1	1961	Mu, Ra, T
9. Botswana	1	1971	Mu, Ma, Ra, A, Ro, T
10. Brunei	11*	1964–74	Mu, H, Ra, A, Ro, T
11. Bulgaria	9	1900–08	Mu, A, T
12. Burma	18*	1953–70	Mu, Ra, Ro, T
13. Cameroon	5	1965–70	Mu, Ra, Ro, T
14. Canada	64***	1901–09, 19–73	Mu, Ma, H, A, Ro, T
15. Central African Republic	4	1967–70	Mu, Ra, Ro, T
16. Chad	2	1967–68	Mu, Ra, Ro
17. Chile	75***	1900–74	H, A, Ro, T
18. China, Republic of	18*	1952–69	Mu, A, Ro, T
19. Colombia	29**	1938–67	H, A, Ro, T
20. Congo (Brazzaville)	7	1964–70	Mu, Ra, Ro, T
21. Cuba	2	1953–54	Mu, Ra, Ro
22. Cyprus	10*	1961–70	Mu, Ra, Ro, T
23. Dahomey	4	1967–70	Mu, Ra, Ro, T
24. Denmark	37**	1921–69	Mu, Ra, A, Ro, T
25. Dominican Republic	2	1969–70	Mu, Ra, Ro, T

Nation	Number of years in CCDF (one or more homicide indicators)[a]	Approximate period(s) covered	Offense categories[b]
26. Egypt	17*	1953–70	Mu, Ra, Ro, T
27. El Salvador	35***	1934–68	Mu, A, Ro, T
28. England (and Wales)	73***	1900–72	Mu, Ma, Ra, A, Ro, T
29. Ethiopia	5	1961–66	Mu, Ra, Ro, T
30. Fiji	9	1962–70	Mu, Ra, Ro, T
31. Finland[c]	55***	1914–70	Mu, Ma, Ra, A, Ro, T
32. France[c]	40***	1931–71	Mu, Ma, Ra, A, Ro, T
33. Germany[c]	51***	1900–30, 53–72	Mu, Ma, H, Ra, A, Ro, T
34. Ghana[c]	14	1955–70	Mu, Ra, Ro, T
35. Greece[c]	5	1965–69	A, T
36. Guam	10*	1965–74	Ma, Ra, A, Ro, T
37. Guyana[c]	12*	1961–72	Mu, Ma, Ra, A, Ro, T
38. Hong Kong	21**	1953–73	H, Ra, A, Ro, T
39. Hungary	58**	1900–38, 51–72	Mu, Ma, Ra, A, Ro, T
40. Iceland	3	1969–71	Mu, Ma, Ra, A, T
41. India (2[c])	19*	1953–71	Mu, Ro, T
42. Indonesia	24*	1920–29, 52–56	Mu, Ma, H, A, Ro, T
43. Iran	3	1966–68	Mu, Ra, Ro, T
44. Iraq	4	1967–70	Mu, Ra, Ro, T
45. Ireland (Eire)[c]	64***	1900–12, 23–73	Mu, Ma, Ra, A, Ro, T
46. Israel[c]	22*	1949–70	Mu, A, Ro, T
47. Italy	72**	1900–71	Mu, Ma, A, Ro, T
48. Ivory Coast	8	1963–70	Mu, Ma, Ro, T
49. Jamaica	9	1960–70	Mu, Ra, Ro, T
50. Japan[c]	71***	1900–70	H, A, Ro, T
51. Jordan	6	1965–70	Mu, Ra, Ro, T
52. Kenya[c]	14*	1955–68	Mu, Ma, Ra, A, Ro, T

Nations Included in the Comparative Crime Data File

Nation	Number of years in CCDF (one or more homicide indicators)[a]	Approximate period(s) covered	Offense categories[b]
53. Khmer Republic (Cambodia)	2	1969–70	Mu, Ra, Ro, T
54. Korea[c]	10*	1964–73	H, Ra, A, Ro, T
55. Kuwait[c]	16*	1957–74	Mu, Ra, A, Ro, T
56. Laos	5	1966–70	Mu, Ra, Ro, T
57. Lebanon[c]	8	1967–74	Mu, Ra, A, Ro, T
58. Libya	14*	1955–69	Mu, Ra, Ro, T
59. Luxembourg	18*	1953–70	Mu, Ra, Ro, T
60. Malagasy Republic[c]	12*	1959–70	Mu, Ra, A, Ro, T
61. Malawi (Nyasaland)	12	1957–70	Mu, Ra, Ro, T
62. Malaya	12*	1959–70	Mu, Ra, Ro, T
63. Mauritania	6	1964–70	Mu, Ra, Ro, T
64. Mauritius	16*	1958–73	Mu, Ma, H, Ra, A, Ro, T
65. Mexico[c]	21*	1950–72	H, Ra, A, Ro
66. Monaco	18*	1953–70	Mu, Ra, Ro, T
67. Morocco	8	1957–66	Mu, Ra, Ro, T
68. Nepal	2	1965–66	Mu, Ra, Ro, T
69. Netherlands[c]	73***	1900–72	H, Ra, A, T
70. Netherlands Antilles	16*	1955–70	Mu, Ra, Ro, T
71. New Zealand[c]	53***	1920–72	Mu, Ra, A, Ro, T
72. Nigeria[c]	12*	1958–70	Mu, Ra, Ro, T
73. Northern Ireland[c]	52***	1922–73	Mu, Ma, Ra, A, Ro
74. Norway[c]	68***	1903–70	Mu, Ma, Ra, A, Ro, T
75. Pakistan	7	1961–68	Mu, Ra, Ro, T
76. Panama[c]	11*	1963–73	H, Ra, A
77. Peru	10*	1961–70	Mu, Ra, Ro, T
78. Philippines (2[c])	11*	1962–72	Mu, H, Ra, Ro, T

Nation	Number of years in CCDF (one or more homicide indicators)[a]	Approximate period(s) covered	Offense categories[b]
79. Poland[c]	15	1923–29, 65–72	Mu, H, A, Ro, T
80. Portugal	62***	1900–68	Ma, H, A, Ro, T
81. Puerto Rico	67***	1900–72	Mu, H, Ra, A, Ro, T
82. Qatar[c]	25**	1950–74	Mu, Ma, Ra, A, Ro, T
83. Rhodesia[c]	37***	1932–72	Mu, H, Ra, A, Ro, T
84. Rumania	2	1919–20	A, T
85. Scotland[c]	74***	1900–73	Mu, H, Ra, A, Ro, T
86. Senegal	4	1965–68	Mu, Ra, Ro, T
87. Sierra Leone[c]	12	1961–74	H, Ra, A, Ro, T
88. Singapore	21**	1953–73	Mu, Ra, A, Ro, T
89. Solomon Islands	8	1963–70	Mu, Ra, Ro, T
90. South Africa[c]	46***	1925–71	Mu, H, Ra, A, Ro, T
91. Spain[c]	23*	1914–18, 53–68	H, Ra, A, Ro, T
92. Sri Lanka (Ceylon)[c]	74***	1900–73	H, Ra, A, Ro, T
93. Sudan[c]	11	1955–68	Mu, Ra, Ro, T
94. Surinam	8	1963–70	Mu, Ra, Ro, T
95. Swaziland	17*	1950–74	Mu, H, Ra, A, Ro, T
96. Sweden[c]	52***	1920–71	H, Ra, A, Ro, T
97. Switzerland[c]	42***	1929–70	Ra, A, T
98. Syria	14*	1960–73	Mu, Ma, H, Ra, A, Ro, T
99. Tangiers	2	1953–54	Mu, Ra, Ro, T
100. Tanzania	11*	1962–72	H, Ra, A, Ro, T
101. Thailand	59*	1911–72	Mu, Ma, A, Ro, T
102. Trinidad and Tobago[c]	25**	1950–74	Mu, Ma, H, Ra, Ro, T

Nations Included in the Comparative Crime Data File

Nation	Number of years in CCDF (one or more homicide indicators)[a]	Approximate period(s) covered	Offense categories[b]
103. Tunisia	14*	1957–70	Mu, Ra, Ro, T
104. Turkey[c]	19*	1955–73	H, Ra, Ro, T
105. Uganda	11	1958–70	Mu, Ra, Ro, T
106. United States[c]	72***	1900–73	Mu, H, Ra, A, Ro, T
107. Venezuela[c]	28**	1943–70	H, A, Ro, T
108. Vietnam, South	12*	1959–70	Mu, Ra, A, Ro, T
109. West Indies (British)	9	1962–70	Mu, Ra, Ro, T
110. Yugoslavia	12	1931–38, 55–58	Mu, Ra, A, Ro, T
111. Zambia	10	1958–70	Mu, Ra, Ro, T

[a] Asterisks next to entries indicate the presence of a continuous series free of measure changes or other interruptions. The *minimum* size of this continuous series in each case is indicated as follows: * = 10 years; ** = 20 years; *** = 30 or more years.

[b] These abbreviations indicate the offense categories for which data is recorded in the CCDF. The categories are abbreviated as follows:

Mu = Murder
Ma = Manslaughter
 H = Homicide
Ra = Rape
 A = Assault
Ro = Robbery
 T = Theft

[c] Indicates that companion data for a major city in this nation are also included in the CCDF (see following table).

International Cities Included in the Comparative Crime Data

City, Nation	Number of years in CCDF (one or more homicide indicators)[a]	Approximate period(s) covered	Offense categories[b]
1. Accra, Ghana	8	1963–72	Mu, Ra, A, Ro, T
2. Amsterdam, Netherlands	43*	1900–70	H, Ra, A, T
3. Athens, Greece	4	1969–72	Mu, Ma, Ra, A, Ro, T
4. Beirut, Lebanon	7	1967–73	Mu, Ra, A, Ro, T
5. Belfast, Northern Ireland	52***	1922–73	Mu, Ma, Ra, A, Ro
6. Bombay, India	16*	1956–71	Mu, Ro, T
7. Brussels, Belgium	27*	1946–73	Mu, Ra, A, Ro, T
8. Calcutta, India	16*	1956–71	Mu, Ro, T
9. Caracas, Venezuela	18*	1956–73	Mu, T
10. Colombo City, Sri Lanka	74***	1900–73	H, Ra, A, Ro, T
11. Daho City, Qatar	19*	1956–74	Mu, Ma, Ra, A, Ro, T
12. Dublin, Ireland	47***	1927–73	Mu, Ma, Ra, A, Ro, T
13. Freetown, Sierra Leone	11	1962–74	H, Ra, A, Ro, T
14. Georgetown, Guyana	18*	1956–73	Mu, Ra, A, Ro, T
15. Glasgow, Scotland	74***	1900–73	Mu, H, Ra, A, Ro, T
16. Helsinki, Finland	43***	1927–70	Mu, Ma, Ra, A, Ro, T
17. Istanbul, Turkey	19*	1955–73	H, Ra, Ro
18. Jerusalem, Israel	6	1968–73	H, Ra, A, Ro, T
19. Johannesburg, South Africa	10*	1963–72	Mu, Ra, A, Ro, T

City, Nation	Number of years in CCDF (one or more homicide indicators)[a]	Approximate period(s) covered	Offense categories[b]
20. Khartoum, Sudan	13*	1960–72	H, Ra, A, Ro, T
21. Kuwait City, Kuwait	5	1970–74	Mu, Ra, A, Ro, T
22. Lagos City, Nigeria	15*	1959–73	Mu, Ma, Ra, A, Ro, T
23. Madrid, Spain	16*	1953–68	H, Ra, A, Ro, T
24. Manila, Philippines	23**	1950–72	Mu, H, Ra, A, Ro, T
25. Mexico City, Mexico	12	1952–72	Mu, Ra, A, Ro
26. Montevideo, Uruguay	31***	1943–73	Mu, Ra, Ro
27. Munich, Germany	28**	1946–73	Mu, Ma, Ra, A, Ro, T
28. Nairobi City, Kenya	21**	1953–73	Mu, Ra, A, Ro, T
29. New York City, U.S.A.	20*	1954–73	Mu, Ra, A, Ro, T
30. Oslo, Norway	20	1923–71	Mu, Ma, Ra, A, T
31. Panama City, Panama	11*	1963–73	H, Ra, A
32. Paris, France	39***	1931–71	Mu, Ma, Ra, A, Ro, T
33. Port of Spain, Trin. & Tob.	25**	1950–74	Mu, Ma, H, Ra, Ro, T
34. Quezon City, Philippines	8	1962–72	Mu, H, Ra, A, Ro, T
35. Salisbury, Rhodesia	22**	1950–71	Mu, H, Ra, A, Ro, T
36. Seoul, Korea	5	1965–69	H, Ra, A, Ro
37. Stockholm, Sweden	23**	1951–73	Mu, H, Ra, A, Ro, T
38. Sydney, Australia	40***	1931–70	Mu, Ma, Ra, A, T
39. Tananarive, Malagasy Rep.	6	1966–71	A, T.

City, Nation	Number of years in CCDF (one or more homicide indicators)[a]	Approximate period(s) covered	Offense categories[b]
40. Tokyo, Japan	73***	1900–72	Mu, Ra, Ro, T
41. Vienna, Austria	21**	1953–73	Mu, Ma, Ra, A, Ro, T
42. Warsaw, Poland	28**	1946–73	H, Ra, A, Ro, T
43. Wellington, New Zealand	17*	1956–73	Mu, Ma, Ra, A, Ro, T
44. Zurich, Switzerland	16	1900–31, 40–72	H, Ra, A, Ro, T

[a] Asterisks next to entries indicate the presence of a continuous series free of measure changes or other interruptions. The *minimum* size of this continuous series in each case is indicated as follows: * = 10 years; ** = 20 years; *** = 30 or more years.
[b] These abbreviations indicate the offense categories for which data is recorded in the CCDF. The categories are abbreviated as follows:

Mu = Murder   A = Assault
Ma = Manslaughter   Ro = Robbery
H = Homicide   T = Theft
Ra = Rape

Comparative Crime Data File: Nations

ADEN *

NUMBER OF OFFENSES REPORTED -- (RATE PER 100,000)

YEAR	MURDER ( )	MANSLTR ( )	HOMICIDE ( )	RAPE (1)	ASSAULT ( )	ROBBERY ( )	THEFT ( )	POP
1960	8 (3.88)			67 (32.52)		925 (449.03)		206
1961	13 (6.19)			77 (36.67)		275 (130.95)	782 (372.38)	210
1962								
1963	18 (8.00)			117 (52.00)		295 (131.11)	616 (273.78)	225
1964	46 (20.00)			90 (39.13)		344 (149.57)	975 (423.91)	230
1965	153 (64.56)			78 (32.91)		411 (173.42)	797 (336.29)	237
1966	354 (141.60)			67 (26.80)		376 (150.40)	730 (292.00)	250

FOOTNOTES:
* BRITISH COLONY IN SOUTH YEMEN UNTIL 1967; RAW CRIME DATA
  FROM INTERPOL, RATES COMPUTED FROM POPULATION FIGURES ABOVE
1. SEX OFFENCES

ARGENTINA *

NUMBER OF OFFENSES REPORTED -- (RATE PER 100,000)

YEAR	MURDER ( )	MANSLTR ( )	HOMICIDE ( )	RAPE (1)	ASSAULT ( )	ROBBERY ( )	THEFT ( )	POP
1965	828 (3.85)			1087 (5.06)		35622 (165.76)	75785 (352.65)	21490
1966	675 (3.09)			1208 (5.54)		30013 (137.55)	68103 (312.11)	21820

FOOTNOTES:
* RAW CRIME DATA FROM INTERPOL; RATES COMPUTED FROM
  POPULATION FIGURES ABOVE
1. SEX OFFENSES

AUSTRALIA *

NUMBER OF CONVICTIONS -- (RATE PER 100,000)

YEAR	MURDER ( )	MANSLTR ( )	HOMICIDE (1)	RAPE (2)	ASSAULT (3)	ROBBERY (4)	THEFT (5)	POP
1903			51 (1.32)	90 (2.34)	244 (6.34)			3850
1904			58 (1.48)	97 (2.47)	225 (5.73)			3926
1905			46 (1.15)	96 (2.40)	256 (6.40)			4002
1906			56 (1.37)	70 (1.72)	239 (5.86)			4078
1907			45 (1.08)	90 (2.17)	255 (6.14)			4154
1908			46 (1.09)	60 (1.42)	278 (6.57)			4230
1909			45 (1.05)	59 (1.37)	260 (6.04)			4306
1910			46 (1.05)	77 (1.76)	250 (5.71)			4382
1911			33 (0.74)	97 (2.18)	235 (5.27)			4455
1912			49 (1.08)	88 (1.93)	221 (4.85)			4556
1913			52 (1.12)	71 (1.52)	298 (6.40)			4657
1914			57 (1.20)	67 (1.41)	300 (6.31)			4758
1915			40 (0.82)	14 (0.29)	226 (4.65)			4859
1916			35 (0.71)	15 (0.30)	193 (3.89)			4960
1917			30 (0.59)	15 (0.30)	239 (4.72)			5061
1918			21 (0.41)	11 (0.21)	155 (3.00)			5162
1919			48 (0.91)	3 (0.06)	220 (4.18)			5263
1920			38 (0.71)	7 (0.13)	223 (4.16)			5360
1921			46 (0.84)	8 (0.15)	235 (4.29)			5476
1922			46 (0.82)	5 (0.09)	240 (4.29)			5592
1923			30 (0.53)	9 (0.16)	246 (4.31)			5708
1924			34 (0.58)	5 (0.09)	217 (3.73)			5824
1925			41 (0.69)	8 (0.13)	253 (4.26)			5939
1926			37 (0.61)	15 (0.25)	235 (3.89)			6044
1927			45 (0.73)	14 (0.23)	224 (3.64)			6149
1928			42 (0.67)	11 (0.18)	222 (3.55)			6252
1929			48 (0.75)	15 (0.24)	244 (3.84)			6359
1930			29 (0.45)	14 (0.22)	224 (3.47)			6463
1931			51 (0.78)	9 (0.14)	211 (3.24)			6516
1932			32 (0.49)	14 (0.21)	217 (3.30)			6569
1933			36 (0.54)	16 (0.24)	216 (3.26)			6622
1934			32 (0.48)	6 (0.09)	191 (2.86)			6675
1935			40 (0.59)	10 (0.15)	188 (2.80)			6726
1936			34 (0.50)	14 (0.21)	182 (2.68)			6789
1937			38 (0.55)	20 (0.29)	227 (3.31)			6852
1938			37 (0.54)	9 (0.13)	60 (0.87)	85 (1.23)	754 (10.90)	6915
1939			34 (0.49)	10 (0.14)	64 (0.92)	117 (1.68)	988 (14.16)	6978
1940			33 (0.46)	28 (0.39)	46 (0.65)	100 (1.41)	697 (9.80)	7110
1941			41 (0.57)	14 (0.19)	74 (1.03)	134 (1.87)	748 (10.42)	7181
1942			37 (0.51)	24 (0.33)	62 (0.86)	148 (2.05)	868 (12.00)	7235
1943								
1944								
1945								
1946			37 (0.50)	25 (0.33)	130 (1.74)	110 (1.47)	1033 (13.84)	7465
1947			51 (0.67)	22 (0.29)	170 (2.24)	128 (1.69)	1027 (13.55)	7579
1948			59 (0.77)	13 (0.17)	173 (2.24)	104 (1.35)	1072 (13.91)	7709

AUSTRALIA *

NUMBER OF CONVICTIONS -- (RATE PER 100,000)   CONTINUED

YEAR	MURDER ( )	MANSLTR ( )	HOMICIDE (1)	RAPE (2)	ASSAULT (3)	ROBBERY (4)	THEFT (5)	POP
1949			60 (0.76)	10 (0.13)	175 (2.21)	138 (1.75)	1073 (13.57)	7908
1950			67 (0.82)	17 (0.21)	215 (2.63)	170 (2.08)	1103 (13.49)	8179
1951			67 (0.80)	19 (0.23)	203 (2.41)	176 (2.09)	1158 (13.75)	8422
1952			61 (0.71)	21 (0.24)	207 (2.40)	165 (1.91)	1457 (16.87)	8636
1953			83 (0.94)	22 (0.25)	318 (3.61)	137 (1.55)	1405 (15.94)	8815
1954			76 (0.85)	26 (0.29)	270 (3.00)	197 (2.19)	1333 (14.83)	8987
1955			83 (0.90)	17 (0.18)	271 (2.95)	158 (1.72)	1373 (14.92)	9201
1956			60 (0.64)	43 (0.46)	268 (2.84)	162 (1.72)	1805 (19.15)	9426
1957			79 (0.82)	13 (0.13)	241 (2.50)	184 (1.91)	2286 (23.71)	9640
1958			80 (0.81)	25 (0.25)	245 (2.49)	158 (1.61)	2533 (25.74)	9842
1959			93 (0.92)	29 (0.29)	212 (2.11)	188 (1.87)	2404 (23.91)	10056
1960			87 (0.85)	39 (0.38)	222 (2.16)	229 (2.23)	2727 (26.54)	10275
1961			90 (0.86)	70 (0.67)	254 (2.42)	223 (2.12)	3235 (30.79)	10508
1962			114 (1.06)	48 (0.45)	231 (2.16)	298 (2.78)	3026 (28.27)	10705
1963			95 (0.87)	83 (0.76)	185 (1.69)	135 (1.24)	3095 (28.35)	10916
1964	143 (1.28)	34 (0.31)	272 (2.44)	262 (2.35)	1924 (17.28)	592 (5.32)	39695 (356.46)	11136
1965	141 (1.24)	29 (0.25)	271 (2.38)	257 (2.26)	1895 (16.64)	730 (6.41)	46626 (409.36)	11390
1966	163 (1.41)	29 (0.25)	321 (2.77)	251 (2.16)	2227 (19.20)	992 (8.55)	56841 (490.01)	11600
1967	137 (1.16)	36 (0.31)	300 (2.54)	311 (2.64)	2158 (18.29)	960 (8.14)	19072 (161.63)	11800
1968	143 (1.19)	43 (0.36)	300 (2.50)	363 (3.02)	2508 (20.90)	1280 (10.67)	23562 (196.35)	12000
1969	157 (1.28)	33 (0.27)	280 (2.28)	364 (2.97)	2483 (20.25)	1599 (13.04)	25597 (208.78)	12260
1970	172 (1.37)	22 (0.18)	339 (2.71)	416 (3.33)	3282 (26.24)	1999 (15.98)	30591 (244.53)	12510
1971	185 (1.45)	39 (0.31)	343 (2.69)	578 (4.53)	3862 (30.27)	2818 (22.08)	33925 (265.87)	12760
1972	207 (1.60)	46 (0.35)	422 (3.26)	544 (4.20)	4285 (33.06)	3045 (23.50)	36976 (285.31)	12960

FOOTNOTES:
* CASES KNOWN AFTER 1963
1. MURDER, MANSLAUGHTER & ATTEMPTED MURDER
2. INCLUDES CRIMES OF LUST BEFORE 1916
3. OFFENSES AGAINST THE PERSON, 1903-1937;
   AGGRAVATED AND COMMON ASSAULT, 1938-1963;
   SERIOUS ASSAULT, 1964-1972
4. ROBBERY AND STEALING FROM THE PERSON
5. BREAKING AND ENTERING: 1967-1972 - EXCLUDES OFFENSES
   INVOLVING PROPERTY VALUED AT $100 OR LESS; 1971 - EXCLUDES
   8,175 ATTEMPTED BREAKING AND ENTERING OFFENSES WHICH WERE
   REPORTED OR BECAME KNOWN; 1972 - EXCLUDES 8,282 ATTEMPTED
   BREAKING AND ENTERING OFFENSES WHICH WERE REPORTED OR
   BECAME KNOWN

CRIME STATISTICS -- (RATE PER 100,000)

YEAR	MURDER ( )	MANSLTR ( )	HOMICIDE ( )	RAPE ( )	ASSAULT (1)	ROBBERY ( )	THEFT (2)	POP
1953	60 (0.86)	23 (0.33)		698 (10.04)	2830 (40.70)	250 (3.60)	20720 (297.96)	6954
1954	68 (0.98)	23 (0.33)		609 (8.74)	2753 (39.50)	272 (3.90)	20930 (300.33)	6969
1955	66 (0.95)	30 (0.43)		730 (10.47)	2888 (41.41)	311 (4.46)	22085 (316.68)	6974
1956	88 (1.26)	20 (0.29)		659 (9.44)	2584 (37.00)	292 (4.18)	24627 (352.67)	6983
1957	59 (0.84)	33 (0.47)		540 (7.72)	2907 (41.55)	338 (4.83)	28287 (404.27)	6997
1958	53 (0.75)	14 (0.20)		640 (9.12)	2914 (41.50)	412 (5.87)	28569 (406.91)	7021
1959	62 (0.88)	30 (0.43)		683 (9.69)	2855 (40.50)	353 (5.01)	29554 (419.27)	7049
1960	55 (0.78)	25 (0.35)		671 (9.52)	2856 (40.52)	362 (5.14)	30569 (433.73)	7048
1961	45 (0.63)	25 (0.35)		641 (9.04)	2424 (34.20)	383 (5.40)	32261 (455.21)	7087
1962	54 (0.76)	20 (0.28)		709 (9.94)	2566 (35.99)	367 (5.15)	36618 (513.58)	7130
1963	47 (0.66)	20 (0.28)		600 (8.37)	2761 (38.50)	378 (5.27)	38618 (538.46)	7172
1964	44 (0.61)	22 (0.30)		669 (9.27)	2695 (37.33)	405 (5.61)	40180 (556.51)	7220
1965	45 (0.62)	29 (0.40)		604 (8.33)	2648 (36.52)	433 (5.97)	45059 (621.50)	7250
1966	49 (0.67)	14 (0.19)		582 (7.98)	2667 (36.58)	461 (6.32)	50667 (695.02)	7290
1967	53 (0.72)	24 (0.33)		583 (7.96)	2954 (40.36)	597 (8.16)	55841 (762.85)	7320
1968	45 (0.61)	10 (0.14)		600 (8.16)	2845 (38.71)	520 (7.07)	62873 (855.41)	7350
1969	52 (0.71)	30 (0.41)		659 (8.94)	2923 (39.66)	550 (7.46)	65496 (888.68)	7370
1970	70 (0.95)	35 (0.47)		673 (9.11)	3178 (43.00)	549 (7.43)	67676 (915.78)	7390
1971	69 (0.92)	36 (0.48)		625 (8.38)	2875 (38.54)	684 (9.17)	67649 (906.82)	7460
1972	63 (0.84)	40 (0.53)		679 (9.07)	3136 (41.87)	761 (10.16)	84127 (1123.19)	7490
1973	70 (0.93)	34 (0.45)		630 (8.38)	3132 (41.64)	825 (10.97)	81687 (1085.97)	7522

FOOTNOTES:
1. SERIOUS BODILY INJURY
2. AGGRAVATED THEFT

NUMBER OF OFFENSES REPORTED -- (RATE PER 100,000)

YEAR	MURDER ( )	MANSLTR ( )	HOMICIDE (1)	RAPE ( )	ASSAULT ( )	ROBBERY ( )	THEFT ( )	POP
1963			2 (1.18)	11 (6.47)	10 (5.88)	20 (11.76)	0 (0.00)	170
1964			4 (2.26)	8 (4.52)	6 (3.39)	13 (7.34)	0 (0.00)	177
1965			3 (1.62)	5 (2.70)	8 (4.32)	22 (11.89)	0 (0.00)	185
1966			2 (1.04)	5 (2.59)	7 (3.63)	16 (8.29)	2 (1.04)	193
1967			1 (0.53)	6 (3.16)	4 (2.11)	14 (7.37)	1 (0.53)	190
1968			5 (2.50)	1 (0.50)	3 (1.50)	7 (3.50)	1 (0.50)	200
1969			2 (0.95)	4 (1.90)	4 (1.90)	15 (7.14)	2 (0.95)	210
1970			2 (0.91)	1 (0.45)	3 (1.36)	14 (6.36)	3 (1.36)	220
1971			2 (0.91)	3 (1.36)	4 (1.82)	16 (7.27)	4 (1.82)	220
1972			1 (0.45)	0 (0.00)	8 (3.64)	16 (7.27)	2 (0.91)	220
1973			2 (0.88)	5 (2.20)	4 (1.76)	28 (12.53)	0 (0.00)	227

FOOTNOTES:
1. MURDER AND MANSLAUGHTER

BELGIUM CRIME STATISTICS -- (RATE PER 100,000)

YEAR	MURDER ( )	MANSLTR ( )	HOMICIDE ( )	RAPE (1)	ASSAULT ( )	ROBBERY ( )	THEFT (2)	POP
1909	57 (0.77)				25725 (347.17)		11937 (161.09)	7410
1910	40 (0.54)				27796 (374.46)		11534 (155.38)	7423
1911	29 (0.39)				26583 (357.49)		10928 (146.96)	7436
1912	55 (0.74)				27696 (371.81)		12239 (164.30)	7449
1913	44 (0.59)				27134 (363.63)		12234 (163.95)	7462
1914								
GAP								
1919	110 (1.48)				5173 (69.81)		19700 (265.86)	7410
1920	93 (1.26)				9427 (127.31)		15899 (214.71)	7405
1921								
GAP								
1941			11 (0.13)	294 (3.55)			15689 (189.62)	8274
1942			15 (0.18)	311 (3.77)			22440 (272.13)	8246
1943			28 (0.34)	308 (3.74)			24018 (291.45)	8241
1944			5 (0.06)	254 (3.06)			12851 (155.00)	8291
1945			33 (0.40)	259 (3.11)			5844 (70.08)	8339
1946			37 (0.44)	399 (4.77)			7520 (89.88)	8367
1947			45 (0.53)	451 (5.34)			6981 (82.62)	8450
1948			49 (0.57)	562 (6.57)			7942 (92.81)	8557
1949			41 (0.48)	783 (9.09)			6884 (79.92)	8614
1950			29 (0.34)	775 (8.97)			4966 (57.48)	8639
1951			22 (0.25)	661 (7.62)			5653 (65.14)	8678
1952			27 (0.31)	747 (8.56)			6932 (79.40)	8730
1953			20 (0.23)	749 (8.53)			5300 (60.38)	8778
1954			11 (0.12)	705 (7.99)			4438 (50.32)	8819
1955			18 (0.20)	713 (8.04)			4266 (48.11)	8868
1956			14 (0.16)	806 (9.03)			4860 (54.46)	8924
1957			15 (0.17)	857 (9.53)			4986 (55.47)	8989
1958			17 (0.19)	825 (9.11)			4974 (54.94)	9053
1959			22 (0.24)	1009 (11.08)			4977 (54.67)	9104
1960			21 (0.23)	1130 (12.35)			5558 (60.72)	9153
1961			11 (0.12)	1114 (12.13)			5667 (61.71)	9184
1962			18 (0.20)	1141 (12.37)			5714 (61.97)	9221
1963			28 (0.30)	1051 (11.31)			5847 (62.94)	9290
1964			16 (0.17)	993 (10.59)			5980 (63.77)	9378
1965			24 (0.25)	990 (10.47)			5577 (58.95)	9460
1966			26 (0.27)	866 (9.09)			6220 (65.27)	9530
1967			27 (0.28)	1049 (10.95)			7158 (74.72)	9580
1968			27 (0.28)	1006 (10.46)			7087 (73.67)	9620
1969			34 (0.35)	908 (9.41)			6274 (65.02)	9650

FOOTNOTES: 1. RAPE AND CRIMES AGAINST MODESTY
2. ROBBERY AND THEFT

BERMUDA

NUMBER OF OFFENSES REPORTED -- (RATE PER 100,000)

YEAR	MURDER (1)	MANSLTR ( )	HOMICIDE ( )	RAPE ( )	ASSAULT (2)	ROBBERY ( )	THEFT ( )	POP
1941	1 (3.13)	1 (3.13)		4 (12.50)	106 (331.25)	4 (12.50)	393 (1228.13)	32
1942	1 (3.03)	0 (0.00)		1 (3.03)	133 (403.03)	2 (6.06)	415 (1257.58)	33
1943	1 (3.03)	1 (3.03)		0 (0.00)	126 (381.82)	5 (15.15)	335 (1015.15)	33
1944	0 (0.00)	1 (2.94)		0 (0.00)	138 (405.88)	3 (8.82)	365 (1073.53)	34
1945	2 (5.71)	1 (2.86)		3 (8.57)	98 (280.00)	6 (17.14)	409 (1168.57)	35
1946	0 (0.00)	1 (2.86)		2 (5.71)	113 (322.86)	2 (5.71)	419 (1197.14)	35
1947	1 (2.86)	1 (2.86)		1 (2.86)	98 (280.00)	9 (25.71)	581 (1660.00)	35
1948	0 (0.00)	0 (0.00)		13 (36.11)	85 (236.11)	4 (11.11)	598 (1661.11)	36
1949	2 (5.56)	0 (0.00)		7 (19.44)	91 (252.78)	3 (8.33)	515 (1430.56)	36
1950	1 (2.70)	2 (5.41)		4 (10.81)	82 (221.62)	2 (5.41)	503 (1359.46)	37
1951	0 (0.00)	1 (2.63)		7 (18.42)	101 (265.79)	5 (13.16)	552 (1452.63)	38
1952								
1953	1 (2.56)	1 (2.56)		4 (10.26)	60 (153.85)	13 (33.33)	752 (1928.21)	39
1954	3 (7.50)	2 (5.00)		0 (0.00)	71 (177.50)	12 (30.00)	796 (1990.00)	40
1955	0 (0.00)	0 (0.00)		3 (7.50)	78 (195.00)	13 (32.50)	832 (2080.00)	40
1956	2 (4.88)	1 (2.44)		5 (12.20)	89 (217.07)	15 (36.59)	1109 (2704.88)	41
1957	0 (0.00)	1 (2.38)		1 (2.38)	113 (269.05)	9 (21.43)	896 (2133.33)	42
1958	0 (0.00)	2 (4.65)		5 (11.63)	96 (223.26)	11 (25.58)	1910 (4441.86)	43
1959	7 (16.28)	1 (2.33)		4 (9.30)	134 (311.63)	11 (25.58)	1757 (4086.05)	43
1960	2 (4.55)	1 (2.27)		3 (6.82)	100 (227.27)	14 (31.82)	2558 (5813.63)	44
1961	1 (2.22)	2 (4.44)		2 (4.44)	97 (215.56)	15 (33.33)	2518 (5595.55)	45
1962	1 (2.17)	0 (0.00)		2 (4.35)	127 (276.09)	21 (45.65)	2909 (6323.91)	46
1963	0 (0.00)	0 (0.00)		7 (14.89)	124 (263.83)	22 (46.81)	3059 (6508.51)	47
1964	2 (4.17)	1 (2.08)		5 (10.42)	132 (275.00)	22 (45.83)	2800 (5833.33)	48
1965	0 (0.00)	0 (0.00)		3 (6.00)	121 (242.00)	18 (36.00)	3416 (6832.00)	50
1966	2 (4.00)	3 (6.00)		5 (10.00)	147 (294.00)	12 (24.00)	3305 (6610.00)	50
1967	2 (4.00)	0 (0.00)		5 (10.00)	176 (352.00)	16 (32.00)	3759 (7518.00)	50
1968	2 (4.00)	4 (8.00)		2 (4.00)	55 (110.00)	11 (22.00)	2509 (5018.00)	50
1969	1 (2.00)	1 (2.00)		4 (8.00)	98 (196.00)	11 (22.00)	3092 (6184.00)	50
1970								
1971	3 (6.00)	0 (0.00)		5 (10.00)	156 (312.00)	26 (52.00)	2120 (4240.00)	50
1972	2 (3.92)	0 (0.00)		3 (5.88)	155 (303.92)	17 (33.33)	1769 (3468.63)	51
1973	7 (13.46)	1 (1.92)		5 (9.62)	100 (192.31)	33 (63.46)	1837 (3553.69)	52
1974	5 (9.62)	1 (1.92)		5 (9.62)	112 (215.38)	39 (75.00)	2594 (4988.46)	52

FOOTNOTES:
1. MURDER AND ATTEMPTED MURDER AFTER 1953
2. INCLUDES ASSAULT AND SERIOUS ASSAULT, 1953-1961

BOLIVIA *

CRIME STATISTICS -- (RATE PER 100,000)

YEAR	MURDER ( )	MANSLTR ( )	HOMICIDE ( )	RAPE ( )	ASSAULT ( )	ROBBERY ( )	THEFT ( )	POP
1961	553 (15.80)			364 (10.40)			1868 (53.37)	3500

FOOTNOTES:
* COEFFICIENT OF OFFENDERS; RAW CRIME DATA FROM INTERPOL.
  RATES COMPUTED FROM POPULATION FIGURES ABOVE

BOTSWANA

NUMBER OF OFFENSES REPORTED -- (RATE PER 100,000)

YEAR	MURDER ( )	MANSLTR ( )	HOMICIDE ( )	RAPE ( )	ASSAULT (1)	ROBBERY ( )	THEFT (2)	POP
1971	29 (4.33)	25 (3.73)		138 (20.60)	2600 (388.06)	38 (5.67)	4352 (649.55)	670

FOOTNOTES:
1. SERIOUS AND COMMON ASSAULT
2. BURGLARY, STEALING STOCK, AND OTHER THEFT

BRUNEI *

CRIME STATISTICS -- (RATE PER 100,000)

YEAR	MURDER ( )	MANSLTR ( )	HOMICIDE (1)	RAPE ( )	ASSAULT ( )	ROBBERY ( )	THEFT ( )	POP
1964	0 (0.00)		0 (0.00)	1 (1.00)	68 (68.00)	0 (0.00)	122 (122.00)	100
1965	0 (0.00)		0 (0.00)	2 (2.00)	56 (56.00)	0 (0.00)	113 (113.00)	100
1966	1 (0.91)		0 (0.00)	3 (2.73)	62 (56.36)	0 (0.00)	185 (168.18)	110
1967	1 (0.91)		0 (0.00)	0 (0.01)	13 (11.82)	0 (0.00)	189 (171.82)	110
1968	0 (0.00)		0 (0.00)	1 (0.83)	31 (25.83)	0 (0.00)	166 (138.33)	120
1969	1 (0.83)		0 (0.00)	1 (0.83)	46 (38.33)	2 (1.67)	245 (204.17)	120
1970	2 (1.54)		0 (0.00)	0 (0.00)	250 (192.31)	4 (3.08)	284 (218.46)	130
1971	2 (0.00)		0 (0.00)	3 (2.14)	363 (259.29)	2 (1.43)	329 (235.00)	140
1972	0 (0.00)		0 (0.00)	0 (0.00)	316 (225.71)	4 (2.86)	335 (239.29)	140
1973	2 (1.40)		0 (0.00)	4 (2.80)	336 (234.97)	4 (2.80)	297 (207.69)	143
1974	2 (1.37)		0 (0.00)	3 (2.05)	175 (119.86)	9 (6.16)	254 (173.97)	146

FOOTNOTES:
* RAW CRIME DATA FROM INTERPOL; RATES COMPUTED FROM
  POPULATION FIGURES ABOVE
1. CULPABLE HOMICIDE

BULGARIA

CRIME STATISTICS -- (RATE PER 100,000)

YEAR	MURDER ( )	MANSLTR ( )	HOMICIDE ( )	RAPE ( )	ASSAULT (1)	ROBBERY ( )	THEFT (2)	POP
1900	884 (23.61)				949 (25.35)		4613 (123.21)	3744
1901	970 (25.51)				815 (21.44)		4851 (127.59)	3802
1902	975 (25.26)				945 (24.48)		5191 (134.48)	3860
1903	1145 (29.22)				839 (21.41)		4826 (123.18)	3918
1904	1241 (31.21)				746 (18.76)		4403 (110.74)	3976
1905	1109 (27.48)				853 (21.13)		5551 (137.54)	4036
1906	1262 (30.81)				731 (17.85)		4474 (109.23)	4096
1907	1252 (30.13)				911 (21.92)		4678 (112.56)	4156
1908	1181 (28.01)				953 (22.60)		4881 (115.77)	4216
1909								
1910					39025 (899.61)		11530 (265.79)	4338
1911					39182 (893.14)		11835 (269.77)	4387
1912					25968 (585.39)		7479 (168.60)	4436
1913								
GAP								
1920					43651 (904.68)		13398 (277.68)	4825
1921					54732 (1111.76)		19466 (395.41)	4923
1922					53118 (1057.92)		17286 (344.27)	5021
1923					42374 (827.78)		20015 (390.99)	5119
1924								
GAP								
1933					36477 (612.54)		21846 (366.85)	5955
1934								
1935					35229 (577.43)		20365 (333.80)	6101
1936					43440 (706.46)		26652 (433.44)	6149

FOOTNOTES:
1. CRIMES AGAINST THE PERSON FROM 1910
2. ROBBERY AND THEFT; CRIMES AGAINST PROPERTY FROM 1910

BURMA *

NUMBER OF OFFENSES REPORTED -- (RATE PER 100,000)

YEAR	MURDER ( )	MANSLTR ( )	HOMICIDE ( )	RAPE (1)	ASSAULT ( )	ROBBERY ( )	THEFT ( )	POP
1953	11495 (58.32)			2207 (11.20)		38573 (195.70)	46164 (234.22)	19710
1954	9072 (45.27)			1944 (9.70)		31482 (157.10)	37613 (187.69)	20040
1955	7246 (35.54)			1737 (8.52)		25379 (124.47)	40999 (201.07)	20390
1956	12034 (58.05)			2504 (12.08)		36154 (174.40)	45860 (221.23)	20730
1957	2302 (10.89)			528 (2.50)		6320 (29.91)	9180 (43.45)	21130
1958	10256 (47.64)			2463 (11.44)		30133 (139.96)	43388 (201.52)	21530
1959	7031 (32.05)			3761 (17.14)		16661 (75.94)	34033 (155.12)	21940
1960	7879 (35.24)			3427 (15.33)		19566 (87.50)	33480 (149.73)	22360
1961	8232 (36.14)			3549 (15.58)		20307 (89.14)	34713 (152.38)	22780
1962	7400 (31.82)			3704 (15.93)		15992 (68.77)	37052 (159.34)	23253
1963	6774 (28.54)			3717 (15.66)		14968 (63.06)	41030 (172.87)	23735
1964	6792 (28.03)			3720 (15.35)		17712 (73.10)	45948 (189.64)	24229
1965	9120 (36.88)			5040 (20.38)		25368 (102.58)	64656 (261.45)	24730
1966	9975 (39.50)			4200 (16.63)		30600 (121.19)	68725 (272.18)	25250
1967	9698 (37.57)			3562 (13.80)		29432 (114.03)	88764 (343.91)	25810
1968	8505 (32.23)			6831 (25.88)		20061 (76.02)	75141 (284.73)	26390
1969	7755 (28.74)			3273 (12.13)		15098 (55.96)	60115 (222.81)	26980
1970	7252 (26.29)			3416 (12.39)		62804 (227.72)	11172 (40.51)	27580

FOOTNOTES: * RAW CRIME DATA FROM INTERPOL; RATES COMPUTED FROM
    POPULATION FIGURES ABOVE
    1. SEX OFFENSES

CAMEROON *

NUMBER OF OFFENSES REPORTED -- (RATE PER 100,000)

YEAR	MURDER ( )	MANSLTR ( )	HOMICIDE ( )	RAPE (1)	ASSAULT ( )	ROBBERY ( )	THEFT ( )	POP
1965	256 (4.82)			49 (0.92)		183 (3.45)	355 (6.69)	5310
1966	146 (2.69)			50 (0.92)		217 (4.00)	267 (4.93)	5420
1967								5630
1968	30 (0.53)			35 (0.62)		160 (2.84)	255 (4.53)	5630
1969	119 (2.07)			138 (2.40)		512 (8.92)	2326 (40.52)	5740
1970	102 (1.75)			149 (2.55)		627 (10.74)	5624 (96.30)	5840

FOOTNOTES: * RAW CRIME DATA FROM INTERPOL; RATES COMPUTED FROM
    POPULATION FIGURES ABOVE
    1. SEX OFFENSES

NUMBER OF CONVICTIONS -- (RATE PER 100,000)

YEAR	MURDER (1)	MANSLTR (2)	HOMICIDE (3)	RAPE ( )	ASSAULT ( )	ROBBERY (4)	THEFT (5)	POP
1901	7 (0.13)	12 (0.22)			346 (6.44)	52 (0.97)	316 (5.88)	5371
1902	11 (0.20)	17 (0.31)			522 (9.40)	29 (0.52)	287 (5.17)	5555
1903	8 (0.14)	14 (0.25)			680 (11.80)	81 (1.41)	346 (6.03)	5739
1904	14 (0.24)	19 (0.32)			699 (11.80)	92 (1.55)	366 (6.18)	5923
1905	12 (0.20)	15 (0.25)			651 (10.66)	84 (1.38)	477 (7.81)	6107
1906	3 (0.05)	15 (0.24)			592 (9.41)	62 (0.99)	392 (6.23)	6291
1907	8 (0.12)	24 (0.37)			728 (11.24)	99 (1.53)	318 (4.91)	6475
1908	14 (0.21)	22 (0.33)			1179 (17.71)	101 (1.52)	507 (7.61)	6659
1909	18 (0.26)	24 (0.35)			1264 (18.47)	92 (1.34)	313 (4.57)	6843
1910 GAP 1919		60 (0.69)			1323 (15.31)	2300 (26.62)	8605 (99.61)	8639
1920		69 (0.78)			1389 (15.75)	1868 (21.18)	6559 (74.37)	8820
1921		56 (0.62)			1474 (16.44)	1966 (21.92)	5938 (66.21)	8968
1922		64 (0.70)			1451 (15.92)	1207 (13.24)	5865 (64.34)	9116
1923		53 (0.57)			1392 (14.05)	1704 (18.39)	6164 (66.54)	9264
1924		47 (0.50)			1440 (15.30)	1905 (20.24)	6610 (70.23)	9412
1925		55 (0.58)			1400 (14.65)	1624 (16.99)	6651 (69.58)	9559
1926		60 (0.62)	126 (1.29)		1743 (17.89)	1896 (19.46)	7108 (72.95)	9744
1927		51 (0.51)	124 (1.25)		1470 (14.81)	2167 (21.82)	7870 (79.26)	9929
1928		54 (0.53)	150 (1.48)		1923 (19.01)	2553 (25.24)	8777 (86.78)	10114
1929		85 (0.83)	182 (1.77)		2202 (21.38)	3696 (35.89)	10540 (102.34)	10299
1930		68 (0.65)	214 (2.04)		2268 (21.63)	4327 (41.27)	11610 (110.74)	10484
1931		77 (0.73)	172 (1.62)		2356 (22.01)	4267 (40.20)	11144 (104.99)	10614
1932		68 (0.63)	158 (1.47)		2144 (19.96)	4347 (40.46)	11257 (104.77)	10744
1933		63 (0.58)	147 (1.35)		2167 (19.93)	4238 (38.97)	10719 (98.57)	10874
1934		58 (0.53)	142 (1.29)		2471 (22.46)	4147 (37.69)	10603 (96.36)	11004
1935		56 (0.50)	153 (1.37)		2667 (23.95)	4841 (43.48)	11026 (99.02)	11135
1936		81 (0.72)	137 (1.22)		2553 (22.71)	4604 (40.95)	11905 (105.88)	11244
1937		57 (0.50)	138 (1.22)		2440 (21.49)	5509 (48.52)	14048 (123.74)	11353
1938		68 (0.59)	155 (1.11)		2639 (23.02)	6147 (53.63)	14763 (128.80)	11462
1939		70 (0.60)	124 (1.07)		2996 (25.89)	5416 (46.81)	13464 (116.36)	11571
1940		65 (0.56)	148 (1.27)		3632 (31.09)	4217 (36.10)	11632 (99.57)	11682
1941		60 (0.51)	130 (1.10)		3914 (33.11)	3920 (33.16)	11056 (93.52)	11822
1942		68 (0.57)	113 (0.94)		4301 (35.96)	4223 (35.30)	12158 (101.64)	11962
1943		44 (0.36)	125 (1.03)		4088 (33.76)	5291 (43.70)	12265 (103.77)	12108
1944		30 (0.24)	106 (0.86)		4183 (34.11)	5297 (43.20)	12280 (100.15)	12262
1945		59 (0.48)	152 (1.23)		4814 (38.84)	5783 (46.66)	12522 (101.03)	12394
1946		87 (0.69)	146 (1.16)		5994 (47.49)	5304 (42.02)	12172 (96.43)	12622
1947		73 (0.57)	146 (1.13)		5462 (42.38)	5541 (42.99)	11719 (90.93)	12888
1948		67 (0.51)	155 (1.18)		4929 (37.43)	5076 (38.55)	11217 (85.19)	13167
1949		77 (0.57)	172 (1.28)		4194 (31.19)	3952 (29.39)	9457 (70.33)	13347
1950		94 (0.69)	112 (0.82)		4153 (30.29)	4292 (31.30)	9162 (66.82)	13712
1951		107 (0.76)	137 (0.98)		3491 (24.92)	3883 (27.72)	9870 (70.45)	14009
1952		95 (0.66)	135 (0.94)		3874 (26.85)	4040 (28.00)	9777 (67.75)	14430

CANADA

YEAR	MURDER (1)	MANSLTR (2)	HOMICIDE (3)	RAPE ( )	ASSAULT ( )	ROBBERY (4)	THEFT (5)	POP
1953	125 ( )	89 (0.60)	149 (1.01)		3864 (26.14)	4174 (28.24)	9001 (60.90)	14781
1954	118 (0.82)	96 (0.63)	157 (1.03)		3765 (24.78)	4743 (31.21)	8746 (57.56)	15195
1955	131 (0.76)	59 (0.38)	157 (1.01)		3483 (22.33)	4606 (29.52)	8229 (52.75)	15601
1956	129 (0.81)	93 (0.58)			3536 (21.93)	4580 (28.41)	9192 (57.01)	16123
1957	153 (0.77)	118 (0.71)			3638 (21.81)	5588 (33.51)	11497 (68.94)	16677
1958	141 (0.89)	98 (0.57)			3457 (20.19)	6896 (40.28)	12847 (75.04)	17120
1959	(0.80)	115 (0.66)			3180 (18.15)	6435 (36.73)	12660 (72.25)	17522
1960	190 (1.06)	112 (0.63)			3550 (19.82)	7642 (42.67)	14435 (80.60)	17909
1961	185 (1.01)	114 (0.62)			3772 (20.65)	7863 (43.04)	15456 (84.60)	18269
1962	217 (1.17)	164 (0.88)			3975 (21.37)	7776 (41.81)	15001 (80.65)	18600
1963	215 (1.14)	151 (0.80)			4077 (21.54)	8701 (45.97)	16765 (88.57)	18928
1964	218 (1.13)	137 (0.71)			4394 (22.84)	8399 (43.66)	16649 (86.55)	19237
1965	243 (1.23)	141 (0.72)			4579 (23.27)	7927 (40.28)	17972 (91.32)	19680
1966	221 (1.10)	142 (0.71)			5097 (25.42)	7965 (39.73)	20480 (102.14)	20050
1967	282 (1.38)	168 (0.82)			4587 (22.47)	8179 (40.07)	20264 (99.28)	20410
1968	315 (1.52)							20730
1969	346 (1.65)							21030
1970	433 (2.03)							21320
1971	427 (1.98)							21600
1972	479 (2.19)							21850
1973	474 (2.14)							22130

FOOTNOTES:
1. OFFENSES KNOWN, 1954-1973
2. MURDER AND MANSLAUGHTER FROM 1919
3. VITAL STATISTICS
4. ROBBERY AND BURGLARY AFTER 1909
5. BREAKING AND ENTERING BEFORE 1919

CENTRAL AFRICAN REPUBLIC *

NUMBER OF OFFENSES REPORTED -- (RATE PER 100,000)

YEAR	MURDER ( )	MANSLTR ( )	HOMICIDE ( )	RAPE (1)	ASSAULT ( )	ROBBERY ( )	THEFT ( )	POP
1967	72 (4.80)			4 (0.27)		196 (13.07)	303 (20.20)	1500
1968	19 (1.23)			23 (1.49)		106 (6.88)	971 (63.05)	1540
1969	66 (4.18)			48 (3.04)		99 (6.27)	459 (29.05)	1580
1970	39 (2.42)			27 (1.68)		126 (7.83)	420 (26.09)	1610

FOOTNOTES:
* COEFFICIENT OF OFFENDERS IN 1967; RAW CRIME DATA FROM INTERPOL. RATES COMPUTED FROM POPULATION FIGURES ABOVE
1. SEX OFFENSES

CHAD *

NUMBER OF OFFENSES REPORTED -- (RATE PER 100,000)

YEAR	MURDER ( )	MANSLTR ( )	HOMICIDE ( )	RAPE (1)	ASSAULT ( )	ROBBERY ( )	THEFT ( )	POP
1967	416 (12.13)			12 (0.35)		2104 (61.34)		3430
1968	452 (12.91)			8 (0.23)		1908 (54.51)		3500

FOOTNOTES:
* RAW CRIME DATA FROM INTERPOL; RATES COMPUTED FROM POPULATION FIGURES ABOVE
1. SEX OFFENSES

CHILE

CRIME STATISTICS -- (RATE PER 100,000)

YEAR	MURDER ( )	MANSLTR ( )	HOMICIDE ( )	RAPE ( )	ASSAULT ( )	ROBBERY ( )	THEFT ( )	POP
1900			855 (29.27)		290 (9.93)	2481 (84.94)		2921
1901			1002 (33.78)		310 (10.45)	2329 (78.52)		2966
1902			1032 (34.27)		362 (12.02)	2475 (82.20)		3011
1903			1068 (34.95)		331 (10.83)	2516 (82.33)		3056
1904			1040 (33.54)		331 (10.67)	2943 (94.90)		3101
1905			1040 (33.06)		317 (10.08)	715 (22.73)		3146
1906			1063 (33.31)		306 (9.59)	2308 (72.33)		3191
1907			941 (29.12)		216 (6.69)	1798 (55.65)		3231
1908			1177 (38.00)		365 (11.79)	1830 (59.09)		3097
1909			1252 (42.25)		260 (8.77)	2005 (67.67)		2963
1910			1252 (44.26)		366 (12.94)	1576 (55.71)		2829
1911			1246 (46.22)		284 (10.53)	1649 (61.16)		2696
1912			1275 (45.26)		298 (10.58)	1707 (60.60)		2817
1913			437 (14.87)		302 (10.28)	10 (0.34)		2938
1914			668 (21.84)		274 (8.96)	2106 (68.85)	4172 (136.38)	3059
1915			458 (14.40)		179 (5.63)	2743 (86.26)	6278 (197.42)	3180
1916			617 (18.69)		208 (6.30)	2226 (67.43)	5752 (174.25)	3301
1917			398 (11.63)		206 (6.02)	2501 (73.09)	7248 (211.81)	3422
1918			473 (13.35)		267 (7.54)	2865 (80.86)	7535 (212.67)	3543
1919			1456 (39.74)		350 (9.55)	58 (1.58)	8737 (238.46)	3664
1920			1272 (33.61)		278 (7.34)	2089 (55.19)	8207 (216.83)	3785
1921			1354 (35.23)		269 (7.00)	2533 (65.91)	8787 (228.65)	3843
1922			1421 (36.43)		325 (8.33)	2012 (51.58)	9420 (241.48)	3901
1923			1473 (37.21)		304 (7.68)	1616 (40.82)	8278 (209.09)	3959
1924			1324 (32.96)		333 (8.29)	1657 (41.25)	8067 (200.82)	4017
1925			1204 (29.56)		326 (8.00)	1647 (40.44)	7639 (187.55)	4073
1926			2251 (54.49)		399 (9.66)	1440 (34.86)		4131
1927			2245 (53.59)		549 (13.11)	1668 (39.82)		4189
1928			851 (20.04)		562 (13.23)	3723 (87.66)	7481 (176.15)	4247
1929			809 (18.79)		598 (13.89)	3338 (77.54)	7530 (174.91)	4305
1930			143 (3.28)		21 (0.48)	123 (2.82)	9229 (211.43)	4365
1931			22 (0.50)		986 (22.25)	39 (0.88)	10865 (245.60)	4432
1932			2656 (59.04)		762 (16.94)	6088 (135.32)	15785 (350.86)	4499
1933			2726 (59.70)		832 (18.22)	6335 (138.74)		4566
1934			2707 (58.43)		837 (18.07)	4887 (105.48)		4633
1935			1047 (22.28)		682 (14.51)	9716 (206.72)	20551 (437.26)	4700
1936			1134 (23.76)		640 (13.41)	9229 (193.36)	19298 (404.32)	4773
1937			1109 (22.88)		615 (12.69)	9079 (187.35)	19268 (397.61)	4846
1938			951 (19.33)		503 (10.23)	9312 (189.31)	17064 (346.90)	4919
1939			988 (19.79)		527 (10.56)	8466 (169.59)	17791 (356.39)	4992
1940			1024 (20.23)		562 (11.10)	7907 (156.17)	17386 (343.39)	5063
1941			1006 (19.52)		566 (10.98)	6996 (135.74)	17321 (336.07)	5154
1942			1152 (21.97)		578 (11.02)	7753 (147.85)	20318 (387.45)	5244
1943			987 (18.48)		671 (12.56)	8067 (151.04)	19701 (368.86)	5341
1944			1069 (19.65)		577 (10.61)	7155 (131.53)	17123 (314.76)	5440

CHILE CRIME STATISTICS -- (RATE PER 100,000) CONTINUED

YEAR	MURDER ( )	MANSLTR ( )	HOMICIDE ( )	RAPE ( )	ASSAULT ( )	ROBBERY ( )	THEFT ( )	POP
1945			747 (13.48)		526 (9.49)	5679 (102.49)	16630 (300.13)	5541
1946			848 (15.03)		501 (8.88)	5318 (94.24)	17548 (310.97)	5643
1947			811 (14.11)		561 (9.76)	5572 (96.94)	19867 (345.63)	5748
1948			943 (16.11)		601 (10.27)	5448 (93.06)	19768 (337.68)	5854
1949			978 (16.40)		615 (10.32)	5000 (85.86)	29859 (500.82)	5962
1950			720 (11.86)		895 (14.74)	5170 (85.13)	19121 (314.85)	6073
1951			710 (11.48)		779 (12.59)	4747 (76.75)	20680 (334.36)	6185
1952			2361 (37.48)		799 (12.68)	3445 (54.69)	19335 (306.95)	6299
1953			696 (10.77)		877 (13.58)	4483 (69.40)	17952 (277.89)	6460
1954			629 (9.50)		1018 (15.38)	4890 (73.87)	19718 (297.85)	6620
1955			661 (9.73)		995 (14.65)	5548 (81.71)	20510 (302.06)	6790
1956			2087 (29.98)		902 (12.96)	3388 (48.66)	20810 (298.91)	6962
1957			633 (8.87)		385 (5.39)	4147 (58.11)		7137
1958			642 (8.78)		1036 (14.16)	5407 (73.91)		7316
1959			312 (4.16)		518 (6.91)	2414 (32.19)		7500
1960			554 (7.21)		926 (11.78)	5016 (65.24)	15129 (192.53)	7689
1961			756 (9.62)		920 (11.46)	6080 (77.37)	14690 (182.96)	7858
1962			657 (8.18)		963 (11.72)	5016 (62.47)		8029
1963			651 (7.92)		772 (9.09)	5828 (70.93)		8217
1964			489 (5.76)		1011 (11.61)	5421 (63.84)		8492
1965			603 (6.92)		893 (10.01)	6453 (74.09)		8710
1966			541 (6.07)		842 (9.21)	4021 (45.08)		8920
1967			640 (7.00)		684 (7.32)	4140 (45.30)		9140
1968			711 (7.60)		542 (5.66)	4105 (43.90)		9350
1969			652 (6.81)			4450 (46.50)		9570
1970			587 (6.04)		418 (4.30)	4737 (48.73)	6313 (62.88)	9720
1971			763 (7.72)		474 (4.80)	4857 (49.16)	5958 (58.24)	9880
1972			823 (8.20)		542 (5.40)		5606 (53.75)	10040
1973			710 (6.94)		583 (5.70)			10230
1974			426 (4.08)		723 (6.93)			10430

CHINA, REPUBLIC OF (TAIWAN)   CRIME STATISTICS -- (RATE PER 100,000)

YEAR	MURDER ( )	MANSLTR ( )	HOMICIDE ( )	RAPE ( )	ASSAULT (1)	ROBBERY (2)	THEFT (3)	POP
1952	553 (6.91)				2534 (31.67)	126 (1.57)	6657 (83.21)	8000
1953	491 (5.94)				3449 (41.75)	182 (2.20)	8688 (105.17)	8261
1954	637 (7.39)				5760 (66.84)	250 (2.90)	10845 (125.86)	8617
1955	942 (10.58)				5865 (65.85)	192 (2.16)	12708 (142.67)	8907
1956	947 (10.25)				6886 (74.52)	317 (3.43)	12782 (138.33)	9240
1957	921 (9.69)				5719 (60.16)	209 (2.20)	12098 (127.27)	9506
1958	1022 (10.37)				6545 (66.44)	226 (2.29)	12516 (127.05)	9851
1959	1199 (11.72)				6616 (64.66)	303 (2.96)	13180 (128.81)	10232
1960	1440 (13.57)				7734 (72.88)	260 (2.45)	13685 (128.96)	10612
1961	1511 (13.77)				8086 (73.70)	337 (3.07)	15549 (141.73)	10971
1962	1556 (13.71)				7827 (68.97)	406 (3.58)	16410 (144.59)	11349
1963	1702 (14.55)				8074 (69.03)	465 (3.98)	18274 (156.24)	11696
1964	1753 (14.52)				8435 (69.88)	319 (2.64)	18659 (154.59)	12070
1965	2042 (16.43)				8927 (71.84)	277 (2.23)	18262 (146.95)	12427
1966	2345 (18.34)				9210 (72.04)	318 (2.49)	17161 (134.24)	12784
1967	2419 (18.41)				9204 (70.04)	313 (2.38)	14101 (107.31)	13141
1968	2469 (18.29)				8763 (64.92)	466 (3.45)	13840 (102.53)	13498
1969	3027 (21.85)				9768 (70.50)	375 (2.71)	15589 (112.52)	13855

FOOTNOTES:
1. INJURY
2. PILLAGE AND ROBBERY
3. BURGLARY

COLOMBIA *

CRIME STATISTICS -- (RATE PER 100,000)

YEAR	MURDER ( )	MANSLTR ( )	HOMICIDE ( )	RAPE ( )	ASSAULT ( )	ROBBERY ( )	THEFT ( )	POP
1938			2700 (30.91)		14083 (161.21)	2317 (26.52)	4257 (48.73)	8736
1939			2922 (32.78)		14205 (159.34)	3101 (34.78)	6128 (68.74)	8915
1940			2450 (26.94)		13352 (146.82)	2924 (32.15)	6026 (66.26)	9094
1941			2781 (30.55)		14229 (153.02)	2691 (28.94)	5449 (58.60)	9299
1942			2599 (27.35)		14195 (149.36)	3487 (36.69)	6096 (64.14)	9504
1943			2453 (25.25)		13679 (140.79)	3753 (38.63)	7402 (76.18)	9716
1944			2495 (25.12)		14964 (150.66)	3617 (36.42)	9139 (92.02)	9932
1945			2687 (26.47)		16189 (159.45)	3533 (34.80)	9973 (98.23)	10153
1946			3321 (31.99)		20668 (199.11)	4418 (42.56)	12030 (115.90)	10380
1947			3787 (35.69)		21884 (206.24)	4704 (44.33)	11916 (112.30)	10611
1948			4267 (39.33)		20184 (186.06)	5379 (49.59)	10064 (92.77)	10848
1949			4967 (44.79)		18056 (162.83)	4866 (43.88)	8807 (79.42)	11089
1950			6319 (55.74)		18371 (162.06)	3860 (34.05)	10639 (93.85)	11336
1951			6129 (52.89)		19417 (167.55)	6651 (57.39)	11662 (100.63)	11589
1952			6881 (58.08)		21808 (184.08)	6672 (56.32)	11338 (95.70)	11847
1953			7742 (64.14)		25304 (209.64)	7214 (59.77)	12420 (102.90)	12070
1954			5919 (47.97)		24509 (198.61)	7468 (60.52)	14110 (114.34)	12340
1955			8342 (63.34)		30469 (231.35)	9908 (75.23)	18504 (140.50)	13170
1956			8141 (59.90)		30945 (227.70)	10773 (79.27)	20845 (153.38)	13590
1957			6525 (46.51)		28259 (201.42)	9908 (70.62)	22085 (157.41)	14030
1958			7797 (53.85)		30624 (211.49)	16440 (113.54)	23168 (160.00)	14480
1959			6611 (44.25)		31936 (213.76)	17168 (114.91)	23220 (155.42)	14940
1960			5981 (38.79)		31783 (206.12)	16113 (104.49)	24517 (158.99)	15420
1961			5497 (34.55)		33090 (207.98)	16105 (101.23)	23806 (149.63)	15910
1962			7775 (47.35)		42085 (256.30)	18927 (115.27)	27775 (169.15)	16420
1963			7862 (46.41)		35633 (210.30)	18535 (109.42)	27993 (165.25)	16940
1964			8210 (46.97)		36902 (211.11)	19602 (112.14)	28431 (162.65)	17480
1965								
1966			9132 (49.04)		25329 (136.03)	29048 (156.00)	28898 (155.20)	18620
1967			10949 (56.97)		28397 (147.75)	32229 (167.68)	34211 (178.00)	19220

FOOTNOTES:
* NUMBER ARRESTED

CONGO (BRAZZAVILLE) *　　　　NUMBER OF OFFENSES REPORTED -- (RATE PER 100,000)

YEAR	MURDER ( )	MANSLTR ( )	HOMICIDE ( )	RAPE (1)	ASSAULT ( )	ROBBERY ( )	THEFT ( )	POP
1964	140 (17.07)			80 (9.76)		429 (52.32)	1297 (158.17)	820
1965	181 (21.55)			50 (5.95)		227 (27.02)	404 (48.10)	840
1966	295 (34.30)			100 (11.63)		90 (10.47)	445 (51.74)	860
1967	272 (30.91)			170 (19.32)		190 (21.59)	824 (93.64)	880
1968	163 (18.11)			117 (13.00)		176 (19.56)	556 (61.78)	900
1969	255 (27.72)			154 (16.74)		171 (18.59)	891 (96.85)	920
1970	166 (17.66)			54 (5.74)		189 (20.11)	646 (68.72)	940

FOOTNOTES:
* RAW CRIME DATA FROM INTERPOL; RATES COMPUTED FROM
  POPULATION FIGURES ABOVE
1. SEX OFFENSES

CUBA *　　　　NUMBER OF OFFENSES REPORTED -- (RATE PER 100,000)

YEAR	MURDER ( )	MANSLTR ( )	HOMICIDE ( )	RAPE (1)	ASSAULT ( )	ROBBERY ( )	THEFT ( )	POP
1953	517 (8.86)			89 (1.53)		1119 (19.19)		5832
1954	1705 (28.75)			238 (4.01)				5930

FOOTNOTES:
* RAW CRIME DATA FROM INTERPOL; RATES COMPUTED FROM
  POPULATION FIGURES ABOVE
1. SEX OFFENSES

CYPRUS *   NUMBER OF OFFENSES REPORTED -- (RATE PER 100,000)

YEAR	MURDER ( )	MANSLTR ( )	HOMICIDE ( )	RAPE (1)	ASSAULT ( )	ROBBERY ( )	THEFT ( )	POP
1961	75 (12.93)			151 (26.03)		1769 (305.00)	1641 (282.93)	580
1962	41 (6.93)			172 (29.05)		1320 (222.97)	1503 (253.89)	592
1963	180 (30.51)			148 (25.08)		1046 (177.29)	1581 (267.97)	590
1964	231 (38.89)			50 (8.42)		1011 (170.20)	1475 (248.32)	594
1965	41 (6.86)			74 (12.37)		553 (92.47)	1198 (200.33)	598
1966	43 (7.08)			109 (17.96)		399 (65.73)	1431 (235.75)	607
1967	45 (7.33)			85 (13.84)		350 (57.00)	1268 (206.51)	614
1968	22 (3.54)			111 (17.87)		405 (65.22)	1320 (212.56)	621
1969	20 (3.17)			99 (15.69)		393 (62.28)	1110 (175.91)	631
1970	20 (3.12)			71 (11.06)		373 (58.10)	1209 (188.32)	642

FOOTNOTES:
  * RAW CRIME DATA FROM INTERPOL; RATES COMPUTED FROM
    POPULATION FIGURES ABOVE
    1. SEX OFFENSES

DAHOMEY *   NUMBER OF OFFENSES REPORTED -- (RATE PER 100,000)

YEAR	MURDER ( )	MANSLTR ( )	HOMICIDE ( )	RAPE (1)	ASSAULT ( )	ROBBERY ( )	THEFT ( )	POP
1967	25 (1.00)			99 (3.98)			1013 (40.68)	2490
1968	25 (0.98)			108 (4.24)			1008 (39.53)	2550
1969	16 (0.61)			78 (2.98)		20 (0.76)	494 (18.85)	2620
1970	10 (0.37)			71 (2.64)		18 (0.67)	463 (17.21)	2690

FOOTNOTES:
  * RAW CRIME DATA FROM INTERPOL; RATES COMPUTED FROM
    POPULATION FIGURES ABOVE
    1. SEX OFFENSES

DENMARK   CRIME STATISTICS -- (RATE PER 100,000)

YEAR	MURDER ( )	MANSLTR ( )	HOMICIDE ( )	RAPE (1)	ASSAULT (2)	ROBBERY ( )	THEFT (3)	POP
1921				1262 (38.49)	938 (28.61)		30249 (922.51)	3279
1922				1190 (35.90)	1092 (32.94)		28299 (853.67)	3315
1923				1191 (35.64)	1135 (33.87)		30804 (919.25)	3351
1924				1306 (38.56)	1329 (39.24)		32804 (968.53)	3387
1925				1551 (45.28)	1371 (40.03)		38244 (1116.61)	3425
1926				1496 (43.39)	1244 (36.08)		41630 (1207.37)	3448
1927				1345 (38.75)	1272 (36.65)		46136 (1329.18)	3471
1928				1595 (45.65)	1276 (36.52)		51259 (1467.06)	3494
1929				1607 (45.69)	1192 (33.89)		48840 (1388.68)	3517
1930				1570 (44.33)	1293 (36.50)		54094 (1527.22)	3542
1931				1635 (45.76)	1275 (35.68)		53763 (1504.70)	3573
1932				2028 (56.27)	1359 (37.71)		55336 (1535.41)	3604
1933	20 (0.55)			495 (13.62)	1376 (37.85)	55 (1.51)	59456 (1635.65)	3635
1934	16 (0.44)				1484 (40.48)	40 (1.09)	61014 (1664.32)	3666
1935	19 (0.51)			1047 (28.34)	1390 (37.62)	48 (1.30)	59195 (1602.03)	3695
1936	29 (0.78)			877 (23.56)	1568 (42.13)	34 (0.91)	59104 (1587.96)	3722
1937	20 (0.53)			1058 (28.22)	1555 (40.94)	30 (0.80)	59694 (1592.26)	3749
1938	15 (0.40)			873 (23.12)	1446 (38.29)	43 (1.14)	60437 (1600.56)	3776
1939	11 (0.29)			1009 (26.53)	1341 (35.26)	32 (0.84)	61047 (1605.23)	3803
1940	20 (0.52)			484 (12.63)	1304 (34.03)	48 (1.25)	77422 (2020.41)	3832
1941	15 (0.39)			633 (16.37)	1614 (41.73)	102 (2.64)	109252 (2824.51)	3868
1942	21 (0.54)			930 (23.83)	1934 (49.55)	110 (2.82)	127485 (3266.33)	3903
1943	13 (0.33)			793 (20.08)	2338 (59.20)	197 (4.99)	137371 (3478.63)	3949
1944								
1945								
1946	51 (1.24)			773 (18.85)	1497 (36.50)	339 (8.27)	97226 (2370.79)	4101
1947	53 (1.28)			753 (18.16)	1472 (35.50)	298 (7.19)	93402 (2252.82)	4146
1948	47 (1.12)			944 (22.53)	1609 (38.40)	223 (5.32)	93543 (2233.53)	4190
1949	67 (1.58)			1000 (23.64)	1557 (36.80)	254 (6.00)	85562 (2022.26)	4231
1950	65 (1.52)			1328 (31.10)	1613 (37.78)	189 (4.43)	81690 (1913.11)	4270
1951	58 (1.35)			1501 (34.87)	1638 (38.06)	166 (3.86)	95699 (2223.49)	4304
1952	55 (1.27)			1499 (34.59)	1553 (35.83)	158 (3.65)	90393 (2085.67)	4334
1953	82 (1.88)			1426 (32.64)	1719 (39.35)	179 (4.10)	86142 (1971.66)	4369
1954	45 (1.02)			1354 (30.73)	1858 (41.72)	106 (2.41)	80686 (1831.28)	4406
1955	50 (1.13)			1600 (36.04)	1289 (29.04)	116 (2.61)	85367 (1923.11)	4439
1956	61 (1.37)			1350 (30.23)	1649 (36.92)	102 (2.28)	83832 (1877.12)	4466
1957	59 (1.31)			1267 (28.23)	1694 (37.75)	125 (2.79)	87833 (1957.06)	4488
1958	56 (1.24)			1162 (25.74)	1859 (40.73)	154 (3.41)	87819 (1945.05)	4515
1959	38 (0.84)			1336 (29.38)	1944 (42.75)	113 (2.49)	91016 (2001.67)	4547
1960	38 (0.83)			2884 (62.96)	1632 (35.63)	344 (7.51)	57164 (1247.85)	4581
1961	34 (0.74)			2751 (59.67)	1572 (34.10)	156 (3.38)	60066 (1302.95)	4610
1962	50 (1.08)			189 (4.07)	1501 (32.30)	168 (3.62)	64473 (1387.41)	4647
1963	62 (1.32)			173 (3.69)	1621 (34.61)	184 (3.93)	70479 (1504.68)	4684
1964	35 (0.74)			259 (5.49)	1799 (38.11)	227 (4.81)	72336 (1553.54)	4720
1965	49 (1.03)			162 (3.40)	1944 (40.84)	222 (4.66)	74916 (1573.87)	4760
1966	32 (0.67)			215 (4.48)	1962 (40.88)	230 (4.79)	76057 (1584.52)	4800

DENMARK — CRIME STATISTICS -- (RATE PER 100,000)   CONTINUED

YEAR	MURDER ( )	MANSLTR ( )	HOMICIDE ( )	RAPE (1)	ASSAULT (2)	ROBBERY ( )	THEFT (3)	POP
1967	55 (1.14)			203 (4.19)	1892 (39.09)	266 (5.50)	86840 (1794.22)	4840
1968	54 (1.11)			217 (4.47)	1999 (41.13)	342 (7.04)	98868 (2034.32)	4860
1969	32 (0.65)			236 (4.83)	2239 (45.79)	309 (6.32)	106751 (2183.05)	4890

FOOTNOTES:
1. SEXUAL CRIMES BEFORE 1933
2. VIOLENT CRIMES BEFORE 1933
3. GRAND LARCENY AND SIMPLE THEFT BEFORE 1933

DOMINICAN REPUBLIC *   NUMBER OF OFFENSES REPORTED -- (RATE PER 100,000)

YEAR	MURDER ( )	MANSLTR ( )	HOMICIDE ( )	RAPE ( )	ASSAULT ( )	ROBBERY ( )	THEFT ( )	POP
1969	396 (10.03)			121 (3.06)		1814 (45.92)	2310 (58.48)	3950
1970	543 (13.54)			137 (3.42)		1779 (44.35)	1653 (41.21)	4011

FOOTNOTES:
* RAW CRIME DATA FROM INTERPOL; RATES COMPUTED FROM POPULATION FIGURES ABOVE

EGYPT *

NUMBER OF OFFENSES REPORTED -- (RATE PER 100,000)

YEAR	MURDER ( )	MANSLTR ( )	HOMICIDE ( )	RAPE (1)	ASSAULT ( )	ROBBERY ( )	THEFT ( )	POP
1953	2307 (10.46)			320 (1.45)		683 (3.10)		22062
1954	2231 (9.85)			283 (1.25)		541 (2.39)		22651
1955	2128 (9.23)			295 (1.28)		439 (1.90)		23063
1956	2243 (9.49)			177 (0.75)		410 (1.73)		23643
1957	1808 (7.48)			166 (0.69)		454 (1.88)		24179
1958	3090 (12.53)			206 (0.84)		446 (1.81)		24666
1959	2843 (11.23)			150 (0.59)		394 (1.56)		25324
1960	2259 (8.70)			154 (0.59)		419 (1.61)		25951
1961	2116 (7.97)			134 (0.50)		321 (1.21)		26557
1962	1521 (5.58)			111 (0.41)		166 (0.61)		27243
1963								28660
1964	1198 (4.18)			117 (0.41)		117 (0.41)	58248 (198.19)	29390
1965	1262 (4.29)			120 (0.41)		120 (0.41)	44266 (146.87)	30140
1966	1160 (3.85)			366 (1.21)		92 (0.31)	39813 (128.80)	30910
1967	1152 (3.73)			156 (0.50)		125 (0.40)	46183 (145.73)	31690
1968	1541 (4.86)			160 (0.50)		193 (0.61)	49289 (151.66)	32500
1969	1446 (4.45)			193 (0.59)		257 (0.79)		
1970	1228 (3.68)			166 (0.50)		232 (0.70)	45170 (135.52)	33330

FOOTNOTES: * RAW CRIME DATA FROM INTERPOL; RATES COMPUTED FROM
POPULATION FIGURES ABOVE
1. SEX OFFENSES

EL SALVADOR

YEAR	MURDER ( )	MANSLTR ( )	HOMICIDE ( )	RAPE ( )	ASSAULT ( )	ROBBERY ( )	THEFT ( )	POP
1934	594 (39.21)				2066 (136.37)	350 (23.10)	833 (54.98)	1515
1935	555 (36.25)				1866 (121.88)	219 (14.30)	770 (50.29)	1531
1936	715 (46.10)				2449 (157.90)	199 (12.83)	495 (31.91)	1551
1937	771 (49.08)				2474 (157.48)	309 (19.67)	553 (35.20)	1571
1938	624 (39.22)				2319 (145.76)	244 (15.34)	546 (34.32)	1591
1939	573 (35.57)				2269 (140.84)	209 (12.97)	493 (30.60)	1611
1940	454 (27.80)				2183 (133.68)	261 (15.98)	667 (40.85)	1633
1941	414 (25.03)				2275 (137.55)	281 (16.99)	564 (34.10)	1654
1942	570 (34.03)				2701 (161.25)	321 (19.16)	765 (45.67)	1675
1943	498 (29.35)				2656 (156.51)	378 (22.27)	1050 (61.87)	1697
1944	672 (39.09)				3038 (176.73)	362 (21.06)	1192 (69.34)	1719
1945	687 (39.44)				2370 (136.05)	521 (29.91)	1300 (74.63)	1742
1946	449 (25.45)				2321 (131.58)	329 (18.65)	1004 (56.92)	1764
1947	553 (30.93)				2742 (153.36)	301 (16.83)	970 (54.25)	1788
1948	649 (35.84)				3122 (172.39)	341 (18.83)	1061 (58.59)	1811
1949	732 (39.89)				3090 (168.39)	359 (19.56)	934 (50.90)	1835
1950	673 (36.03)				3450 (184.69)	348 (18.63)	1310 (70.13)	1868
1951	814 (42.40)				4226 (220.10)	433 (22.55)	1482 (77.19)	1920
1952	812 (40.89)				4397 (221.40)	355 (17.88)	1412 (71.10)	1986
1953	798 (38.85)				4691 (228.38)	388 (18.89)	1285 (62.56)	2054
1954	775 (36.52)				5060 (238.45)	389 (18.33)	1406 (66.26)	2122
1955	805 (37.70)				4696 (219.95)	404 (18.92)	1374 (64.36)	2135
1956	932 (42.44)				4916 (223.86)	294 (13.39)	1149 (52.32)	2196
1957	691 (30.62)				4201 (186.13)	300 (13.29)	1146 (50.78)	2257
1958	774 (33.35)				4478 (192.93)	367 (15.81)	1381 (59.50)	2321
1959	754 (31.60)				4317 (180.94)	428 (17.94)	1601 (67.10)	2386
1960	763 (31.09)				4098 (166.99)	473 (19.27)	1385 (56.44)	2454
1961	893 (35.35)				4559 (180.48)	441 (17.46)	1296 (51.31)	2526
1962	869 (33.08)				4501 (171.34)	368 (14.01)	1255 (47.77)	2627
1963	862 (31.68)				4207 (154.61)	447 (16.43)	1416 (52.04)	2721
1964	827 (29.28)				4456 (157.79)	439 (15.55)	1325 (46.92)	2824
1965	861 (29.39)				4284 (146.21)	422 (14.40)	1237 (42.22)	2930
1966	844 (27.76)				3945 (129.77)	426 (14.01)	1563 (51.41)	3040
1967	860 (27.30)				4231 (134.32)	528 (16.76)	1474 (46.79)	3150
1968	790 (24.16)				4650 (142.20)	616 (18.84)	1475 (45.11)	3270

ENGLAND (AND WALES)   NUMBER OF OFFENSES REPORTED -- (RATE PER 100,000)

YEAR	MURDER	( )	MANSLTR	( )	HOMICIDE	( )	RAPE	( )	ASSAULT	( )	ROBBERY	( )	THEFT	( )	POP
1900	136	0.42	176	0.55			231	0.72	1260	3.92	256	0.80	59736	185.67	32173
1901	161	0.49	180	0.55			236	0.73	1307	4.02	234	0.72	60863	187.12	32527
1902	149	0.45	181	0.55			216	0.66	1295	3.94	274	0.83	62134	188.97	32881
1903	171	0.51	141	0.42			190	0.57	1221	3.67	241	0.73	63613	191.40	33235
1904	160	0.48	156	0.46			213	0.63	1096	3.26	251	0.75	68837	204.94	33589
1905	137	0.40	150	0.44			172	0.51	1171	3.45	223	0.66	70177	206.75	33943
1906	134	0.39	129	0.38			203	0.59	1311	3.82	242	0.71	67012	195.39	34297
1907	132	0.38	142	0.41			185	0.53	1433	4.14	232	0.67	72776	210.03	34651
1908	159	0.45	161	0.46			202	0.58	1332	3.81	310	0.89	76837	219.50	35005
1909	161	0.46	138	0.39			172	0.49	1369	3.87	226	0.64	75927	214.73	35359
1910	148	0.41	140	0.39			156	0.44	1325	3.71	211	0.59	73916	206.97	35713
1911	144	0.40	147	0.41			146	0.40	1368	3.79	198	0.55	69345	192.25	36070
1912	152	0.42	154	0.44			175	0.48	1359	3.75	195	0.54	73841	203.76	36240
1913	178	0.49	153	0.42			177	0.49	1222	3.36	155	0.43	69942	192.10	36410
1914	141	0.39	145	0.39			154	0.42	1084	2.96	133	0.36	63657	174.02	36580
1915	130	0.35	128	0.35			124	0.34	769	2.09	85	0.23	57766	157.19	36750
1916	146	0.40	111	0.30			98	0.27	572	1.55	114	0.31	60768	164.59	36920
1917	127	0.34	99	0.27			74	0.20	388	1.05	134	0.36	67104	180.92	37090
1918	131	0.35	73	0.20			78	0.21	420	1.13	100	0.27	65296	175.24	37260
1919	176	0.47	122	0.33			121	0.32	761	2.03	203	0.54	60673	162.10	37430
1920	179	0.48	134	0.36			130	0.35	826	2.20	235	0.63	69408	184.62	37596
1921	138	0.36	113	0.30			125	0.33	742	1.96	211	0.56	70637	186.55	37864
1922	145	0.38	98	0.26			118	0.31	635	1.67	164	0.43	70923	185.99	38132
1923	150	0.39	109	0.28			116	0.29	646	1.68	151	0.39	73145	190.48	38400
1924	150	0.39	110	0.28			116	0.30	646	1.67	122	0.32	74742	193.29	38668
1925	160	0.41	133	0.34			125	0.32	774	1.99	136	0.35	75839	194.78	38935
1926	154	0.39	128	0.33			113	0.29	1067	2.73	120	0.31	90910	232.46	39108
1927	143	0.36	138	0.35			107	0.27	1168	2.97	110	0.28	82603	210.29	39281
1928	136	0.34	122	0.31			99	0.25	1264	3.20	128	0.32	84566	214.34	39454
1929	131	0.33	157	0.40			89	0.22	1342	3.39	167	0.42	87156	219.94	39627
1930	122	0.31	162	0.41			89	0.22	1470	3.69	217	0.55	94716	237.97	39801
1931	138	0.35	124	0.31			90	0.23	1377	3.44	208	0.52	100718	251.98	39970
1932	125	0.31	141	0.35			72	0.18	1277	3.18	342	0.85	137980	343.76	40139
1933	141	0.35	192	0.48			75	0.19	1483	3.68	219	0.54	158711	393.75	40308
1934	120	0.30	171	0.42			84	0.21	1609	3.98	215	0.53	164488	406.37	40477
1935	145	0.35	197	0.48			104	0.26	1765	4.34	182	0.45	165003	405.96	40645
1936	114	0.28	171	0.42			99	0.24	1807	4.42	189	0.46	176653	432.04	40888
1937	116	0.28	172	0.42			108	0.26	1983	4.82	209	0.51	188962	459.42	41131
1938	156	0.37	155	0.37			99	0.24	2020	4.88	287	0.69	199951	483.28	41374
1939	141	0.34	147	0.35			109	0.26	2179	5.24	265	0.64	219478	527.38	41617
1940	123	0.29	134	0.32			125	0.30	1794	4.29	342	0.82	225671	539.08	41862
1941	146	0.35	145	0.35			169	0.40	1931	4.61	483	1.15	267386	638.69	41880
1942	209	0.50	158	0.38			200	0.48	2035	4.86	685	1.63	267789	639.16	41897
1943	174	0.41	114	0.27			257	0.61	2303	5.45	730	1.73	272186	644.09	42259
1944	166	0.39	147	0.35			416	0.98	2749	6.48	821	1.93	297930	701.85	42449

ENGLAND (AND WALES)

NUMBER OF OFFENSES REPORTED -- (RATE PER 100,000)   CONTINUED

YEAR	MURDER ( )	MANSLTR ( )	HOMICIDE ( )	RAPE ( )	ASSAULT ( )	ROBBERY ( )	THEFT ( )	POP
1945	218 (0.51)	217 (0.51)		377 (0.88)	3292 (7.72)	1033 (2.42)	323310 (758.30)	42636
1946	148 (0.35)	151 (0.35)		251 (0.59)	3020 (7.07)	921 (2.16)	310650 (727.52)	42700
1947	175 (0.41)	138 (0.32)		240 (0.56)	3495 (8.12)	979 (2.27)	330918 (768.68)	43050
1948	171 (0.39)	138 (0.32)		252 (0.58)	4224 (9.71)	1101 (2.53)	349358 (803.99)	43502
1949	136 (0.31)	131 (0.30)		233 (0.53)	4376 (9.99)	990 (2.26)	301591 (688.80)	43785
1950	139 (0.32)	176 (0.40)		314 (0.72)	5258 (12.00)	1021 (2.33)	301075 (686.92)	43830
1951	132 (0.30)	176 (0.40)		335 (0.76)	5619 (12.82)	800 (1.83)	355407 (811.15)	43815
1952	146 (0.33)	233 (0.53)		260 (0.59)	5980 (13.60)	1002 (2.28)	341512 (776.96)	43955
1953	143 (0.32)	158 (0.36)		295 (0.67)	6187 (14.03)	980 (2.22)	308578 (699.58)	44109
1954	146 (0.33)	138 (0.31)		294 (0.66)	6586 (14.88)	812 (1.83)	285199 (644.17)	44274
1955	135 (0.30)	122 (0.27)		340 (0.77)	7076 (15.92)	823 (1.85)	295035 (663.88)	44441
1956	156 (0.35)	142 (0.32)		329 (0.73)	8433 (18.81)	965 (2.15)	323561 (721.90)	44821
1957	166 (0.37)	147 (0.33)		408 (0.91)	9774 (21.70)	1194 (2.65)	360985 (801.42)	45043
1958	137 (0.30)	108 (0.24)		391 (0.86)	10945 (24.19)	1692 (3.74)	409388 (904.84)	45244
1959	149 (0.33)	92 (0.20)		512 (1.13)	12707 (27.93)	1900 (4.18)	445000 (977.94)	45504
1960	153 (0.33)	108 (0.24)		515 (1.12)	14391 (31.38)	2014 (4.39)	489258 (1066.80)	45862
1961	147 (0.32)	105 (0.23)		503 (1.09)	16197 (34.98)	2349 (5.07)	531430 (1147.60)	46308
1962	159 (0.34)	114 (0.24)		473 (1.01)	16430 (35.10)	2517 (5.38)	585566 (1257.43)	46807
1963	153 (0.32)	135 (0.29)		422 (0.90)	18655 (39.59)	2483 (5.27)	635627 (1348.84)	47124
1964	170 (0.36)	108 (0.23)		517 (1.09)	21868 (46.19)	3066 (6.48)	704116 (1487.36)	47340
1965	171 (0.36)	134 (0.28)		618 (1.30)	23876 (50.07)	3736 (7.83)	744155 (1560.40)	47690
1966	169 (0.35)	172 (0.36)		644 (1.34)	25027 (52.15)	4474 (9.32)	775990 (1616.98)	47990
1967	200 (0.41)	193 (0.40)		702 (1.45)	27123 (56.16)	4564 (9.45)	784093 (1623.38)	48300
1968	203 (0.42)	196 (0.40)		829 (1.71)	30094 (61.93)	4815 (9.91)	826311 (1700.58)	48590
1969	182 (0.37)	188 (0.39)		869 (1.78)	35928 (73.58)	6041 (12.37)	878710 (1799.53)	48830
1970	186 (0.38)	181 (0.37)		884 (1.80)	39266 (80.15)	6273 (12.80)	914723 (1867.16)	48990
1971	247 (0.51)	193 (0.40)		784 (1.61)	45165 (92.51)	7465 (15.29)	962992 (1972.54)	48820
1972	251 (0.51)	204 (0.42)		893 (1.82)	50519 (103.04)	8126 (16.57)		49030

ETHIOPIA *

NUMBER OF OFFENSES REPORTED -- (RATE PER 100,000)

YEAR	MURDER ( )	MANSLTR ( )	HOMICIDE ( )	RAPE (1)	ASSAULT ( )	ROBBERY ( )	THEFT ( )	POP
1961	5337 (25.41)					10525 (50.12)	13805 (65.74)	21000
1962	4805 (22.35)					10828 (50.36)	14164 (65.88)	21500
1963	5414 (24.83)					9095 (41.72)	12727 (58.38)	21800
1964	5315 (23.94)			227 (1.02)		4259 (19.18)	18407 (82.91)	22200
1965								
1966	5947 (25.70)			935 (4.04)		2444 (10.56)	1883 (8.14)	23140

FOOTNOTES:
* RAW CRIME DATA FROM INTERPOL; RATES COMPUTED FROM
  POPULATION FIGURES ABOVE
1. SEX OFFENSES

FIJI *

NUMBER OF OFFENSES REPORTED -- (RATE PER 100,000)

YEAR	MURDER ( )	MANSLTR ( )	HOMICIDE ( )	RAPE (1)	ASSAULT ( )	ROBBERY ( )	THEFT ( )	POP
1962	13 (3.04)			248 (58.08)		372 (87.12)	539 (126.23)	427
1963	9 (2.04)			190 (43.08)		327 (74.15)	1443 (327.21)	441
1964	14 (3.07)			78 (17.11)		306 (67.11)	799 (175.22)	456
1965	5 (1.08)			70 (15.09)		158 (34.05)	673 (145.04)	464
1966	9 (1.92)			80 (17.06)		207 (44.14)	714 (152.24)	469
1967	15 (2.99)			75 (14.94)		387 (77.09)	533 (106.18)	502
1968	10 (1.95)			118 (23.05)		51 (9.96)	159 (31.05)	512
1969	11 (2.09)			116 (22.05)		437 (83.08)	1201 (228.33)	526
1970	16 (3.05)			178 (33.97)		619 (118.13)	1773 (338.36)	524

FOOTNOTES:
* RAW CRIME DATA FROM INTERPOL; RATES COMPUTED FROM
  POPULATION FIGURES ABOVE
1. SEX OFFENSES

FINLAND *

NUMBER OF OFFENSES REPORTED -- (RATE PER 100,000)

YEAR	MURDER ( ) 61 (1.95)	MANSLTR ( ) 33 (1.06)	HOMICIDE ( )	RAPE ( )	ASSAULT (1) 1358 (43.50)	ROBBERY ( ) 61 (1.95)	THEFT (2) 1524 (48.81)	POP 3122
1914	61 (1.95)	33 (1.06)			1358 (43.50)	61 (1.95)	1524 (48.81)	3122
1915								
1916	38 (1.22)	37 (1.18)			749 (23.97)	33 (1.06)	2068 (66.18)	3125
1917	32 (1.02)	31 (0.99)			832 (26.61)	40 (1.28)	3938 (125.94)	3127
1918	42 (1.34)	86 (2.75)			248 (7.93)	33 (1.05)	3902 (124.70)	3129
1919	62 (1.98)	38 (1.21)			502 (16.03)	42 (1.34)	5020 (160.33)	3131
1920	69 (2.20)	50 (1.60)			747 (23.84)	50 (1.60)	2978 (95.05)	3133
1921	121 (3.82)	47 (1.48)			820 (25.89)	65 (2.05)	2454 (77.49)	3167
1922	106 (3.31)	46 (1.44)			921 (28.77)	35 (1.09)	1735 (54.20)	3201
1923	103 (3.18)	60 (1.85)			869 (26.86)	56 (1.73)	1445 (44.67)	3235
1924	95 (2.91)	45 (1.38)			1100 (33.65)	54 (1.65)	1335 (40.84)	3269
1925	109 (3.30)	62 (1.88)			1395 (42.22)	61 (1.85)	1686 (51.03)	3304
1926	91 (2.73)	55 (1.65)			1385 (41.55)	46 (1.38)	1719 (51.58)	3333
1927	51 (1.52)	224 (6.66)		77 (2.29)	1271 (37.80)	298 (8.86)	3970 (118.08)	3362
1928	74 (2.18)	262 (7.73)		77 (2.27)	1349 (39.78)	277 (8.17)	3458 (101.98)	3391
1929	55 (1.61)	302 (8.83)		94 (2.75)	1511 (44.18)	276 (8.07)	4333 (126.70)	3420
1930	60 (1.74)	275 (7.97)		104 (3.02)	1575 (45.67)	268 (7.77)	4633 (134.33)	3449
1931	53 (1.53)	251 (7.23)		80 (2.30)	1777 (50.29)	308 (8.87)	5030 (144.79)	3474
1932	71 (2.03)	263 (7.52)		77 (2.20)	1720 (49.16)	282 (8.06)	6698 (191.43)	3499
1933	44 (1.25)	234 (6.64)		76 (2.16)	1853 (52.58)	286 (8.12)	6399 (181.58)	3524
1934	54 (1.52)	171 (4.82)		93 (2.62)	1718 (48.41)	231 (6.51)	5384 (151.70)	3549
1935	53 (1.48)	153 (4.28)		90 (2.52)	1604 (44.85)	197 (5.51)	5000 (139.82)	3576
1936	60 (1.67)	131 (3.64)		91 (2.53)	1592 (44.22)	197 (5.47)	4511 (125.31)	3600
1937	57 (1.57)	135 (3.73)		88 (2.43)	1580 (43.60)	197 (5.44)	4199 (115.87)	3624
1938	50 (1.37)	120 (3.29)		86 (2.36)	1350 (37.01)	148 (4.06)	4178 (114.53)	3648
1939	48 (1.31)	114 (3.10)		80 (2.18)	1101 (29.98)	120 (3.27)	3599 (98.01)	3672
1940	38 (1.03)	114 (3.08)		47 (1.27)	872 (23.58)	282 (7.63)	5868 (158.68)	3698
1941	39 (1.05)	116 (3.13)		41 (1.11)		328 (8.86)	6712 (181.26)	3703
1942	38 (1.02)	107 (2.89)		48 (1.29)		461 (12.43)	9965 (268.74)	3708
1943	61 (1.64)	107 (2.88)		70 (1.88)		580 (15.59)	8574 (230.42)	3721
1944	54 (1.45)	126 (3.37)		86 (2.30)		901 (24.12)	11045 (295.72)	3735
1945	84 (2.24)	186 (4.95)		123 (3.27)		1730 (46.04)	21747 (578.69)	3758
1946	51 (1.34)	148 (3.89)		135 (3.55)		1097 (28.82)	16051 (421.73)	3806
1947	63 (1.63)	115 (2.98)		124 (3.21)	1261 (32.68)	696 (18.04)	13456 (348.69)	3859
1948	41 (1.05)	143 (3.66)		79 (2.02)	1038 (26.53)	469 (11.99)	9570 (244.63)	3912
1949	38 (0.96)	95 (2.40)		171 (4.31)	969 (24.45)	332 (8.38)	6528 (164.72)	3963
1950	29 (0.72)	108 (2.69)		158 (3.94)	956 (23.85)	259 (6.46)	5630 (140.43)	4009
1951	34 (0.84)	77 (1.90)		183 (4.52)	940 (23.23)	193 (4.77)	4897 (121.00)	4047
1952	38 (0.93)	94 (2.30)		79 (1.93)	937 (22.90)	188 (4.60)	2848 (69.62)	4091
1953	50 (1.21)	74 (1.79)		172 (4.15)	925 (22.34)	211 (5.10)	5337 (128.88)	4141
1954	40 (0.95)	76 (1.81)		163 (3.75)	776 (18.52)	221 (5.27)	4651 (111.00)	4190
1955	39 (0.92)	71 (1.68)		157 (3.85)	802 (18.92)	186 (4.39)	4626 (109.16)	4238
1956	23 (0.54)	80 (1.87)		118 (2.76)	643 (15.02)	186 (4.34)	5556 (129.75)	4282
1957	25 (0.58)	74 (1.71)		161 (3.72)	634 (14.66)	204 (4.72)	7325 (169.40)	4324
1958	33 (0.76)	63 (1.44)		158 (3.62)	677 (15.53)	226 (5.18)	7711 (176.86)	4360
1959	12 (0.27)	67 (1.52)		181 (4.12)	719 (16.36)	254 (5.78)	7972 (181.39)	4395

FINLAND *

NUMBER OF OFFENSES REPORTED -- (RATE PER 100,000)   CONTINUED

YEAR	MURDER ( )	MANSLTR ( )	HOMICIDE ( )	RAPE ( )	ASSAULT (1)	ROBBERY ( )	THEFT (2)	POP
1960	37 (0.84)	72 (1.63)		222 (5.01)	674 (15.21)	294 (6.64)	7626 (172.14)	4430
1961	18 (0.40)	79 (1.77)		211 (4.72)	631 (14.13)	250 (5.60)	8162 (182.72)	4467
1962	21 (0.47)	88 (1.95)		186 (4.13)	701 (15.56)	269 (5.97)	8899 (197.54)	4505
1963	19 (0.42)	75 (1.65)		237 (5.22)	681 (14.99)	351 (7.73)	10909 (240.13)	4543
1964	16 (0.35)	71 (1.55)		299 (6.52)	692 (15.09)	315 (6.87)	12561 (273.90)	4586
1965	20 (0.43)	59 (1.28)		320 (6.94)	742 (16.10)	334 (7.25)	13802 (299.39)	4610
1966	14 (0.30)	80 (1.72)		371 (8.00)	794 (17.11)	444 (9.57)	12967 (279.46)	4640
1967	12 (0.26)	80 (1.71)		386 (8.27)	774 (16.57)	607 (13.00)	16917 (362.25)	4670
1968								
1969	22 (0.47)	93 (1.98)		407 (8.66)	1111 (23.64)	809 (17.21)	19154 (407.53)	4700
1970	14 (0.30)	42 (0.90)		325 (6.93)		947 (20.19)	21234 (452.75)	4690

FOOTNOTES:
* CONVICTIONS BEFORE 1927
1. WOUNDING WITH INJURY FROM 1941
2. LARCENY

FRANCE

CRIME STATISTICS -- (RATE PER 100,000)

YEAR	MURDER (1)	MANSLTR	HOMICIDE	RAPE	ASSAULT	ROBBERY	THEFT	POP
1931	330 (0.80)	2278 (5.53)		253 (0.61)	55 (0.13)	380 (0.92)	47105 (114.36)	41190
1932	358 (0.87)	1753 (4.25)		250 (0.61)	92 (0.22)	165 (0.40)	46188 (112.03)	41230
1933	379 (0.92)	2324 (5.63)		271 (0.66)	88 (0.21)	374 (0.91)	41379 (100.26)	41270
1934	397 (0.96)	2744 (6.64)		297 (0.72)	98 (0.24)	355 (0.86)	38506 (93.21)	41310
1935	414 (1.00)	2770 (6.70)		301 (0.73)	91 (0.22)	322 (0.78)	36810 (89.02)	41350
1936	369 (0.90)	2389 (5.82)		286 (0.70)	117 (0.29)	341 (0.83)	35512 (86.53)	41040
1937	289 (0.71)	2324 (5.71)		274 (0.67)	52 (0.13)	338 (0.83)	35791 (87.87)	41030
1938	328 (0.81)	2553 (6.32)		288 (0.71)	88 (0.22)	221 (0.55)	37400 (92.53)	40420
1939								
1940	174 (0.44)	1707 (4.29)		155 (0.39)	42 (0.11)	112 (0.28)	60438 (151.85)	39800
1941	184 (0.47)	1385 (3.57)		249 (0.64)	51 (0.13)	223 (0.58)	128776 (332.32)	38750
1942	185 (0.48)	1093 (2.82)		299 (0.77)	76 (0.20)	278 (0.72)	134070 (346.43)	38700
1943	161 (0.42)	935 (2.43)		202 (0.52)	44 (0.11)	333 (0.86)	121437 (315.42)	38500
1944	171 (0.45)	929 (2.43)		187 (0.49)	72 (0.19)	373 (0.97)	103695 (270.74)	38300
1945	319 (0.82)	1137 (2.91)		187 (0.48)	81 (0.21)	555 (1.42)	98759 (252.58)	39100
1946	641 (1.59)	1717 (4.26)		318 (0.79)	102 (0.25)	825 (2.05)	122191 (303.07)	40018
1947	668 (1.64)	1753 (4.30)		377 (0.93)	95 (0.23)	1069 (2.62)	118225 (290.17)	40743
1948	562 (1.36)	1967 (4.77)		527 (1.28)	127 (0.31)	1345 (3.26)	117341 (284.73)	41212
1949	619 (1.49)	1805 (4.34)		495 (1.19)	140 (0.34)	1266 (3.04)	87920 (211.34)	41602
1950	461 (1.10)	2124 (5.06)		602 (1.44)	96 (0.23)	1058 (2.52)	78312 (186.71)	41944
1951	344 (0.81)	2149 (5.09)		522 (1.24)	113 (0.27)	842 (1.99)	60479 (143.19)	42258
1952	277 (0.65)	2057 (4.83)		469 (1.10)	110 (0.26)	616 (1.45)	51693 (121.50)	42545
1953	158 (0.37)	1975 (4.61)		415 (0.97)	134 (0.31)	360 (0.84)	34546 (80.60)	42860
1954	163 (0.38)	2186 (5.08)		409 (0.95)	157 (0.37)	338 (0.79)	32846 (76.39)	43000
1955	153 (0.35)	2209 (5.10)		357 (0.82)	146 (0.34)	285 (0.66)	30414 (70.24)	43300
1956	127 (0.29)	2371 (5.41)		369 (0.84)	172 (0.39)	216 (0.49)	30605 (69.81)	43843
1957	173 (0.39)	3176 (7.17)		350 (0.79)	139 (0.31)	241 (0.54)	34078 (76.91)	44311
1958	217 (0.48)	3102 (6.93)		342 (0.76)	140 (0.31)	218 (0.49)	34973 (78.08)	44789
1959	149 (0.33)	2671 (5.90)		313 (0.69)	102 (0.23)	242 (0.53)	33419 (73.87)	45240
1960	179 (0.39)	2753 (6.03)		300 (0.66)	85 (0.19)	291 (0.64)	38030 (83.25)	45684
1961	182 (0.39)	1808 (3.92)		284 (0.62)	84 (0.18)	248 (0.54)	39644 (85.88)	46163
1962	207 (0.44)	3328 (7.08)		323 (0.69)	93 (0.20)	281 (0.60)	42081 (89.54)	46998
1963	238 (0.50)	3602 (7.53)		359 (0.75)	134 (0.28)	367 (0.77)	44859 (93.74)	47853
1964	238 (0.49)	3940 (8.13)		336 (0.69)	134 (0.28)	475 (0.98)	46507 (96.01)	48440
1965	264 (0.54)	4368 (8.96)		418 (0.86)	135 (0.28)	479 (0.98)	50014 (102.57)	48760
1966	251 (0.51)	4590 (9.34)		443 (0.90)	134 (0.27)	586 (1.19)	53685 (109.20)	49160
1967	231 (0.47)	4754 (9.59)		475 (0.96)	117 (0.24)	436 (0.88)	60656 (122.41)	49550
1968	219 (0.44)	4745 (9.51)		381 (0.76)	137 (0.27)	406 (0.81)	61776 (123.77)	49910
1969	221 (0.44)	3306 (6.57)		325 (0.65)	150 (0.30)	400 (0.79)	54971 (109.24)	50320
1970	199 (0.39)	3846 (7.58)		264 (0.52)	171 (0.34)	335 (0.66)	67370 (132.70)	50770
1971	181 (0.35)	4912 (9.58)		163 (0.32)	144 (0.28)	400 (0.78)	73412 (143.24)	51250

FOOTNOTES:
1. MURDER, ASSASSINATION, PARRICIDE, POISONING

GERMANY *

NUMBER OF OFFENSES REPORTED -- (RATE PER 100,000)

YEAR	MURDER ( )	MANSLTR ( )	HOMICIDE (1)	RAPE ( )	ASSAULT (2)	ROBBERY ( )	THEFT (3)	POP
1900	89 (0.18)	162 (0.32)			93079 (185.76)	446 (0.89)	94801 (189.20)	50106
1901	84 (0.17)	158 (0.31)			98110 (192.85)	527 (1.04)	101558 (199.62)	50875
1902	103 (0.20)	179 (0.35)			97376 (188.55)	597 (1.16)	103875 (201.14)	51644
1903	86 (0.16)	189 (0.36)			96177 (183.50)	516 (0.98)	100859 (192.43)	52413
1904	94 (0.18)	179 (0.34)			98985 (186.13)	566 (1.06)	98882 (185.93)	53182
1905	91 (0.17)	180 (0.33)			97673 (181.04)	556 (1.03)	100183 (185.69)	53951
1906	93 (0.17)	168 (0.31)			97943 (178.99)	564 (1.03)	104255 (190.52)	54720
1907	82 (0.15)	190 (0.34)			94471 (170.25)	602 (1.08)	105999 (191.03)	55489
1908	80 (0.14)	210 (0.37)			97235 (172.84)	708 (1.26)	115964 (206.13)	56258
1909	96 (0.17)	193 (0.34)			93175 (163.59)	675 (1.18)	115418 (202.39)	57027
1910	93 (0.16)	210 (0.36)			92193 (159.51)	695 (1.20)	114207 (197.60)	57798
1911	93 (0.16)	229 (0.39)			90881 (156.16)	662 (1.14)	110748 (190.30)	58198
1912	94 (0.16)	229 (0.39)			96848 (165.28)	695 (1.19)	118062 (201.48)	58598
1913	110 (0.19)	257 (0.44)			90990 (154.23)	754 (1.28)	114707 (194.43)	58998
1914	82 (0.14)	230 (0.39)			70604 (118.87)	687 (1.16)	98177 (165.29)	59398
1915	68 (0.11)	102 (0.17)			33081 (55.32)	511 (0.85)	91912 (153.70)	59798
1916	74 (0.12)	91 (0.15)			27905 (46.36)	614 (1.02)	109332 (181.62)	60198
1917	71 (0.12)	71 (0.12)			20475 (33.79)	435 (0.72)	137604 (227.08)	60598
1918	87 (0.14)	91 (0.15)			23121 (37.90)	316 (0.52)	161059 (264.04)	60998
1919	164 (0.27)	267 (0.43)			23092 (37.61)	972 (1.58)	159755 (260.20)	61398
1920	209 (0.34)	393 (0.64)			37406 (60.53)	1327 (2.15)	265331 (429.38)	61794
1921	243 (0.39)	383 (0.62)			33159 (53.42)	1789 (2.88)	251912 (405.86)	62068
1922	200 (0.32)	330 (0.53)			25491 (40.89)	1517 (2.43)	251529 (403.47)	62342
1923	139 (0.22)	280 (0.45)			24971 (39.88)	999 (1.60)	367435 (586.81)	62616
1924	193 (0.31)	409 (0.65)			25189 (40.05)	1155 (1.84)	224530 (357.02)	62890
1925	185 (0.29)	385 (0.61)			28371 (44.91)	864 (1.37)	112596 (178.25)	63166
1926	170 (0.27)	404 (0.64)			32146 (50.58)	811 (1.28)	95347 (150.03)	63550
1927	124 (0.19)	385 (0.60)			33064 (51.72)	707 (1.11)	89902 (140.62)	63934
1928	90 (0.14)	317 (0.49)			32677 (50.81)	683 (1.06)	86349 (134.25)	64318
1929	69 (0.11)	348 (0.54)			34950 (54.02)	811 (1.25)	91109 (140.81)	64702
1930	90 (0.14)	345 (0.53)			35429 (54.44)	1028 (1.58)	97596 (149.95)	65084
1931								
GAP								
1953			325 (0.63)	4377 (8.54)	26830 (52.37)	3584 (7.00)	541110 (1062.16)	51227
1954			390 (0.75)	4340 (8.39)	26419 (51.09)	3540 (6.85)	534507 (1033.12)	51707
1955			371 (0.71)	4574 (8.74)	26824 (51.23)	3685 (7.04)	576619 (1101.20)	52363
1956			332 (0.63)	4824 (9.10)	27986 (52.81)	4316 (8.14)	622385 (1174.42)	52995
1957			326 (0.61)	5186 (9.67)	28149 (52.47)	4471 (8.33)	714087 (1331.03)	53649
1958			330 (0.61)	5426 (10.00)	27962 (51.51)	5124 (9.44)	735679 (1355.27)	54283
1959			354 (0.65)	6030 (10.99)	29161 (53.13)	5250 (9.57)	781797 (1424.51)	54882
1960			355 (0.64)	6436 (11.61)	29072 (52.45)	5790 (10.45)	855033 (1542.74)	55423
1961			382 (0.68)	6630 (11.79)	28852 (50.96)	6158 (10.95)	906094 (1611.49)	56227
1962			397 (0.70)	6451 (11.33)	29210 (51.29)	6410 (11.26)	908186 (1594.79)	56947
1963			442 (0.77)	6572 (11.41)	30239 (52.49)	6721 (11.67)	943425 (1637.99)	57607
1964			471 (0.81)	6159 (10.57)	29858 (51.22)	7218 (12.38)	994714 (1706.49)	58290

GERMANY *

NUMBER OF OFFENSES REPORTED -- (RATE PER 100,000)   CONTINUED

YEAR	MURDER ( )	MANSLTR ( )	HOMICIDE (1)	RAPE ( )	ASSAULT (2)	ROBBERY ( )	THEFT (3)	POP
1965	482 (0.82)		5923 (10.03)	30403 (51.50)	7655 (12.97)	1034957 (1752.98)	59040	
1966	534 (0.89)		6060 (10.15)	30663 (51.38)	9010 (15.10)	1140764 (1911.47)	59680	
1967	599 (1.00)		6255 (10.45)	31860 (53.22)	9784 (16.34)	1242510 (2075.35)	59870	
1968	539 (0.90)		6319 (10.50)	32668 (54.29)	9737 (16.18)	1308067 (2217.95)	60170	
1969	662 (1.09)		6766 (11.12)	34955 (57.45)	11503 (18.91)	1360812 (2236.71)	60840	
1970	779 (1.28)		6889 (11.36)	37895 (62.48)	13230 (21.81)	1549694 (2555.14)	60650	
1971	666 (1.09)		6555 (10.70)	35133 (57.32)	15531 (25.34)	1608645 (2624.65)	61290	
1972	779 (1.26)		7001 (11.35)	39218 (63.59)	18786 (30.46)	1702493 (2760.65)	61670	

FOOTNOTES:
* WEST GERMANY FROM 1953, CONVICTIONS 1900-1930
1. MURDER AND NON-NEGLIGENT MANSLAUGHTER
2. DANGEROUS (AND FROM 1953 GRIEVOUS) ASSAULT
3. GRAND LARCENY AND PLAIN THEFT BEFORE 1952

GHANA *

NUMBER OF OFFENSES REPORTED -- (RATE PER 100,000)

YEAR	MURDER ( )	MANSLTR ( )	HOMICIDE ( )	RAPE (1)	ASSAULT ( )	ROBBERY ( )	THEFT ( )	POP
1955	280 (4.80)			554 (9.50)		1616 (27.72)	13841 (237.41)	5830
1956	333 (5.53)			629 (10.45)		1862 (30.93)	14857 (246.79)	6020
1957	261 (4.21)			601 (9.69)		2096 (33.81)	17320 (279.35)	6200
1958	246 (3.85)			880 (13.77)		1653 (25.87)	17888 (279.94)	6390
1959	215 (3.27)			835 (12.69)		1455 (22.11)	18271 (277.67)	6580
1960	246 (3.63)			864 (12.75)		1233 (18.19)	19591 (289.08)	6777
1961	195 (2.80)			546 (7.84)		594 (8.53)	20473 (294.15)	6960
1962	183 (2.56)			469 (6.56)		653 (9.14)	23202 (324.59)	7148
1963								
1964								
1965	161 (2.09)			469 (6.08)		539 (6.99)	28103 (364.41)	7712
1966	195 (2.47)			383 (4.85)		654 (8.28)	32188 (407.55)	7898
1967	213 (2.63)			380 (4.70)			32996 (408.16)	8084
1968	240 (2.90)			373 (4.51)			33920 (410.16)	8270
1969	288 (3.41)			446 (5.27)		738 (8.73)	35642 (421.50)	8456
1970	193 (2.23)			366 (4.24)		807 (9.34)	37175 (430.27)	8640

FOOTNOTES:
* 1965-1970: RAW CRIME DATA FROM INTERPOL; RATES COMPUTED FROM POPULATION FIGURES ABOVE
1. SEX OFFENSES

GREECE * CRIME STATISTICS -- (RATE PER 100,000)

YEAR	MURDER ( )	MANSLTR ( )	HOMICIDE ( )	RAPE ( )	ASSAULT (1)	ROBBERY ( )	THEFT (2)	POP
1965					14362 (167.98)		8416 (98.43)	8550
1966					16301 (189.53)		9988 (116.00)	8610
1967					15997 (183.45)		7877 (90.33)	8720
1968					10820 (123.80)		5983 (68.46)	8740
1969					14212 (162.05)		6874 (78.38)	8770

FOOTNOTES:
* PERSONS SENTENCED
1. CRIMES AGAINST THE PERSON
2. CRIMES AGAINST PROPERTY

GUAM NUMBER OF OFFENSES REPORTED -- (RATE PER 100,000)

YEAR	MURDER ( )	MANSLTR ( )	HOMICIDE ( )	RAPE ( )	ASSAULT (1)	ROBBERY ( )	THEFT (2)	POP
1965		15 (18.75)		2 (2.50)	25 (31.25)	8 (10.00)	535 (668.75)	80
1966		7 (8.75)		6 (7.50)	25 (31.25)	8 (10.00)	667 (833.75)	80
1967		8 (8.89)		2 (2.22)	31 (34.44)	18 (20.00)	687 (763.33)	90
1968		17 (17.00)		6 (6.00)	32 (32.00)	10 (10.00)	929 (929.00)	100
1969		15 (15.00)		6 (6.00)	31 (31.00)	26 (26.00)	895 (895.00)	100
1970		13 (14.44)		8 (8.89)	43 (47.78)	10 (11.11)	918 (1020.00)	90
1971		21 (23.33)		14 (15.56)	57 (63.33)	15 (16.67)	887 (985.56)	90
1972		29 (32.22)		24 (26.67)	103 (114.44)	66 (73.33)	1147 (1274.44)	90
1973		28 (31.11)		22 (24.44)	85 (94.44)	79 (87.78)	1246 (1384.44)	90
1974		33 (36.67)		20 (22.22)	95 (105.56)	86 (95.56)	1422 (1580.00)	90

FOOTNOTES:
1. AGGRAVATED ASSAULT
2. LARCENY

GUYANA

NUMBER OF OFFENSES REPORTED -- (RATE PER 100,000)

YEAR	MURDER ( )	MANSLTR ( )	HOMICIDE ( )	RAPE (1)	ASSAULT (2)	ROBBERY (3)	THEFT (4)	POP
1961	25 (4.29)	8 (1.37)		54 (9.26)	146 (25.04)	107 (18.35)	647 (110.98)	583
1962	31 (5.18)	15 (2.51)		66 (11.04)	154 (25.75)	169 (28.26)	1158 (193.65)	598
1963	46 (7.54)	15 (2.46)		56 (9.18)	174 (28.52)	264 (43.28)	1022 (167.54)	610
1964	166 (26.43)	5 (0.80)		84 (13.38)	218 (34.71)	267 (42.52)	678 (107.96)	628
1965	43 (6.69)	6 (0.93)		96 (14.93)	251 (39.04)	338 (52.57)	794 (123.48)	643
1966	40 (6.08)	1 (0.15)		99 (15.05)	241 (36.63)	308 (46.81)	863 (131.16)	658
1967	30 (4.46)	3 (0.45)		94 (13.97)	224 (33.28)	252 (37.44)	1285 (190.94)	673
1968	52 (7.56)	3 (0.44)		118 (17.15)	178 (25.87)	299 (43.46)	1011 (146.95)	688
1969	44 (6.26)	2 (0.28)		122 (17.35)	219 (31.15)	459 (65.29)	859 (122.19)	703
1970	47 (6.53)	3 (0.42)		148 (20.56)	259 (35.97)	434 (60.28)	966 (134.17)	720
1971	49 (6.62)	6 (0.81)		128 (17.30)	290 (39.19)	571 (77.16)	855 (115.54)	740
1972	63 (8.40)	2 (0.27)		138 (18.40)	246 (32.80)	452 (60.27)	943 (125.73)	750

FOOTNOTES:
1. RAPE AND SEXUAL CRIMES
2. WOUNDING AND WOUNDING WITH INTENT
3. ROBBERY AND EXTORTION
4. HOUSE AND SHOP BREAKING, LARCENY IN DWELLING HOUSES

HONG KONG

NUMBER OF OFFENSES REPORTED -- (RATE PER 100,000)

YEAR	MURDER ( )	MANSLTR ( )	HOMICIDE (1)	RAPE ( )	ASSAULT ( )	ROBBERY ( )	THEFT ( )	POP
1953			28 (1.24)	3 (0.13)	194 (8.62)	102 (4.53)	11780 (523.56)	2250
1954			38 (1.61)	4 (0.17)	336 (14.24)	109 (4.62)	13477 (571.06)	2360
1955			28 (1.12)	1 (0.04)	316 (12.69)	141 (5.66)	13261 (532.57)	2490
1956			39 (1.49)	3 (0.11)	414 (15.83)	127 (4.86)	14534 (555.79)	2615
1957			17 (0.62)	3 (0.11)	341 (12.46)	122 (4.46)	12413 (453.69)	2736
1958			30 (1.05)	4 (0.14)	432 (15.14)	104 (3.64)	9665 (338.65)	2854
1959			24 (0.81)	1 (0.03)	404 (13.62)	82 (2.76)	9241 (311.46)	2967
1960			30 (0.98)	2 (0.07)	539 (17.53)	89 (2.89)	8578 (278.96)	3075
1961			25 (0.79)	1 (0.03)	638 (20.08)	114 (3.59)	9821 (309.03)	3178
1962			20 (0.60)	4 (0.12)	675 (20.39)	130 (3.93)	8902 (268.94)	3310
1963			25 (0.73)	3 (0.09)	633 (18.51)	153 (4.47)	8274 (241.93)	3420
1964			42 (1.20)	2 (0.06)	941 (26.89)	230 (6.57)	8779 (250.83)	3500
1965			33 (0.92)	5 (0.14)	905 (25.14)	380 (10.56)	11329 (314.69)	3600
1966			40 (1.10)	12 (0.33)	1054 (29.04)	520 (14.33)	11664 (321.32)	3630
1967			73 (1.96)	13 (0.35)	1065 (28.63)	1224 (32.90)	10854 (291.77)	3720
1968			50 (1.32)	10 (0.26)	1060 (27.89)	1801 (47.39)	10610 (279.21)	3800
1969			55 (1.42)	31 (0.80)	1266 (32.80)	2327 (60.28)	10452 (270.78)	3860
1970			71 (1.79)	28 (0.71)	1337 (33.76)	3006 (75.91)	11579 (292.40)	3960
1971			98 (2.42)	45 (1.11)	1598 (39.46)	5146 (127.06)	11937 (294.74)	4050
1972			115 (2.82)	62 (1.52)	1726 (42.30)	7404 (181.47)	10728 (262.94)	4080
1973			110 (2.64)	64 (1.54)	2237 (53.77)	8717 (209.54)	13210 (317.55)	4160

FOOTNOTES:
1. MURDER AND MANSLAUGHTER

HUNGARY *

NUMBER OF CONVICTIONS -- (RATE PER 100,000)

YEAR	MURDER (1)	MANSLTR ( )	HOMICIDE ( )	RAPE ( )	ASSAULT ( )	ROBBERY ( )	THEFT ( )	POP
1900	231 (1.30)	347 (1.96)		91 (0.51)	3258 (18.36)	82 (0.46)	15331 (86.38)	17748
1901	319 (1.78)	456 (2.55)		144 (0.80)	4837 (27.03)	80 (0.45)	18193 (101.67)	17894
1902	388 (2.15)	455 (2.52)		191 (1.06)	5990 (33.20)	101 (0.56)	20511 (113.70)	18040
1903	353 (1.95)	551 (3.04)		253 (1.40)	6581 (36.32)	124 (0.68)	22296 (123.06)	18118
1904	422 (2.30)	512 (2.79)		281 (1.53)	25584 (139.53)	144 (0.79)	20025 (110.30)	18336
1905	439 (2.37)	463 (2.50)		212 (1.15)	28246 (152.80)	213 (1.15)	25822 (139.68)	18486
1906	419 (2.25)	487 (2.61)		239 (1.28)	30268 (162.41)	197 (1.06)	24424 (131.05)	18637
1907	429 (2.28)	520 (2.77)		285 (1.52)	27753 (147.70)	142 (0.76)	23306 (124.03)	18790
1908	471 (2.49)	480 (2.53)		311 (1.64)	27993 (147.77)	158 (0.83)	24505 (129.35)	18944
1909	511 (2.68)	521 (2.73)		355 (1.86)	24929 (130.53)	182 (0.95)	21105 (110.51)	19098
1910	478 (2.48)	520 (2.70)		369 (1.92)	25934 (134.69)	214 (1.11)	19769 (102.67)	19255
1911	504 (2.60)	587 (3.02)		428 (2.20)	25177 (129.70)	197 (1.01)	20093 (103.51)	19412
1912	460 (2.35)	616 (3.15)		418 (2.14)	25571 (130.67)	161 (0.82)	14208 (72.60)	19569
1913	489 (2.48)	637 (3.23)		374 (1.90)	23293 (118.08)	189 (0.96)	21165 (107.29)	19727
1914	391 (1.97)	609 (3.06)		366 (1.84)	18115 (91.09)	143 (0.72)	18409 (92.57)	19887
1915	316 (1.58)	593 (2.96)		228 (1.14)	10894 (54.34)	137 (0.68)	22198 (110.72)	20048
1916	260 (1.29)	530 (2.62)		170 (0.84)	8893 (44.00)	123 (0.61)	20523 (101.54)	20211
1917	215 (1.06)	474 (2.33)		113 (0.55)	8250 (40.49)	107 (0.53)	23867 (117.14)	20374
1918								
1919								
1920								
1921	194 (2.41)	100 (1.24)		50 (0.62)	5171 (64.24)	118 (1.47)	16269 (202.12)	8049
1922	222 (2.74)	161 (1.98)		88 (1.08)	6347 (78.25)	140 (1.73)	22644 (279.18)	8111
1923	251 (3.07)	195 (2.39)		96 (1.17)	8121 (99.36)	107 (1.31)	27647 (338.27)	8173
1924	269 (3.27)	242 (2.94)		148 (1.80)	8882 (107.86)	127 (1.54)	26268 (318.98)	8235
1925	266 (3.21)	331 (3.99)		240 (2.89)	8447 (101.78)	103 (1.24)	18276 (220.22)	8299
1926	238 (2.84)	284 (3.39)		226 (2.70)	8374 (100.06)	99 (1.18)	12941 (154.63)	8369
1927	238 (2.82)	309 (3.66)		214 (2.54)	8136 (96.41)	80 (0.95)	12466 (147.72)	8439
1928	238 (2.80)	375 (4.41)		234 (2.75)	8697 (102.21)	73 (0.86)	12268 (144.18)	8509
1929	265 (3.09)	417 (4.86)		325 (3.79)	8805 (102.63)	70 (0.82)	11534 (134.44)	8579
1930	338 (3.91)	429 (4.96)		386 (4.46)	9864 (114.05)	70 (0.81)	11905 (137.65)	8649
1931	400 (4.59)	526 (6.04)		355 (4.07)	11423 (131.07)	93 (1.07)	12746 (146.25)	8715
1932	423 (4.82)	490 (5.58)		347 (3.95)	12749 (145.19)	131 (1.49)	16422 (187.02)	8781
1933	335 (3.79)	484 (5.47)		351 (3.97)	13573 (153.42)	111 (1.25)	18735 (211.77)	8847
1934	330 (3.70)	397 (4.45)		314 (3.52)	12130 (136.09)	104 (1.17)	17506 (196.41)	8913
1935	301 (3.35)	377 (4.20)		260 (2.90)	11797 (131.37)	108 (1.20)	19240 (214.25)	8980
1936	354 (3.92)	449 (4.97)		312 (3.45)	12074 (133.56)	129 (1.43)	20859 (230.74)	9040
1937	372 (4.09)	476 (5.23)		306 (3.36)	11684 (128.40)	95 (1.04)	19143 (210.36)	9100
1938	413 (4.51)	467 (5.10)		287 (3.13)	11647 (127.15)	141 (1.54)	17929 (195.73)	9160
1939								
GAP								
1951	347 (3.68)	305 (3.24)				107 (1.14)	18556 (197.01)	9419
1952	268 (2.82)	222 (2.34)				115 (1.21)	27251 (286.70)	9498
1953	253 (2.64)	166 (1.73)				178 (1.86)	26791 (279.51)	9585
1954	269 (2.78)	86 (0.89)			7105 (73.32)	156 (1.61)	23647 (244.01)	9691
1955	515 (5.25)	90 (0.92)			8243 (84.04)	188 (1.92)	34622 (353.00)	9808

HUNGARY *

NUMBER OF CONVICTIONS -- (RATE PER 100,000)   CONTINUED

YEAR	MURDER (1)	MANSLTR ( )	HOMICIDE ( )	RAPE ( )	ASSAULT ( )	ROBBERY ( )	THEFT ( )	POP
1956	336 (3.39)	74 (0.75)				107 (1.08)	17774 (179.34)	9911
1957	447 (4.54)	62 (0.63)				104 (1.06)	9617 (97.73)	9840
1958	458 (4.63)	96 (0.97)		290 (2.93)	7160 (72.24)	109 (1.10)	10770 (108.99)	9882
1959	409 (4.12)	118 (1.19)		413 (4.16)	7856 (79.84)	136 (1.37)	11009 (110.79)	9937
1960	340 (3.41)	82 (0.82)		382 (3.83)	8456 (85.57)	159 (1.59)	8867 (88.81)	9984
1961	301 (3.00)	94 (0.94)		371 (3.70)	12749 (128.30)	113 (1.13)	10474 (104.45)	10028
1962	393 (3.91)	56 (0.56)		475 (4.72)	8785 (87.99)	130 (1.29)	11133 (110.66)	10061
1963	386 (3.83)	46 (0.46)		370 (3.67)	8940 (89.15)	165 (1.64)	7798 (77.30)	10088
1964	480 (4.75)	49 (0.49)		468 (4.63)	9049 (89.94)	173 (1.71)	10163 (100.62)	10100
1965	485 (4.79)	59 (0.58)		469 (4.63)	6426 (63.70)	189 (1.87)	12554 (123.73)	10130
1966	466 (4.58)	62 (0.61)		439 (4.32)	7560 (74.85)	199 (1.96)	13953 (137.20)	10170
1967	424 (4.15)	63 (0.62)		528 (5.17)	7778 (76.78)	279 (2.73)	13671 (133.90)	10210
1968	372 (3.63)	32 (0.31)		429 (4.19)	7735 (76.06)	294 (2.87)	10934 (106.67)	10250
1969	406 (3.95)	46 (0.45)		521 (5.06)	8715 (85.36)	261 (2.54)	8095 (78.67)	10290
1970	430 (4.17)	27 (0.26)		680 (6.59)	7988 (77.93)	376 (3.64)	5775 (55.96)	10320
1971	370 (3.57)	52 (0.50)		604 (5.84)	7144 (69.43)	495 (4.78)	8592 (83.01)	10350
1972	422 (4.07)	41 (0.39)		560 (5.39)	6343 (61.46)	482 (4.64)	9515 (91.67)	10380

FOOTNOTES:
* BORDER CHANGE AFTER 1920; COMPUTED RATES BASED ON
  QUESTIONABLE POPULATION ESTIMATES: 1900-1917
1. FROM 1962 INCLUDES INTENT TO COMMIT MURDER

ICELAND

NUMBER OF OFFENSES REPORTED -- (RATE PER 100,000)

YEAR	MURDER ( )	MANSLTR ( )	HOMICIDE ( )	RAPE ( )	ASSAULT ( )	ROBBERY ( )	THEFT ( )	POP
1969	1 (0.50)	0 (0.00)		0 (0.00)	5 (2.50)		99 (49.50)	200
1970	1 (0.50)	1 (0.50)		2 (1.00)	3 (1.50)		63 (31.50)	200
1971	1 (0.48)	5 (2.38)		3 (1.43)	11 (5.24)		82 (39.05)	210

INDIA

NUMBER OF OFFENSES REPORTED -- (RATE PER 100,000)

YEAR	MURDER ( )	MANSLTR ( )	HOMICIDE ( )	RAPE ( )	ASSAULT ( )	ROBBERY (1)	THEFT ( )	POP
1953	9802 (2.63)					13986 (3.76)	256567 (68.97)	372000
1954	9765 (2.59)					12995 (3.45)	223866 (59.38)	377000
1955	9700 (2.51)					11489 (2.97)	212028 (54.84)	386621
1956	10025 (2.54)					13015 (3.30)	236214 (59.92)	394217
1957	10419 (2.59)					12968 (3.22)	233239 (57.99)	402225
1958	10661 (2.60)					11778 (2.87)	236103 (57.49)	410686
1959	10712 (2.55)					10141 (2.42)	233052 (55.54)	419613
1960	10910 (2.54)					10244 (2.39)	228842 (53.34)	429027
1961	11188 (2.55)					10641 (2.42)	232868 (53.05)	439000
1962	11586 (2.58)					12441 (2.77)	252453 (56.15)	449641
1963	10754 (2.34)					12691 (2.76)	242487 (52.66)	460490
1964	11748 (2.49)					13623 (2.89)	273676 (58.03)	471627
1965	12310 (2.55)					13022 (2.69)	273702 (56.62)	483410
1966	12631 (2.56)					13402 (2.71)	298701 (60.45)	494110
1967	13398 (2.65)					16552 (3.28)	339861 (67.29)	505080
1968	13841 (2.68)					16551 (3.21)	315513 (61.10)	516350
1969	14732 (2.79)					15971 (3.03)	300140 (56.85)	527950
1970	15708 (2.91)					26795 (4.96)	337211 (62.46)	539860
1971	16180 (2.93)					29595 (5.36)	335204 (60.74)	551830

FOOTNOTES:
   1. INCLUDES "DACOITY" (ROBBERY COMMITTED BY GROUPS)

INDONESIA *

NUMBER OF OFFENSES REPORTED -- (RATE PER 100,000)

YEAR	MURDER ( )	MANSLTR ( )	HOMICIDE (1)	RAPE ( )	ASSAULT (2)	ROBBERY ( )	THEFT ( )	POP
1920	594 (1.14)	462 (0.88)			2920 (5.58)		24077 (46.01)	52327
1921	613 (1.15)	517 (0.97)			3684 (6.93)		21280 (40.05)	53130
1922	586 (1.09)	464 (0.86)			3732 (6.92)		18440 (34.18)	53945
1923	556 (1.02)	592 (1.08)			3945 (7.20)		15929 (29.09)	54754
1924			1104 (1.99)		4230 (7.61)		16094 (28.97)	55563
1925			1155 (2.05)		4748 (8.42)		16545 (29.35)	56371
1926			1095 (1.91)		4860 (8.49)		17898 (31.27)	57242
1927			1305 (2.25)		4931 (8.49)		16661 (28.67)	58113
1928			1257 (2.13)		5345 (9.06)		14612 (24.77)	58984
1929								
GAP								
1952	4015 (5.10)					48460 (61.58)	187034 (237.65)	78700
1953	3823 (4.78)					14893 (18.64)	160465 (200.83)	79900
1954	3464 (4.27)					12569 (15.50)	163357 (201.43)	81100
1955	2979 (3.55)					13108 (15.63)	193537 (230.79)	83858
1956	3216 (3.75)					16357 (19.10)	199556 (232.98)	85654
1957	3056 (3.49)					15595 (17.82)	190780 (218.00)	87514
1958	2615 (2.92)					16006 (17.90)	235934 (263.79)	89441
1959	2720 (2.97)					13818 (15.11)	235617 (257.68)	91438
1960	2310 (2.47)					11618 (12.42)	226372 (242.09)	93506
1961	2117 (2.21)					9033 (9.44)	197882 (206.87)	95655
1962	1301 (1.33)					6198 (6.34)	246192 (251.82)	97765
1963	1270 (1.27)					4831 (4.83)	213760 (213.66)	100045
1964	1225 (1.20)					5412 (5.30)	237031 (232.22)	102070
1965	3497 (3.35)					6229 (5.97)	192387 (184.38)	104340
1966	1634 (1.53)					4434 (4.16)	144886 (135.90)	106610

FOOTNOTES:
* NUMBER SENTENCED BEFORE 1929
1. MURDER AND MANSLAUGHTER
2. WOUNDING

IRAN *

NUMBER OF OFFENSES REPORTED -- (RATE PER 100,000)

YEAR	MURDER ( )	MANSLTR ( )	HOMICIDE ( )	RAPE (1)	ASSAULT ( )	ROBBERY ( )	THEFT ( )	POP
1966	129 (0.51)			2939 (11.51)		851 (3.33)	2939 (11.51)	25540
1967	103 (0.39)			2655 (10.10)		825 (3.14)	3867 (14.70)	26300
1968	49 (0.18)			1774 (6.55)		1215 (4.49)	2700 (9.97)	27080

FOOTNOTES:
* RAW CRIME DATA FROM INTERPOL; RATES COMPUTED FROM
  POPULATION FIGURES ABOVE
  1. SEX OFFENSES

IRAQ *

NUMBER OF OFFENSES REPORTED -- (RATE PER 100,000)

YEAR	MURDER ( )	MANSLTR ( )	HOMICIDE ( )	RAPE (1)	ASSAULT ( )	ROBBERY ( )	THEFT ( )	POP
1967	2083 (24.28)			213 (2.48)		213 (2.48)	952 (11.10)	8580
1968	1896 (21.40)			162 (1.83)		137 (1.55)	714 (8.06)	8860
1969	1890 (20.66)			180 (1.97)		360 (3.93)	900 (9.84)	9150
1970	1935 (20.50)			333 (3.53)		468 (4.96)	1323 (14.01)	9440

FOOTNOTES:
* RAW CRIME DATA FROM INTERPOL; RATES COMPUTED FROM
  POPULATION FIGURES ABOVE
  1. SEX OFFENSES

IRELAND (EIRE) *

NUMBER OF OFFENSES REPORTED -- (RATE PER 100,000)

YEAR	MURDER ( )	MANSLTR ( )	HOMICIDE ( )	RAPE (1)	ASSAULT (2)	ROBBERY ( )	THEFT (3)	POP
1900	38 (0.85)	54 (1.21)		88 (1.97)	20199 (452.28)	61 (1.37)	782 (17.51)	4466
1901	25 (0.56)	37 (0.83)		97 (2.18)	20199 (452.99)	94 (2.11)	807 (18.10)	4459
1902	39 (0.88)	36 (0.81)		78 (1.75)	20199 (453.71)	108 (2.43)	678 (15.23)	4452
1903	26 (0.58)	47 (1.06)		77 (1.73)	16260 (365.72)	90 (2.02)	616 (13.86)	4446
1904	29 (0.65)	43 (0.97)		87 (1.96)	16260 (366.30)	81 (1.82)	644 (14.51)	4439
1905	36 (0.81)	45 (1.02)		81 (1.83)	16260 (366.88)	88 (1.99)	588 (13.27)	4432
1906	19 (0.43)	44 (0.99)		60 (1.36)	16260 (367.37)	68 (1.54)	550 (12.43)	4426
1907	23 (0.52)	41 (0.93)		62 (1.40)	16260 (367.96)	82 (1.86)	539 (12.20)	4419
1908	28 (0.63)	29 (0.66)		59 (1.34)	13704 (310.54)	102 (2.31)	534 (12.10)	4413
1909	29 (0.66)	40 (0.91)		60 (1.36)	13704 (311.03)	36 (0.82)	383 (8.69)	4406
1910	33 (0.75)	55 (1.25)		76 (1.73)	13704 (311.53)	33 (0.75)	408 (9.27)	4399
1911	25 (0.57)	35 (0.80)		75 (1.71)	13704 (312.09)	48 (1.09)	445 (10.13)	4391
1912	25 (0.57)	55 (1.25)		65 (1.48)	13151 (299.77)	43 (0.98)	387 (8.82)	4387
GAP								
1923	83 (2.74)	63 (2.11)		102 (3.42)	813 (27.24)	308 (10.32)	3426 (114.77)	3031
1924	48 (1.60)	68 (2.29)		134 (4.51)	890 (29.94)	207 (6.96)	4301 (144.67)	3007
1925	33 (1.11)	80 (2.70)		130 (4.39)	55 (1.86)	88 (2.97)	3943 (133.16)	2985
1926	50 (1.68)	23 (0.78)		152 (5.15)	88 (2.98)	59 (2.00)	3292 (111.16)	2973
1927	28 (0.95)	32 (1.09)		16 (0.54)	1118 (38.07)	40 (1.36)	3462 (117.88)	2961
1928	22 (0.75)							2949
1929	21 (0.72)							2937
1930	16 (0.55)	38 (1.30)		13 (0.44)	967 (33.04)	33 (1.13)	3521 (120.29)	2927
1931	17 (0.58)	35 (1.19)		23 (0.78)	963 (32.80)	38 (1.29)	3527 (120.13)	2936
1932	13 (0.44)	42 (1.43)		8 (0.27)	857 (29.10)	55 (1.87)	3621 (122.95)	2945
1933	19 (0.64)	30 (1.02)		138 (4.67)	993 (33.62)	56 (1.90)	3933 (133.14)	2954
1934	7 (0.24)	45 (1.52)		154 (5.20)	1353 (45.66)	86 (2.90)	3793 (128.01)	2963
1935	17 (0.57)	51 (1.72)		18 (0.61)	1314 (44.23)	34 (1.14)	3423 (115.21)	2971
1936	16 (0.54)	50 (1.68)		15 (0.51)	1257 (42.35)	32 (1.08)	3712 (125.07)	2968
1937	12 (0.40)	58 (1.96)		13 (0.44)	896 (30.22)	15 (0.51)	3840 (129.51)	2965
1938	14 (0.47)	8 (0.27)		4 (0.14)	1064 (35.92)	27 (0.91)	4360 (147.20)	2962
1939	10 (0.34)	12 (0.41)			1137 (38.43)	32 (1.08)	5707 (192.87)	2959
1940	12 (0.41)	12 (0.41)		6 (0.20)	904 (30.56)	41 (1.39)	6293 (212.75)	2958
1941	9 (0.30)	15 (0.51)		9 (0.30)	971 (32.79)	56 (1.89)	9760 (329.62)	2961
1942	8 (0.27)	11 (0.37)		14 (0.47)	1238 (41.78)	42 (1.42)	12790 (431.66)	2963
1943	13 (0.44)	19 (0.64)		10 (0.34)	1314 (44.60)	75 (2.55)	12630 (428.72)	2946
1944	8 (0.27)	13 (0.44)		11 (0.37)	1245 (42.29)	33 (1.12)	11532 (391.71)	2944
1945	6 (0.20)	14 (0.47)		16 (0.54)	1612 (54.61)	32 (1.08)	12116 (410.43)	2952
1946	8 (0.27)	7 (0.24)		12 (0.41)	1514 (51.20)	31 (1.05)	10900 (368.62)	2957
1947	3 (0.10)	14 (0.47)		12 (0.40)	1138 (38.26)	24 (0.81)	10886 (366.04)	2974
1948	17 (0.57)	5 (0.17)		18 (0.60)	1330 (44.56)	33 (1.11)	10221 (342.41)	2985
1949	6 (0.20)	9 (0.30)		16 (0.54)	1369 (45.92)	28 (0.94)	8388 (281.38)	2981
1950	9 (0.30)	5 (0.17)		14 (0.47)	1258 (42.37)	32 (1.08)	8414 (283.40)	2969
1951	5 (0.17)	3 (0.10)		9 (0.30)	1395 (47.11)	24 (0.81)	9797 (330.87)	2961
1952	10 (0.34)	3 (0.10)		17 (0.58)	1412 (47.88)	23 (0.78)	10561 (358.12)	2949

IRELAND (EIRE) *   NUMBER OF OFFENSES REPORTED -- (RATE PER 100,000)   CONTINUED

YEAR	MURDER ( )	MANSLTR ( )	HOMICIDE ( )	RAPE (1)	ASSAULT (2)	ROBBERY ( )	THEFT (3)	POP
1953	12 (0.41)	7 (0.24)		9 (0.31)	1497 (50.83)	36 (1.22)	11229 (381.29)	2945
1954	4 (0.14)	1 (0.03)		12 (0.41)	1466 (49.98)	24 (0.82)	8243 (281.04)	2933
1955	5 (0.17)	3 (0.10)		12 (0.41)	1388 (47.71)	41 (1.41)	8141 (279.86)	2909
1956	4 (0.14)	3 (0.10)		6 (0.21)	1563 (53.93)	27 (0.93)	8900 (307.11)	2898
1957	12 (0.42)	2 (0.07)		9 (0.31)	1402 (48.60)	33 (1.14)	9842 (341.14)	2885
1958	10 (0.35)	2 (0.07)		10 (0.35)	1500 (52.58)	61 (2.14)	11766 (412.41)	2853
1959	9 (0.32)	2 (0.07)		5 (0.18)	1545 (54.29)	59 (2.07)	12655 (444.66)	2846
1960	4 (0.14)	2 (0.07)		12 (0.42)	1592 (56.18)	59 (2.08)	10709 (377.88)	2834
1961	11 (0.39)	2 (0.07)		7 (0.25)	1779 (63.13)	42 (1.49)	9861 (349.93)	2818
1962	6 (0.21)	6 (0.21)		12 (0.42)	1824 (64.59)	39 (1.38)	9817 (347.63)	2824
1963	4 (0.14)	1 (0.04)		13 (0.46)	2236 (78.70)	42 (1.48)	10002 (352.06)	2841
1964	9 (0.32)	5 (0.18)		19 (0.67)	2363 (82.94)	62 (2.18)	11150 (391.37)	2849
1965	7 (0.24)	5 (0.17)		22 (0.76)	2692 (93.47)	77 (2.67)	10140 (352.08)	2880
1966	8 (0.28)	7 (0.24)		13 (0.45)	2876 (99.86)	73 (2.53)	11791 (409.41)	2880
1967	9 (0.31)	4 (0.14)		15 (0.52)	3047 (105.07)	86 (2.97)	12481 (430.38)	2900
1968	12 (0.41)	3 (0.10)		16 (0.55)	3364 (115.60)	101 (3.47)	13893 (477.42)	2910
1969	8 (0.27)	5 (0.17)		10 (0.34)	3680 (125.60)	147 (5.02)	15477 (528.23)	2930
1970	12 (0.41)	7 (0.24)		15 (0.51)	3645 (123.56)	215 (7.29)	18570 (629.49)	2950
1971	10 (0.34)	4 (0.13)		24 (0.81)	4365 (146.97)	314 (10.57)	23242 (782.56)	2970
1972	22 (0.73)	6 (0.20)		26 (0.86)	4840 (160.80)	618 (20.53)	24280 (806.64)	3010
1973	23 (0.76)	6 (0.20)		42 (1.38)	6258 (206.33)	619 (20.41)	22206 (732.15)	3033

FOOTNOTES:
* ENTIRE NATION OF IRELAND, 1900-1912;
  REPUBLIC OF IRELAND, 1923-1973
  1. RAPE AND INDECENT ASSAULT
  2. ASSAULT FIGURES YEARLY AVERAGE FOR 1900-1902,
     1903-1907,1908-1911
  3. LARCENIES

ISRAEL

NUMBER OF OFFENSES REPORTED -- (RATE PER 100,000)

YEAR	MURDER ( )	MANSLTR ( )	HOMICIDE ( )	RAPE ( )	ASSAULT (1)	ROBBERY ( )	THEFT ( )	POP
1949	47 (4.41)				1334 (125.14)	196 (18.39)	7257 (680.77)	1066
1950	50 (3.97)				1982 (157.55)	201 (15.98)	9142 (726.71)	1258
1951	61 (4.02)				2618 (172.69)	165 (10.88)	12774 (842.61)	1516
1952	61 (3.80)				3035 (188.86)	157 (9.77)	16840 (1047.92)	1607
1953	66 (4.00)				2584 (156.61)	125 (7.58)	14571 (883.09)	1650
1954	55 (3.26)				3051 (180.75)	85 (5.04)	15291 (905.87)	1688
1955	30 (1.72)				3827 (218.94)	60 (3.43)	14462 (827.35)	1748
1956	56 (3.07)				7233 (395.90)	49 (2.68)	16434 (899.51)	1827
1957	30 (1.55)				8091 (417.71)	72 (3.72)	17800 (918.95)	1937
1958	30 (1.50)				8740 (437.66)	67 (3.36)	18643 (933.55)	1997
1959	34 (1.65)				8906 (432.12)	55 (2.67)	19391 (940.85)	2061
1960	26 (1.23)				6616 (312.96)	46 (2.18)	21611 (1022.28)	2114
1961	24 (1.10)				6120 (280.09)	63 (2.88)	24287 (1111.53)	2185
1962	23 (1.00)				6522 (284.55)	71 (3.10)	25921 (1130.93)	2292
1963	24 (1.01)				7191 (302.65)	111 (4.67)	28936 (1217.85)	2376
1964	35 (1.41)				6810 (275.15)	58 (2.34)	35382 (1429.58)	2475
1965	29 (1.13)				7373 (288.01)	47 (1.84)	40417 (1578.79)	2560
1966	30 (1.14)				6846 (260.30)	75 (2.85)	44478 (1691.18)	2630
1967	29 (1.09)				5751 (215.39)	66 (2.47)	47552 (1780.97)	2670
1968	45 (1.64)				5774 (210.73)	97 (3.54)	47668 (1739.71)	2740
1969	19 (0.67)				5858 (207.73)	97 (3.44)	52561 (1863.87)	2820
1970	46 (1.58)				5655 (194.33)	181 (6.22)	67459 (2318.18)	2910

FOOTNOTES:
   1. INCLUDES CAUSING DAMAGE TO PROPERTY 1956-59

ITALY

NUMBER OF OFFENSES REPORTED -- (RATE PER 100,000)

YEAR	MURDER (1)	MANSLTR (2)	HOMICIDE ( )	RAPE ( )	ASSAULT (3)	ROBBERY ( )	THEFT ( )	POP
1900	3479 (10.78)				87996 (272.59)	3210 (9.94)	135021 (418.25)	32282
1901	3168 (9.76)				81251 (250.20)	3333 (10.26)	147452 (454.05)	32475
1902	3202 (9.80)				89589 (274.24)	3656 (11.19)	135489 (414.75)	32668
1903	3106 (9.45)				93768 (285.35)	3910 (11.90)	145594 (443.06)	32861
1904	3011 (9.11)				94793 (286.78)	3462 (10.47)	134610 (407.24)	33054
1905	2847 (8.56)				91471 (275.13)	4131 (12.43)	134676 (405.08)	33247
1906	2612 (7.81)				85593 (255.95)	4391 (13.13)	138144 (413.10)	33441
1907	2662 (7.91)				87856 (261.10)	4127 (12.26)	136028 (404.26)	33649
1908	3807 (11.24)				93583 (276.41)	4382 (12.94)	132501 (391.35)	33857
1909	4290 (12.59)				105500 (309.70)	4557 (13.38)	146103 (428.89)	34065
1910	3494 (10.19)				98673 (287.90)	4610 (13.45)	152962 (446.30)	34273
1911	3061 (8.83)				88018 (255.27)	4111 (11.92)	156420 (453.64)	34481
1912	3411 (9.83)				86632 (249.75)	4229 (12.19)	148378 (427.76)	34687
1913	3356 (9.52)				91160 (258.69)	4867 (13.81)	149003 (422.84)	35239
1914	2975 (8.36)				106740 (299.85)	3663 (10.29)	166740 (468.40)	35598
1915	2966 (8.21)				110572 (306.12)	4360 (12.07)	177831 (492.33)	36120
1916	2429 (6.69)				77691 (214.04)	3804 (10.48)	172865 (476.25)	36297
1917	2206 (6.05)				64137 (175.84)	2899 (7.95)	168216 (461.67)	36474
1918	1983 (5.41)				58148 (158.65)	4185 (11.42)	172712 (471.23)	36651
1919	3100 (8.42)				75534 (204.56)	5185 (14.08)	229960 (624.42)	36828
1920	5034 (13.60)				92792 (250.75)	8493 (22.95)	267808 (723.69)	37006
1921	5735 (15.37)				101710 (272.60)	8908 (23.88)	237146 (635.59)	37311
1922	6278 (16.69)				108208 (287.66)	8447 (22.46)	191296 (508.55)	37616
1923	5477 (14.44)				122624 (323.37)	7690 (20.28)	214802 (566.45)	37921
1924	4259 (11.14)				115431 (301.97)	7025 (18.38)	196740 (514.68)	38226
1925	4281 (11.11)				129985 (337.33)	5706 (14.81)	205532 (532.87)	38533
1926	3495 (8.99)				117299 (301.66)	4318 (11.10)	201064 (517.07)	38885
1927	2915 (7.43)				99176 (252.76)	3304 (8.42)	189665 (483.38)	39237
1928	2331 (5.89)				90717 (229.15)	2665 (6.73)	203110 (513.05)	39589
1929	2109 (5.28)				87719 (219.62)	2595 (6.50)	190097 (475.94)	39941
1930	2127 (5.28)	2725 (6.65)			85801 (212.94)	2487 (6.17)	194704 (483.22)	40293
1931	2270 (5.59)	2595 (6.28)			72925 (179.45)	2623 (6.45)	205781 (506.38)	40638
1932	1971 (4.81)	3087 (7.41)			81060 (199.45)	2352 (5.74)	226651 (553.04)	40983
1933	1760 (4.26)	3006 (7.15)			65486 (158.45)	1941 (4.70)	210038 (508.22)	41328
1934	1740 (4.18)	2651 (6.26)			66626 (160.36)	2077 (4.98)	208061 (499.27)	41673
1935	1628 (3.87)	3066 (7.17)			58239 (138.60)	1891 (4.50)	227361 (541.10)	42018
1936	1578 (3.72)	3146 (7.30)			56065 (132.28)	1632 (3.85)	241630 (570.12)	42382
1937	1537 (3.60)	2828 (6.51)			63574 (148.73)	1937 (4.53)	281678 (658.96)	42746
1938	1438 (3.34)				52590 (121.99)	1784 (4.14)	250749 (581.65)	43110
1939	1242 (2.86)				52584 (120.96)	1665 (3.83)	230890 (531.10)	43474
1940	1001 (2.28)	2597 (5.92)			47358 (108.02)	1254 (2.86)	229160 (522.72)	43840
1941	784 (1.78)	2033 (4.60)			35669 (80.78)	975 (2.21)	232103 (525.66)	44155
1942	830 (1.87)	2039 (4.59)			46201 (103.89)	1067 (2.40)	348329 (783.31)	44469
1943	1554 (3.48)	2252 (5.04)			43437 (97.24)	2110 (4.72)	416572 (932.53)	44671
1944	5126 (11.44)	3101 (6.92)			51890 (115.76)	11822 (26.37)	581597 (1297.46)	44826

ITALY

NUMBER OF OFFENSES REPORTED -- (RATE PER 100,000)   CONTINUED

YEAR	MURDER (1)	MANSLTR (2)	HOMICIDE ( )	RAPE ( )	ASSAULT (3)	ROBBERY ( )	THEFT ( )	POP
1945	12060 (26.81)	3249 (7.22)			67108 (149.19)	20884 (46.43)	593867 (1320.20)	44983
1946	6027 (13.31)	3213 (7.09)			95115 (210.03)	18720 (41.34)	653073 (1442.08)	45287
1947	3992 (8.74)	2874 (6.29)			75398 (165.11)	10442 (22.87)	493964 (1081.74)	45664
1948	3071 (6.68)	3604 (7.83)			85551 (185.96)	6983 (15.18)	369891 (804.04)	46004
1949	2873 (6.20)	3713 (8.02)			95186 (205.55)	5077 (10.96)	312481 (674.80)	46307
1950	2275 (4.88)	3645 (7.82)			99534 (213.58)	3593 (7.71)	280460 (601.81)	46603
1951	2259 (4.81)	3788 (8.07)			106258 (226.41)	3690 (7.86)	269270 (573.75)	46932
1952	1966 (4.16)	4477 (9.48)			110428 (233.89)	3074 (6.51)	248571 (526.49)	47213
1953	1674 (3.53)	4674 (9.85)			80253 (169.13)	2590 (5.46)	230909 (486.75)	47439
1954	1696 (3.56)	5524 (11.59)			85045 (178.42)	2766 (5.80)	252494 (529.73)	47665
1955	1834 (3.83)	6101 (12.75)			66387 (138.78)	3086 (6.45)	236284 (493.94)	47837
1956	1829 (3.77)	6608 (13.63)			65388 (134.91)	3017 (6.22)	259809 (536.03)	48469
1957	1667 (3.42)	6980 (14.32)			66076 (135.56)	2752 (5.65)	274240 (562.62)	48743
1958	1615 (3.29)	6962 (14.20)			64786 (132.11)	2984 (6.08)	274895 (560.54)	49041
1959	1611 (3.26)	7030 (14.24)			75728 (153.43)	2876 (5.83)	288413 (584.35)	49356
1960	1601 (3.23)	3785 (7.62)			29886 (60.20)	2218 (4.47)	206002 (414.98)	49642
1961	1458 (2.92)	4738 (9.49)			30460 (61.04)	2102 (4.21)	208154 (417.12)	49903
1962	1309 (2.61)	5024 (10.01)			27862 (55.51)	1849 (3.68)	210209 (418.83)	50190
1963	1337 (2.65)	5451 (10.79)			25104 (49.71)	1940 (3.84)	230627 (456.71)	50498
1964	1302 (2.56)	5370 (10.58)			24403 (48.07)	2068 (4.07)	241280 (475.32)	50762
1965	1375 (2.65)	5215 (10.04)			25206 (48.53)	2193 (4.22)	239219 (460.57)	51940
1966	1308 (2.50)	5285 (10.11)			27836 (53.24)	2070 (3.96)	248082 (474.53)	52280
1967	1334 (2.54)	5901 (11.22)			29780 (56.61)	2341 (4.45)	254034 (482.86)	52610
1968	1371 (2.59)	6278 (11.87)			30168 (57.02)	2438 (4.61)	268802 (508.04)	52910
1969	1289 (2.42)	5919 (11.12)			26877 (50.49)	2254 (4.23)	275136 (516.88)	53230
1970	1264 (2.36)	6064 (11.32)			24521 (45.77)	2931 (5.47)	340545 (635.70)	53570
1971	1594 (2.96)	5963 (11.06)			25892 (48.04)	4092 (7.59)	404295 (750.08)	53900

FOOTNOTES:
1. MURDER, ATTEMPTED MURDER, AND MURDER WITH OTHER INTENTIONS
2. UNKNOWN MEASURE CHANGE AFTER 1959
3. UNKNOWN MEASURE CHANGE AFTER 1959

IVORY COAST *

NUMBER OF OFFENSES REPORTED -- (RATE PER 100,000)

YEAR	MURDER ( )	MANSLTR ( )	HOMICIDE ( )	RAPE (1)	ASSAULT ( )	ROBBERY ( )	THEFT ( )	POP
1963	109 (2.97)			228 (6.21)		816 (22.23)	7690 (209.54)	3670
1964	102 (2.72)			266 (7.09)		1015 (27.07)	8334 (222.24)	3750
1965	106 (2.76)			287 (7.47)		865 (22.53)	5117 (133.26)	3840
1966	91 (2.32)			347 (8.85)		1001 (25.54)	4624 (117.96)	3920
1967	84 (2.09)			438 (10.90)		1456 (36.22)	5856 (145.67)	4020
1968	112 (2.73)			486 (11.82)		1516 (36.89)	6840 (166.42)	4110
1969	162 (3.85)			455 (10.81)		1370 (32.54)	6853 (162.78)	4210
1970	162 (3.76)			355 (8.24)		1444 (33.50)	7896 (183.20)	4310

FOOTNOTES:
* RAW CRIME DATA FROM INTERPOL; RATES COMPUTED FROM
  POPULATION FIGURES ABOVE
  1. SEX OFFENSES

JAMAICA *

NUMBER OF OFFENSES REPORTED -- (RATE PER 100,000)

YEAR	MURDER ( )	MANSLTR ( )	HOMICIDE ( )	RAPE (1)	ASSAULT ( )	ROBBERY ( )	THEFT ( )	POP
1960	121 (7.49)			253 (15.66)		4671 (289.05)	5814 (359.78)	1616
1961								
1962								
1963	77 (4.56)			317 (18.79)		6337 (375.64)	7378 (437.34)	1687
1964	65 (3.76)			311 (18.00)		6481 (375.06)	7068 (409.03)	1728
1965	66 (3.77)			196 (11.20)		6805 (388.86)	6535 (373.43)	1750
1966	87 (4.91)			330 (18.62)		6806 (384.09)	7934 (447.74)	1772
1967	100 (5.57)			389 (21.68)		3737 (208.31)	5141 (286.57)	1794
1968	108 (5.95)			310 (17.07)		3188 (175.55)	4288 (236.12)	1816
1969	158 (8.59)			428 (23.26)		10991 (597.34)	4106 (223.15)	1840
1970	154 (8.24)			552 (29.52)		8551 (457.27)	5407 (289.14)	1870

FOOTNOTES:
* RAW CRIME DATA FROM INTERPOL; RATES COMPUTED FROM
  POPULATION FIGURES ABOVE
  1. SEX OFFENSES

NUMBER OF OFFENSES REPORTED -- (RATE PER 100,000)

YEAR	MURDER ( )	MANSLTR ( )	HOMICIDE ( )	RAPE ( )	ASSAULT ( )	ROBBERY ( )	THEFT ( )	POP
1900			1511 (3.45)		10209 (23.28)	1108 (2.53)	51601 (117.68)	43847
1901			1582 (3.57)		10605 (23.91)	1132 (2.55)	52145 (117.55)	44359
1902			1652 (3.67)		10424 (23.18)	981 (2.18)	52275 (116.26)	44964
1903			1524 (3.35)		9937 (21.82)	1229 (2.70)	65770 (144.40)	45546
1904			1571 (3.41)		8541 (18.51)	1149 (2.49)	71231 (154.40)	46135
1905			1511 (3.24)		8110 (17.40)	1012 (2.17)	64224 (137.76)	46620
1906			1625 (3.45)		10318 (21.94)	1037 (2.20)	67393 (143.27)	47038
1907			1717 (3.62)		11875 (25.04)	883 (1.86)	62258 (131.30)	47416
1908			1690 (3.52)		12363 (25.78)	891 (1.86)	58430 (121.82)	47965
1909			1412 (2.91)		15727 (32.39)	1093 (2.25)	55607 (114.53)	48554
1910			1389 (2.82)		15957 (32.44)	1035 (2.10)	53059 (107.88)	49184
1911			1538 (3.09)		16303 (32.70)	1041 (2.09)	57854 (116.05)	49852
1912			1603 (3.17)		15571 (30.79)	1179 (2.33)	65522 (129.55)	50577
1913			1962 (3.82)		16852 (32.85)	1131 (2.20)	74593 (145.39)	51305
1914			2021 (3.88)		18522 (35.59)	1069 (2.05)	75056 (144.23)	52039
1915			1833 (3.47)		18864 (35.76)	1214 (2.30)	73151 (138.67)	52752
1916			1886 (3.53)		19022 (35.56)	1083 (2.02)	81063 (151.53)	53496
1917			1943 (3.59)		19873 (36.71)	903 (1.67)	82775 (152.91)	54134
1918			1874 (3.42)		19808 (36.19)	1540 (2.81)	92558 (169.09)	54739
1919			1935 (3.52)		21412 (38.91)	994 (1.81)	85523 (155.40)	55033
1920			1869 (3.34)		22132 (39.55)	835 (1.49)	76847 (137.32)	55963
1921			1878 (3.31)		19303 (34.06)	743 (1.31)	58426 (103.11)	56666
1922			1889 (3.29)		21746 (37.89)	894 (1.56)	58418 (101.79)	57390
1923			2502 (4.30)		24050 (41.38)	880 (1.51)	69062 (118.83)	58119
1924			2330 (3.97)		27265 (46.49)	1127 (1.92)	159870 (272.59)	58649
1925			2391 (4.04)		28919 (48.87)	1516 (2.56)	187190 (316.31)	59179
1926			2620 (4.36)		30868 (51.35)	1437 (2.39)	268391 (446.44)	60118
1927			2447 (4.01)		29929 (49.02)	1570 (2.57)	282483 (462.65)	61057
1928			2293 (3.70)		22977 (37.06)	1875 (3.02)	299738 (482.48)	61996
1929			2028 (3.22)		22911 (36.40)	2181 (3.47)	347878 (552.76)	62935
1930			2286 (3.58)		24355 (38.13)	2112 (3.31)	402863 (630.73)	63872
1931			2379 (3.67)		24513 (37.61)	2127 (3.28)	455904 (703.23)	64830
1932			2661 (4.04)		24658 (37.48)	2268 (3.45)	514202 (781.60)	65788
1933			2670 (4.00)		26219 (39.28)	2050 (3.07)	546472 (818.73)	66746
1934			2586 (3.82)		28893 (42.68)	1909 (2.82)	571295 (841.81)	67704
1935			2441 (3.56)		29374 (42.78)	2045 (2.98)	498465 (725.97)	68662
1936			2459 (3.55)		27675 (39.99)	1755 (2.54)	469388 (678.21)	69210
1937			2206 (3.16)		25485 (36.53)	1598 (2.29)	436409 (625.60)	69758
1938			1922 (2.73)		23098 (32.65)	1303 (1.85)	455187 (647.44)	70306
1939			1661 (2.34)		21622 (30.52)	1099 (1.55)	370341 (522.68)	70854
1940			1463 (2.05)		18151 (25.42)	1221 (1.71)	382014 (535.03)	71400
1941			1433 (1.99)		19663 (27.37)	939 (1.31)	358389 (498.80)	71850
1942			1139 (1.58)		15442 (21.36)	1076 (1.49)	269387 (372.60)	72300
1943			1056 (1.44)		13418 (18.31)	1151 (1.57)	439671 (599.82)	73300
1944			861 (1.17)		9746 (13.21)	1235 (1.67)	448463 (607.67)	73800

JAPAN

NUMBER OF OFFENSES REPORTED -- (RATE PER 100,000)   CONTINUED

YEAR	MURDER ( )	MANSLTR ( )	HOMICIDE ( )	RAPE ( )	ASSAULT ( )	ROBBERY ( )	THEFT (2)	POP
1945			926 (1.28)		5134 (7.11)	1303 (1.80)	321559 (445.37)	72200
1946			1953 (2.58)		10788 (14.23)	10800 (14.25)	568637 (750.18)	75800
1947			2098 (2.69)		15835 (20.28)	11597 (14.85)	443575 (567.95)	78101
1948			2895 (3.62)		26161 (32.70)	13588 (16.98)	466682 (583.28)	80010
1949			2969 (3.63)		38251 (46.77)	10349 (12.65)	504021 (616.31)	81780
1950			3076 (3.71)		49188 (59.33)	8941 (10.79)	526921 (635.61)	82900
1951			3109 (3.69)		51204 (60.74)	7100 (8.42)	585383 (694.40)	84300
1952			3061 (3.58)		56194 (65.72)	6463 (7.56)	558064 (652.71)	85500
1953			3090 (3.56)		60681 (69.99)	5419 (6.25)	557996 (643.59)	86700
1954			3356 (3.81)		68863 (78.25)	5856 (6.65)	555628 (631.40)	88000
1955			3269 (3.68)		79426 (89.34)	6641 (7.47)	605411 (681.00)	88900
1956			2862 (3.18)		81444 (90.54)	5814 (6.46)	512241 (569.47)	89950
1957			2652 (2.92)		86368 (95.19)	5510 (6.07)	506172 (557.89)	90730
1958			2906 (3.17)		90414 (98.77)	6113 (6.68)	474895 (518.78)	91540
1959			2965 (3.21)		88756 (96.03)	5764 (6.24)	491044 (531.26)	92430
1960			2844 (3.05)		83449 (89.53)	5560 (5.97)	519984 (557.86)	93210
1961			2921 (3.11)		85056 (90.44)	4974 (5.29)	561746 (597.28)	94050
1962			2503 (2.64)		79202 (83.43)	4541 (4.78)	574645 (605.34)	94930
1963			2452 (2.56)		73612 (76.76)	4200 (4.38)	574583 (599.15)	95899
1964			2501 (2.58)		76791 (79.24)	4019 (4.15)	575420 (593.79)	96906
1965			2379 (2.43)		73802 (75.24)	4106 (4.19)	514805 (525.58)	97950
1966			2278 (2.30)		74222 (75.09)	3799 (3.84)	484549 (490.19)	98850
1967			2225 (2.23)		73633 (73.73)	3143 (3.15)	450144 (450.73)	99870
1968			2297 (2.27)		71179 (70.42)	2974 (2.94)		101080
1969			2351 (2.30)		66553 (65.04)	2935 (2.87)		102320
1970			2146 (2.07)		61675 (59.57)	2845 (2.75)		103540

FOOTNOTES:
1. INJURY
2. OFFENDERS PRIOR TO 1924

JORDAN *

NUMBER OF OFFENSES REPORTED -- (RATE PER 100,000)

YEAR	MURDER ( )	MANSLTR ( )	HOMICIDE ( )	RAPE (1)	ASSAULT ( )	ROBBERY ( )	THEFT ( )	POP
1965	178 (9.13)			220 (11.28)		558 (28.62)	1606 (82.36)	1950
1966	194 (9.65)			246 (12.24)		524 (26.07)	1496 (74.43)	2010
1967	272 (13.08)			216 (10.38)		330 (15.87)	1075 (51.68)	2080
1968	233 (10.84)			214 (9.95)		260 (12.09)	1116 (51.91)	2150
1969	220 (9.87)			149 (6.68)				2230
1970	209 (9.05)			97 (4.20)		217 (9.39)	706 (30.56)	2310

FOOTNOTES:
* RAW CRIME DATA FROM INTERPOL; RATES COMPUTED FROM
  POPULATION FIGURES ABOVE
  1. SEX OFFENSES

KENYA

NUMBER OF OFFENSES REPORTED -- (RATE PER 100,000)

YEAR	MURDER (1)	MANSLTR ( )	HOMICIDE ( )	RAPE ( )	ASSAULT ( )	ROBBERY ( )	THEFT (2)	POP
1955	631 (9.02)	59 (0.84)		70 (1.00)	2274 (32.52)	645 (9.22)	3228 (46.16)	6993
1956	446 (6.19)	52 (0.72)		179 (2.48)	3214 (44.58)	732 (10.15)	4528 (62.81)	7209
1957	317 (4.27)	45 (0.61)		200 (2.69)	3977 (53.51)	1154 (15.53)	6153 (82.79)	7432
1958	293 (3.83)	33 (0.43)		115 (1.50)	3417 (44.65)	1219 (15.93)	6331 (82.74)	7652
1959	324 (4.11)	28 (0.36)		79 (1.00)	3482 (44.19)	1215 (15.42)	6721 (85.29)	7880
1960	338 (4.17)	17 (0.21)		97 (1.20)	4301 (53.00)	1759 (21.68)	8372 (103.17)	8115
1961	361 (4.32)	12 (0.14)		73 (0.87)	3917 (46.90)	2153 (25.78)	8331 (99.75)	8352
1962	470 (5.47)	13 (0.15)		64 (0.74)	4390 (51.08)	2087 (24.28)	8022 (93.33)	8595
1963	509 (5.75)	26 (0.29)		68 (0.77)	5089 (57.52)	1940 (21.93)	8256 (93.32)	8847
1964	621 (6.82)	9 (0.10)		59 (0.65)	5379 (59.08)	2359 (25.91)	8396 (92.22)	9104
1965	552 (5.85)	13 (0.14)		129 (1.37)	5000 (52.95)	2160 (22.88)	7516 (79.60)	9442
1966	548 (5.60)	7 (0.07)		128 (1.31)	5547 (56.72)	2326 (23.78)	7109 (72.69)	9780
1967	509 (5.03)	7 (0.07)		178 (1.76)	5876 (58.06)	2354 (23.26)	7424 (73.36)	10120
1968	529 (5.05)	8 (0.08)		256 (2.44)	6872 (65.57)	2278 (21.74)	6947 (66.29)	10480

FOOTNOTES:
1. INCLUDES ATTEMPTED MURDER
2. BREAK-INS

KHMER REPUBLIC (CAMBODIA) *   NUMBER OF OFFENSES REPORTED -- (RATE PER 100,000)

YEAR	MURDER ( )	MANSLTR ( )	HOMICIDE ( )	RAPE (1)	ASSAULT ( )	ROBBERY ( )	THEFT ( )	POP
1969	42 (0.63)			28 (0.42)		56 (0.84)	126 (1.88)	6700
1970	46 (0.67)			5 (0.07)		51 (0.74)	75 (1.09)	6900

FOOTNOTES:
* RAW CRIME DATA FROM INTERPOL; RATES COMPUTED FROM
  POPULATION FIGURES ABOVE
1. SEX OFFENSES

KOREA   NUMBER OF OFFENSES REPORTED -- (RATE PER 100,000)

YEAR	MURDER ( )	MANSLTR ( )	HOMICIDE ( )	RAPE ( )	ASSAULT ( )	ROBBERY ( )	THEFT ( )	POP
1964			518 (1.88)	879 (3.19)	18558 (67.41)	1618 (5.88)	140815 (511.50)	27530
1965			568 (2.02)	1017 (3.61)	18127 (64.37)	1542 (5.48)	127663 (453.35)	28160
1966			567 (1.97)	1111 (3.86)	19670 (68.32)	1307 (4.54)	98505 (342.15)	28790
1967			818 (2.78)	1225 (4.16)	16492 (56.06)	1097 (3.73)	89010 (302.55)	29420
1968			500 (1.66)	1350 (4.49)	15947 (53.07)	946 (3.15)	77376 (257.49)	30050
1969			570 (1.86)	1369 (4.46)	12887 (42.00)	805 (2.62)	66204 (215.79)	30680
1970			570 (1.82)	1659 (5.30)	12320 (39.34)	929 (2.97)	63704 (203.40)	31320
1971			620 (1.94)	2022 (6.33)	11001 (34.46)	1067 (3.34)	66838 (209.39)	31920
1972			609 (1.87)	2058 (6.33)	10914 (33.55)	955 (2.94)	66228 (203.59)	32530
1973			438 (1.33)	1994 (6.04)	9489 (28.76)	819 (2.48)	63276 (191.76)	32998

KUWAIT

NUMBER OF OFFENSES REPORTED -- (RATE PER 100,000)

YEAR	MURDER (1)	MANSLTR ( )	HOMICIDE ( )	RAPE (2)	ASSAULT ( )	ROBBERY ( )	THEFT ( )	POP
1957	15 (6.82)			24 (10.91)	1056 (480.00)		808 (367.27)	220
1958	11 (4.58)			322 (13.17)	1990 (829.17)		1155 (481.25)	240
1959	18 (7.20)			350 (140.00)	2072 (828.80)		1500 (600.00)	250
1960	26 (9.56)			384 (141.18)	1628 (598.53)		1786 (656.62)	272
1961	78 (24.22)			298 (92.55)	1696 (526.71)		1783 (553.73)	322
1962	61 (17.28)			250 (70.82)	1820 (515.58)		2373 (672.24)	353
1963	77 (19.85)			1064 (274.23)	2943 (758.51)		3014 (776.80)	388
1964	44 (10.33)			491 (115.26)	2377 (557.98)		3181 (746.71)	426
1965	74 (15.42)			410 (85.42)	1931 (402.29)		2906 (605.42)	480
1966	28 (5.38)			404 (77.69)	1844 (354.62)		2789 (536.35)	520
1967	50 (8.77)			303 (53.16)	1489 (261.23)		2444 (428.77)	570
1968								
1969								
1970	26 (3.47)			216 (28.80)	1034 (137.87)	24 (3.20)	1010 (134.67)	750
1971	28 (3.54)			208 (26.33)	1154 (146.08)	29 (3.67)	1106 (140.00)	790
1972	37 (4.40)			248 (29.52)	1121 (133.45)	56 (6.67)	921 (109.64)	840
1973	27 (3.07)			231 (26.25)	769 (87.39)	355 (40.34)	1028 (116.82)	880
1974	54 (5.84)			228 (24.65)	958 (103.57)	90 (9.73)	718 (77.62)	925

FOOTNOTES:
1. INCLUDES ATTEMPTED MURDER AND ROBBERY BEFORE 1970
2. MORAL OFFENSES BEFORE 1970

LAOS *

NUMBER OF OFFENSES REPORTED -- (RATE PER 100,000)

YEAR	MURDER ( )	MANSLTR ( )	HOMICIDE ( )	RAPE (1)	ASSAULT ( )	ROBBERY ( )	THEFT ( )	POP
1966	66 (2.45)			18 (0.67)		82 (3.05)	626 (23.27)	2690
1967	45 (1.63)			18 (0.65)		48 (1.74)	591 (21.41)	2760
1968	57 (2.01)			21 (0.74)		54 (1.91)	492 (17.39)	2830
1969	62 (2.15)			23 (0.80)		71 (2.46)	712 (24.64)	2890
1970	60 (2.03)			19 (0.64)		70 (2.36)	664 (22.43)	2960

FOOTNOTES:
* RAW CRIME DATA FROM INTERPOL; RATES COMPUTED FROM POPULATION FIGURES ABOVE
1. SEX OFFENSES

NUMBER OF OFFENSES REPORTED -- (RATE PER 100,000)

YEAR	MURDER ( )	MANSLTR ( )	HOMICIDE ( )	RAPE ( )	ASSAULT ( )	ROBBERY ( )	THEFT ( )	POP
1967	133 (5.22)			809 (31.73)	463 (18.16)	78 (3.06)	4062 (159.29)	2550
1968	106 (4.05)			412 (15.73)	251 (9.58)	78 (2.98)	3343 (127.60)	2620
1969	172 (6.37)			337 (12.48)	82 (3.04)	68 (2.52)	3462 (128.22)	2700
1970	324 (11.61)			66 (2.37)	1043 (37.38)	150 (5.38)	4461 (159.89)	2790
1971	151 (5.26)			55 (1.92)	623 (21.71)	117 (4.08)	4772 (166.27)	2870
1972	121 (4.09)			49 (1.66)	615 (20.78)	92 (3.11)	4146 (140.07)	2960
1973	191 (6.24)			47 (1.54)	578 (18.89)	137 (4.48)	3718 (121.50)	3060
1974	173 (5.47)			52 (1.65)	506 (16.01)	291 (9.21)	4143 (131.11)	3160

NUMBER OF OFFENSES REPORTED -- (RATE PER 100,000)

YEAR	MURDER ( )	MANSLTR ( )	HOMICIDE ( )	RAPE (1)	ASSAULT ( )	ROBBERY ( )	THEFT ( )	POP
1955	235 (20.78)			321 (28.38)		1782 (157.56)	2266 (200.35)	1131
1956	210 (17.90)			212 (18.07)		1655 (141.09)	2658 (226.60)	1173
1957	261 (21.48)			336 (27.65)		793 (65.27)	3150 (259.26)	1215
1958	148 (11.77)			307 (24.42)		1024 (81.46)	2490 (198.09)	1257
1959	139 (10.64)			319 (24.43)		1576 (120.67)	1956 (149.77)	1306
1960	129 (9.52)			303 (22.36)		974 (71.88)	2855 (210.70)	1355
1961	136 (9.69)			342 (24.36)		960 (68.38)	2216 (157.83)	1404
1962	293 (20.17)			397 (27.32)		815 (56.09)	2240 (154.16)	1453
1963	189 (12.57)			401 (26.66)		1001 (66.56)	1894 (125.93)	1504
1964	193 (12.34)			466 (29.80)		1065 (68.09)	1500 (95.91)	1564
1965	146 (9.00)			475 (29.28)		885 (54.56)	1472 (90.75)	1622
1966								
1967	145 (8.34)			523 (30.09)		802 (46.15)	1952 (112.31)	1738
1968	46 (2.55)			542 (30.04)		596 (33.04)	1850 (102.55)	1804
1969	96 (5.14)			568 (30.39)		831 (44.46)	2337 (125.04)	1869

FOOTNOTES:
* RAW CRIME DATA FROM INTERPOL; RATES COMPUTED FROM
  POPULATION FIGURES ABOVE
  1. SEX OFFENSES

LUXEMBOURG

NUMBER OF OFFENSES REPORTED -- (RATE PER 100,000)

YEAR	MURDER ( )	MANSLTR ( )	HOMICIDE ( )	RAPE (1)	ASSAULT ( )	ROBBERY ( )	THEFT ( )	POP
1953	3 (0.99)			92 (30.26)		314 (103.29)	1486 (488.82)	304
1954	0 (0.00)			113 (36.93)		204 (66.67)	464 (151.63)	306
1955	1 (0.33)			102 (33.44)		240 (78.69)	499 (163.61)	305
1956	3 (0.98)			97 (31.60)		135 (43.97)	394 (128.34)	307
1957	6 (1.95)			102 (33.12)		533 (173.05)	1380 (448.05)	308
1958	3 (0.97)			103 (33.23)		435 (140.32)	1559 (502.90)	310
1959	20 (6.41)			117 (37.50)		429 (137.50)	1651 (529.17)	312
1960	67 (21.34)			129 (41.08)		564 (179.62)	1685 (536.62)	314
1961	22 (6.94)			165 (52.05)		821 (258.99)	1803 (568.77)	317
1962	10 (3.11)			128 (39.75)		783 (243.17)	1627 (505.28)	322
1963	11 (3.37)			160 (49.08)		792 (242.94)	1689 (518.10)	326
1964	5 (1.52)			211 (63.94)		910 (275.76)	1903 (576.67)	330
1965	21 (6.36)			108 (32.73)		968 (293.33)	1982 (600.61)	330
1966	28 (8.48)			135 (40.91)		690 (209.09)	1694 (513.33)	330
1967	29 (8.53)			129 (37.94)		1093 (321.47)	1582 (465.29)	340
1968	23 (6.76)			133 (39.12)		945 (277.94)	1842 (541.76)	340
1969	20 (5.88)			101 (29.71)		1081 (317.94)	1903 (559.71)	340
1970	38 (11.18)			101 (29.71)		1361 (400.29)	1953 (574.41)	340

FOOTNOTES:
1. SEX OFFENSES

MALAGASY REPUBLIC *

NUMBER OF OFFENSES REPORTED -- (RATE PER 100,000)

YEAR	MURDER ( )	MANSLTR ( )	HOMICIDE ( )	RAPE (1)	ASSAULT ( )	ROBBERY ( )	THEFT ( )	POP
1959	218 (4.16)			229 (4.37)		1537 (29.30)	2742 (52.28)	5245
1960	283 (5.25)			82 (1.52)		1181 (21.90)	3456 (64.08)	5393
1961	248 (4.45)			87 (1.56)		621 (11.15)	3468 (62.24)	5572
1962	248 (4.31)			104 (1.81)		717 (12.46)	3165 (54.99)	5756
1963	451 (7.83)			147 (2.55)		817 (14.18)	3231 (56.09)	5760
1964	614 (10.39)			183 (3.10)		1305 (22.08)	4378 (74.08)	5910
1965	416 (6.84)			87 (1.43)		484 (7.96)	1510 (24.84)	6080
1966	198 (3.19)			134 (2.16)	3121 (50.34)	1062 (17.13)	2726 (43.97)	6200
1967	255 (4.03)			161 (2.54)	3465 (54.74)	1347 (21.28)	2312 (36.52)	6330
1968	286 (4.43)			234 (3.62)	4300 (66.56)	575 (8.90)	4466 (69.13)	6460
1969	298 (4.52)			144 (2.18)	4285 (64.92)	507 (7.68)	2246 (34.03)	6600
1970	270 (4.00)			119 (1.76)	4570 (67.70)	797 (11.81)	2218 (32.86)	6750
1971					5046 (73.13)			6900

FOOTNOTES: * RAW CRIME DATA FROM INTERPOL EXCLUDING ASSAULT; RATES
COMPUTED FROM POPULATION FIGURES ABOVE
1. SEX OFFENSES

MALAWI (NYASALAND) *

NUMBER OF OFFENSES REPORTED -- (RATE PER 100,000)

YEAR	MURDER ( )	MANSLTR ( )	HOMICIDE ( )	RAPE (1)	ASSAULT ( )	ROBBERY ( )	THEFT ( )	POP
1957	93 (3.51)			92 (3.47)		2864 (108.08)	5925 (223.58)	2650
1958								
1959								
1960	145 (5.12)			179 (6.33)		3594 (127.00)	6588 (232.79)	2830
1961	141 (4.88)			204 (7.06)		6855 (237.20)	4275 (147.92)	2890
1962	66 (2.24)			204 (6.92)		7638 (258.92)	4791 (162.41)	2950
1963	116 (3.09)			180 (4.80)		8540 (227.55)	5432 (144.74)	3753
1964	160 (4.22)			260 (6.86)		9380 (247.49)	5844 (154.20)	3790
1965	192 (4.91)			232 (5.93)		9176 (234.68)	5252 (134.32)	3910
1966	140 (3.47)			224 (5.56)		8180 (202.98)	4852 (120.40)	4030
1967	166 (4.03)			297 (7.21)		5060 (122.82)	8652 (209.51)	4120
1968	128 (3.03)			315 (7.46)		5240 (124.17)	8700 (206.16)	4220
1969	156 (3.60)			292 (6.74)		5518 (127.44)	10320 (238.34)	4330
1970	150 (3.38)			322 (7.25)		6518 (146.80)	11685 (263.18)	4440

FOOTNOTES:
* POPULATION MEASURE CHANGE 1963; RAW CRIME DATA FROM INTERPOL. RATES COMPUTED FROM POPULATION FIGURES ABOVE
1. SEX OFFENSES

MALAYA *

NUMBER OF OFFENSES REPORTED -- (RATE PER 100,000)

YEAR	MURDER ( )	MANSLTR ( )	HOMICIDE ( )	RAPE (1)	ASSAULT ( )	ROBBERY ( )	THEFT ( )	POP
1959	798 (11.91)			309 (4.61)		497 (7.42)	14357 (214.35)	6698
1960	894 (12.94)			357 (5.17)		564 (8.16)	14450 (209.15)	6909
1961	189 (2.65)			340 (4.76)		747 (10.47)	18815 (263.63)	7137
1962	182 (2.47)			372 (5.05)		1056 (14.32)	20041 (271.71)	7376
1963	161 (2.12)			497 (6.53)		1094 (14.38)	22124 (290.84)	7607
1964	242 (2.70)			510 (5.70)		1915 (21.40)	29938 (334.50)	8950
1965	201 (2.19)			488 (5.32)		1225 (13.34)	27389 (298.35)	9180
1966	207 (2.20)			552 (5.87)		1597 (16.97)	32493 (345.30)	9410
1967	253 (2.62)			505 (5.23)		2212 (22.90)	37061 (383.65)	9660
1968	261 (2.64)			595 (6.02)		2276 (23.01)	37567 (379.85)	9890
1969	387 (3.82)			481 (4.74)		1493 (14.72)	32245 (318.00)	10140
1970	230 (2.21)			536 (5.15)		919 (8.84)	27035 (259.95)	10400

FOOTNOTES:
* MALAYSIA FROM 1964; RAW CRIME DATA FROM INTERPOL. RATES COMPUTED FROM POPULATION FIGURES ABOVE
1. SEX OFFENSES

MAURITANIA *

NUMBER OF OFFENSES REPORTED -- (RATE PER 100,000)

YEAR	MURDER ( )	MANSLTR ( )	HOMICIDE ( )	RAPE (1)	ASSAULT ( )	ROBBERY ( )	THEFT ( )	POP
1964	83 (8.06)			11 (1.07)		73 (7.09)	244 (23.69)	1030
1965								
1966	17 (1.50)			7 (0.65)		350 (32.71)		1070
1967	18 (1.64)			9 (0.82)		360 (32.73)		1100
1968	25 (2.23)			11 (0.98)		385 (34.38)		1120
1969	27 (2.37)			17 (1.49)		405 (35.53)		1140
1970	30 (2.56)			19 (1.62)		424 (36.24)		1170

FOOTNOTES:
* RAW CRIME DATA FROM INTERPOL; RATES COMPUTED FROM POPULATION FIGURES ABOVE
  1. SEX OFFENSES

MAURITIUS *

CRIME STATISTICS -- (RATE PER 100,000)

YEAR	MURDER (1)	MANSLTR ( )	HOMICIDE (2)	RAPE ( )	ASSAULT ( )	ROBBERY (3)	THEFT (4)	POP
1958	5 (0.83)	12 (1.99)		4 (0.66)				603
1959	5 (0.81)	25 (4.03)		3 (0.48)				621
1960	1 (0.16)	11 (1.72)	9 (1.41)	1 (0.16)	2827 (442.41)	539 (84.35)	603 (94.37)	639
1961	2 (0.30)	3 (0.45)	12 (1.81)	2 (0.30)	2590 (391.24)	406 (61.33)	775 (117.07)	662
1962	2 (0.29)	3 (0.44)	12 (1.76)	0 (0.00)	2772 (406.45)	379 (55.57)	897 (131.52)	682
1963	3 (0.43)	7 (1.00)	8 (1.14)	5 (0.71)	2647 (377.60)	254 (36.23)	880 (125.53)	701
1964	9 (1.25)	8 (1.11)	8 (1.11)	2 (0.28)	3000 (415.51)	240 (33.24)	912 (126.32)	722
1965	1 (0.14)	10 (1.35)	25 (3.38)	4 (0.54)	2850 (385.14)	354 (47.84)	921 (124.46)	740
1966	0 (0.00)	9 (1.18)	9 (1.18)	1 (0.13)	2801 (368.53)	284 (37.37)	888 (116.84)	760
1967	2 (0.26)	9 (1.15)		2 (0.26)	3357 (429.28)	419 (53.58)	873 (111.64)	782
1968	9 (1.13)	14 (1.76)	3 (0.38)	1 (0.13)	2743 (345.03)	268 (33.71)	843 (106.04)	795
1969	3 (0.38)	18 (2.25)	19 (2.38)	7 (0.88)	3413 (427.16)	651 (81.48)	1014 (126.91)	799
1970	2 (0.24)	21 (2.56)	27 (3.30)	6 (0.73)	2953 (360.56)	304 (37.12)	1064 (129.91)	819
1971	5 (0.61)	10 (1.22)	15 (1.83)	3 (0.37)	2467 (300.85)	436 (53.17)	911 (111.10)	820
1972	4 (0.48)	2 (0.24)	26 (3.13)	1 (0.12)	2827 (340.60)	423 (50.96)	697 (83.98)	830
1973	4 (0.48)	5 (0.60)	22 (2.62)	1 (0.12)	2876 (342.38)	494 (58.81)	894 (106.43)	840

FOOTNOTES:
* TOTAL ARRESTED OR SUMMONED TO COURT
  1. MURDER AND COMPLICITY IN MURDER
  2. INVOLUNTARY HOMICIDE
  3. LARCENY WITH VIOLENCE OR AGGRAVATING CIRCUMSTANCES
  4. SIMPLE LARCENY

MEXICO *

CRIME STATISTICS -- (RATE PER 100,000)

YEAR	MURDER ( )	MANSLTR ( )	HOMICIDE ( )	RAPE (1)	ASSAULT ( )	ROBBERY ( )	THEFT ( )	POP
1950			7276 (27.69)	2117 (8.06)	15656 (59.57)	12939 (49.24)		26280
1951			7658 (28.32)	2199 (8.13)	15062 (55.70)	15370 (56.84)		27040
1952			7498 (26.92)	2249 (8.08)	15241 (54.73)	15579 (55.94)		27850
1953			4512 (15.72)	1505 (5.24)	9261 (32.27)	9120 (31.78)		28700
1954								
1955			6011 (19.67)	1691 (5.53)	12955 (42.39)	11275 (36.89)		30560
1956			6048 (19.16)	1583 (5.02)	13207 (41.85)	10630 (33.68)		31560
1957								
1958			5748 (17.06)	1564 (4.64)	13337 (39.58)	10419 (30.92)		33700
1959			6078 (17.44)	1755 (5.03)	14403 (41.32)	10841 (31.10)		34860
1960			6124 (16.99)	1858 (5.15)	13965 (38.74)	10678 (29.62)		36050
1961			5873 (15.76)	1689 (4.53)	13273 (35.61)	10743 (28.82)		37270
1962			5769 (14.97)	1689 (4.38)	13058 (33.88)	10556 (26.87)		38540
1963			5843 (14.66)	1861 (4.67)	14630 (36.69)	10808 (27.11)		39870
1964			6172 (14.96)	2076 (5.03)	15775 (38.24)	11043 (26.77)		41250
1965			6124 (14.35)	2145 (5.02)	16475 (38.59)	11884 (27.84)		42690
1966			6052 (13.71)	2181 (4.94)	16291 (36.90)	11449 (25.93)		44150
1967			6036 (13.22)	1882 (4.12)	16317 (35.73)	11044 (24.18)		45670
1968			6012 (12.72)	1967 (4.16)	16255 (34.39)	10778 (22.80)		47270
1969			6153 (12.58)	2163 (4.42)	17470 (35.70)	11469 (23.44)		48930
1970			6280 (12.39)	2163 (4.27)	17001 (33.55)	11180 (22.06)		50670
1971			6050 (11.53)	2184 (4.16)	18838 (35.92)	13054 (24.89)		52450
1972			5999 (11.05)	2227 (4.10)	18011 (33.19)	12039 (22.18)		54270

FOOTNOTES:
* COURT CASES
1. ABDUCTION AND RAPE

MONACO *

NUMBER OF OFFENSES REPORTED -- (RATE PER 100,000)

YEAR	MURDER ( )	MANSLTR ( )	HOMICIDE ( )	RAPE (1)	ASSAULT ( )	ROBBERY ( )	THEFT ( )	POP
1953	0 (0.00)			4 (18.18)		93 (422.73)	347 (1577.27)	22
1954	0 (0.00)			1 (4.55)		50 (227.27)	200 (909.09)	22
1955	1 (4.76)			0 (0.00)		8 (38.10)	74 (352.38)	21
1956	0 (0.00)			0 (0.00)		20 (100.00)	101 (505.00)	20
1957	0 (0.00)			1 (4.76)		33 (157.14)	79 (376.19)	21
1958	0 (0.00)			2 (9.52)		6 (28.57)	192 (914.29)	21
1959	0 (0.00)			2 (8.70)		10 (43.48)	211 (917.39)	23
1960	0 (0.00)			2 (8.70)		19 (82.61)	223 (969.57)	23
1961	0 (0.00)			2 (9.09)		9 (40.91)	182 (827.27)	22
1962	0 (0.00)			0 (0.00)		9 (40.91)	285 (1295.45)	22
1963	1 (4.55)			2 (9.09)		8 (36.36)	221 (1004.55)	22
1964	0 (0.00)			2 (9.09)		9 (40.91)	297 (1350.00)	22
1965	0 (0.00)			2 (8.70)		11 (47.83)	305 (1326.09)	23
1966	0 (0.00)			0 (0.00)		9 (39.13)	218 (947.83)	23
1967	0 (0.00)			2 (8.70)		28 (121.74)	395 (1717.39)	23
1968	0 (0.00)			1 (4.17)		41 (170.83)	483 (2012.50)	24
1969	0 (0.00)			10 (41.67)		23 (95.83)	373 (1554.17)	24
1970	0 (0.00)			9 (37.50)		37 (154.17)	414 (1725.00)	24

FOOTNOTES:
* RAW CRIME DATA FROM INTERPOL; RATES COMPUTED FROM
* POPULATION FIGURES ABOVE
  1. SEX OFFENSES

MOROCCO *

NUMBER OF OFFENSES REPORTED -- (RATE PER 100,000)

YEAR	MURDER ( )	MANSLTR ( )	HOMICIDE ( )	RAPE (1)	ASSAULT ( )	ROBBERY ( )	THEFT ( )	POP
1957	412 (3.85)			856 (8.01)		5285 (45.45)	22026 (206.08)	10668
1958	446 (4.06)			1204 (10.96)		4481 (40.78)	23402 (213.00)	10987
1959								
1960								
1961	683 (5.68)			7292 (60.62)		4949 (41.14)	15444 (128.38)	12030
1962	115 (0.93)			3031 (24.52)		3070 (24.84)	12182 (98.56)	12360
1963	181 (1.43)			2517 (19.87)		2981 (23.54)	13283 (104.88)	12665
1964	215 (1.66)			2314 (17.86)		3084 (23.80)	17465 (134.77)	12959
1965	129 (0.97)			2948 (22.13)		2925 (21.96)	14400 (108.11)	13320
1966	167 (1.22)			3516 (25.61)		3174 (23.12)	16400 (119.45)	13730

FOOTNOTES:
* RAW CRIME DATA FROM INTERPOL; RATES COMPUTED FROM
  POPULATION FIGURES ABOVE
  1. SEX OFFENSES

NEPAL *

NUMBER OF OFFENSES REPORTED -- (RATE PER 100,000)

YEAR	MURDER ( )	MANSLTR ( )	HOMICIDE ( )	RAPE (1)	ASSAULT ( )	ROBBERY ( )	THEFT ( )	POP
1965	192 (1.90)			37 (0.37)		258 (2.55)	1107 (10.96)	10100
1966	198 (1.93)			35 (0.34)		219 (2.13)	1253 (12.19)	10280

FOOTNOTES:
* RAW CRIME DATA FROM INTERPOL; RATES COMPUTED FROM
  POPULATION FIGURES ABOVE
  1. SEX OFFENSES

NETHERLANDS

NUMBER OF CONVICTIONS -- (RATE PER 100,000)

YEAR	MURDER ( )	MANSLTR ( )	HOMICIDE (1)	RAPE ( )	ASSAULT ( )	ROBBERY ( )	THEFT (2)	POP
1900			17 (0.33)	7 (0.14)	4144 (80.02)		2381 (45.97)	5179
1901			19 (0.36)	3 (0.06)	4011 (76.34)		2787 (53.05)	5254
1902			19 (0.36)	9 (0.17)	4159 (78.04)		2590 (48.60)	5329
1903			20 (0.37)	8 (0.15)	4181 (77.37)		2545 (47.09)	5404
1904			26 (0.47)	5 (0.09)	3796 (69.28)		2752 (50.23)	5479
1905			26 (0.47)	6 (0.11)	3691 (66.46)		2735 (49.24)	5554
1906			21 (0.37)	8 (0.14)	3452 (61.33)		2733 (48.55)	5629
1907			21 (0.37)	7 (0.12)	3297 (57.80)		2761 (48.40)	5704
1908			40 (0.69)	8 (0.14)	3457 (59.82)		3068 (53.09)	5779
1909			42 (0.72)	7 (0.12)	3392 (57.90)		3247 (55.43)	5858
1910			35 (0.59)	13 (0.22)	3514 (59.11)		3483 (58.59)	5945
1911			29 (0.48)	12 (0.20)	3517 (58.31)		3485 (57.78)	6032
1912			37 (0.60)	12 (0.20)	3704 (60.53)		3612 (59.03)	6119
1913			41 (0.66)	11 (0.18)	3767 (60.70)		3468 (55.88)	6206
1914			40 (0.64)	6 (0.10)	3428 (54.47)		3336 (53.01)	6293
1915			28 (0.44)	6 (0.09)	2928 (45.89)		3848 (60.31)	6380
1916			29 (0.45)	5 (0.08)	2613 (40.41)		4401 (68.05)	6467
1917			32 (0.49)	6 (0.09)	2105 (32.12)		6367 (97.15)	6554
1918			25 (0.38)	6 (0.09)	1807 (27.21)		10254 (154.40)	6641
1919			26 (0.39)	17 (0.25)	2196 (32.64)		13495 (200.58)	6728
1920			51 (0.75)	18 (0.26)	3387 (49.66)		9722 (142.55)	6820
1921			45 (0.65)	9 (0.13)	3362 (48.52)		5919 (85.42)	6929
1922			37 (0.53)	14 (0.20)	3618 (51.41)		4282 (60.84)	7038
1923			47 (0.66)	14 (0.20)	3768 (52.72)		4366 (61.09)	7147
1924			21 (0.29)	19 (0.26)	3652 (50.33)		4420 (60.92)	7256
1925			36 (0.49)	14 (0.19)	3932 (53.38)		4691 (63.68)	7366
1926			28 (0.37)	13 (0.17)	4024 (53.87)		4156 (55.64)	7470
1927			33 (0.44)	11 (0.15)	4326 (57.12)		4322 (57.06)	7574
1928			46 (0.60)	11 (0.14)	4252 (55.38)		4140 (53.92)	7678
1929			24 (0.31)	10 (0.13)	4081 (52.44)		3720 (47.80)	7782
1930			28 (0.36)	12 (0.15)	4258 (54.01)		3710 (47.06)	7884
1931			37 (0.46)	14 (0.18)	3903 (48.82)		4097 (51.25)	7994
1932			45 (0.56)	17 (0.21)	4028 (49.70)		4331 (53.44)	8104
1933			40 (0.49)	7 (0.09)	3855 (46.93)		5082 (61.87)	8214
1934			33 (0.40)	19 (0.23)	3823 (45.93)		5695 (68.42)	8324
1935			31 (0.37)	12 (0.14)	3824 (45.35)		6302 (74.73)	8433
1936			39 (0.46)	16 (0.19)	3567 (41.86)		7213 (84.64)	8522
1937			30 (0.35)	16 (0.19)	3572 (41.48)		8222 (95.48)	8611
1938			32 (0.37)	12 (0.14)	3597 (41.34)		7110 (81.72)	8700
1939			43 (0.49)	13 (0.15)	3383 (38.49)		6149 (69.96)	8789
1940			25 (0.28)	16 (0.18)	2686 (30.25)		7047 (79.37)	8879
1941			24 (0.27)	7 (0.08)	3348 (37.36)		12135 (135.42)	8961
1942			21 (0.23)	11 (0.12)	3045 (33.68)		23795 (263.16)	9042
1943			22 (0.24)	7 (0.08)	3052 (33.53)		23553 (258.77)	9102
1944								

NETHERLANDS

NUMBER OF CONVICTIONS -- (RATE PER 100,000)   CONTINUED

YEAR	MURDER ( )	MANSLTR ( )	HOMICIDE (1)	RAPE ( )	ASSAULT ( )	ROBBERY ( )	THEFT (2)	POP
1946			44 (0.47)	19 (0.20)	2345 (24.89)		21953 (232.97)	9423
1947			57 (0.59)	21 (0.22)	2843 (29.53)		18597 (193.14)	9629
1948			45 (0.46)	23 (0.23)	3770 (38.47)		16619 (169.58)	9800
1949			51 (0.51)	28 (0.28)	4276 (42.95)		12378 (124.33)	9956
1950			28 (0.28)	25 (0.25)	4336 (42.87)		10834 (107.12)	10114
1951			34 (0.33)	21 (0.20)	4264 (41.54)		13391 (130.47)	10264
1952			43 (0.41)	24 (0.23)	4894 (47.14)		13030 (125.51)	10382
1953			39 (0.37)	24 (0.23)	4430 (42.22)		9812 (93.51)	10493
1954			26 (0.24)	23 (0.22)	4299 (40.50)		8624 (81.24)	10615
1955			27 (0.25)	27 (0.25)	4371 (40.67)		9053 (84.24)	10747
1956			28 (0.25)	30 (0.28)	4077 (37.44)		9103 (83.60)	10889
1957			28 (0.25)	30 (0.27)	4292 (38.94)		9674 (87.78)	11021
1958			41 (0.37)	32 (0.29)	4289 (38.34)		10814 (90.42)	11186
1959			35 (0.31)	41 (0.36)	4269 (37.63)		9575 (84.39)	11346
1960			26 (0.23)	53 (0.46)	4724 (41.15)		9932 (86.52)	11480
1961			30 (0.26)	52 (0.45)	4433 (38.09)		10376 (89.16)	11637
1962			30 (0.25)	55 (0.47)	3880 (32.89)		10914 (92.52)	11797
1963			31 (0.26)	55 (0.46)	4120 (34.43)		11430 (95.51)	11967
1964			41 (0.34)	39 (0.32)	4570 (37.69)		12464 (102.80)	12124
1965			59 (0.48)	55 (0.45)	4197 (34.15)		12575 (102.32)	12290
1966			65 (0.52)	53 (0.43)	4289 (34.45)		13197 (106.00)	12450
1967			57 (0.45)	63 (0.50)	4453 (35.34)		14510 (115.16)	12600
1968			63 (0.50)	65 (0.51)	4226 (33.22)		14832 (116.60)	12720
1969			74 (0.57)	84 (0.65)	4071 (31.63)		14339 (111.41)	12870
1970			63 (0.48)	68 (0.52)	4034 (30.96)		14712 (112.91)	13030
1971			80 (0.61)	92 (0.70)	3627 (27.50)		15097 (114.46)	13190
1972			73 (0.55)	85 (0.64)	3659 (27.45)		15595 (116.99)	13330

FOOTNOTES:
1. MURDER AND MANSLAUGHTER
2. THEFT, ROBBERY, HOUSEBREAKING

NETHERLANDS ANTILLES *   NUMBER OF OFFENSES REPORTED -- (RATE PER 100,000)

YEAR	MURDER ( )	MANSLTR ( )	HOMICIDE ( )	RAPE (1)	ASSAULT ( )	ROBBERY ( )	THEFT ( )	POP
1955	35 (19.44)			91 (50.56)		367 (203.89)	677 (376.11)	180
1956	24 (13.19)			204 (112.09)		278 (152.75)	732 (402.20)	182
1957	22 (11.89)			116 (62.70)		313 (169.19)	730 (394.59)	185
1958	38 (20.32)			105 (56.15)		432 (231.02)	853 (456.15)	187
1959	45 (23.94)			140 (74.47)		493 (262.23)	852 (453.19)	188
1960	22 (11.58)			139 (73.16)		604 (317.89)	863 (454.21)	190
1961	12 (6.19)			101 (52.06)		566 (291.75)	871 (448.97)	194
1962	34 (17.17)			160 (80.81)		547 (276.26)	781 (394.44)	198
1963	31 (15.35)			132 (65.35)		504 (249.51)	785 (388.61)	202
1964	29 (14.15)			134 (65.37)		741 (361.46)	773 (377.07)	205
1965	27 (12.92)			122 (58.37)		702 (335.89)	924 (442.11)	209
1966	33 (15.64)			156 (73.93)		723 (342.65)	988 (468.25)	211
1967	25 (11.74)			151 (70.89)		719 (337.56)	985 (462.44)	213
1968	45 (20.83)			150 (69.44)		925 (428.24)	1081 (500.46)	216
1969	31 (14.22)			116 (53.21)		1031 (472.94)	1026 (470.64)	218
1970	45 (20.27)			122 (54.95)		932 (419.82)	1433 (645.50)	222

FOOTNOTES:
   * RAW CRIME DATA FROM INTERPOL; RATES COMPUTED FROM
     POPULATION FIGURES ABOVE
   1. SEX OFFENSES

NEW ZEALAND

NUMBER OF CONVICTIONS -- (RATE PER 100,000)

YEAR	MURDER ( )	MANSLTR ( )	HOMICIDE ( )	RAPE ( )	ASSAULT (1)	ROBBERY ( )	THEFT ( )	POP
1920	3 (0.24)			0 (0.00)	696 (52.53)	13 (0.98)	1762 (132.98)	1241
1921	2 (0.16)			2 (0.15)	549 (40.58)	12 (0.89)	1785 (131.93)	1269
1922	0 (0.00)							1297
1923	2 (0.15)							1325
1924	2 (0.15)							1353
1925	0 (0.00)							1382
1926	0 (0.00)			5 (0.36)	697 (49.64)	5 (0.36)	2049 (145.94)	1404
1927	0 (0.00)			4 (0.28)	636 (44.60)	3 (0.21)	3000 (210.38)	1426
1928	1 (0.07)			3 (0.21)	569 (39.30)	12 (0.83)	2862 (197.65)	1448
1929	1 (0.07)			2 (0.14)	566 (38.50)	3 (0.20)	3031 (206.19)	1470
1930	3 (0.20)			4 (0.27)	507 (34.00)	3 (0.20)	3496 (234.47)	1491
1931	4 (0.27)			2 (0.13)	512 (34.02)	8 (0.53)	3880 (257.81)	1505
1932	4 (0.26)							1519
1933	2 (0.13)			0 (0.00)	486 (31.70)	6 (0.39)	8377 (546.44)	1533
1934	1 (0.06)			1 (0.06)	428 (27.67)	4 (0.26)	3713 (240.01)	1547
1935	1 (0.06)							1560
1936	0 (0.00)			2 (0.13)	508 (32.25)	5 (0.32)	3820 (242.54)	1575
1937	0 (0.00)			0 (0.00)	471 (29.62)	1 (0.06)	4005 (251.89)	1590
1938	2 (0.12)			2 (0.12)	578 (36.01)	4 (0.25)	2631 (163.93)	1605
1939	1 (0.06)			4 (0.25)	635 (39.20)	6 (0.37)	2890 (178.40)	1620
1940	1 (0.06)			0 (0.00)	661 (40.40)	4 (0.24)	3253 (198.84)	1636
1941	1 (0.06)			3 (0.18)	553 (33.76)		3061 (186.87)	1638
1942	2 (0.12)							1639
1943	2 (0.12)							1633
1944	0 (0.00)							1654
1945	4 (0.24)							1688
1946	2 (0.11)			4 (0.22)	618 (34.39)	5 (0.28)	2755 (153.31)	1759
1947	4 (0.22)			5 (0.27)	587 (32.02)	1 (0.05)	2712 (147.95)	1797
1948	6 (0.33)			5 (0.27)	651 (34.79)	6 (0.32)	2630 (140.57)	1833
1949	3 (0.16)							1871
1950	8 (0.42)			8 (0.42)	678 (35.53)	4 (0.21)	2420 (126.83)	1908
1951	3 (0.15)			1 (0.05)	731 (37.54)	12 (0.62)	2256 (115.87)	1947
1952	2 (0.10)			16 (0.80)	671 (33.63)	4 (0.20)	2516 (126.12)	1995
1953	6 (0.29)			21 (1.03)	701 (34.25)	39 (1.91)	2693 (131.56)	2047
1954	4 (0.19)			9 (0.43)	786 (37.55)	83 (3.97)	2847 (136.02)	2093
1955	5 (0.23)			5 (0.23)	774 (36.24)	76 (3.56)	2639 (123.55)	2136
1956	1 (0.05)			22 (1.01)	910 (41.78)	30 (1.38)	1705 (78.28)	2178
1957	1 (0.04)			10 (0.45)	880 (39.48)	36 (1.62)	3559 (159.67)	2229
1958	1 (0.04)			17 (0.74)	973 (42.64)	27 (1.18)	4514 (197.81)	2282
1959	3 (0.13)			10 (0.43)	865 (37.11)	33 (1.42)	4002 (171.69)	2331
1960	1 (0.04)			17 (0.72)	1003 (42.29)	42 (1.77)	3953 (166.65)	2372
1961	2 (0.08)			47 (1.94)	1471 (60.79)	23 (0.95)	3523 (145.58)	2420
1962	2 (0.08)			20 (0.80)	1337 (53.80)	25 (1.01)	3971 (159.80)	2485
1963	3 (0.12)			23 (0.91)	1439 (56.70)	16 (0.63)	3932 (154.93)	2538
1964	4 (0.15)			8 (0.31)	1550 (59.75)	21 (0.81)	4092 (157.75)	2594

NEW ZEALAND   NUMBER OF CONVICTIONS -- (RATE PER 100,000)   CONTINUED

YEAR	MURDER ( )	MANSLTR ( )	HOMICIDE ( )	RAPE ( )	ASSAULT (1)	ROBBERY ( )	THEFT ( )	POP
1965	2 (0.08)			20 (0.76)	1469 (55.86)	17 (0.65)	4330 (164.64)	2630
1966	6 (0.22)			30 (1.12)	1871 (69.81)	24 (0.90)	5194 (193.81)	2680
1967	3 (0.11)			36 (1.32)	1813 (66.65)	17 (0.63)	5545 (203.86)	2720
1968	4 (0.15)			11 (0.40)	2349 (85.42)	57 (2.07)	6376 (231.85)	2750
1969	2 (0.07)			11 (0.40)	2324 (83.90)	55 (1.99)	6671 (240.83)	2770
1970	7 (0.25)			19 (0.68)	2612 (92.95)	59 (2.10)	6749 (240.18)	2810
1971	5 (0.18)			9 (0.32)	3107 (109.02)	91 (3.19)	7436 (260.91)	2850
1972	2 (0.07)					91 (3.14)	7456 (257.10)	2900

FOOTNOTES:
    1. COMMON ASSAULT

NIGERIA *   NUMBER OF OFFENSES REPORTED -- (RATE PER 100,000)

YEAR	MURDER ( )	MANSLTR ( )	HOMICIDE ( )	RAPE (1)	ASSAULT ( )	ROBBERY ( )	THEFT ( )	POP
1958	566 (1.38)			640 (1.56)		8122 (19.84)	26864 (65.63)	40930
1959								
1960	606 (1.41)			1834 (4.27)		9489 (22.09)	30516 (71.05)	42950
1961	522 (1.19)			1985 (4.51)		10171 (23.09)	34927 (79.29)	44050
1962	651 (1.44)			2058 (4.56)		11581 (25.64)	37153 (82.25)	45170
1963	644 (1.39)			2420 (5.22)		11512 (24.85)	35838 (77.37)	46320
1964	1045 (2.20)			2695 (5.67)		11330 (23.86)	41415 (87.21)	47490
1965	1111 (2.28)			2107 (4.33)		12535 (25.75)	39958 (82.08)	48680
1966	1265 (2.54)			2294 (4.60)		16005 (32.09)	52718 (105.69)	49880
1967	550 (1.08)			2090 (4.09)		9020 (17.64)	23760 (46.48)	51120
1968	660 (1.26)			1210 (2.31)		8195 (15.64)	20460 (39.05)	52390
1969	770 (1.43)			1430 (2.66)		7370 (13.72)	27005 (50.29)	53700
1970	1100 (2.00)			1925 (3.50)		12100 (21.97)	46695 (84.79)	55070

FOOTNOTES:
    * RAW CRIME DATA FROM INTERPOL; RATES COMPUTED FROM POPULATION FIGURES ABOVE
    1. SEX OFFENSES

NORTHERN IRELAND *   CRIME STATISTICS -- (RATE PER 100,000)

YEAR	MURDER ( )	MANSLTR ( )	HOMICIDE ( )	RAPE ( )	ASSAULT ( )	ROBBERY ( )	THEFT ( )	POP
1922	295 (23.45)	14 (1.11)		1 (0.08)	365 (29.01)	528 (41.97)		1258
1923	2 (0.16)	8 (0.64)		6 (0.48)	51 (4.06)	88 (7.00)		1257
1924	2 (0.16)	2 (0.16)		6 (0.48)	31 (2.47)	54 (4.30)		1257
1925	2 (0.16)	4 (0.32)		2 (0.16)	29 (2.31)	57 (4.53)		1257
1926	3 (0.24)	5 (0.40)		2 (0.16)	26 (2.08)	47 (3.75)		1253
1927	1 (0.08)	3 (0.24)		1 (0.08)	26 (2.08)	15 (1.20)		1249
1928	5 (0.40)	11 (0.88)		2 (0.16)	23 (1.85)	19 (1.53)		1245
1929	3 (0.24)	11 (0.89)		2 (0.16)	39 (3.14)	17 (1.37)		1241
1930	2 (0.16)	6 (0.49)		5 (0.40)	26 (2.10)	10 (0.81)		1237
1931	5 (0.40)	8 (0.64)		3 (0.24)	33 (2.65)	13 (1.05)		1244
1932	2 (0.16)	4 (0.32)		1 (0.08)	41 (3.28)	24 (1.92)		1251
1933	5 (0.40)	7 (0.56)		3 (0.24)	28 (2.23)	11 (0.87)		1258
1934	5 (0.40)	6 (0.47)		2 (0.16)	45 (3.56)	29 (2.29)		1265
1935	13 (1.02)	1 (0.08)		0 (0.00)	39 (3.07)	26 (2.05)		1271
1936	1 (0.08)	2 (0.16)		3 (0.23)	36 (2.82)	9 (0.70)		1277
1937	1 (0.08)	2 (0.16)		0 (0.00)	40 (3.12)	11 (0.86)		1283
1938	2 (0.16)	1 (0.08)		8 (0.62)	30 (2.33)	7 (0.54)		1290
1939	1 (0.08)	2 (0.15)		2 (0.15)	18 (1.39)	15 (1.16)		1295
1940	2 (0.15)	3 (0.23)		1 (0.08)	21 (1.62)	35 (2.69)		1299
1941	3 (0.23)	5 (0.38)		3 (0.23)	28 (2.13)	22 (1.67)		1314
1942	8 (0.60)	5 (0.38)		2 (0.15)	21 (1.58)	20 (1.50)		1329
1943	3 (0.22)	1 (0.07)		3 (0.22)	27 (2.01)	13 (0.97)		1341
1944	3 (0.22)	3 (0.22)		4 (0.29)	24 (1.77)	19 (1.40)		1357
1945	0 (0.00)	1 (0.07)		4 (0.30)	23 (1.69)	27 (1.99)		1359
1946	0 (0.00)	4 (0.30)		3 (0.22)	29 (2.15)	26 (1.93)		1350
1947	0 (0.00)	1 (0.07)		4 (0.29)	57 (4.22)	13 (0.96)		1350
1948	1 (0.07)	2 (0.15)		3 (0.22)	62 (4.55)	25 (1.84)		1362
1949	2 (0.15)	2 (0.15)		3 (0.22)	75 (5.47)	19 (1.39)		1371
1950	1 (0.07)	0 (0.00)		11 (0.80)	81 (5.92)	21 (1.53)		1369
1951	0 (0.00)	2 (0.15)		2 (0.15)	76 (5.54)	24 (1.75)		1373
1952	3 (0.22)	3 (0.22)		0 (0.00)	73 (5.31)	22 (1.60)		1375
1953	2 (0.14)	2 (0.14)		4 (0.29)	79 (5.71)	18 (1.30)		1384
1954	2 (0.14)	6 (0.43)		2 (0.14)	94 (6.78)	18 (1.30)		1387
1955	1 (0.07)	0 (0.00)		3 (0.22)	101 (7.25)	10 (0.72)		1394
1956	1 (0.07)	1 (0.07)		3 (0.21)	106 (7.56)	22 (1.57)		1402
1957	3 (0.21)	3 (0.21)		2 (0.14)	97 (6.91)	15 (1.07)		1403
1958	3 (0.21)	4 (0.29)		3 (0.21)	111 (7.91)	29 (2.07)		1403
1959	0 (0.00)	0 (0.00)		4 (0.28)	111 (7.86)	31 (2.20)		1412
1960	9 (0.63)	7 (0.49)		6 (0.42)	133 (9.35)	35 (2.46)		1423
1961	5 (0.35)	1 (0.07)		7 (0.49)	91 (6.36)	39 (2.73)		1430
1962	3 (0.21)	0 (0.00)		7 (0.49)	160 (11.13)	48 (3.34)		1437
1963	0 (0.00)	0 (0.00)		4 (0.28)	235 (16.23)	27 (1.86)		1448
1964	1 (0.07)	0 (0.00)		5 (0.34)	231 (15.82)	23 (1.58)		1460
1965	1 (0.07)	0 (0.00)		18 (1.22)	194 (13.20)	43 (2.93)		1470
1966	3 (0.20)	0 (0.00)		14 (0.95)	248 (16.76)	37 (2.50)		1480
1967	8 (0.54)	1 (0.07)		15 (1.01)	230 (15.44)	45 (3.02)		1490

NORTHERN IRELAND *   CRIME STATISTICS -- (RATE PER 100,000)   CONTINUED

YEAR	MURDER ( )	MANSLTR ( )	HOMICIDE ( )	RAPE ( )	ASSAULT ( )	ROBBERY ( )	THEFT ( )	POP
1968	2 (0.13)	0 (0.00)		27 (1.80)	362 (24.13)	50 (3.53)		1500
1969	5 (0.33)	7 (0.46)		15 (0.99)	1064 (70.46)	89 (5.89)		1510
1970	15 (0.99)	5 (0.33)		17 (1.12)	478 (31.45)	109 (7.17)		1520
1971	123 (8.04)	11 (0.72)		15 (0.98)	998 (65.23)	640 (41.83)		1530
1972	376 (24.26)	17 (1.10)		28 (1.81)	1097 (70.77)	2310 (149.03)		1550
1973	200 (12.93)	15 (0.97)		17 (1.10)	892 (57.66)	1886 (121.91)		1547

FOOTNOTES: * YEARS OF POLITICAL TURMOIL: 1922,
1933-35, 1941-42, 1956-61, 1969-73

YEAR	MURDER ( )	MANSLTR ( )	HOMICIDE ( )	RAPE ( )	ASSAULT ( )	ROBBERY ( )	THEFT (1)	POP
1903	7 (0.31)			3 (0.13)	443 (19.39)	11 (0.48)	1779 (77.86)	2285
1904	8 (0.35)			5 (0.22)	336 (14.61)	18 (0.77)	1710 (74.35)	2300
1905	7 (0.30)			6 (0.26)	310 (13.39)	10 (0.43)	1512 (65.31)	2315
1906	9 (0.39)			7 (0.30)	296 (12.70)	10 (0.43)	1567 (67.25)	2330
1907	11 (0.47)			5 (0.21)	309 (13.18)	14 (0.59)	1214 (51.77)	2345
1908	15 (0.64)			4 (0.17)	255 (10.81)	14 (0.59)	1479 (62.67)	2360
1909	6 (0.25)			12 (0.51)	268 (11.28)	12 (0.51)	1594 (67.12)	2375
1910	14 (0.59)			5 (0.21)	280 (11.71)	14 (0.59)	1556 (65.05)	2392
1911	9 (0.37)			5 (0.21)	287 (11.88)	13 (0.54)	1371 (56.75)	2416
1912	6 (0.25)			7 (0.29)	274 (11.23)	7 (0.29)	1465 (60.04)	2440
1913	12 (0.49)			7 (0.28)	262 (10.63)	17 (0.69)	1573 (63.84)	2464
1914	13 (0.52)			7 (0.28)	248 (9.97)	21 (0.84)	1815 (72.95)	2488
1915	6 (0.24)			10 (0.40)	480 (19.11)	9 (0.36)	1883 (74.96)	2512
1916	11 (0.43)			7 (0.28)	476 (18.77)	9 (0.35)	2156 (85.02)	2536
1917	6 (0.23)			7 (0.27)	435 (16.99)	18 (0.70)	2365 (92.38)	2560
1918	6 (0.23)			4 (0.15)	437 (16.91)	10 (0.39)	2884 (111.61)	2584
1919	4 (0.15)			7 (0.27)	582 (22.32)	15 (0.58)	2385 (91.45)	2608
1920	4 (0.15)			12 (0.46)	545 (20.68)	10 (0.38)	1774 (67.32)	2635
1921	10 (0.38)			11 (0.41)	591 (22.24)	18 (0.68)	1843 (69.36)	2657
1922	13 (0.49)			9 (0.34)	617 (23.03)	29 (1.08)	1617 (60.36)	2679
1923	4 (0.15)	8 (0.30)		14 (0.52)	568 (21.03)		2317 (85.78)	2701
1924	3 (0.11)	3 (0.11)		13 (0.48)	512 (18.80)		2348 (86.23)	2723
1925	6 (0.22)	6 (0.22)		9 (0.33)	457 (16.64)		2944 (107.17)	2747
1926	2 (0.07)	15 (0.54)		21 (0.76)	512 (18.56)		2898 (105.04)	2759
1927	2 (0.07)	4 (0.14)		5 (0.18)	495 (17.86)		2905 (104.84)	2771
1928	5 (0.18)	6 (0.22)		9 (0.32)	439 (15.77)		2847 (102.30)	2783
1929	4 (0.14)	3 (0.11)		8 (0.29)	413 (14.78)		2840 (101.61)	2795
1930	6 (0.21)	9 (0.32)		10 (0.36)	489 (17.42)		2984 (106.31)	2807
1931	4 (0.14)	9 (0.32)		12 (0.43)	489 (17.32)		2603 (92.21)	2823
1932	2 (0.07)	8 (0.28)		16 (0.56)	477 (16.80)		2751 (96.90)	2839
1933	4 (0.14)	6 (0.21)		12 (0.42)	403 (14.12)		2792 (97.79)	2855
1934	7 (0.24)	5 (0.17)		14 (0.49)	446 (15.53)		2809 (97.84)	2871
1935	5 (0.17)	6 (0.21)		3 (0.10)	452 (15.65)		2557 (88.51)	2889
1936	7 (0.24)	6 (0.21)		4 (0.14)	448 (15.42)		2590 (89.13)	2906
1937	5 (0.17)	9 (0.31)		14 (0.48)	443 (15.16)		2562 (87.65)	2923
1938	2 (0.07)	7 (0.24)		13 (0.44)	424 (14.42)		2573 (87.52)	2940
1939	1 (0.03)	8 (0.27)		13 (0.44)	470 (15.89)		2565 (86.74)	2957
1940	2 (0.07)	4 (0.13)		7 (0.24)	280 (9.42)		2334 (78.51)	2973
1941	3 (0.10)	4 (0.13)		7 (0.23)	314 (10.50)		3063 (102.44)	2990
1942	7 (0.23)	2 (0.07)		6 (0.20)	307 (10.21)		3755 (124.92)	3006
1943	6 (0.20)	6 (0.20)		12 (0.40)	287 (9.47)		4421 (145.91)	3030
1944	4 (0.13)	8 (0.26)		12 (0.39)	269 (8.80)		4208 (137.65)	3057
1945	4 (0.13)	12 (0.39)		10 (0.32)	229 (7.42)		3212 (104.02)	3088
1946	5 (0.17)	4 (0.13)		13 (0.42)	384 (12.29)		3566 (114.15)	3124
1947	10 (0.32)	9 (0.28)		12 (0.38)	389 (12.30)		3392 (107.24)	3163
1948	7 (0.22)	8 (0.25)		12 (0.38)	389 (12.16)		2733 (85.41)	3200

NORWAY *

CRIME STATISTICS -- (RATE PER 100,000)   CONTINUED

YEAR	MURDER ( )		MANSLTR ( )		HOMICIDE ( )		RAPE ( )		ASSAULT ( )		ROBBERY ( )		THEFT (1)		POP
1949	8 (	0.25)	4 (	0.12)	(	)	9 (	0.28)	382 (	11.82)	(	)	2363 (	73.09)	3233
1950	6 (	0.18)	0 (	0.00)			17 (	0.52)	378 (	11.58)			2235 (	68.45)	3265
1951	8 (	0.24)	5 (	0.15)			10 (	0.30)	353 (	10.71)			2225 (	67.51)	3296
1952	3 (	0.09)	4 (	0.12)			15 (	0.45)	315 (	9.47)			2392 (	71.90)	3327
1953	1 (	0.03)	5 (	0.15)			12 (	0.36)	353 (	10.51)			2258 (	67.22)	3359
1954	6 (	0.18)	1 (	0.03)			13 (	0.38)	372 (	10.97)			2172 (	64.03)	3392
1955	7 (	0.20)	4 (	0.12)			5 (	0.15)	355 (	10.36)			2307 (	67.32)	3427
1956	6 (	0.17)	11 (	0.32)			10 (	0.29)	346 (	10.00)			2793 (	80.72)	3460
1957	4 (	0.11)	7 (	0.20)			10 (	0.29)	346 (	9.91)			3106 (	88.95)	3492
1958	6 (	0.17)	11 (	0.31)			9 (	0.26)	325 (	9.23)			3342 (	94.86)	3523
1959	6 (	0.17)	6 (	0.17)			14 (	0.39)	314 (	8.84)			3531 (	99.38)	3553
1960	7 (	0.20)	10 (	0.28)			11 (	0.31)	324 (	9.05)			3751 (	104.75)	3581
1961	7 (	0.19)	5 (	0.14)			18 (	0.50)	318 (	8.81)			4177 (	115.71)	3610
1962	3 (	0.08)	8 (	0.22)			15 (	0.41)	342 (	9.40)			4391 (	120.67)	3639
1963	8 (	0.22)	11 (	0.30)			28 (	0.76)	337 (	9.19)			4495 (	122.58)	3667
1964	10 (	0.27)	7 (	0.19)			24 (	0.65)	389 (	10.54)			4997 (	135.42)	3690
1965	7 (	0.19)	9 (	0.24)			18 (	0.48)	385 (	10.35)			5004 (	134.52)	3720
1966	5 (	0.13)	14 (	0.37)			16 (	0.43)	468 (	12.48)			5305 (	141.47)	3750
1967	11 (	0.29)	17 (	0.45)			26 (	0.69)	357 (	9.42)			5678 (	149.82)	3790
1968	5 (	0.13)	9 (	0.24)			10 (	0.26)	454 (	11.88)			5780 (	151.31)	3820
1969	12 (	0.31)	15 (	0.39)			22 (	0.57)	533 (	13.84)			6129 (	159.19)	3850
1970	9 (	0.23)	17 (	0.44)			26 (	0.67)	556 (	14.33)			6136 (	158.14)	3880

FOOTNOTES:
* PERSONS PROCEEDED AGAINST
1. THEFT AND ROBBERY

PAKISTAN *

NUMBER OF OFFENSES REPORTED -- (RATE PER 100,000)

YEAR	MURDER ( )	MANSLTR ( )	HOMICIDE ( )	RAPE (1)	ASSAULT ( )	ROBBERY ( )	THEFT ( )	POP
1961	6803 (6.62)			2064 (2.01)		27286 (26.55)	36135 (35.16)	102770
1962	7225 (6.85)			2214 (2.10)		28084 (26.64)	36238 (34.37)	105440
1963	7084 (6.55)			2074 (1.92)		29951 (27.69)	27615 (25.53)	108180
1964								113930
1965	7752 (6.80)			1699 (1.49)		28540 (25.05)	28737 (25.22)	117000
1966	8418 (7.19)			3200 (2.74)		30107 (25.73)	32313 (27.62)	120160
1967	8380 (6.97)			1990 (1.66)		30680 (25.53)	33467 (27.85)	123410
1968	8287 (6.72)			1943 (1.57)		30586 (24.78)	33720 (27.32)	

FOOTNOTES:
* RAW CRIME DATA FROM INTERPOL; RATES COMPUTED FROM POPULATION FIGURES ABOVE
1. SEX OFFENSES

PANAMA

CRIME STATISTICS -- (RATE PER 100,000)

YEAR	MURDER ( )	MANSLTR ( )	HOMICIDE ( )	RAPE (1)	ASSAULT ( )	ROBBERY ( )	THEFT ( )	POP
1963			189 (16.15)	107 (9.15)	65 (5.56)			1170
1964			109 (9.01)	84 (6.94)	40 (3.31)			1210
1965			141 (11.46)	129 (10.49)	38 (3.09)			1230
1966			158 (12.44)	110 (8.66)	65 (5.12)			1270
1967			146 (11.15)	105 (8.02)	74 (5.65)			1310
1968			168 (12.44)	125 (9.26)	102 (7.56)			1350
1969			153 (11.01)	142 (10.22)	144 (10.36)			1390
1970			119 (8.32)	125 (8.74)	204 (14.27)			1430
1971			154 (10.41)	137 (9.26)	144 (9.73)			1480
1972			132 (8.68)	125 (8.22)	155 (10.20)			1520
1973			146 (9.31)	155 (9.89)	170 (10.84)			1568

FOOTNOTES:
1. SEX OFFENSES

PERU *

NUMBER OF OFFENSES REPORTED -- (RATE PER 100,000)

YEAR	MURDER ( )	MANSLTR ( )	HOMICIDE ( )	RAPE (1)	ASSAULT ( )	ROBBERY ( )	THEFT ( )	POP
1961	992 (10.01)			1810 (18.27)		7897 (79.71)	4147 (41.86)	9907
1962	1423 (13.58)			1822 (17.14)		9970 (93.77)	3886 (36.55)	10632
1963	1448 (13.21)			2220 (20.26)		6983 (63.73)	10838 (98.90)	10958
1964	2024 (17.82)			2243 (19.75)		6962 (61.30)	10851 (95.54)	11357
1965	780 (6.70)			2307 (19.80)		4156 (35.67)	8820 (75.71)	11650
1966	1062 (8.84)			1764 (14.69)		4100 (34.14)	7627 (63.51)	12010
1967	269 (2.17)			1980 (15.98)		13638 (110.07)		12390
1968	180 (1.41)			2100 (16.44)		15504 (121.41)		12770
1969	1963 (14.91)			1950 (14.81)		1248 (9.48)		13170
1970	2474 (18.20)			2288 (16.84)				13590

FOOTNOTES:
* RAW CRIME DATA FROM INTERPOL; RATES COMPUTED FROM
  POPULATION FIGURES ABOVE
1. SEX OFFENSES

PHILIPPINES *

NUMBER OF OFFENSES REPORTED -- (RATE PER 100,000)

YEAR	MURDER (1)	MANSLTR ( )	HOMICIDE ( )	RAPE (2)	ASSAULT ( )	ROBBERY ( )	THEFT ( )	POP
1962	663 (2.27)		1314 (4.49)	147 (0.50)		966 (3.30)	738 (2.52)	29257
1963	674 (2.23)		1286 (4.25)	149 (0.49)		1005 (3.32)	689 (2.28)	30241
1964	770 (2.46)		1469 (4.70)	137 (0.44)		1012 (3.24)	906 (2.90)	31270
1965	825 (2.60)		1398 (4.41)	147 (0.46)		962 (3.04)	851 (2.69)	31670
1966	1029 (3.15)		1618 (4.96)	137 (0.42)		1120 (3.43)	933 (2.86)	32630
1967	926 (2.75)		1680 (5.00)	175 (0.52)		1700 (5.06)	917 (2.73)	33630
1968	1084 (3.13)		1910 (5.51)	214 (0.62)		1327 (3.83)	1021 (2.95)	34660
1969	1302 (3.64)		1999 (5.59)	219 (0.61)		1431 (4.00)	909 (2.54)	35740
1970	817 (2.22)		1448 (3.93)	141 (0.38)		1237 (3.36)	764 (2.07)	36850
1971	638 (1.68)		1508 (3.98)			1297 (3.42)	575 (1.52)	37920
1972	834 (2.14)		1968 (5.04)			1574 (4.03)	467 (1.20)	39040

FOOTNOTES:
* CRIMES ARE FOR FISCAL YEARS BEGINNING IN YEAR INDICATED
1. PARRICIDE AND MURDER
2. RAPE AND OTHER SEX OFFENSES

POLAND *   NUMBER OF OFFENSES REPORTED -- (RATE PER 100,000)

YEAR	MURDER ( )	MANSLTR ( )	HOMICIDE (1)	RAPE ( )	ASSAULT (2)	ROBBERY (3)	THEFT ( )	POP
1923	2897 (10.25)				25175 (89.07)	42127 (149.04)	149726 (529.72)	28265
1924	2562 (8.90)				28085 (97.62)	26392 (91.73)	124764 (433.65)	28771
1925	2729 (9.32)				34801 (118.88)	24493 (83.67)	123909 (423.26)	29275
1926	2798 (9.42)				50491 (169.92)	30654 (103.16)	162277 (546.13)	29714
1927	2587 (8.58)				57150 (189.53)	33547 (111.26)	190575 (632.03)	30153
1928	2811 (9.19)				72334 (236.45)	33764 (110.37)	191889 (627.25)	30592
1929	2933 (9.45)				72203 (232.68)	32953 (106.19)	192880 (621.57)	31031
1930								
GAP								
1965			439 (1.39)		6310 (20.03)	2569 (8.16)	94509 (300.03)	31500
1966			442 (1.39)		6342 (20.01)	4286 (13.52)	120052 (378.71)	31700
1967			398 (1.25)		5770 (18.07)	3996 (12.51)	112784 (353.11)	31940
1968			380 (1.18)		4920 (15.23)	3888 (12.03)	104969 (324.88)	32310
1969			416 (1.28)		4876 (14.98)	5347 (16.42)	115198 (353.80)	32560
1970			500 (1.54)		4700 (14.45)		92700 (284.97)	32530
1971			600 (1.83)		6400 (19.51)		99600 (303.57)	32810
1972			600 (1.81)		6000 (18.14)		76600 (231.63)	33070

FOOTNOTES:
* RAW FIGURES ROUNDED FROM 1970
1. HOMICIDE AND ATTEMPTED HOMICIDE FROM 1965
2. FIGHTS FROM 1965
3. BURGLARY BEFORE 1931

PORTUGAL

NUMBER OF CONVICTIONS -- (RATE PER 100,000)

YEAR	MURDER ( )	MANSLTR (1)	HOMICIDE (2)	RAPE ( )	ASSAULT (3)	ROBBERY (4)	THEFT (5)	POP
		33 (0.61)	117 (2.16)		8449 (155.80)	194 (3.58)	2541 (46.86)	5423
1900								
1901								
1902								
1903		47 (0.84)	78 (1.40)		8518 (152.93)	125 (2.24)	2463 (44.22)	5570
1904		50 (0.89)	98 (1.74)		8477 (150.86)	109 (1.94)	2412 (42.93)	5619
1905		57 (1.01)	102 (1.80)		9386 (165.60)	132 (2.33)	2629 (46.38)	5668
1906		66 (1.15)	100 (1.75)		9266 (162.08)	222 (3.88)	2323 (40.63)	5717
1907		48 (0.83)	106 (1.84)		9403 (163.08)	79 (1.37)	2519 (43.69)	5766
1908		53 (0.91)	139 (2.39)		9487 (163.15)	142 (2.44)	2880 (49.53)	5815
1909		53 (0.90)	123 (2.10)		9809 (167.27)	109 (1.86)	2797 (47.70)	5864
1910		50 (0.85)	113 (1.91)		8593 (145.32)	133 (2.25)	2548 (43.09)	5913
1911		35 (0.59)	122 (2.05)		6381 (107.06)	130 (2.18)	2355 (39.51)	5960
1912		32 (0.54)	129 (2.16)		5899 (98.84)	74 (1.24)	2385 (39.96)	5968
1913		34 (0.57)	167 (2.79)		5980 (100.07)	129 (2.16)	2511 (42.02)	5976
1914		63 (1.05)	178 (2.97)		5820 (97.26)	168 (2.81)	2440 (40.78)	5984
1915		38 (0.63)	146 (2.44)		6041 (100.82)	193 (3.22)	2628 (43.86)	5992
1916		41 (0.68)	149 (2.48)		5937 (98.95)	160 (2.67)	2963 (49.38)	6000
1917		44 (0.73)	146 (2.43)		5956 (99.13)	214 (3.56)	3285 (54.68)	6008
1918		44 (0.73)	150 (2.49)		5162 (85.80)	181 (3.01)	2983 (49.58)	6016
1919		38 (0.63)	169 (2.81)		5127 (85.11)	180 (2.99)	2732 (45.35)	6024
1920		43 (0.71)	211 (3.50)		4840 (80.23)	245 (4.06)	2383 (39.50)	6033
1921		54 (0.88)	214 (3.50)		4954 (81.13)	271 (4.44)	2394 (39.21)	6106
1922		66 (1.07)	219 (3.54)		4790 (77.52)	238 (3.85)	1983 (32.09)	6179
1923		63 (1.01)	188 (3.01)		4859 (77.72)	173 (2.77)	2193 (35.08)	6252
1924		54 (0.85)	192 (3.04)		4408 (69.69)	147 (2.32)	1864 (29.47)	6325
1925		114 (1.78)	190 (2.97)		5249 (82.07)	167 (2.61)	1914 (29.92)	6396
1926		54 (0.83)	203 (3.13)		5215 (80.45)	159 (2.45)	1857 (28.65)	6482
1927		74 (1.13)	175 (2.66)		5044 (76.80)	157 (2.39)	1779 (27.09)	6568
1928		59 (0.89)	189 (2.84)		4880 (73.34)	160 (2.40)	1730 (26.00)	6654
1929		76 (1.13)	254 (3.77)		5215 (77.37)	223 (3.31)	1848 (27.42)	6740
1930		86 (1.26)	215 (3.15)		5336 (78.17)	119 (1.74)	2102 (30.79)	6826
1931		73 (1.06)	202 (2.92)		5074 (73.45)	73 (1.06)	1622 (23.48)	6908
1932		72 (1.03)	204 (2.92)		5679 (81.24)	56 (0.80)	1675 (23.96)	6990
1933		64 (0.90)	200 (2.83)		6201 (87.68)	119 (1.68)	2329 (32.93)	7072
1934		79 (1.10)	227 (3.17)		6776 (94.72)	101 (1.41)	2435 (34.04)	7154
1935		111 (1.53)	219 (3.03)		6989 (96.57)	121 (1.67)	2914 (40.27)	7237
1936		61 (0.83)	154 (2.10)		4952 (67.52)	43 (0.59)	2352 (32.07)	7334
1937		84 (1.13)	86 (1.16)		5108 (68.74)	60 (0.81)	1164 (15.66)	7431
1938		83 (1.10)	75 (1.00)		5414 (71.92)	56 (0.74)	1337 (17.76)	7528
1939		92 (1.21)	88 (1.15)		5882 (77.14)	39 (0.51)	1431 (18.77)	7625
1940		74 (0.96)	72 (0.93)		5408 (70.03)	39 (0.51)	1479 (19.15)	7722
1941		59 (0.76)	37 (0.48)		5231 (67.27)	80 (1.03)	2186 (28.11)	7776
1942		81 (1.03)	71 (0.91)		5434 (69.40)		2406 (30.73)	7830
1943								
1944		51 (0.64)	58 (0.73)		6353 (79.67)		3150 (39.50)	7974

PORTUGAL

NUMBER OF CONVICTIONS -- (RATE PER 100,000)   CONTINUED

YEAR	MURDER ( )	MANSLTR (1)	HOMICIDE (2)	RAPE ( )	ASSAULT (3)	ROBBERY (4)	THEFT (5)	POP
1945								
1946								
1947								
1948								
1949		69 (0.84)	75 (0.91)		7709 (93.31)	4055 (49.08)	3135 (37.94)	8262
1950		137 (1.63)	111 (1.32)		9655 (114.87)	5352 (63.68)	4278 (50.90)	8405
1951		165 (1.95)	125 (1.47)		9862 (116.34)	5116 (60.35)	4233 (49.94)	8477
1952		156 (1.82)	119 (1.39)		10845 (126.86)	5151 (60.25)	4399 (51.46)	8549
1953		166 (1.93)	94 (1.09)		10035 (116.40)	5119 (59.38)	3992 (46.31)	8621
1954		191 (2.20)	83 (0.95)		12034 (138.43)	4938 (56.80)	4056 (46.66)	8693
1955		148 (1.69)	82 (0.94)		15285 (174.39)	4892 (55.81)	3993 (45.56)	8765
1956		183 (2.12)	55 (0.64)		16221 (187.59)	4429 (51.22)	3593 (41.55)	8647
1957		188 (2.17)	78 (0.90)		10670 (122.93)	4892 (56.36)	3936 (45.35)	8680
1958		231 (2.65)	83 (0.95)		7243 (83.01)	4623 (52.99)	3813 (43.70)	8725
1959		272 (3.10)	92 (1.05)		6402 (72.95)	4204 (47.90)	3387 (38.59)	8776
1960		203 (2.30)	83 (0.94)		6424 (72.78)	4467 (50.61)	3552 (40.24)	8826
1961		291 (3.27)	96 (1.08)		6940 (78.03)	4109 (46.20)	3155 (35.47)	8894
1962		270 (3.03)	87 (0.97)		6675 (74.41)	3845 (42.86)	2944 (32.79)	8971
1963		270 (2.99)	73 (0.81)		6441 (71.27)	4071 (45.05)	2944 (32.58)	9037
1964		126 (1.38)	91 (1.00)		6435 (70.66)	3671 (40.31)	2382 (26.16)	9107
1965		62 (0.67)	74 (0.80)		6467 (70.29)	3494 (37.98)	2155 (23.42)	9200
1966		84 (0.90)	74 (0.80)		5677 (61.04)	3354 (36.06)	1979 (21.28)	9300
1967		98 (1.04)	65 (0.69)		4832 (51.51)	3084 (32.88)	1807 (19.26)	9380
1968		28 (0.30)	59 (0.62)		4865 (51.43)	2950 (31.18)	1728 (18.27)	9460

FOOTNOTES:
1. INVOLUNTARY HOMICIDE.
2. VOLUNTARY HOMICIDE; MEASURE CHANGE TO "SIMPLE VOLUNTARY HOMICIDE", PROBABLY IN 1937
3. BODILY OFFENSES (AND INJURY BEFORE 1937)
4. INCLUDES THEFT AND IMMORAL USURPATION AFTER 1947
5. SIMPLE THEFT AFTER 1936

PUERTO RICO *

NUMBER OF CONVICTIONS -- (RATE PER 100,000)

YEAR	MURDER ( )	MANSLTR ( )	HOMICIDE ( )	RAPE ( )	ASSAULT (1)	ROBBERY ( )	THEFT (2)	POP
1900	8 (0.83)		28 (2.89)	3 (0.31)	17 (1.76)	117 (12.09)	5 (0.52)	968
1901	3 (0.31)		25 (2.54)	5 (0.51)	13 (1.32)	79 (8.04)	5 (0.51)	983
1902	5 (0.50)		21 (2.10)	7 (0.70)	7 (0.70)	50 (5.01)	5 (0.50)	998
1903	9 (0.89)		30 (2.96)	7 (0.69)	7 (0.69)	14 (1.38)	32 (3.16)	1013
1904	9 (0.88)		25 (2.43)	9 (0.88)	3 (0.29)	8 (0.78)	26 (2.53)	1028
1905	25 (2.40)		15 (1.44)	20 (1.92)	14 (1.34)	2 (0.19)	58 (5.56)	1043
1906	16 (1.51)		21 (1.98)	16 (1.51)	15 (1.42)	1 (0.09)	82 (7.75)	1058
1907	9 (0.84)		19 (1.77)	18 (1.68)	19 (1.77)	3 (0.28)	90 (8.39)	1073
1908	9 (0.83)		20 (1.84)	11 (1.01)	6 (0.55)	4 (0.37)	96 (8.82)	1088
1909	5 (0.45)		17 (1.54)	6 (0.54)	15 (1.36)	4 (0.36)	129 (11.70)	1103
1910	12 (1.07)		48 (4.29)	10 (0.89)	6 (0.54)	2 (0.18)	141 (12.61)	1118
1911	17 (1.50)		22 (1.93)	6 (0.53)	12 (1.06)	0 (0.00)	32 (2.81)	1137
1912	10 (0.87)		33 (2.85)	9 (0.78)	5 (0.43)	1 (0.09)	69 (5.97)	1156
1913	8 (0.68)		21 (1.79)	4 (0.34)	5 (0.43)	1 (0.09)	74 (6.30)	1175
1914	12 (1.01)		15 (1.26)	11 (0.92)	10 (0.84)	0 (0.00)	43 (3.60)	1194
1915	6 (0.49)		22 (1.81)	16 (1.32)	5 (0.41)	0 (0.00)	72 (5.94)	1213
1916	25 (2.03)		45 (3.65)	9 (0.73)	10 (0.81)	0 (0.00)	121 (9.82)	1232
1917	17 (1.36)		16 (1.28)	8 (0.64)	10 (0.80)	0 (0.00)	56 (4.48)	1251
1918	14 (1.10)		12 (0.94)	6 (0.47)	19 (1.50)	7 (0.55)	67 (5.28)	1270
1919	6 (0.47)		24 (1.86)	12 (0.93)	4 (0.31)	2 (0.16)	59 (4.58)	1289
1920	12 (0.91)		17 (1.30)	5 (0.38)	2 (0.15)	1 (0.08)	57 (4.34)	1312
1921	8 (0.60)		47 (3.52)	9 (0.67)	3 (0.22)	1 (0.07)	65 (4.87)	1336
1922	17 (1.25)		46 (3.38)	6 (0.44)	11 (0.81)	1 (0.07)	56 (4.12)	1360
1923	19 (1.37)		56 (4.05)	8 (0.58)	8 (0.58)	0 (0.00)	61 (4.41)	1384
1924	27 (1.92)		72 (5.11)	6 (0.43)	8 (0.57)	5 (0.36)	67 (4.76)	1408
1925	21 (1.47)		55 (3.84)	10 (0.70)	10 (0.70)	3 (0.21)	90 (6.29)	1431
1926	37 (2.54)		88 (6.05)	11 (0.76)	11 (0.76)	7 (0.48)	149 (10.24)	1455
1927	27 (1.83)		65 (4.39)	17 (1.15)	10 (0.68)	7 (0.47)	152 (10.28)	1479
1928	23 (1.53)		59 (3.93)	18 (1.20)	10 (0.67)	4 (0.27)	129 (8.58)	1503
1929	31 (2.03)		88 (5.76)	17 (1.11)	18 (1.18)	5 (0.33)	153 (10.02)	1527
1930	28 (1.80)		85 (5.48)	17 (1.10)	18 (1.16)	8 (0.52)	148 (9.54)	1552
1931	33 (2.08)		87 (5.49)	17 (1.07)	21 (1.33)	5 (0.32)	153 (9.66)	1584
1932	44 (2.72)		99 (6.13)	15 (0.93)	12 (0.74)	11 (0.68)	145 (8.97)	1616
1933	38 (2.31)		100 (7.07)	15 (0.91)	20 (1.21)	9 (0.55)	165 (10.01)	1648
1934	46 (2.74)		87 (5.18)	29 (1.73)	22 (1.31)	15 (0.89)	153 (9.11)	1680
1935	61 (3.57)		94 (5.50)	16 (0.94)	27 (1.58)	25 (1.46)	189 (11.05)	1710
1936	55 (3.15)		108 (6.19)	22 (1.26)	20 (1.15)	11 (0.63)	173 (9.92)	1744
1937	64 (3.60)		115 (6.47)	34 (1.91)	35 (1.97)	20 (1.12)	198 (11.14)	1778
1938	44 (2.43)		123 (6.79)	34 (1.88)	39 (2.15)	27 (1.49)	209 (11.53)	1812
1939	59 (3.20)		107 (5.80)	24 (1.30)	24 (1.30)	19 (1.03)	290 (15.71)	1846
1940	43 (2.29)		128 (6.81)	13 (0.69)	26 (1.38)	26 (1.38)	169 (8.99)	1880
1941	47 (2.43)		95 (4.91)	22 (1.14)	95 (4.91)	22 (1.14)	179 (9.26)	1934
1942	50 (2.52)		118 (5.94)	19 (0.96)	108 (5.44)	29 (1.46)	221 (11.12)	1987
1943	57 (2.80)		101 (4.97)	33 (1.62)	32 (1.57)	29 (1.43)	265 (13.03)	2033
1944	72 (3.49)		102 (4.95)	33 (1.60)	46 (2.23)	60 (2.91)	165 (8.00)	2062

PUERTO RICO *

NUMBER OF CONVICTIONS -- (RATE PER 100,000) CONTINUED

YEAR	MURDER ( )	MANSLTR ( )	HOMICIDE ( )	RAPE ( )	ASSAULT (1)	ROBBERY ( )	THEFT (2)	POP
1945	34 (1.62)		70 (3.33)	13 (0.62)	41 (1.95)	18 (0.86)	101 (4.81)	2099
1946	111 (5.18)		163 (7.61)	60 (2.80)	86 (4.02)	31 (1.45)	212 (9.90)	2141
1947	54 (2.50)		83 (3.84)	60 (2.78)	29 (1.34)	31 (1.43)	201 (9.30)	2162
1948	96 (4.39)		78 (3.57)	51 (2.33)	31 (1.42)	38 (1.74)	229 (10.47)	2187
1949	62 (2.82)		42 (1.91)	22 (1.00)	23 (1.05)	26 (1.18)	121 (5.51)	2197
1950 GAP								
1956	64 (2.85)		64 (2.85)	19 (0.84)	14 (0.62)	35 (1.56)	297 (13.21)	2249
1957	58 (2.57)		48 (2.12)	34 (1.50)	12 (0.53)	9 (0.40)	252 (11.15)	2260
1958	56 (2.44)		50 (2.17)	33 (1.44)	32 (1.39)	22 (0.96)	218 (9.48)	2299
1959	61 (2.63)		47 (2.02)	35 (1.51)	11 (0.47)	24 (1.03)	355 (15.29)	2322
1960	71 (3.01)		55 (2.33)	32 (1.35)	18 (0.76)	56 (2.37)	379 (16.05)	2362
1961	76 (3.15)		44 (1.83)	45 (1.87)	17 (0.71)	76 (3.15)	436 (18.10)	2409
1962	37 (1.50)		29 (1.18)	15 (0.61)	15 (0.61)	34 (1.38)	208 (8.46)	2460
1963	37 (1.47)		31 (1.23)	12 (0.48)	22 (0.87)	60 (2.38)	319 (12.66)	2520
1964	36 (1.42)		32 (1.26)	42 (1.65)	11 (0.43)	59 (2.32)	280 (11.02)	2540
1965	49 (1.90)		36 (1.40)	33 (1.28)	8 (0.31)	80 (3.10)	320 (12.40)	2580
1966	45 (1.72)		36 (1.38)	41 (1.57)	0 (0.00)	95 (3.64)	342 (13.10)	2610
1967	42 (1.60)		30 (1.14)	28 (1.06)	10 (0.38)	67 (2.55)	312 (11.86)	2630
1968	38 (1.42)		34 (1.27)	26 (0.97)	4 (0.15)	82 (3.07)	308 (11.54)	2670
1969	30 (1.11)		34 (1.25)	20 (0.74)	1 (0.04)	65 (2.40)	260 (9.59)	2710
1970	20 (0.74)		19 (0.70)	21 (0.77)	0 (0.00)	53 (1.95)	280 (10.29)	2720
1971	20 (0.72)		32 (1.16)	11 (0.40)	3 (0.11)	79 (2.85)	254 (9.17)	2770
1972	17 (0.60)		26 (0.93)	11 (0.39)	4 (0.14)	61 (2.17)	203 (7.22)	2810

FOOTNOTES: * FISCAL YEARS FROM 1956
1. ATTEMPT TO KILL
2. BURGLARY

QATAR

NUMBER OF OFFENSES REPORTED -- (RATE PER 100,000)

YEAR	MURDER ( )	MANSLTR ( )	HOMICIDE ( )	RAPE ( )	ASSAULT ( )	ROBBERY ( )	THEFT ( )	POP
1950	0 (0.00)	0 (0.00)		0 (0.00)	14 (70.00)	1 (5.00)	22 (110.00)	20
1951	1 (4.55)	0 (0.00)		0 (0.00)	18 (81.82)	1 (4.55)	7 (31.82)	22
1952	5 (20.00)	5 (20.00)		3 (12.00)	15 (60.00)	0 (0.00)	37 (148.00)	25
1953	0 (0.00)	0 (0.00)		4 (14.29)	12 (42.86)	2 (7.14)	43 (153.57)	28
1954	0 (0.00)	0 (0.00)		0 (0.00)	19 (61.29)	2 (6.45)	7 (22.58)	31
1955	0 (0.00)	0 (0.00)		4 (11.43)	29 (82.86)	0 (0.00)	39 (111.43)	35
1956	0 (0.00)	0 (0.00)		5 (13.51)	32 (86.49)	0 (0.00)	80 (216.22)	37
1957	1 (2.56)	0 (0.00)		0 (0.00)	22 (56.41)	0 (0.00)	136 (348.72)	39
1958	1 (2.44)	2 (4.88)		12 (29.27)	56 (136.59)	3 (7.32)	126 (307.32)	41
1959	1 (2.33)	2 (4.65)		10 (23.26)	69 (160.47)	0 (0.00)	135 (313.95)	43
1960	0 (0.00)	2 (4.44)		13 (28.89)	64 (142.22)	0 (0.00)	124 (275.56)	45
1961	2 (3.64)	2 (3.64)		2 (3.64)	311 (565.45)	1 (1.82)	227 (412.73)	55
1962	2 (3.51)	3 (5.26)		2 (3.51)	158 (277.19)	0 (0.00)	220 (385.96)	57
1963	4 (6.78)	5 (8.47)		9 (15.25)	174 (294.92)	2 (3.39)	273 (462.71)	59
1964	0 (0.00)	3 (4.84)		11 (17.74)	211 (340.32)	7 (11.29)	200 (322.58)	62
1965	0 (0.00)	2 (3.08)		3 (4.62)	186 (286.15)	6 (9.23)	211 (324.62)	65
1966	2 (2.94)	3 (4.41)		9 (13.24)	143 (210.29)	3 (4.41)	216 (317.65)	68
1967	2 (2.78)	3 (4.17)		5 (6.94)	151 (209.72)	0 (0.00)	171 (237.50)	72
1968	5 (6.67)	14 (18.67)		6 (8.00)	162 (216.00)	1 (1.33)	135 (180.00)	75
1969	7 (9.09)	12 (15.58)		11 (14.29)	218 (283.12)	0 (0.00)	206 (267.53)	77
1970	4 (5.06)	9 (11.39)		13 (16.46)	312 (394.94)	4 (5.06)	229 (289.87)	79
1971	3 (3.66)	12 (14.63)		11 (13.41)	206 (251.22)	2 (2.44)	143 (174.39)	82
1972	4 (4.76)	14 (16.67)		20 (23.81)	395 (470.24)	0 (0.00)	571 (679.76)	84
1973	5 (5.81)	9 (10.47)		5 (5.81)	384 (446.51)	2 (2.33)	764 (888.37)	86
1974	2 (2.17)	3 (3.26)		4 (4.35)	148 (160.87)	0 (0.00)	154 (167.39)	92

RHODESIA *

CRIME STATISTICS -- (RATE PER 100,000)

YEAR	MURDER ( )	MANSLTR ( )	HOMICIDE (1)	RAPE ( )	ASSAULT (2)	ROBBERY ( )	THEFT ( )	POP
1932	160 (10.53)		63 (4.14)	232 (15.26)	2587 (170.20)	50 (3.29)	6861 (451.38)	1520
1933	171 (10.89)		95 (6.05)	256 (16.31)	2606 (165.99)	56 (3.57)		1570
1934	168 (10.37)		82 (5.06)	304 (18.77)	2913 (179.81)	68 (4.20)	8338 (514.69)	1620
1935	208 (12.46)		101 (6.05)	317 (18.98)	2995 (179.34)	58 (3.47)	8901 (532.99)	1670
1936	170 (9.88)		99 (5.76)	298 (17.33)	3445 (200.29)	73 (4.24)	9453 (549.59)	1720
1937	193 (10.90)		109 (6.16)	319 (18.02)	3726 (210.51)	86 (4.86)	9498 (536.61)	1770
1938	163 (8.91)		111 (6.07)	267 (14.59)	3499 (191.20)	60 (3.28)	10084 (551.04)	1830
1939							10204 (539.89)	1890
1940							10072 (519.18)	1940
1941							10805 (537.56)	2010
1942								
1943	129 (6.00)		120 (5.58)	254 (11.81)	3162 (147.07)	58 (2.70)	13406 (623.53)	2150
1944	93 (4.21)		104 (4.71)	276 (12.49)	3752 (169.77)	59 (2.67)	11876 (537.38)	2210
1945	102 (4.45)		122 (5.33)	284 (12.40)	3931 (171.66)	39 (1.70)	11048 (482.45)	2290
1946	120 (5.08)		117 (4.96)	271 (11.48)	3951 (167.42)	50 (2.12)	13138 (556.70)	2360
1947	65 (2.65)		110 (4.49)	243 (9.92)	3705 (151.22)	128 (5.22)	15106 (616.57)	2450
1948	100 (3.94)		130 (5.12)	305 (12.01)	4339 (170.83)	122 (4.80)	14974 (589.53)	2540
1949	122 (4.64)		177 (6.73)	294 (11.18)	4382 (166.62)	139 (5.29)	14791 (562.40)	2630
1950	65 (2.42)		86 (3.20)	235 (8.74)	4205 (156.32)	105 (3.90)	16569 (615.95)	2690
1951	68 (2.49)		109 (3.99)	196 (7.18)	3900 (142.86)	78 (2.86)	18766 (687.40)	2730
1952	56 (1.98)		92 (3.25)	208 (7.35)	4556 (160.99)	127 (4.49)	21005 (742.23)	2830
1953	67 (2.27)		106 (3.59)	220 (7.46)	4739 (160.64)	191 (6.47)	22211 (752.92)	2950
1954	79 (2.49)		125 (3.94)	235 (7.41)	5219 (164.64)	203 (6.40)	22613 (713.34)	3170
1955	77 (2.35)		13 (0.40)	186 (5.69)	5517 (168.72)	221 (6.76)	23033 (704.37)	3270
1956	57 (1.69)		213 (6.30)	225 (6.66)	5816 (172.07)	210 (6.21)	23141 (684.65)	3380
1957	72 (2.06)		179 (5.11)	216 (6.17)	4888 (139.66)	218 (6.23)	27037 (772.49)	3500
1958	62 (1.72)		122 (3.38)	208 (5.76)	6800 (188.37)	292 (8.09)	27747 (768.00)	3610
1959	102 (2.73)		141 (3.78)	297 (7.96)	7289 (195.42)	413 (11.07)	30959 (830.00)	3730
1960	94 (2.45)		119 (3.10)	240 (6.25)	7066 (184.01)	449 (11.69)	32254 (839.95)	3840
1961	124 (3.12)		244 (6.15)	275 (6.93)	7084 (178.44)	445 (11.21)	32226 (811.74)	3970
1962	105 (2.57)		247 (6.04)	310 (7.58)	7291 (178.26)	543 (13.28)	31203 (762.91)	4090
1963	118 (2.80)		129 (3.06)	306 (7.25)	7166 (169.81)	770 (18.25)	32139 (761.59)	4220
1964	98 (2.25)		157 (3.61)	286 (6.57)	8274 (190.21)	837 (19.24)	30002 (689.70)	4350
1965	128 (2.86)		112 (2.50)	421 (9.40)	6551 (146.23)	942 (21.03)	30833 (688.24)	4480
1966	128 (2.77)		109 (2.36)	399 (8.64)	5811 (125.78)	875 (18.94)	28761 (622.53)	4620
1967	127 (2.65)		114 (2.38)	483 (10.08)	5707 (119.14)	635 (13.26)	25936 (541.46)	4790
1968	133 (2.68)		117 (2.36)	424 (8.55)	6382 (128.67)	733 (14.78)	26168 (527.58)	4960
1969	155 (3.02)		128 (2.50)	430 (8.38)	6518 (127.06)	772 (15.05)	25120 (489.67)	5130
1970	181 (3.41)		133 (2.50)	475 (8.95)	7540 (142.00)	1174 (22.11)	29542 (556.35)	5310
1971	211 (3.84)		231 (4.20)	555 (10.09)	8489 (154.35)	1604 (29.16)	34300 (623.64)	5500
1972	237 (4.17)		158 (2.78)	628 (11.04)	8154 (143.30)	2122 (37.29)	31865 (560.02)	5690

FOOTNOTES:
* BEFORE 1954 COMPUTED RATES BASED ON QUESTIONABLE
  POPULATION ESTIMATES
1. CULPABLE HOMICIDE
2. GRIEVOUS BODILY HARM AND COMMON ASSAULT

RUMANIA

NUMBER OF CONVICTIONS -- (RATE PER 100,000)

YEAR	MURDER ( )	MANSLTR ( )	HOMICIDE ( )	RAPE ( )	ASSAULT (1)	ROBBERY ( )	THEFT (2)	POP
1919					25712 (177.36)		52056 (359.08)	14497
1920					38615 (248.47)		72225 (464.74)	15541

FOOTNOTES:
1. CRIMES AGAINST THE PERSON
2. CRIMES AGAINST PROPERTY

SCOTLAND

NUMBER OF OFFENSES REPORTED -- (RATE PER 100,000)

YEAR	MURDER ( )	MANSLTR ( )	HOMICIDE (1)	RAPE ( )	ASSAULT ( )	ROBBERY ( )	THEFT ( )	POP
1900	10 (0.22)		58 (1.30)	18 (0.40)	4024 (90.41)	140 (3.15)	18641 (418.80)	4451
1901	8 (0.18)		34 (0.76)	26 (0.58)	4055 (90.68)	127 (2.84)	19253 (430.52)	4472
1902	14 (0.31)		37 (0.82)	21 (0.47)	3984 (88.67)	183 (4.07)	18948 (421.72)	4493
1903	8 (0.18)		46 (1.02)	20 (0.44)	3945 (87.39)	228 (5.05)	19430 (430.44)	4514
1904	13 (0.29)		26 (0.57)	12 (0.26)	3588 (79.12)	270 (5.95)	23007 (507.52)	4535
1905	19 (0.42)		43 (0.94)	23 (0.50)	3424 (75.15)	302 (6.63)	23999 (526.76)	4556
1906	11 (0.22)		48 (1.05)	22 (0.48)	3713 (81.12)	223 (4.87)	24799 (541.82)	4577
1907	11 (0.24)		50 (1.09)	25 (0.54)	3778 (82.17)	195 (4.24)	26247 (570.83)	4598
1908	11 (0.24)		39 (0.84)	9 (0.19)	3487 (75.49)	214 (4.63)	25629 (554.86)	4619
1909	10 (0.22)		28 (0.60)	17 (0.37)	2511 (54.12)	142 (3.06)	24331 (524.38)	4640
1910	9 (0.19)		32 (0.69)	22 (0.47)	2625 (56.32)	149 (3.20)	23427 (502.62)	4661
1911	6 (0.13)		32 (0.68)	23 (0.49)	2925 (62.47)	152 (3.25)	22064 (471.25)	4682
1912	11 (0.23)		40 (0.85)	18 (0.38)	3185 (67.72)	122 (2.59)	22451 (477.38)	4703
1913	10 (0.21)		31 (0.66)	23 (0.49)	3409 (72.16)	135 (2.86)	22540 (477.14)	4724
1914	8 (0.17)		31 (0.65)	13 (0.27)	3379 (71.21)	124 (2.61)	21783 (459.07)	4745
1915	12 (0.25)		45 (0.94)	9 (0.19)	2462 (51.66)	17 (0.36)	19559 (410.39)	4766
1916	9 (0.19)		44 (0.92)	13 (0.27)	1541 (32.19)	113 (2.36)	20174 (421.43)	4787
1917	6 (0.12)		23 (0.48)	9 (0.19)	1065 (22.15)	99 (2.06)	19422 (403.95)	4808
1918	9 (0.19)		23 (0.48)	17 (0.35)	855 (17.71)	48 (0.99)	17787 (368.34)	4829
1919	12 (0.25)		38 (0.78)	11 (0.23)	1673 (34.49)	149 (3.07)	19096 (393.73)	4850
1920	18 (0.37)		41 (0.84)	39 (0.80)	2900 (59.62)	184 (3.78)	22787 (468.18)	4864
1921	17 (0.35)		35 (0.72)	21 (0.43)	2146 (44.11)	138 (2.84)	23361 (480.18)	4865
1922	12 (0.25)		33 (0.68)	24 (0.49)	1731 (35.58)	84 (1.73)	21170 (435.15)	4865
1923	12 (0.25)		32 (0.66)	19 (0.39)	1839 (37.79)	44 (0.90)	20387 (418.97)	4866
1924	12 (0.25)		33 (0.68)	16 (0.33)	1810 (37.20)	33 (0.68)	17754 (364.86)	4866
1925	17 (0.35)		42 (0.86)	23 (0.47)	1704 (35.01)	38 (0.78)	17723 (364.15)	4867
1926	10 (0.21)		35 (0.72)	17 (0.35)	1589 (32.70)	81 (1.67)	20761 (427.27)	4859
1927	13 (0.27)		51 (1.05)	10 (0.21)	1607 (33.13)	39 (0.80)	15153 (312.37)	4851
1928	19 (0.39)		41 (0.85)	15 (0.31)	1650 (34.07)	18 (0.37)	15642 (322.58)	4843
1929	9 (0.19)		46 (0.95)	24 (0.50)	1725 (35.68)	10 (0.21)	16522 (341.72)	4835
1930	13 (0.27)		32 (0.66)	14 (0.29)	1828 (37.86)	25 (0.52)	16879 (349.61)	4828
1931	8 (0.16)		29 (0.60)	15 (0.31)	1732 (35.69)	28 (0.58)	16588 (341.81)	4853
1932	10 (0.21)		29 (0.59)	23 (0.47)	1588 (32.55)	112 (2.30)	22842 (468.27)	4878
1933	16 (0.33)		32 (0.65)	16 (0.33)	1694 (34.55)	159 (3.24)	23154 (472.24)	4903
1934	12 (0.24)		37 (0.75)	11 (0.22)	1725 (35.00)	99 (2.01)	24558 (498.34)	4928
1935	16 (0.32)		25 (0.50)	16 (0.32)	1789 (36.12)	120 (2.42)	31545 (636.89)	4953
1936	19 (0.38)		32 (0.64)	11 (0.22)	1795 (36.08)	164 (3.30)	30284 (608.72)	4975
1937	10 (0.20)		14 (0.28)	20 (0.40)	1802 (36.06)	107 (2.14)	30374 (607.84)	4997
1938	15 (0.30)		23 (0.46)	36 (0.72)	1794 (35.74)	114 (2.27)	29394 (585.65)	5019
1939	8 (0.16)		22 (0.44)	10 (0.20)	1674 (33.21)	21 (0.42)	30439 (603.83)	5041
1940	8 (0.16)		27 (0.53)	9 (0.18)	1363 (26.91)	129 (2.55)	33068 (652.87)	5065
1941	11 (0.21)		19 (0.37)	11 (0.21)	1427 (27.87)	333 (6.50)	37170 (725.98)	5120
1942	15 (0.29)		29 (0.56)	17 (0.33)	1273 (24.60)	411 (7.94)	37915 (732.80)	5174
1943	8 (0.15)		18 (0.35)	16 (0.31)	1376 (26.52)	465 (8.96)	38970 (751.01)	5189
1944	12 (0.23)		18 (0.35)	18 (0.35)	1456 (27.95)	383 (7.35)	36764 (705.64)	5210

SCOTLAND

NUMBER OF OFFENSES REPORTED -- (RATE PER 100,000)   CONTINUED

YEAR	MURDER ( )	MANSLTR ( )	HOMICIDE (1)	RAPE ( )	ASSAULT ( )	ROBBERY ( )	THEFT ( )	POP
1945	24 (0.46)		14 (0.27)	24 (0.46)	1015 (19.57)	436 (8.41)	38867 (749.32)	5187
1946	18 (0.35)		19 (0.37)	13 (0.25)	529 (10.24)	381 (7.37)	35800 (692.86)	5167
1947	16 (0.31)		14 (0.27)	20 (0.39)	555 (10.82)	386 (7.52)	35284 (687.66)	5131
1948	14 (0.27)		20 (0.39)	17 (0.33)	485 (9.40)	353 (6.84)	36869 (714.24)	5162
1949	14 (0.27)		10 (0.19)	26 (0.50)	424 (8.20)	325 (6.29)	31708 (613.54)	5168
1950	21 (0.41)		14 (0.27)	20 (0.39)	395 (7.71)	346 (6.75)	32462 (633.28)	5126
1951	9 (0.18)		12 (0.23)	18 (0.35)	694 (13.57)	305 (5.96)	38346 (749.82)	5114
1952	13 (0.25)		14 (0.27)	22 (0.43)	608 (11.89)	304 (5.94)	37217 (727.60)	5115
1953	18 (0.35)		23 (0.45)	27 (0.53)	577 (11.27)	301 (5.88)	33486 (654.28)	5118
1954	14 (0.27)		18 (0.35)	26 (0.51)	516 (10.07)	266 (5.19)	31406 (613.04)	5123
1955	11 (0.21)		24 (0.47)	21 (0.41)	497 (9.68)	333 (6.49)	33522 (655.07)	5133
1956	13 (0.25)		16 (0.31)	23 (0.44)	550 (10.61)	339 (6.54)	34945 (674.22)	5183
1957	12 (0.23)		14 (0.27)	35 (0.67)	690 (13.31)	483 (9.31)	35163 (678.04)	5186
1958	18 (0.35)		24 (0.46)	27 (0.52)	751 (14.45)	629 (12.11)	38450 (739.99)	5196
1959	14 (0.27)		20 (0.38)	34 (0.65)	804 (15.43)	617 (11.84)	40734 (781.54)	5212
1960	16 (0.31)		19 (0.36)	40 (0.77)	966 (18.50)	606 (11.60)	44540 (852.77)	5223
1961	14 (0.27)		23 (0.44)	40 (0.77)	1063 (20.34)	612 (11.71)	46220 (884.42)	5226
1962	27 (0.52)		31 (0.59)	42 (0.80)	1162 (22.19)	766 (14.63)	49141 (938.52)	5236
1963	16 (0.31)		30 (0.57)	55 (1.05)	1218 (23.24)	830 (15.84)	51764 (987.86)	5240
1964	27 (0.52)		24 (0.46)	39 (0.75)	1462 (28.06)	1012 (19.24)	56335 (1081.29)	5210
1965	32 (0.61)		31 (0.60)	58 (1.11)	1763 (33.84)	1301 (24.97)	58696 (1126.60)	5210
1966	30 (0.58)		56 (1.08)	64 (1.23)	2101 (40.40)	1356 (26.08)	61405 (1180.87)	5200
1967	41 (0.79)		29 (0.56)	101 (1.94)	2440 (46.92)	1644 (31.62)	63297 (1217.25)	5200
1968	41 (0.79)		32 (0.62)	81 (1.56)	2431 (46.75)	1852 (35.23)	65636 (1262.23)	5200
1969	31 (0.60)		51 (0.98)	91 (1.75)	2150 (41.27)	1804 (34.63)	66248 (1271.55)	5210
1970	29 (0.56)		54 (1.04)	77 (1.48)	2108 (40.46)	2138 (41.04)	71310 (1368.71)	5210
1971	45 (0.86)		27 (0.52)	102 (1.95)	2446 (46.86)	2333 (44.69)	74207 (1421.59)	5220
1972	47 (0.90)		38 (0.73)	131 (2.51)	2593 (49.77)	2334 (44.99)	73368 (1408.22)	5210
1973	43 (0.83)		34 (0.65)	161 (3.09)	2354 (45.18)	2136 (41.00)	71983 (1381.63)	5210

FOOTNOTES:
1. CULPABLE HOMICIDE

NUMBER OF OFFENSES REPORTED -- (RATE PER 100,000)

SENEGAL *

YEAR	MURDER ( )	MANSLTR ( )	HOMICIDE ( )	RAPE (1)	ASSAULT ( )	ROBBERY ( )	THEFT ( )	POP
1965	153 (4.38)			70 (2.01)		493 (14.13)	3007 (86.16)	3490
1966	195 (5.46)			159 (4.45)		1284 (35.97)	3333 (93.36)	3570
1967	60 (1.66)			180 (4.97)		1161 (32.07)	3114 (86.02)	3620
1968	39 (1.06)			159 (4.31)		990 (26.83)	3114 (84.39)	3690

FOOTNOTES:
* RAW CRIME DATA FROM INTERPOL; RATES COMPUTED FROM
  POPULATION FIGURES ABOVE
1. SEX OFFENSES

CRIME STATISTICS -- (RATE PER 100,000)

SIERRA LEONE

YEAR	MURDER ( )	MANSLTR ( )	HOMICIDE ( )	RAPE ( )	ASSAULT ( )	ROBBERY ( )	THEFT ( )	POP
1961			49 (2.00)	183 (7.47)	601 (24.53)	47 (1.92)	5935 (242.24)	2450
1962			56 (2.41)	159 (6.85)	932 (40.17)	112 (4.83)	6217 (267.97)	2320
1963			76 (3.30)	191 (8.30)	1246 (54.17)	76 (3.30)	7804 (339.30)	2300
1964			69 (2.96)	164 (7.04)	994 (42.66)	69 (2.96)	8437 (362.10)	2330
1965			75 (3.16)	157 (6.62)	1040 (43.88)	91 (3.84)	8974 (378.65)	2370
1966								
1967								
1968			70 (2.82)	115 (4.64)	893 (36.01)	221 (8.91)	6359 (256.41)	2480
1969			92 (3.67)	147 (5.86)	1190 (47.41)	257 (10.24)	7932 (316.02)	2510
1970			108 (4.24)	139 (5.45)	1334 (52.31)	258 (10.12)	8895 (348.82)	2550
1971			127 (4.90)	124 (4.79)	1062 (41.00)	181 (6.99)	9108 (351.66)	2590
1972			143 (5.44)	113 (4.30)	881 (33.50)	157 (5.97)	8476 (322.28)	2630
1973			97 (3.63)	114 (4.27)	992 (37.15)	225 (8.43)	8390 (341.23)	2670
1974			113 (4.17)	191 (7.05)	1180 (43.54)	152 (5.61)	8131 (300.04)	2710

SINGAPORE *

NUMBER OF OFFENSES REPORTED -- (RATE PER 100,000)

YEAR	MURDER ( )	MANSLTR ( )	HOMICIDE ( )	RAPE (1)	ASSAULT ( )	ROBBERY ( )	THEFT ( )	POP
1953	40 (3.36)			21 (1.76)		397 (33.36)	3662 (307.73)	1190
1954	59 (4.72)			28 (2.24)		438 (35.04)	5313 (425.04)	1250
1955	58 (4.43)			31 (2.37)		281 (21.45)	4351 (332.14)	1310
1956	56 (4.08)			47 (3.43)		332 (24.20)	5127 (373.69)	1372
1957	48 (3.32)			27 (1.87)		329 (22.75)	5464 (377.87)	1446
1958	57 (3.76)			36 (2.38)		642 (42.40)	5899 (389.63)	1514
1959	58 (3.67)			45 (2.85)		1386 (87.72)	5573 (352.72)	1580
1960	51 (3.12)			40 (2.45)	503 (29.55)	858 (52.51)	556 (34.03)	1634
1961	53 (3.11)			32 (1.88)	519 (29.66)	880 (51.70)	8961 (526.50)	1702
1962	43 (2.46)			36 (2.06)	478 (26.63)	1039 (59.37)	8460 (483.43)	1750
1963	29 (1.62)			46 (2.56)	419 (22.75)	885 (49.30)	8773 (488.75)	1795
1964	76 (4.13)			36 (1.95)	446 (23.64)	969 (52.61)	8546 (463.95)	1842
1965	36 (1.91)			41 (2.17)	395 (20.42)	1180 (62.53)	9648 (511.29)	1887
1966	43 (2.22)			39 (2.02)	423 (21.39)	844 (43.64)	9565 (494.57)	1934
1967	42 (2.12)			47 (2.38)	381 (18.94)	1063 (53.74)	10218 (516.58)	1978
1968	50 (2.49)			41 (2.04)	421 (20.61)	1097 (54.52)	9962 (495.13)	2012
1969	70 (3.43)			42 (2.06)		1024 (50.12)	9357 (458.00)	2043
1970	52 (2.51)			47 (2.27)	391 (18.84)	1408 (67.86)	9634 (464.29)	2075
1971	57 (2.70)			51 (2.42)	447 (21.18)	2182 (103.41)	10565 (500.71)	2110
1972	65 (3.03)			62 (2.89)	477 (22.22)	1753 (81.65)	8597 (400.42)	2147
1973	57 (2.59)			53 (2.40)	483 (21.91)	1767 (80.17)	9810 (445.10)	2204

FOOTNOTES:
* 1953-1960: RAW CRIME DATA FROM INTERPOL, RATES COMPUTED
  FROM POPULATION FIGURES ABOVE
1. SEX OFFENSES PRIOR TO 1961

SOLOMON ISLANDS *

NUMBER OF OFFENSES REPORTED -- (RATE PER 100,000)

YEAR	MURDER ( )	MANSLTR ( )	HOMICIDE ( )	RAPE (1)	ASSAULT ( )	ROBBERY ( )	THEFT ( )	POP
1963	3 (2.29)			22 (16.79)		64 (48.85)	260 (198.47)	131
1964	7 (5.11)			70 (51.09)		38 (27.74)	388 (283.21)	137
1965	4 (2.86)			58 (41.43)		63 (45.00)	27 (19.29)	140
1966	2 (1.41)			45 (31.69)		75 (52.82)	414 (291.55)	142
1967	4 (2.76)			67 (46.21)		117 (80.69)	502 (346.21)	145
1968	1 (0.67)			70 (46.67)		73 (48.67)	474 (316.00)	150
1969	2 (1.33)			78 (52.00)		119 (79.33)	442 (294.67)	150
1970	4 (2.48)			89 (55.28)		140 (86.96)	524 (325.47)	161

FOOTNOTES:
* RAW CRIME DATA FROM INTERPOL; RATES COMPUTED FROM
  POPULATION FIGURES ABOVE
1. SEX OFFENSES

NUMBER OF CONVICTIONS -- (RATE PER 100,000)

YEAR	MURDER ( )	MANSLTR ( )	HOMICIDE (1)	RAPE (2)	ASSAULT (3)	ROBBERY ( )	THEFT (4)	POP
1925	79 (1.03)		436 (5.69)	422 (5.51)	20494 (267.41)	409 (5.34)	29115 (379.89)	7664
1926	85 (1.08)		557 (7.11)	406 (5.18)	22016 (280.85)	421 (5.37)	30142 (384.51)	7839
1927	93 (1.16)		579 (7.22)	487 (6.08)	22599 (281.99)	575 (7.17)	31217 (389.53)	8014
1928	82 (1.00)		588 (7.18)	478 (5.84)	25105 (306.57)	540 (6.59)	31276 (381.93)	8189
1929	71 (0.85)		804 (9.61)	502 (6.00)	24435 (292.14)	563 (6.73)	31299 (374.21)	8364
1930	71 (0.83)		916 (10.72)	513 (6.01)	24011 (281.13)	647 (7.58)	32477 (380.25)	8541
1931	92 (1.06)		761 (8.73)	511 (5.86)	22566 (258.78)	821 (9.42)	36418 (417.64)	8720
1932	126 (1.42)		952 (10.70)	455 (5.11)	22560 (253.51)	867 (9.74)	40793 (458.40)	8899
1933	101 (1.11)		1026 (11.30)	513 (5.65)	22684 (249.88)	909 (10.01)	44404 (489.14)	9078
1934	92 (0.99)		820 (8.86)	591 (6.38)	22537 (243.46)	832 (8.99)	43397 (468.80)	9257
1935	120 (1.27)		1286 (13.63)	544 (5.77)	23816 (252.42)	1033 (10.95)	40555 (429.84)	9435
1936	120 (1.25)		990 (10.29)	555 (5.77)	24859 (258.44)	949 (9.87)	42958 (446.60)	9619
1937	145 (1.48)		1002 (10.22)	534 (5.45)	28175 (287.41)	1052 (10.73)	39255 (400.44)	9803
1938	144 (1.44)		1046 (10.47)	635 (6.36)	28850 (288.88)	1072 (10.73)	41022 (410.75)	9987
1939	170 (1.67)		1600 (15.73)	637 (6.26)	28605 (281.24)	1164 (11.44)	41786 (410.83)	10171
1940	124 (1.20)		1160 (11.20)	573 (5.53)	29757 (287.37)	1233 (11.91)	45108 (435.62)	10355
1941	173 (1.64)		1055 (10.01)	619 (5.87)	31166 (295.78)	1391 (13.20)	46683 (443.04)	10537
1942	220 (2.05)		1113 (10.38)	569 (5.31)	32247 (300.87)	1851 (17.27)	50314 (469.43)	10718
1943	256 (2.35)		964 (8.84)	677 (6.21)	32680 (299.82)	1766 (16.20)	52430 (481.01)	10900
1944	349 (3.15)		1207 (10.89)	725 (6.54)	36058 (325.32)	1825 (16.47)	52626 (474.79)	11084
1945	228 (2.02)		1159 (10.29)	728 (6.46)	37311 (331.15)	2122 (18.83)	56900 (505.01)	11267
1946	277 (2.42)		1133 (9.89)	673 (5.88)	37268 (325.40)	2330 (20.34)	63346 (553.10)	11453
1947	235 (2.01)		1457 (12.46)	700 (5.99)	38869 (332.44)	2508 (21.45)	64942 (555.44)	11692
1948	343 (2.87)		1394 (11.66)	788 (6.59)	41638 (348.20)	2722 (22.76)	61863 (517.34)	11958
1949	356 (2.92)		1253 (10.26)	882 (7.22)	40923 (335.10)	2799 (22.92)	61420 (502.95)	12212
1950	356 (2.86)		1354 (10.88)	837 (6.72)	43304 (347.82)	2939 (23.61)	67175 (539.56)	12450
1951	296 (2.33)		1480 (11.64)	886 (6.97)	44755 (351.85)	3101 (24.38)	70362 (553.16)	12720
1952	313 (2.40)		1362 (10.44)	944 (7.24)	44900 (344.32)	2965 (22.74)	75626 (579.95)	13040
1953	387 (2.89)		1654 (12.36)	913 (6.82)	45373 (339.11)	3038 (22.71)	72920 (544.99)	13380
1954	343 (2.50)		1742 (12.70)	1156 (8.43)	48677 (354.79)	2970 (21.65)	70852 (516.41)	13720
1955	353 (2.51)		1576 (11.20)	1102 (7.83)	49455 (351.49)	2991 (21.26)	74465 (529.25)	14070
1956	591 (4.10)		1585 (10.99)	1141 (7.91)	52271 (362.46)	3414 (23.67)	75948 (526.65)	14421
1957	786 (5.32)		1350 (9.13)	1170 (7.91)	50377 (340.71)	3869 (26.17)	77441 (523.75)	14786
1958	727 (4.80)		1790 (11.81)	1391 (9.18)	49070 (323.68)	3803 (25.09)	77779 (513.05)	15160
1959	652 (4.19)		1790 (11.51)	1681 (10.81)	50105 (322.30)	4218 (27.13)	78435 (504.53)	15546
1960	615 (3.86)		2053 (12.88)	1767 (11.09)	54222 (340.21)	4850 (30.43)	79406 (498.22)	15938
1961	808 (4.96)		2339 (14.35)	2095 (12.86)	54487 (334.34)	4714 (28.93)	82659 (507.20)	16297
1962	845 (5.01)		2235 (13.26)	2123 (12.60)	54360 (322.61)	4600 (27.30)	84356 (500.63)	16850
1963	929 (5.35)		2013 (11.60)	1980 (11.41)	51644 (297.66)	4243 (24.46)	77130 (444.55)	17350
1964								
1965	1440 (7.81)		2379 (12.91)	2318 (12.58)	49665 (269.48)	5183 (28.12)	79137 (429.39)	18430
1966	1653 (8.70)		2801 (14.74)	2878 (15.15)	50150 (263.95)	6311 (33.22)	89329 (470.15)	19000
1967	1352 (6.91)		2273 (11.61)	2384 (12.18)	50546 (258.15)	5627 (28.74)	78361 (400.21)	19580
1968	1260 (6.25)		2434 (12.07)	2856 (14.17)	52854 (262.17)	5893 (29.23)	81517 (404.35)	20160
1969	1258 (6.06)		2605 (12.54)	2898 (13.95)	53172 (256.00)	5705 (27.47)	76130 (366.54)	20770

SOUTH AFRICA *

NUMBER OF CONVICTIONS -- (RATE PER 100,000)   CONTINUED

YEAR	MURDER ( )	MANSLTR ( )	HOMICIDE (1)	RAPE (2)	ASSAULT (3)	ROBBERY ( )	THEFT (4)	POP
1970	1380 (6.41)		3146 (14.61)	3195 (14.84)	57464 (266.90)	6399 (29.72)	84515 (392.55)	21530
1971	1133 (5.13)		3659 (16.56)	3239 (14.66)	60828 (275.36)	6749 (30.55)	84376 (381.96)	22090

FOOTNOTES:
* FROM 1965, FISCAL YEARS (BEGINNING IN YEAR INDICATED)
1. CULPABLE HOMICIDE
2. RAPE AND ATTEMPTED RAPE
3. COMMON ASSAULT
4. THEFT AND OTHER OFFENCES IN RESPECT OF PROPERTY

SPAIN

CRIME STATISTICS -- (RATE PER 100,000)

YEAR	MURDER ( )	MANSLTR ( )	HOMICIDE ( )	RAPE ( )	ASSAULT ( )	ROBBERY ( )	THEFT ( )	POP
1914			789 (3.82)	58 (0.28)	3441 (16.66)	120 (0.58)	3699 (17.91)	20655
1915			743 (3.58)	40 (0.19)	3465 (16.70)	140 (0.67)	3469 (16.72)	20745
1916			823 (3.95)	51 (0.24)	3430 (16.46)	190 (0.91)	3616 (17.36)	20835
1917			679 (3.24)	45 (0.22)	3022 (14.44)	134 (0.64)	3718 (17.77)	20925
1918			624 (2.97)	42 (0.20)	2496 (11.88)	120 (0.57)	3540 (16.85)	21015
1919								
GAP								
1929			13914 (59.93)		8532 (36.75)	7616 (32.80)	14519 (62.54)	23216
1930			13018 (55.53)		8400 (35.83)	6933 (29.57)	13844 (59.05)	23445
1931								
GAP								
1953			293 (1.03)	17 (0.06)	1855 (6.50)	5146 (18.04)	8575 (30.06)	28528
1954			265 (0.92)	39 (0.14)	1900 (6.61)	5069 (17.63)	7516 (26.14)	28751
1955			280 (0.97)	29 (0.10)	1905 (6.57)	4245 (14.65)	6819 (23.53)	28876
1956			282 (0.96)	35 (0.12)	2031 (6.93)	4047 (13.81)	6580 (22.46)	29301
1957			298 (1.01)	48 (0.16)	2094 (7.09)	3941 (13.34)	6850 (23.18)	29548
1958			269 (0.90)	38 (0.13)	2011 (6.75)	3463 (11.62)	6520 (21.88)	29798
1959			201 (0.67)	21 (0.07)	1684 (5.60)	2755 (9.17)	5414 (18.02)	30049
1960			201 (0.66)	44 (0.15)	1632 (5.39)	3146 (10.38)	6118 (20.19)	30303
1961			170 (0.56)	33 (0.11)	1637 (5.36)	3305 (10.82)	5838 (19.10)	30559
1962			177 (0.57)	35 (0.11)	1482 (4.81)	2953 (9.58)	4985 (16.18)	30817
1963			199 (0.64)	24 (0.08)	1412 (4.54)	2536 (8.16)	4763 (15.33)	31077
1964			159 (0.51)	32 (0.10)	1244 (3.97)	3099 (9.89)	4858 (15.50)	31339
1965			139 (0.43)	36 (0.11)	1386 (4.32)	3537 (11.03)	5456 (17.02)	32060
1966			182 (0.56)	39 (0.12)	1349 (4.16)	3383 (10.44)	5191 (16.03)	32390
1967			161 (0.49)	48 (0.15)	1278 (3.90)	3363 (10.27)	3566 (10.90)	32730
1968			156 (0.47)	59 (0.18)	1506 (4.55)	4471 (13.52)	3265 (9.87)	33080

SRI LANKA (CEYLON)

NUMBER OF OFFENSES REPORTED -- (RATE PER 100,000)

YEAR	MURDER ( )	MANSLTR ( )	HOMICIDE (1)	RAPE ( )	ASSAULT (2)	ROBBERY ( )	THEFT (3)	POP
1900			146 (4.14)	32 (0.91)	1253 (35.50)	289 (8.19)		3530
1901			160 (4.47)	36 (1.01)	1315 (36.75)	382 (10.68)		3578
1902			146 (4.03)	22 (0.61)	1189 (32.79)	326 (8.99)		3626
1903			134 (3.65)	31 (0.84)	1324 (36.04)	294 (8.00)		3674
1904			144 (3.87)	20 (0.54)	1240 (33.32)	280 (7.52)		3722
1905			170 (4.51)	23 (0.61)	1345 (35.68)	290 (7.69)		3770
1906			187 (4.90)	19 (0.50)	1294 (33.89)	327 (8.56)		3818
1907			171 (4.42)		1220 (31.56)	329 (8.51)		3866
1908			179 (4.57)	61 (1.58)	2146 (54.83)	211 (5.39)		3914
1909			157 (3.96)		1438 (36.29)	257 (6.49)		3962
1910			186 (4.64)		1525 (38.03)	194 (4.84)		4010
1911			156 (3.84)		1307 (32.21)	226 (5.57)		4058
1912			172 (4.19)		1253 (30.52)	226 (5.50)		4106
1913			175 (4.21)		1595 (38.40)	193 (4.65)		4154
1914			238 (5.66)	53 (1.26)	1831 (43.57)	303 (7.21)		4202
1915			204 (4.80)	56 (1.32)	1829 (43.04)	381 (8.96)		4250
1916			158 (3.68)		1734 (40.34)			4298
1917			163 (3.75)		1749 (40.24)			4346
1918			170 (3.87)		1869 (42.54)			4394
1919			200 (4.50)		1743 (39.24)			4442
1920			176 (3.92)		1822 (40.62)			4486
1921			221 (4.85)		1782 (39.10)	331 (7.26)		4558
1922			202 (4.36)		1873 (40.45)	285 (6.16)		4630
1923			189 (4.02)		1702 (36.20)	298 (6.34)		4702
1924			217 (4.55)		1954 (40.93)	310 (6.49)		4774
1925			184 (3.80)		2268 (46.79)	347 (7.16)		4847
1926			223 (4.53)		2350 (47.89)	370 (7.51)		4928
1927			208 (4.15)		2364 (47.20)	388 (7.75)		5009
1928			248 (4.87)		2466 (48.45)	477 (9.37)		5090
1929			243 (4.70)		2545 (49.22)	480 (9.28)		5171
1930			334 (6.36)		2665 (50.73)	475 (9.04)	3175 (60.44)	5253
1931			277 (5.20)		2901 (54.51)	531 (9.98)	3229 (60.67)	5322
1932			294 (5.45)		3082 (57.17)	543 (10.07)	3472 (64.40)	5391
1933			367 (6.72)		3154 (57.77)	526 (9.63)	3474 (63.63)	5460
1934			255 (4.61)		3070 (55.53)	524 (9.48)	3384 (61.20)	5529
1935			295 (5.27)		2771 (49.50)	471 (8.41)	3692 (65.95)	5598
1936			316 (5.57)		3421 (60.35)	565 (9.97)	3971 (70.05)	5669
1937			326 (5.68)		4298 (74.88)	1219 (21.24)	4062 (70.77)	5740
1938			390 (6.71)		4958 (85.32)	1418 (24.40)	4830 (83.12)	5811
1939			359 (6.10)		4750 (80.75)	1304 (22.17)	4657 (79.17)	5882
1940			439 (7.35)		4746 (79.47)	1241 (20.78)	4849 (81.20)	5972
1941			280 (4.53)		4717 (76.35)	1252 (20.27)	5199 (84.15)	6178
1942			464 (7.51)	147 (2.38)	4983 (80.64)	1416 (22.92)	6758 (109.37)	6179
1943			525 (8.34)	168 (2.67)	5757 (91.44)	1784 (28.34)	11403 (181.12)	6296
1944			617 (9.58)	156 (2.42)	6204 (96.31)	2275 (35.32)	14508 (225.21)	6442

SRI LANKA (CEYLON) NUMBER OF OFFENSES REPORTED -- (RATE PER 100,000) CONTINUED

YEAR	MURDER ( )	MANSLTR ( )	HOMICIDE (1)	RAPE ( )	ASSAULT (2)	ROBBERY ( )	THEFT (3)	POP
1945			592 (8.90)	163 (2.45)	5842 (87.85)	2216 (33.32)	13014 (195.70)	6650
1946			543 (7.92)	138 (2.01)	5599 (81.69)	2194 (32.01)	11347 (165.55)	6854
1947			561 (7.97)	159 (2.26)	6320 (89.81)	2384 (33.88)	9982 (141.85)	7037
1948			462 (6.38)	153 (2.11)	5535 (76.41)	2006 (27.69)	8962 (123.72)	7244
1949			403 (5.41)	150 (2.01)	5158 (69.19)	1603 (21.50)	7822 (104.92)	7455
1950			374 (4.87)	144 (1.88)	4936 (64.29)	1382 (18.00)	6928 (90.23)	7678
1951			383 (4.86)	148 (1.88)	5086 (64.58)	1667 (21.17)	6850 (86.97)	7876
1952			411 (5.09)	115 (1.42)	4941 (61.20)	949 (11.75)	6035 (74.75)	8074
1953			429 (5.17)	117 (1.41)	5507 (66.43)	975 (11.76)	5665 (68.34)	8290
1954			492 (5.77)	126 (1.48)	5796 (68.03)	1114 (13.08)	6377 (74.85)	8520
1955			466 (5.34)	123 (1.41)	5540 (63.51)	926 (10.62)	5035 (57.72)	8723
1956			497 (5.57)	119 (1.33)	5773 (64.65)	1236 (13.84)	6352 (71.14)	8929
1957			527 (5.75)	99 (1.08)	5950 (64.92)	1156 (12.61)	5730 (62.52)	9165
1958			703 (7.49)	100 (1.07)	6463 (68.84)	1129 (12.03)	5055 (53.85)	9388
1959			585 (6.08)	94 (0.98)	6661 (69.21)	947 (9.84)	5123 (53.23)	9625
1960			536 (5.42)	98 (0.99)	6954 (70.27)	881 (8.90)	4913 (49.65)	9896
1961			538 (5.29)	99 (0.97)	7020 (69.04)	973 (9.57)	5022 (49.39)	10168
1962			602 (5.77)	98 (0.94)	7306 (69.97)	1084 (10.38)	5254 (50.32)	10442
1963			575 (5.41)	94 (0.88)	7705 (72.52)	1269 (11.94)	5981 (56.29)	10625
1964			614 (5.60)	116 (1.06)	7691 (70.14)	1410 (12.86)	5937 (54.15)	10965
1965			654 (5.86)	123 (1.10)	8429 (75.53)	1530 (13.71)	6239 (55.91)	11160
1966			634 (5.57)	113 (0.99)	8303 (72.90)	1496 (13.13)	6681 (58.66)	11390
1967			766 (6.55)	129 (1.10)	8837 (75.53)	2083 (17.80)	8281 (70.78)	11700
1968			697 (5.81)	146 (1.22)	9124 (76.10)	2399 (20.01)	9178 (76.55)	11990
1969			706 (5.76)	189 (1.54)	9772 (79.77)	2700 (22.04)	10298 (84.07)	12250
1970			845 (6.75)	166 (1.33)	9951 (79.54)	3250 (25.98)	10762 (86.03)	12510
1971			1194 (9.36)	598 (4.69)	10483 (82.16)	5631 (44.13)	11050 (86.60)	12760
1972			928 (7.12)	200 (1.53)	10989 (84.34)	3389 (26.01)	15691 (120.42)	13030
1973			1028 (7.76)	211 (1.59)	10406 (78.51)	5084 (38.36)	17755 (133.95)	13255

FOOTNOTES:
1. HOMICIDE OR MURDER
2. INCLUDES ATTEMPTED MURDER AFTER 1917
3. THEFT OF CATTLE AND PRAEDIAL PRODUCTS

SUDAN *

NUMBER OF OFFENSES REPORTED -- (RATE PER 100,000)

YEAR	MURDER ( )	MANSLTR ( )	HOMICIDE ( )	RAPE (1)	ASSAULT ( )	ROBBERY ( )	THEFT ( )	POP
1955	613 (6.00)			250 (2.45)		208 (2.04)	15296 (149.81)	10210
1956	613 (5.83)			296 (2.81)		238 (2.26)	17868 (169.85)	10520
1957	621 (5.73)			289 (2.67)		257 (2.37)	17655 (162.96)	10834
1958	579 (5.19)			343 (3.08)		205 (1.84)	22729 (203.92)	11146
1959	575 (5.02)			473 (4.13)		2209 (19.28)	21526 (187.85)	11459
1960	658 (5.55)			510 (4.30)		2198 (18.55)	20658 (174.33)	11850
1961	612 (5.02)			336 (2.75)		180 (1.48)	24768 (203.02)	12200
1962	708 (5.63)			360 (2.86)		264 (2.10)	23196 (184.53)	12570
1963	735 (5.68)			535 (4.13)		281 (2.17)	24750 (191.27)	12940
1964	828 (6.21)			586 (4.40)		567 (4.25)	25926 (194.49)	13330
1965								
1966								
1967								
1968	858 (5.74)			607 (4.06)		2012 (13.47)	3684 (24.66)	14990

FOOTNOTES:
* RAW CRIME DATA FROM INTERPOL; RATES COMPUTED FROM
  POPULATION FIGURES ABOVE
  1. SEX OFFENSES

SURINAM *

NUMBER OF OFFENSES REPORTED -- (RATE PER 100,000)

YEAR	MURDER ( )	MANSLTR ( )	HOMICIDE ( )	RAPE (1)	ASSAULT ( )	ROBBERY ( )	THEFT ( )	POP
1963	3 (0.94)			108 (33.75)		1635 (510.94)	5016 (1567.50)	320
1964	9 (2.73)			150 (45.45)		1788 (541.82)	4248 (1287.27)	330
1965	11 (3.24)			228 (67.06)		2678 (787.65)	4449 (1308.53)	340
1966	11 (3.14)			105 (30.00)		2118 (605.14)	5495 (1570.00)	350
1967	11 (3.06)			165 (45.83)		2216 (615.56)	5282 (1467.22)	360
1968	35 (9.46)			137 (37.03)		2916 (788.11)	5404 (1460.54)	370
1969	25 (6.58)			139 (36.58)		3393 (892.89)	4674 (1230.00)	380
1970	31 (7.95)			120 (30.77)		3798 (973.85)	5094 (1306.15)	390

FOOTNOTES:
* RAW CRIME DATA FROM INTERPOL; RATES COMPUTED FROM
  POPULATION FIGURES ABOVE
  1. SEX OFFENSES

SWAZILAND

CRIME STATISTICS -- (RATE PER 100,000)

YEAR	MURDER ( )	MANSLTR ( )	HOMICIDE (1)	RAPE ( )	ASSAULT (2)	ROBBERY ( )	THEFT ( )	POP
1950							1246 (498.40)	250
1951							1441 (554.23)	260
1952							1576 (606.15)	260
1953				31 (11.48)			1614 (597.78)	270
1954				11 (3.93)	97 (34.64)		262 (93.57)	280
1955				3 (1.07)	368 (131.43)		272 (97.14)	280
1956				16 (5.52)	717 (247.24)	37 (12.76)	389 (134.14)	290
1957				150 (50.00)	2812 (937.33)	27 (9.00)	2859 (953.00)	300
1958	52 (16.77)		34 (10.97)	52 (16.77)	2549 (822.26)	23 (7.42)	2628 (847.74)	310
1959	70 (22.58)		48 (15.48)	89 (28.71)	3262 (1052.26)	37 (11.94)	3279 (1057.74)	310
1960	43 (13.44)		39 (12.19)	53 (16.56)	2882 (900.63)	48 (15.00)	3156 (986.25)	320
1961	63 (19.09)		44 (13.33)	56 (16.97)	3144 (952.73)	61 (18.48)	3950 (1196.97)	330
1962	81 (24.55)		36 (10.91)	63 (19.09)	3455 (1046.97)	92 (27.88)	4432 (1343.03)	330
1963	60 (17.65)		50 (14.71)	62 (18.24)	3522 (1035.88)	71 (20.88)	4446 (1307.65)	340
1964	84 (24.00)		40 (11.43)	73 (20.86)	3396 (970.29)	141 (40.29)	5082 (1452.00)	350
1965	92 (25.56)		38 (10.56)	53 (14.72)	2539 (705.28)	143 (39.72)	4664 (1295.56)	360
1966	116 (31.35)		38 (10.27)	75 (20.27)	2363 (638.65)	157 (42.43)	4567 (1234.32)	370
1967	171 (43.85)		28 (7.18)	82 (21.03)	2130 (546.15)	158 (40.51)	4538 (1163.59)	390
1968	93 (23.25)		31 (7.75)	12 (3.00)	2174 (543.50)	201 (50.25)	4753 (1188.25)	400
1969	136 (33.17)		42 (10.24)	118 (28.78)	3168 (772.68)	153 (37.32)	5078 (1238.54)	410
1970	129 (30.71)		41 (9.76)	100 (23.81)	3624 (862.86)	160 (38.10)	4867 (1158.81)	420
1971	137 (31.14)		44 (10.00)	93 (21.14)	3735 (848.86)	121 (27.50)	4579 (1040.68)	440
1972	141 (31.33)		53 (11.78)	94 (20.89)	4153 (922.89)	134 (29.78)	4991 (1109.11)	450
1973	159 (34.57)		60 (15.04)	107 (23.26)	4394 (955.22)	192 (41.74)	5405 (1175.00)	460
1974	85 (17.71)		57 (11.88)	98 (20.42)	4927 (1026.46)	183 (38.13)	5908 (1230.83)	480

FOOTNOTES:
1. CULPABLE HOMICIDE
2. COMMON ASSAULT AND GRIEVOUS BODILY HARM

SWEDEN *

NUMBER OF CONVICTIONS -- (RATE PER 100,000)

YEAR	MURDER ( )	MANSLTR ( )	HOMICIDE (1)	RAPE ( )	ASSAULT (2)	ROBBERY (3)	THEFT (4)	POP
1920			25 (0.43)	18 (0.31)	2587 (44.03)	2569 (43.72)		5876
1921			19 (0.32)	13 (0.22)	2162 (36.58)	1955 (33.08)		5910
1922			9 (0.15)	8 (0.13)	1753 (29.49)	1666 (28.03)		5944
1923			14 (0.23)	10 (0.17)	1911 (31.97)	1695 (28.35)		5978
1924			9 (0.15)	10 (0.17)	1879 (31.25)	1557 (25.90)		6012
1925			15 (0.25)	15 (0.25)	2335 (38.63)	2040 (33.75)		6045
1926			12 (0.20)	13 (0.21)	2130 (35.14)	2003 (33.04)		6062
1927			13 (0.21)	16 (0.26)	2208 (36.32)	2146 (35.30)		6079
1928			8 (0.13)	10 (0.16)	2383 (39.09)	2178 (35.73)		6096
1929			15 (0.25)	10 (0.16)	2502 (40.93)	2286 (37.40)		6113
1930			11 (0.18)	8 (0.13)	2753 (44.90)	2443 (39.85)		6131
1931			11 (0.18)	4 (0.07)	2901 (47.15)	2402 (35.04)		6153
1932			19 (0.31)	7 (0.11)	2558 (41.43)	2725 (44.13)		6175
1933			9 (0.15)	11 (0.18)	2573 (41.52)	2726 (43.99)		6197
1934			13 (0.21)	10 (0.16)	2557 (41.12)	2654 (42.68)		6219
1935			4 (0.06)	9 (0.14)	2608 (41.78)	2748 (44.02)		6242
1936			10 (0.16)	6 (0.10)	2651 (42.31)	2801 (44.71)		6265
1937			10 (0.16)	9 (0.14)	2821 (44.86)	2902 (46.15)		6288
1938			7 (0.11)	19 (0.30)	3051 (48.34)	2911 (46.13)		6311
1939			4 (0.06)	41 (0.65)	2912 (45.97)	2987 (47.16)		6334
1940			2 (0.03)	17 (0.27)	2314 (36.41)	3130 (49.24)		6356
1941			8 (0.13)	16 (0.25)	2810 (43.95)	4001 (62.57)		6394
1942			5 (0.08)	37 (0.58)	3246 (50.47)	6610 (102.77)		6432
1943			10 (0.15)	32 (0.49)	3646 (56.17)	6450 (99.37)		6491
1944			13 (0.20)	22 (0.34)	3378 (51.49)	5434 (82.84)		6560
1945			12 (0.18)	25 (0.38)	3498 (52.71)	4585 (69.09)		6636
1946			8 (0.12)	12 (0.18)	3494 (52.00)	5160 (76.80)		6719
1947			11 (0.16)	21 (0.31)	3247 (47.73)	5319 (78.19)		6803
1948			14 (0.20)	12 (0.17)	2717 (39.47)	4505 (65.45)		6883
1949			12 (0.17)	29 (0.42)	3257 (46.82)	5549 (79.77)		6956
1950			53 (0.76)	350 (4.99)	8441 (120.29)	110660 (1577.03)	20714 (295.20)	7017
1951			60 (0.85)	449 (6.35)	8809 (124.54)	134324 (1899.11)	24159 (341.57)	7073
1952			50 (0.70)	310 (4.35)	8485 (119.09)	131530 (1846.03)	26511 (372.08)	7125
1953			59 (0.82)	330 (4.60)	8517 (118.77)	138365 (1922.51)	25889 (361.02)	7171
1954			64 (0.89)	339 (4.70)	9057 (125.55)	142909 (1981.00)	28348 (392.96)	7214
1955			49 (0.67)	375 (5.17)	9816 (135.21)	163723 (2225.14)	33319 (458.94)	7260
1956			76 (1.04)	333 (4.55)	9704 (132.66)	172849 (2362.94)	34357 (469.68)	7315
1957			61 (0.83)	356 (4.83)	9789 (132.93)	194060 (2635.25)	42717 (580.08)	7364
1958			51 (0.69)	427 (5.76)	9440 (127.41)	213385 (2880.08)	53645 (724.05)	7409
1959			57 (0.77)	474 (6.37)	9284 (124.68)	207998 (2793.42)	53230 (714.88)	7446
1960			46 (0.61)	512 (6.84)	9823 (131.32)	204144 (2729.20)	56302 (752.70)	7480
1961			127 (1.69)	428 (5.69)	9880 (131.38)	208330 (2770.35)	56460 (750.80)	7520
1962			120 (1.59)	431 (5.74)	9735 (128.74)	218593 (2890.68)	62002 (819.92)	7562
1963			184 (2.42)	516 (6.79)	10067 (132.39)	233135 (3065.95)	66120 (869.54)	7604
1964			146 (1.91)	590 (7.70)	10514 (137.24)	255674 (3337.35)	72530 (946.74)	7661

SWEDEN *

NUMBER OF CONVICTIONS -- (RATE PER 100,000)   CONTINUED

YEAR	MURDER ( )	MANSLTR ( )	HOMICIDE (1)	RAPE ( )	ASSAULT (2)	ROBBERY (3)	THEFT (4)	POP
1965			166 (2.15)	587 (7.59)	12931 (167.28)	285691 (3695.87)	80584 (1042.48)	7730
1966			172 (2.20)	660 (8.45)	14370 (183.99)	291698 (3734.93)	80520 (1030.99)	7810
1967			172 (2.19)	652 (8.28)	14855 (188.75)	309945 (3938.31)	85469 (1086.01)	7870
1968			225 (2.84)	603 (7.62)	18048 (228.17)	335469 (4241.07)	97493 (1232.53)	7910
1969			207 (2.60)	603 (7.57)	19201 (240.92)	330059 (4141.27)	86353 (1083.48)	7970
1970			222 (2.76)	664 (8.26)	18832 (234.23)	379379 (4718.64)	104874 (1304.40)	8040
1971			197 (2.43)	618 (7.63)	18268 (225.53)	442312 (5460.64)	130808 (1614.91)	8100

FOOTNOTES:
* OFFENSES KNOWN FROM 1950; NEW PENAL CODE TOOK EFFECT
  JAN. 1,1965 WHICH MEANT FIGURES FROM 1960 ON WERE REVISED
1. MURDER AND MANSLAUGHTER AFTER 1949;
   UNSPECIFIED MEASURE CHANGE AFTER 1960
2. VIOLENT CRIMES
3. ROBBERY AND LARCENY
4. BURGLARY AND HOUSEBREAKING

SWITZERLAND

NUMBER OF CONVICTIONS -- (RATE PER 100,000)

YEAR	MURDER ( )	MANSLTR ( )	HOMICIDE ( )	RAPE (1)	ASSAULT (2)	ROBBERY ( )	THEFT (3)	POP
1929				881 (21.90)	2787 (69.29)		8320 (206.86)	4022
1930				1053 (25.99)	3187 (78.67)		8896 (219.60)	4051
1931				865 (21.24)	3333 (81.85)		8503 (208.82)	4072
1932				1043 (25.48)	3162 (77.25)		8481 (207.21)	4093
1933				1077 (26.18)	3238 (78.71)		8987 (218.45)	4114
1934				1156 (27.96)	3414 (82.56)		9336 (225.78)	4135
1935				1198 (28.83)	3426 (82.45)		9775 (235.26)	4155
1936				1302 (31.23)	3278 (78.63)		10636 (255.12)	4169
1937				1230 (29.40)	3041 (72.70)		10291 (246.02)	4183
1938				1502 (35.79)	3064 (73.00)		9441 (224.95)	4197
1939				1238 (29.40)	2864 (68.01)		8135 (193.18)	4211
1940				1094 (25.89)	2290 (54.19)		7436 (175.96)	4226
1941				1106 (25.99)	1926 (45.25)		8842 (207.75)	4256
1942				1127 (26.29)	1505 (35.11)		9197 (214.58)	4286
1943				1254 (29.01)	1541 (35.65)		9562 (221.19)	4323
1944				1216 (27.86)	1852 (42.44)		9093 (208.36)	4364
1945				1265 (28.67)	1620 (36.72)		10109 (229.13)	4412
1946				1523 (34.09)	1958 (43.83)		9556 (213.92)	4467
1947				1565 (34.59)	1950 (43.10)		9158 (202.43)	4524
1948					2162 (47.18)		9483 (206.96)	4582
1949					2059 (44.38)		9131 (196.79)	4640
1950					2290 (48.79)		9575 (203.98)	4694
1951					1934 (40.72)		8823 (185.79)	4749
1952					1802 (37.42)		8956 (186.00)	4815
1953					2068 (42.40)		8786 (180.15)	4877
1954					1968 (39.98)		8660 (175.91)	4923
1955					1820 (36.56)		8297 (166.67)	4978
1956					2005 (39.74)		8574 (169.95)	5045
1957					1982 (38.67)		9118 (177.88)	5126
1958					2152 (41.39)		9391 (180.63)	5139
1959					2046 (36.90)		9348 (177.75)	5259
1960					2044 (38.12)		9648 (179.93)	5362
1961					2277 (41.43)		9783 (178.00)	5496
1962					2132 (37.67)		10013 (176.91)	5560
1963					2104 (36.46)		9871 (171.07)	5770
1964					2281 (38.86)		10100 (172.06)	5870
1965					2169 (36.45)		9811 (164.89)	5950
1966					1977 (32.95)		9899 (164.98)	6000
1967					2032 (33.48)		10273 (169.24)	6070
1968					2008 (32.65)		10543 (171.43)	6150
1969					2076 (33.38)		11095 (178.38)	6220
1970					2353 (37.53)		12036 (191.96)	6270

FOOTNOTES:
1. OFFENSES AGAINST MORALITY
2. LIFE AND BODY
3. PROPERTY OFFENSES

SYRIA

NUMBER OF CONVICTIONS -- (RATE PER 100,000)

YEAR	MURDER (1)	MANSLTR ( )	HOMICIDE ( )	RAPE (2)	ASSAULT (3)	ROBBERY (4)	THEFT (5)	POP
1960	111 (2.43)	165 (3.61)	411 (9.00)	28 (0.61)	11096 (243.07)	494 (10.82)	2305 (50.49)	4565
1961	82 (1.75)	240 (5.13)	342 (7.31)	29 (0.62)	11628 (248.46)	400 (8.55)	2214 (47.31)	4680
1962	34 (0.70)	153 (3.17)	145 (3.00)	25 (0.52)	10461 (216.58)	331 (6.85)	2397 (49.63)	4830
1963	48 (0.96)	130 (2.61)	255 (5.11)	32 (0.64)	6682 (133.91)	393 (7.88)	2100 (42.08)	4990
1964	33 (0.64)	224 (4.35)	165 (3.20)	21 (0.41)	7751 (150.50)	337 (6.54)	2449 (47.55)	5150
1965	21 (0.39)	263 (4.94)	159 (2.99)	20 (0.38)	9578 (180.04)	379 (7.12)	2206 (41.47)	5320
1966	27 (0.49)	287 (5.23)	167 (3.04)	19 (0.35)	6867 (125.08)	377 (6.87)	1620 (29.51)	5490
1967	28 (0.49)	380 (6.70)	222 (3.92)	18 (0.32)	7710 (135.98)	468 (8.25)	2179 (38.43)	5670
1968	43 (0.73)	451 (7.70)	135 (2.30)	22 (0.38)	8069 (137.70)	484 (8.26)	2151 (36.71)	5860
1969	35 (0.58)	468 (7.74)	176 (2.91)	21 (0.35)	9693 (160.21)	550 (9.09)	2314 (38.25)	6050
1970	41 (0.66)	569 (9.10)	219 (3.50)	27 (0.43)	8590 (137.44)	659 (10.54)	2315 (37.04)	6250
1971	49 (0.76)	269 (4.17)	294 (4.56)	28 (0.43)	4568 (70.82)	701 (10.87)	2140 (33.18)	6450
1972	31 (0.46)	360 (5.39)	170 (2.54)	27 (0.40)	6097 (91.27)	615 (9.21)	2220 (33.23)	6680
1973	38 (0.55)	453 (6.58)	168 (2.44)	12 (0.17)	5973 (86.82)	509 (7.40)	2194 (31.89)	6880

FOOTNOTES:
1. ATTEMPTED MURDER
2. EXTORTION, RAVISHMENT
3. BATTERY
4. ARMED ROBBERY
5. LARCENY, BURGLARY

TANGIERS *

NUMBER OF OFFENSES REPORTED -- (RATE PER 100,000)

YEAR	MURDER ( )	MANSLTR ( )	HOMICIDE ( )	RAPE (1)	ASSAULT ( )	ROBBERY ( )	THEFT ( )	POP
1953	9 (4.89)			93 (50.54)		405 (220.11)	171 (92.93)	184
1954	6 (3.28)			59 (32.24)		399 (218.03)	1903 (1039.89)	183

FOOTNOTES:
* RAW CRIME DATA FROM INTERPOL; RATES COMPUTED FROM
  POPULATION FIGURES ABOVE
1. SEX OFFENSES

TANZANIA *

NUMBER OF OFFENSES REPORTED -- (RATE PER 100,000)

YEAR	MURDER ( )	MANSLTR ( )	HOMICIDE (1)	RAPE (2)	ASSAULT ( )	ROBBERY (3)	THEFT (4)	POP
1962			586 (5.57)	2481 (23.58)	16021 (152.29)	619 (5.88)	33279 (316.34)	10520
1963			533 (4.94)	2172 (20.13)	15619 (144.75)	562 (5.21)	27984 (259.35)	10790
1964			690 (6.24)	1522 (13.76)	20589 (186.16)	250 (2.26)	31376 (283.69)	11060
1965			747 (6.59)	1625 (14.34)	23685 (209.05)	1008 (8.90)	37341 (329.58)	11330
1966			887 (7.64)	1645 (14.17)	24347 (209.71)	1155 (9.95)	35987 (309.97)	11610
1967			813 (6.83)	1659 (13.93)	26462 (222.18)	1472 (12.36)	40205 (337.57)	11910
1968			806 (6.59)	1623 (13.27)	27377 (223.85)	1627 (13.30)	43639 (356.82)	12230
1969			882 (7.02)	1597 (12.71)	30544 (243.18)	2167 (17.25)	46388 (369.33)	12560
1970			929 (7.20)	1578 (12.23)	33064 (256.31)	2722 (21.10)	43916 (340.43)	12900
1971			1018 (7.69)	1383 (10.45)	29570 (223.34)	2692 (20.33)	40640 (306.95)	13240
1972			924 (6.79)	1286 (9.46)	26766 (196.81)	3218 (23.66)	38998 (286.75)	13600

FOOTNOTES:
* FIGURES FOR MAINLAND (TANGANYIKA)
1. MANSLAUGHTER AND MURDER
2. AGAINST PUBLIC MORALITY
3. ROBBERY AND EXTORTION
4. THEFT AND OTHER STEALING

NUMBER OF CONVICTIONS -- (RATE PER 100,000)

YEAR	MURDER ( )	MANSLTR ( )	HOMICIDE ( )	RAPE ( )	ASSAULT (1)	ROBBERY (2)	THEFT ( )	POP
1911	11 (0.13)	25 (0.30)			1073 (12.98)	133 (1.61)	2290 (27.70)	8266
1912	15 (0.18)	8 (0.10)			935 (11.15)	146 (1.74)	2460 (29.34)	8384
1913	6 (0.07)	15 (0.18)			866 (10.19)	102 (1.20)	2014 (23.69)	8502
1914	18 (0.21)	15 (0.17)			1048 (12.16)	89 (1.03)	1966 (22.81)	8620
1915	15 (0.17)	27 (0.31)			1141 (13.06)	98 (1.12)	2056 (23.53)	8738
1916	16 (0.18)	14 (0.16)			731 (8.25)	119 (1.34)	2108 (23.80)	8856
1917	14 (0.16)	14 (0.16)			702 (7.82)	71 (0.79)	2005 (22.34)	8974
1918	36 (0.40)	12 (0.13)			774 (8.51)	107 (1.18)	2149 (23.64)	9092
1919	11 (0.12)	8 (0.09)			698 (7.58)	140 (1.52)	2333 (25.34)	9207
1920	26 (0.27)	18 (0.19)			667 (7.05)	131 (1.38)	2269 (23.99)	9460
1921	22 (0.23)	19 (0.20)			742 (7.67)	112 (1.16)	1710 (17.67)	9676
1922	35 (0.35)	32 (0.32)			805 (8.14)	156 (1.58)	1893 (19.14)	9892
1923	51 (0.50)	27 (0.27)			877 (8.68)	146 (1.44)	1829 (18.09)	10108
1924	44 (0.43)	24 (0.23)			932 (9.03)	193 (1.87)	2083 (20.18)	10324
1925	43 (0.41)	50 (0.47)			997 (9.46)	191 (1.81)	2109 (20.01)	10542
1926	55 (0.51)	47 (0.44)			1253 (11.60)	199 (1.84)	2167 (20.06)	10801
1927	61 (0.55)	31 (0.28)			1188 (10.74)	172 (1.56)	2111 (19.09)	11060
1928	57 (0.50)	25 (0.22)			1417 (12.52)	172 (1.52)	2141 (18.92)	11319
1929	76 (0.66)	39 (0.34)			1478 (12.77)	191 (1.65)	2114 (18.26)	11578
1930	622 (5.25)	199 (1.68)			7442 (62.87)	931 (7.86)	12674 (107.06)	11838
1931	541 (4.43)	196 (1.61)			7274 (59.58)	1682 (13.78)	12857 (105.31)	12209
1932	550 (4.56)	181 (1.44)			7308 (58.09)	2026 (16.10)	12308 (97.84)	12580
1933	591 (4.56)	189 (1.46)			7459 (57.59)	1920 (14.83)	10393 (80.25)	12951
1934	802 (6.02)	278 (2.09)			8657 (64.98)	2595 (19.48)	10854 (81.47)	13322
1935	659 (4.81)	255 (1.86)			8528 (62.28)	2359 (17.30)	12600 (92.01)	13594
1936	776 (5.54)	272 (1.94)			10395 (74.18)	2097 (14.96)	12743 (90.93)	14014
1937	673 (4.70)	254 (1.77)			9748 (68.01)	2127 (14.84)	14076 (98.20)	14334
1938	764 (5.21)	252 (1.72)			9889 (67.48)	1787 (12.19)	12103 (82.59)	14654
1939	741 (4.95)	254 (1.70)			9883 (66.00)	1644 (10.98)	11889 (79.40)	14974
1940	437 (2.86)	132 (0.86)			6639 (43.40)	1018 (6.66)	9670 (63.22)	15296
1941	586 (3.76)	160 (1.03)			7140 (45.84)	1349 (8.66)	11778 (75.61)	15577
1942	252 (1.59)	58 (0.37)			2539 (16.01)	663 (4.18)	6834 (43.10)	15857
1943	528 (3.27)	137 (0.85)			5544 (34.34)	1099 (6.81)	11635 (72.05)	16145
1944	513 (3.12)	149 (0.91)			4943 (30.07)	869 (5.29)	10522 (64.01)	16439
1945								
1946	716 (4.20)	171 (1.00)			4815 (28.26)	2029 (11.91)	9063 (53.18)	17041
1947								
1948	777 (4.36)	207 (1.16)			5280 (29.65)	1739 (5.77)	7565 (42.48)	17808
1949								
1950	779 (3.97)	241 (1.23)			6257 (31.86)	1255 (6.39)	5715 (29.10)	19640
1951	847 (4.19)	255 (1.26)			6249 (30.91)	1210 (5.98)	5386 (26.64)	20220
1952	884 (4.24)	231 (1.11)			6659 (31.97)	1308 (6.28)	5292 (25.41)	20830
1953	1068 (4.98)	272 (1.27)			8139 (37.93)	1388 (6.47)	6155 (28.68)	21460
1954	1248 (5.65)	290 (1.31)			9276 (41.97)	1575 (7.13)	7143 (32.32)	22100
1955	1189 (5.22)	274 (1.20)			9343 (41.05)	1556 (6.84)	7596 (33.37)	22760
1956	1211 (5.17)	284 (1.21)			9476 (40.42)	1744 (7.44)	8037 (34.28)	23445

THAILAND *

YEAR	MURDER ( )	MANSLTR ( )	HOMICIDE ( )	RAPE ( )	ASSAULT (1)	ROBBERY (2)	THEFT ( )	POP
1957	1278 (5.29)	283 (1.17)			7979 (33.04)	2269 (9.40)	7860 (32.55)	24148
1958	1459 (5.87)	320 (1.29)			7121 (28.63)	2723 (10.95)	8197 (32.96)	24873
1959	1984 (7.74)	406 (1.58)			8726 (34.06)	2848 (11.12)	10773 (42.05)	25619
1960	1873 (7.10)	367 (1.39)			8608 (32.62)	2492 (5.44)	10889 (41.26)	26388
1961	3656 (13.45)					2889 (10.63)	17930 (65.97)	27180
1962	4028 (14.39)					3037 (10.85)	21814 (77.92)	27995
1963	4377 (15.18)					3411 (11.83)	21778 (75.53)	28835
1964	5232 (17.44)					3909 (13.03)	24133 (80.44)	30000
1965	5494 (17.71)					3507 (11.30)	23630 (76.15)	31030
1966	5504 (17.20)					2606 (8.14)		32000
1967	5884 (17.83)					2179 (6.60)	24415 (73.98)	33000
1968	6308 (18.53)					2584 (7.59)	26076 (76.60)	34040
1969	6977 (19.87)					4306 (12.26)	23309 (66.39)	35110
1970	7285 (20.12)					3982 (11.00)		36210
1971	7373 (19.72)					3925 (10.50)		37380
1972	5266 (13.65)					2550 (6.61)		38580

FOOTNOTES:
* PROBABLE CRIME MEASURE CHANGE, 1930;
  FISCAL YEARS (BEGINNING IN YEAR INDICATED) UNTIL 1940;
  POPULATION MEASURE CHANGE, 1950;
  CONVICTIONS UNTIL 1960, THEN CASES KNOWN
1. BODILY HARM
2. ROBBERY AND GANG ROBBERY

TRINIDAD AND TOBAGO

NUMBER OF OFFENSES REPORTED -- (RATE PER 100,000)

YEAR	MURDER ( )	MANSLTR ( )	HOMICIDE ( )	RAPE ( )	ASSAULT ( )	ROBBERY ( )	THEFT ( )	POP
1950	32 (5.06)	66 (10.44)	9 (1.42)	54 (8.54)		87 (13.77)	326 (51.58)	632
1951	35 (5.39)	4 (0.62)	59 (9.09)	76 (11.71)		77 (11.86)	330 (50.85)	649
1952	49 (7.39)	0 (0.00)	59 (8.90)	46 (6.94)		69 (10.41)	344 (51.89)	663
1953	48 (7.08)	3 (0.44)	57 (8.41)	69 (10.18)		50 (7.37)	311 (45.87)	678
1954	44 (6.30)	3 (0.43)	48 (6.88)	46 (6.59)		51 (7.31)	310 (44.41)	698
1955	32 (4.44)	1 (0.14)	65 (9.02)	40 (5.55)		47 (6.52)	345 (47.85)	721
1956	49 (6.59)	2 (0.27)	65 (8.75)	48 (6.46)		72 (9.69)	371 (49.93)	743
1957	46 (6.01)	16 (2.09)	87 (11.37)	60 (7.84)		70 (9.15)	351 (45.88)	765
1958	29 (3.68)	21 (2.66)	55 (6.97)	46 (5.83)		95 (12.04)	323 (40.94)	789
1959	45 (5.51)	9 (1.10)	58 (7.10)	69 (8.45)		118 (14.44)	335 (41.00)	817
1960	50 (5.95)	18 (2.14)	54 (6.42)	45 (5.35)		94 (11.18)	344 (40.90)	841
1961	46 (5.31)	25 (2.88)	57 (6.57)	45 (5.19)		82 (9.46)	509 (58.71)	867
1962	51 (5.70)	17 (1.90)	65 (7.27)	60 (6.71)		95 (10.63)	548 (61.30)	894
1963	61 (6.62)	32 (3.47)	62 (6.72)	96 (10.41)		142 (15.40)	559 (60.63)	922
1964	48 (5.05)	34 (3.58)	67 (7.05)	97 (10.21)		196 (20.63)	546 (57.47)	950
1965	65 (6.70)	29 (2.99)	63 (6.49)	121 (12.47)		250 (25.77)	790 (81.44)	970
1966	52 (5.25)	28 (2.83)	86 (8.69)	113 (11.41)		261 (26.36)	975 (98.48)	990
1967	68 (6.73)	21 (2.08)	72 (7.13)	109 (10.79)		268 (26.53)	1057 (104.65)	1010
1968	51 (5.00)	21 (2.06)	100 (9.80)	118 (11.57)		228 (22.35)	1250 (122.55)	1020
1969	44 (4.27)	19 (1.84)	93 (9.03)	99 (9.61)		97 (9.42)	1474 (143.11)	1030
1970	56 (5.44)	15 (1.46)	89 (8.64)	92 (8.93)		287 (27.86)	1283 (124.56)	1030
1971	49 (4.76)	19 (1.84)	64 (6.21)	134 (13.01)		273 (26.50)	1713 (166.31)	1030
1972	57 (5.48)	21 (2.02)	89 (8.56)	144 (13.85)		400 (38.46)	1707 (164.13)	1040
1973	60 (5.69)	25 (2.37)	92 (8.72)	139 (13.18)		398 (37.73)	1730 (163.98)	1055
1974	58 (5.42)	17 (1.59)	88 (8.22)	127 (11.87)		384 (35.89)	2238 (209.16)	1070

TUNISIA *

NUMBER OF OFFENSES REPORTED -- (RATE PER 100,000)

YEAR	MURDER ( )	MANSLTR ( )	HOMICIDE ( )	RAPE (1)	ASSAULT ( )	ROBBERY ( )	THEFT ( )	POP
1957	165 (4.12)			575 (14.36)				4003
1958	103 (2.54)			846 (20.89)				4050
1959	184 (4.48)			1504 (36.62)		2385 (58.07)	6095 (148.41)	4107
1960	101 (2.39)			1482 (35.02)		1608 (38.00)	6320 (149.34)	4232
1961	80 (1.86)			1240 (28.77)		1600 (37.12)	5920 (137.36)	4310
1962	86 (1.96)			1504 (34.21)		1465 (33.33)	6636 (150.96)	4396
1963	57 (1.27)			862 (19.18)		1626 (36.18)	6628 (147.49)	4494
1964	57 (1.25)			990 (21.67)		1131 (24.75)	7708 (168.70)	4569
1965	45 (0.97)			1233 (26.55)		786 (16.93)	9995 (215.22)	4644
1966	57 (1.21)			1257 (26.63)		839 (17.78)	10916 (231.27)	4720
1967	31 (0.64)			1447 (30.02)		862 (17.88)	10687 (221.72)	4820
1968	50 (1.02)			1556 (31.63)		722 (14.67)	12126 (246.46)	4920
1969	51 (1.01)			2000 (39.76)		946 (18.81)	12508 (248.67)	5030
1970	52 (1.01)			2366 (46.03)		977 (19.01)	15671 (304.88)	5140

FOOTNOTES:
* RAW CRIME DATA FROM INTERPOL; RATES COMPUTED FROM
  POPULATION FIGURES ABOVE
  1. SEX OFFENSES

TURKEY *

NUMBER OF OFFENSES REPORTED -- (RATE PER 100,000)

YEAR	MURDER ( )	MANSLTR ( )	HOMICIDE (1)	RAPE ( )	ASSAULT ( )	ROBBERY ( )	THEFT ( )	POP
1955			1593 (6.68)	718 (3.01)		257 (1.08)	9984 (41.84)	23860
1956			1832 (7.50)	696 (2.85)		219 (0.90)	9917 (40.58)	24440
1957			1943 (7.70)	690 (2.73)		266 (1.05)	11144 (44.13)	25250
1958			2041 (7.86)	611 (2.35)		304 (1.17)	10615 (40.86)	25980
1959			1903 (7.12)	606 (2.27)		316 (1.18)	9174 (34.31)	26740
1960			1691 (6.15)	147 (0.53)		342 (1.24)	11049 (40.16)	27510
1961			1718 (6.08)	152 (0.54)		356 (1.26)	13579 (48.08)	28240
1962			1915 (6.62)	186 (0.64)		618 (2.14)	13474 (46.57)	28930
1963			2223 (7.49)	155 (0.52)		463 (1.56)	13592 (45.83)	29660
1964			2269 (7.47)	158 (0.52)		474 (1.56)	13145 (43.25)	30390
1965			2520 (8.09)	42 (0.13)		484 (1.55)	17704 (56.83)	31150
1966			3055 (9.57)	115 (0.36)		497 (1.56)	18026 (56.45)	31930
1967			3111 (9.51)	117 (0.36)		307 (0.94)	16859 (51.53)	32220
1968			3417 (10.19)	112 (0.33)		328 (0.98)	17040 (50.81)	33540
1969			3334 (9.70)	175 (0.51)		337 (0.98)	15780 (45.90)	34380
1970			3271 (9.28)	223 (0.63)		417 (1.18)	15703 (44.57)	35230
1971			2844 (7.88)	219 (0.61)		414 (1.15)	14127 (39.12)	36110
1972			2495 (6.74)	158 (0.43)		309 (0.83)	15453 (41.75)	37010
1973			2767 (7.29)	127 (0.33)		298 (0.79)	14534 (38.30)	37943

FOOTNOTES:
* SOME CRIME FIGURES MAY BE FOR TOWNS AND CITIES ONLY;
  COMPUTED RATES BASED ON QUESTIONABLE POPULATION
  ESTIMATES FOR ENTIRE NATION OF TURKEY
1. MURDER AND MANSLAUGHTER

UGANDA *

NUMBER OF OFFENSES REPORTED -- (RATE PER 100,000)

YEAR	MURDER ( )	MANSLTR ( )	HOMICIDE ( )	RAPE (1)	ASSAULT ( )	ROBBERY ( )	THEFT ( )	POP
1958	551 (8.67)			241 (3.79)		9484 (149.21)	11191 (176.07)	6356
1959								
1960	930 (13.93)			546 (8.18)		17035 (255.13)	10875 (162.87)	6677
1961	950 (13.88)			377 (5.51)		1320 (19.28)	18220 (266.18)	6845
1962	955 (13.61)			482 (6.87)		1460 (20.81)	19073 (271.85)	7016
1963								7583
1964	1530 (20.18)			585 (7.71)		16920 (223.13)	9450 (124.62)	7976
1965	1680 (21.06)			704 (8.83)		17632 (221.06)	10440 (130.89)	8369
1966	1832 (21.89)			1200 (14.34)		18784 (224.45)	15416 (184.20)	8762
1967	1767 (20.17)			1254 (14.31)		17604 (200.91)	18611 (212.41)	9155
1968	2005 (21.90)			1444 (15.77)		19513 (213.14)	21081 (230.27)	9550
1969	2320 (24.29)			1580 (16.54)				9810
1970	2460 (25.08)			1330 (13.56)				

FOOTNOTES: * RAW CRIME DATA FROM INTERPOL; RATES COMPUTED FROM
POPULATION FIGURES ABOVE
1. SEX OFFENSES

NUMBER OF OFFENSES REPORTED -- (RATE PER 100,000)

YEAR	MURDER (1)	MANSLTR ( )	HOMICIDE (2)	RAPE ( )	ASSAULT ( )	ROBBERY ( )	THEFT (3)	POP
1900			1596 (2.10)					75995
1901			1785 (2.30)					77593
1902			1821 (2.30)					79191
1903			2101 (2.60)					80789
1904			2307 (2.60)					82387
1905			3779 (4.50)					83985
1906			4279 (5.00)					85583
1907			5492 (6.30)					87181
1908			5682 (6.40)					88779
1909			5061 (5.60)					90377
1910			5426 (5.90)					91972
1911			6166 (6.60)					93421
1912			6167 (6.50)					94870
1913			6935 (7.20)					96319
1914			7137 (7.30)					97768
1915			6846 (6.90)					99217
1916			7147 (7.10)					100666
1917			7761 (7.60)					102115
1918			7042 (6.80)					103564
1919			7876 (7.50)					105013
1920			7559 (7.10)					106466
1921			9209 (8.50)					108339
1922			9258 (8.40)					110212
1923			9079 (8.10)					112085
1924			9601 (8.43)					113958
1925			9962 (8.60)					115832
1926			10323 (8.80)					117303
1927			10333 (8.70)					118774
1928			10582 (8.80)					120245
1929			10346 (8.50)					121716
1930			11086 (9.00)					123188
1931			11534 (9.30)					124023
1932			11487 (9.20)					124858
1933	9678 (7.70)		12067 (9.60)	4902 (3.90)	70891 (56.40)	136753 (108.80)	846165 (673.20)	125693
1934	7718 (6.10)		12020 (9.50)	5314 (4.20)	69084 (54.60)	108814 (86.00)	761825 (602.10)	126528
1935	8915 (7.00)		10571 (8.30)	5986 (4.70)	65591 (51.50)	90045 (70.70)	661772 (519.60)	127362
1936	9110 (7.10)		10265 (8.00)	6929 (5.40)	66467 (51.80)	74165 (57.80)	621296 (484.20)	128314
1937	9049 (7.00)		9824 (7.60)	7368 (5.70)	63728 (49.30)	79757 (61.70)	639737 (494.90)	129266
1938	8594 (6.60)		8855 (6.80)	6250 (4.80)	62374 (47.90)	79042 (60.70)	619707 (475.90)	130218
1939	8657 (6.60)		8395 (6.40)	7346 (5.60)	65060 (47.60)	73586 (56.10)	623844 (475.60)	131170
1940	8720 (6.60)		8192 (6.20)	7267 (5.50)	64740 (49.00)	70817 (53.60)	622955 (471.50)	132122
1941	8677 (6.50)		8009 (6.00)	7609 (5.70)	67546 (50.60)	66078 (49.50)	629009 (471.20)	133491
1942	8766 (6.50)		7822 (5.80)	8226 (6.10)	72959 (54.10)	62845 (46.60)	583808 (432.90)	134860
1943	7657 (5.60)		6837 (5.00)	10255 (7.50)	70421 (51.50)	60986 (44.60)	635015 (464.40)	136739
1944	7750 (5.60)		6781 (4.90)	11072 (8.00)	79301 (57.30)	60203 (43.50)	677453 (489.50)	138397

UNITED STATES *

NUMBER OF OFFENSES REPORTED -- (RATE PER 100,000)   CONTINUED

YEAR	MURDER (1)	MANSLTR ( )	HOMICIDE (2)	RAPE ( )	ASSAULT ( )	ROBBERY ( )	THEFT (3)	POP
1945	8256 (5.90)		7836 (5.60)	12454 (8.90)	87734 (62.70)	75701 (54.10)	807524 (577.10)	139928
1946	9756 (6.90)		8908 (6.30)	12301 (8.70)	95013 (67.20)	83985 (55.40)	840982 (594.80)	141389
1947	8936 (6.20)		8648 (6.00)	12595 (8.60)	100312 (69.60)	80422 (55.80)	808259 (560.80)	144126
1948	8797 (6.00)		8505 (5.80)	11291 (7.70)	103815 (70.80)	75955 (51.80)	809550 (552.10)	146631
1949	8056 (5.40)		8056 (5.40)	10891 (7.30)	105774 (70.90)	81755 (54.80)	828739 (555.50)	149188
1950	8039 (5.30)		8039 (5.30)	11073 (7.30)	108605 (71.60)	73566 (48.50)	847756 (558.90)	151683
1951	7872 (5.10)		7564 (4.90)	11731 (7.60)	105736 (68.50)	72240 (46.80)	900691 (583.50)	154360
1952	8322 (5.30)		8165 (5.20)	11306 (7.20)	118399 (75.40)	80712 (51.40)	1026806 (653.90)	157028
1953	8301 (5.20)		7663 (4.80)	11654 (7.30)	124681 (78.10)	87644 (54.90)	1088446 (681.80)	159643
1954	7958 (4.90)		7796 (4.80)	11206 (6.90)	125867 (77.50)	93385 (57.50)	1132278 (697.30)	162409
1955	7932 (4.80)		7601 (4.60)	13385 (8.10)	124432 (75.30)	79484 (48.10)	1109640 (671.50)	163248
1956	8107 (4.80)		7770 (4.60)	14357 (8.50)	129886 (76.90)	78709 (46.60)	1245660 (737.50)	168903
1957	8083 (4.70)		7739 (4.50)	14619 (8.50)	134835 (78.40)	85132 (49.50)	1363661 (792.90)	171984
1958	8219 (4.70)		7870 (4.50)	16439 (9.40)	138157 (79.00)	96010 (54.90)	1496116 (855.50)	174882
1959	8536 (4.80)		8180 (4.60)	16716 (9.40)	145287 (81.70)	91049 (51.20)	1513867 (851.30)	177830
1960	9034 (5.00)		8492 (4.70)	17165 (9.50)	153762 (85.10)	108230 (59.90)	1764471 (976.70)	180684
1961	8637 (4.70)		8637 (4.70)	17089 (9.30)	155641 (84.70)	106578 (58.00)	1791989 (975.20)	183756
1962	8586 (4.60)		9146 (4.90)	17546 (9.40)	163511 (87.60)	110874 (59.40)	1928716 (1033.30)	186656
1963	8524 (4.50)		9281 (4.90)	17616 (9.30)	173127 (91.40)	116491 (61.50)	2137571 (1128.50)	189417
1964	9414 (4.90)		9798 (5.10)	21325 (11.10)	201533 (104.90)	130257 (67.80)	2410517 (1254.70)	192119
1965	9909 (5.10)		10687 (5.50)	23316 (12.00)	213341 (109.80)	138342 (71.20)	2595903 (1317.50)	194300
1966	11007 (5.60)		11597 (5.90)	25749 (13.10)	233513 (118.80)	157838 (80.30)	2855820 (1452.90)	196560
1967	12121 (6.10)		13512 (6.80)	27722 (13.80)	255342 (128.50)	202883 (102.10)	3329585 (1675.60)	198710
1968	12644 (6.30)		14652 (7.30)	31511 (15.70)	284607 (141.80)	262729 (130.90)	3903408 (1944.80)	200710
1969	14796 (7.30)		14593 (7.20)	36888 (18.20)	308682 (152.30)	298548 (147.30)	4373024 (2157.60)	202660
1970	15980 (7.80)		15571 (7.60)	37903 (18.50)	333954 (163.00)	351164 (171.40)	4898886 (2391.10)	204880
1971	17599 (8.50)		17599 (8.50)	42031 (20.30)	366064 (176.80)	387391 (187.10)	5163827 (2494.00)	207050
1972	18587 (8.90)			46571 (22.30)	389695 (186.60)	375703 (179.90)	5078571 (2431.80)	208840
1973	19510 (9.07)			51000 (23.72)	416270 (193.61)	382680 (177.99)	5228000 (2431.63)	215000

FOOTNOTES:

* RAW FIGURES FOR ALL CRIMES EXCEPT HOMICIDE ARE
  EXTRAPOLATIONS FROM UNIFORM CRIME REPORT RATES
  USING TOTAL U.S. POPULATION FIGURES. (UCR RATES
  ARE COMPUTED FROM POPULATION FIGURES FOR REPORTING
  AREAS ONLY)

1. MURDER AND NON-NEGLIGENT MANSLAUGHTER
2. NUMBER OF DEATHS CAUSED (VITAL STATISTICS)
3. BURGLARY, LARCENY AND AUTO THEFTS

VENEZUELA   CRIME STATISTICS -- (RATE PER 100,000)

YEAR	MURDER ( )	MANSLTR ( )	HOMICIDE ( )	RAPE ( )	ASSAULT ( )	ROBBERY ( )	THEFT ( )	POP
1943			253 (6.28)		1061 (26.34)	38 (0.94)	440 (10.92)	4028
1944			366 (8.83)		1132 (27.30)	28 (0.68)	594 (14.33)	4146
1945			322 (7.55)		1153 (27.02)	17 (0.40)	404 (9.47)	4267
1946			388 (8.84)		1437 (32.73)	30 (0.68)	363 (8.27)	4391
1947			492 (10.82)		1430 (31.44)	6 (0.13)	368 (8.09)	4548
1948			426 (9.09)		1635 (34.89)	7 (0.15)	326 (6.96)	4686
1949			395 (8.18)		1345 (27.86)	5 (0.10)	239 (4.95)	4828
1950			335 (6.75)		1462 (29.48)	10 (0.20)	176 (3.55)	4960
1951			357 (6.91)		1568 (30.33)	13 (0.25)	188 (3.64)	5170
1952			431 (8.00)		1640 (30.43)	29 (0.54)	292 (5.42)	5390
1953			369 (6.57)		1606 (28.58)	19 (0.34)	231 (4.11)	5620
1954			475 (8.12)		1958 (33.47)	48 (0.82)	285 (4.87)	5850
1955			476 (7.82)		1935 (31.77)	33 (0.54)	469 (7.70)	6090
1956			518 (8.10)		2520 (39.42)	53 (0.83)	532 (8.32)	6393
1957			508 (7.66)		2582 (38.91)	49 (0.74)	465 (7.01)	6636
1958			587 (8.53)		2498 (36.31)	58 (0.84)	327 (4.75)	6879
1959			763 (10.71)		3593 (47.64)	120 (1.68)	621 (8.72)	7122
1960			762 (10.35)		3435 (46.65)	67 (0.91)	849 (11.53)	7364
1961			629 (8.26)		3413 (44.84)	64 (0.84)	939 (12.34)	7612
1962			774 (9.83)		2730 (34.68)	132 (1.68)	1126 (14.30)	7872
1963			704 (8.64)		2175 (26.71)	219 (2.69)	959 (11.53)	8144
1964			807 (9.58)		2317 (27.49)	278 (3.30)	1047 (12.42)	8427
1965			844 (9.68)		2357 (27.03)	229 (2.63)	1220 (13.99)	8720
1966			710 (7.86)		2422 (26.82)	231 (2.56)	1217 (13.48)	9030
1967			703 (7.52)		2255 (23.90)	269 (2.88)	1270 (13.58)	9350
1968			718 (7.41)		1951 (20.13)	288 (2.97)	1344 (13.87)	9690
1969			809 (8.06)		2035 (20.27)	294 (2.93)	1357 (13.52)	10040
1970			764 (7.35)		2125 (20.43)	374 (3.60)	1360 (13.08)	10400

VIETNAM, SOUTH *   CRIME STATISTICS -- (RATE PER 100,000)

YEAR	MURDER ( )	MANSLTR ( )	HOMICIDE ( )	RAPE (1)	ASSAULT ( )	ROBBERY ( )	THEFT ( )	POP
1959	536 (3.89)				619 (4.49)	339 (2.46)	399 (2.89)	13789
1960	94 (0.67)				206 (1.46)	235 (1.67)	197 (1.40)	14100
1961	153 (1.06)				160 (1.10)	286 (1.97)	171 (1.18)	14494
1962	129 (0.86)				355 (2.38)	313 (2.10)	184 (1.23)	14929
1963	235 (1.53)				362 (2.36)	300 (1.96)	163 (1.06)	15317
1964	286 (1.82)				527 (3.35)	297 (1.89)	189 (1.20)	15715
1965	296 (1.84)				190 (1.18)	254 (1.58)	178 (1.10)	16120
1966	271 (1.64)				117 (0.71)	221 (1.34)	241 (1.46)	16540
1967	124 (0.73)				40 (0.24)	59 (0.35)	83 (0.49)	16970
1968	148 (0.85)				117 (0.67)	205 (1.18)	138 (0.79)	17410
1969	454 (2.54)			221 (1.24)		530 (2.96)		17876
1970	198 (1.08)			232 (1.27)		209 (1.14)		18330

FOOTNOTES:
* FIGURES SHOW NUMBER ACCUSED; 1969-1970: RAW CRIME DATA FROM
  INTERPOL. RATES COMPUTED FROM POPULATION FIGURES ABOVE
  1. RAPE AND INDECENT EXPOSURE

WEST INDIES (BRITISH) *   NUMBER OF OFFENSES REPORTED -- (RATE PER 100,000)

YEAR	MURDER ( )	MANSLTR ( )	HOMICIDE ( )	RAPE (1)	ASSAULT ( )	ROBBERY ( )	THEFT ( )	POP
1962	7 (11.67)			16 (26.67)		42 (70.00)	429 (715.00)	60
1963	5 (8.33)			15 (25.00)		28 (46.67)	175 (291.67)	60
1964	3 (5.00)			18 (30.00)		18 (30.00)	358 (596.67)	60
1965	8 (13.33)			21 (35.00)				60
1966	4 (6.67)			20 (33.33)				60
1967	3 (5.00)			18 (30.00)		57 (95.00)	301 (501.67)	60
1968	7 (11.67)			22 (36.67)		65 (108.33)	315 (525.00)	60
1969	4 (6.67)			15 (25.00)		73 (121.67)	242 (403.33)	60
1970	3 (5.00)			13 (21.67)		101 (168.33)	242 (403.33)	60

FOOTNOTES:
* ST. KITTS-NEVIS-ANGUILLA; RAW CRIME DATA FROM INTERPOL.
  RATES COMPUTED FROM POPULATION FIGURES ABOVE
  1. SEX OFFENSES

YUGOSLAVIA *

NUMBER OF CONVICTIONS -- (RATE PER 100,000)

YEAR	MURDER ( )	MANSLTR ( )	HOMICIDE ( )	RAPE (1)	ASSAULT ( )	ROBBERY ( )	THEFT ( )	POP
1931	580 (4.15)			227 (1.62)	4148 (29.68)	530 (3.79)	8151 (58.32)	13977
1932	657 (4.64)			219 (1.55)	3424 (24.16)	415 (2.93)	5238 (36.95)	14174
1933	831 (5.78)			265 (1.84)	2736 (19.04)	348 (2.42)	5988 (41.67)	14371
1934	843 (5.79)			304 (2.09)	2643 (18.14)	364 (2.50)	6604 (45.33)	14568
1935	939 (6.36)			294 (1.99)	2937 (19.89)	398 (2.70)	4769 (32.29)	14767
1936	1056 (7.05)			285 (1.90)	3374 (22.53)	352 (2.35)	5073 (33.87)	14767
1937	1059 (6.97)			324 (2.13)	3156 (20.78)	352 (2.32)	5183 (34.13)	14976
1938	924 (6.00)			312 (2.03)	2832 (18.40)	377 (2.45)	5050 (32.80)	15185
1939								15394
GAP								
1955	1172 (6.69)			669 (3.82)		13887 (79.27)	53568 (305.77)	17519
1956	1306 (7.58)			674 (3.81)		15013 (84.89)	53502 (300.53)	17685
1957	1211 (6.78)			839 (4.70)		13509 (75.64)	53725 (300.83)	17859
1958	966 (5.36)			731 (4.06)		13955 (77.45)	51452 (285.56)	18018

FOOTNOTES: * 1955-1958: RAW CRIME DATA FROM INTERPOL, RATES COMPUTED
FROM POPULATION FIGURES ABOVE
1. SEX OFFENSES FROM 1955

ZAMBIA *

NUMBER OF OFFENSES REPORTED -- (RATE PER 100,000)

YEAR	MURDER ( )	MANSLTR ( )	HOMICIDE ( )	RAPE (1)	ASSAULT ( )	ROBBERY ( )	THEFT ( )	POP
1958	132 (4.34)			157 (5.16)		6788 (223.29)	10298 (338.75)	3040
1959								
1960	187 (5.83)			257 (8.01)		5515 (171.81)	13204 (411.34)	3210
1961	150 (4.55)			202 (6.12)		4418 (133.88)	12514 (379.21)	3300
1962	186 (5.47)			250 (7.35)		6231 (183.26)	14567 (428.44)	3400
1963								
1964								
1965	192 (5.19)			364 (9.84)		436 (11.78)	31484 (850.92)	3700
1966	222 (5.84)			421 (11.08)		545 (14.34)	28839 (758.92)	3800
1967	302 (7.74)			479 (12.28)		11000 (282.05)	21095 (540.90)	3900
1968	366 (9.13)			588 (14.66)		12034 (300.10)	24972 (622.74)	4010
1969	373 (9.19)			661 (16.28)		13659 (336.43)	29165 (718.35)	4060
1970	425 (10.17)			731 (17.49)		13815 (330.50)	27793 (664.90)	4180

FOOTNOTES: * RAW CRIME DATA FROM INTERPOL; RATES COMPUTED FROM
POPULATION FIGURES ABOVE
1. SEX OFFENSES

Comparative Crime Data File: Cities

ACCRA, GHANA *

NUMBER OF OFFENSES REPORTED -- (RATE PER 100,000)

YEAR	MURDER ( )	MANSLTR ( )	HOMICIDE ( )	RAPE ( )	ASSAULT ( )	ROBBERY ( )	THEFT ( )	POP
1963	13 (2.34)			69 (12.41)	6315 (1135.79)	0 (0.00)	7631 (1372.48)	556
1964	8 (1.38)			75 (12.95)	6193 (1069.60)	22 (3.80)	7377 (1274.09)	579
1965								
1966	10 (1.59)			81 (12.90)	1332 (212.10)	17 (2.71)	8714 (1387.58)	628
1967	13 (1.99)			67 (10.24)	6825 (1043.58)	20 (3.06)	10421 (1593.43)	654
1968								
1969	19 (2.68)			84 (11.85)	7933 (1118.90)	43 (6.06)	10197 (1438.22)	709
1970	6 (0.81)			36 (4.88)	3962 (536.86)	65 (8.81)	4934 (668.56)	738
1971	4 (0.52)			28 (3.64)	2340 (304.29)	48 (6.24)	3543 (460.73)	769
1972	14 (1.75)			46 (5.74)	2804 (350.06)	22 (2.75)	3607 (450.31)	801

FOOTNOTES:
* COMPUTED RATES BASED ON VERY QUESTIONABLE POPULATION ESTIMATES

AMSTERDAM, NETHERLANDS   NUMBER OF CONVICTIONS -- (RATE PER 100,000)

YEAR	MURDER ( )	MANSLTR ( )	HOMICIDE (1)	RAPE ( )	ASSAULT ( )	ROBBERY ( )	THEFT (2)	POP
1900			3 (0.57)	0 (0.00)	151 (28.82)		292 (55.73)	524
1901			6 (1.14)	0 (0.00)	122 (23.11)		308 (58.33)	528
1902			1 (0.19)	0 (0.00)	146 (27.44)		346 (65.04)	532
1903			8 (1.49)	0 (0.00)	120 (22.39)		274 (51.12)	536
1904			1 (0.19)	0 (0.00)	116 (21.48)		304 (56.30)	540
1905			1 (0.18)	0 (0.00)	131 (24.04)		320 (58.72)	545
1906			0 (0.00)	0 (0.00)	108 (19.67)		260 (47.36)	549
1907			4 (0.72)	0 (0.00)	71 (12.84)		273 (49.37)	553
1908			4 (0.72)	0 (0.00)	94 (16.88)		282 (50.63)	557
1909			3 (0.53)	1 (0.18)	77 (13.70)		268 (47.69)	562
1910			7 (1.24)	0 (0.00)	164 (28.98)		342 (60.42)	566
1911			0 (0.00)	0 (0.00)	203 (35.37)		348 (60.63)	574
1912			4 (0.69)	0 (0.00)	215 (36.94)		375 (64.43)	582
1913			1 (0.17)	1 (0.17)	161 (27.29)		370 (62.71)	590
1914							359 (60.03)	598
1915							370 (61.06)	606
1916							491 (79.97)	614
1917							603 (96.95)	622
1918			1 (0.16)	0 (0.00)	74 (11.75)		886 (140.63)	630
1919			4 (0.63)	0 (0.00)	53 (8.31)		1165 (182.60)	638
1920			6 (0.93)	0 (0.00)	108 (16.69)		1249 (193.04)	647
1921								
GAP								
1926			1 (0.14)	0 (0.00)	162 (22.34)		403 (55.59)	725
1927			4 (0.55)	0 (0.00)	194 (26.50)		365 (49.86)	732
1928			6 (0.81)	0 (0.00)	206 (27.88)		365 (49.39)	739
1929			6 (0.80)	0 (0.00)	250 (33.51)		348 (46.65)	746
1930			2 (0.27)	0 (0.00)	235 (31.25)		366 (48.67)	752
1931								
GAP								
1935			2 (0.26)	0 (0.00)	284 (36.79)		705 (91.32)	772
1936								
GAP								
1940			6 (0.75)	3 (0.38)	188 (23.62)		711 (89.32)	796
1941								
GAP								
1950			3 (0.36)	4 (0.48)	360 (43.27)		1460 (175.48)	832
1951								
1952								
1953			6 (0.73)	0 (0.00)	358 (43.29)		1591 (192.38)	827
1954			6 (0.72)	1 (0.12)	324 (38.62)		1205 (143.62)	839
1955			0 (0.00)	0 (0.00)	303 (35.48)		984 (115.22)	854
1956			0 (0.12)	0 (0.00)	358 (41.68)		1231 (143.31)	859
1957			1 (0.12)	1 (0.12)	300 (34.76)		1216 (140.90)	863

AMSTERDAM, NETHERLANDS   NUMBER OF CONVICTIONS -- (RATE PER 100,000)   CONTINUED

YEAR	MURDER ( )	MANSLTR ( )	HOMICIDE (1)	RAPE ( )	ASSAULT ( )	ROBBERY ( )	THEFT (2)	POP
1958			3 (0.35)	1 (0.12)	271 (31.26)		1353 (156.06)	867
1959			6 (0.69)	0 (0.00)	291 (33.45)		1196 (137.47)	870
1960			3 (0.34)	3 (0.34)	338 (38.76)		1203 (137.96)	872
1961			5 (0.57)	0 (0.00)	277 (31.80)		1295 (148.68)	871
1962			5 (0.57)	6 (0.69)	290 (33.33)		1326 (152.41)	870
1963			4 (0.46)	4 (0.46)	304 (34.98)		1533 (176.41)	869
1964			3 (0.35)	6 (0.69)	341 (39.29)		1750 (201.61)	868
1965			1 (0.12)	3 (0.35)	376 (43.37)		1616 (186.39)	867
1966			9 (1.04)	3 (0.35)	303 (35.15)		1501 (174.13)	862
1967			6 (0.70)	6 (0.70)	334 (39.16)		1701 (199.41)	853
1968			11 (1.30)	4 (0.47)	336 (39.62)		1678 (197.88)	848
1969			12 (1.43)	6 (0.72)	348 (41.48)		1742 (207.63)	839
1970			14 (1.69)	9 (1.09)	308 (37.24)		1782 (215.48)	827

FOOTNOTES:
1. MURDER AND MANSLAUGHTER
2. THEFT, ROBBERY AND HOUSEBREAKING

ATHENS, GREECE *

CRIME STATISTICS -- (RATE PER 100,000)

YEAR	MURDER (1)		MANSLTR ( )		HOMICIDE ( )	RAPE ( )		ASSAULT ( )		ROBBERY ( )		THEFT ( )		POP
1969	15 (	0.59)	141 (	5.56)		15 (	0.59)	2029 (	80.04)	9 (	0.36)	4125 (	162.72)	2535
1970	12 (	0.46)	167 (	6.41)		21 (	0.81)	1995 (	76.58)	11 (	0.42)	3666 (	140.73)	2605
1971	19 (	0.71)	164 (	6.12)		20 (	0.75)	2477 (	92.43)	16 (	0.60)	4091 (	152.65)	2680
1972	18 (	0.64)	193 (	6.89)		21 (	0.75)	1813 (	64.75)	19 (	0.68)	3880 (	138.57)	2800

FOOTNOTES:
* INCLUDES PIRAEUS, PATRAS, AND KERKYRA;
* COMPUTED RATES BASED ON VERY QUESTIONABLE
  POPULATION ESTIMATES
  1. HOMICIDE OR MURDER

BEIRUT, LEBANON *

NUMBER OF OFFENSES REPORTED -- (RATE PER 100,000)

YEAR	MURDER ( )		MANSLTR ( )	HOMICIDE ( )	RAPE ( )		ASSAULT ( )		ROBBERY ( )		THEFT ( )		POP
1967	8 (	1.56)					244 (	47.66)	28 (	5.47)	2166 (	423.05)	512
1968	18 (	3.11)					160 (	27.63)	29 (	5.01)	2018 (	348.53)	579
1969	3 (	0.46)					59 (	9.09)	5 (	0.77)	2008 (	309.40)	649
1970	50 (	7.55)			29 (	4.38)	188 (	28.40)	36 (	5.44)	3046 (	460.12)	662
1971	23 (	3.41)			23 (	3.41)	232 (	34.42)	34 (	5.04)	3193 (	473.74)	674
1972	19 (	2.77)			23 (	3.35)	265 (	38.57)	30 (	4.37)	3082 (	448.62)	687
1973	31 (	4.43)			15 (	2.14)	303 (	43.29)	43 (	6.14)	2738 (	391.14)	700

FOOTNOTES:
* COMPUTED RATES BASED ON VERY QUESTIONABLE
  POPULATION ESTIMATES

BELFAST, NORTHERN IRELAND *   CRIME STATISTICS -- (RATE PER 100,000)

YEAR	MURDER ( )	MANSLTR ( )	HOMICIDE ( )	RAPE ( )	ASSAULT ( )	ROBBERY ( )	THEFT ( )	POP
1922	231 (56.07)	2 (0.49)		0 (0.00)	185 (44.90)	315 (76.46)		412
1923	1 (0.24)	6 (1.45)		0 (0.00)	16 (3.86)	38 (9.16)		415
1924	1 (0.24)	0 (0.00)		0 (0.00)	12 (2.87)	22 (5.26)		418
1925	1 (0.24)	2 (0.48)		1 (0.24)	11 (2.61)	31 (7.36)		421
1926	2 (0.47)	0 (0.00)		0 (0.00)	8 (1.88)	12 (2.82)		425
1927	0 (0.00)	0 (0.00)		1 (0.23)	9 (2.11)	5 (1.17)		426
1928	1 (0.23)	2 (0.47)		1 (0.23)	11 (2.58)	5 (1.17)		427
1929	0 (0.00)	5 (1.17)		0 (0.00)	14 (3.26)	4 (0.93)		429
1930	0 (0.00)	1 (0.23)		1 (0.23)	15 (3.49)	5 (1.16)		430
1931	0 (0.00)	0 (0.00)		1 (0.23)	14 (3.25)	5 (1.16)		431
1932	0 (0.00)	1 (0.23)		0 (0.00)	15 (3.47)	10 (2.31)		432
1933	3 (0.69)	0 (0.00)		0 (0.00)	15 (3.46)	5 (1.15)		433
1934	1 (0.23)	1 (0.23)		0 (0.00)	25 (5.76)	9 (2.07)		434
1935	11 (2.52)	1 (0.23)		0 (0.00)	25 (5.73)	14 (3.21)		436
1936	1 (0.23)	2 (0.46)		2 (0.46)	19 (4.35)	3 (0.69)		437
1937	1 (0.23)	1 (0.23)		0 (0.00)	18 (4.11)	5 (1.14)		438
1938	0 (0.00)	0 (0.00)		2 (0.46)	10 (2.28)	5 (1.14)		439
1939	0 (0.00)	0 (0.00)		0 (0.00)	7 (1.59)	6 (1.37)		439
1940	0 (0.00)	2 (0.45)		0 (0.00)	10 (2.27)	21 (4.77)		440
1941	3 (0.68)	3 (0.68)		1 (0.23)	6 (1.36)	20 (4.54)		441
1942	3 (0.68)	1 (0.23)		1 (0.23)	5 (1.13)	11 (2.49)		441
1943	2 (0.45)	1 (0.23)		0 (0.00)	7 (1.58)	6 (1.36)		442
1944	1 (0.23)	0 (0.00)		1 (0.23)	11 (2.48)	12 (2.71)		443
1945	0 (0.00)	0 (0.00)		1 (0.23)	4 (0.90)	15 (3.39)		443
1946	0 (0.00)	2 (0.45)		0 (0.00)	11 (2.48)	18 (4.05)		444
1947	0 (0.00)	0 (0.00)		1 (0.23)	37 (8.31)	8 (1.80)		445
1948	0 (0.00)	1 (0.22)		0 (0.00)	30 (6.73)	18 (4.04)		446
1949	1 (0.22)	1 (0.22)		1 (0.22)	40 (8.97)	9 (2.02)		446
1950	0 (0.00)	0 (0.00)		6 (1.34)	54 (12.08)	14 (3.13)		447
1951	0 (0.00)	0 (0.00)		0 (0.00)	45 (10.04)	14 (3.13)		448
1952	1 (0.22)	2 (0.45)		0 (0.00)	53 (11.83)	15 (3.35)		448
1953	0 (0.00)	1 (0.22)		0 (0.00)	47 (10.44)	14 (3.11)		450
1954	0 (0.00)	2 (0.44)		1 (0.22)	61 (13.50)	11 (2.43)		452
1955	1 (0.22)	0 (0.00)		0 (0.00)	68 (14.98)	4 (0.88)		454
1956	0 (0.00)	0 (0.00)		0 (0.00)	71 (15.99)	4 (0.90)		444
1957	0 (0.00)	0 (0.00)		0 (0.00)	52 (11.82)	8 (1.82)		440
1958	1 (0.23)	1 (0.23)		0 (0.00)	71 (16.28)	13 (2.98)		436
1959	0 (0.00)	0 (0.00)		1 (0.23)	64 (14.88)	20 (4.65)		430
1960	0 (0.00)	3 (0.71)		1 (0.24)	74 (17.49)	24 (5.67)		423
1961	0 (0.00)	0 (0.00)		0 (0.00)	47 (11.30)	31 (7.45)		416
1962	1 (0.24)	0 (0.00)		1 (0.24)	86 (20.82)	27 (6.54)		413
1963	0 (0.00)	0 (0.00)		0 (0.00)	127 (31.05)	16 (3.91)		409
1964	1 (0.25)	0 (0.00)		0 (0.00)	143 (35.22)	11 (2.71)		406
1965	1 (0.25)	0 (0.00)		3 (0.75)	91 (22.64)	26 (6.47)		402
1966	2 (0.50)	0 (0.00)		5 (1.26)	94 (23.62)	21 (5.28)		398
1967	3 (0.76)	0 (0.00)		6 (1.52)	111 (28.17)	30 (7.61)		394

BELFAST, NORTHERN IRELAND *   CRIME STATISTICS -- (RATE PER 100,000)   CONTINUED

YEAR	MURDER ( )	MANSLTR ( )	HOMICIDE ( )	RAPE ( )	ASSAULT ( )	ROBBERY ( )	THEFT ( )	POP
1968	1 (0.26)	0 (0.00)		4 (1.03)	151 (38.72)	35 (8.97)		390
1969	3 (0.78)	1 (0.26)		3 (0.78)	224 (58.03)	44 (11.40)		386
1970	9 (2.42)	0 (0.00)		7 (1.88)	312 (83.87)	66 (17.74)		372
1971	88 (24.44)	10 (2.78)		6 (1.67)	596 (165.56)	419 (116.39)		360
1972	213 (58.84)	14 (3.87)		3 (0.83)	675 (186.46)	1440 (397.79)		362
1973	111 (30.66)	6 (1.66)		10 (2.76)	322 (88.95)	1213 (335.08)		362

FOOTNOTES:
 * YEARS OF POLITICAL TURMOIL: 1922, 1933-35,
   1941-42, 1956-61, AND 1969-73

BOMBAY, INDIA *   NUMBER OF OFFENSES REPORTED -- (RATE PER 100,000)

YEAR	MURDER ( )	MANSLTR ( )	HOMICIDE ( )	RAPE ( )	ASSAULT ( )	ROBBERY (1)	THEFT ( )	POP
1956	131 (3.47)					574 (15.19)	9117 (241.19)	3780
1957	125 (3.24)					182 (4.72)	9041 (234.22)	3860
1958	112 (2.84)					161 (4.09)	8851 (224.64)	3940
1959	130 (3.23)					140 (3.48)	9164 (227.96)	4020
1960	134 (3.27)					244 (5.95)	10424 (254.24)	4100
1961	125 (2.99)					258 (6.17)	11004 (263.25)	4180
1962	121 (2.83)					227 (5.32)	10724 (251.15)	4270
1963	125 (2.86)					174 (3.99)	9681 (221.84)	4364
1964	152 (3.35)					296 (6.52)	11537 (254.23)	4538
1965	152 (3.22)					371 (7.86)	14477 (306.78)	4719
1966	133 (2.71)					320 (6.52)	16134 (328.80)	4907
1967	164 (3.21)					361 (7.07)	16620 (325.69)	5103
1968	148 (2.79)					315 (5.94)	15089 (284.32)	5307
1969	168 (3.04)					235 (4.26)	13587 (246.23)	5518
1970	146 (2.54)					255 (4.44)	13640 (237.67)	5739
1971	131 (2.20)					233 (3.90)	12758 (213.77)	5968

FOOTNOTES:
 * COMPUTED RATES BASED ON QUESTIONABLE POPULATION ESTIMATES
 1. INCLUDES "DACOITY" (ROBBERY COMMITTED BY GROUPS)

CRIME STATISTICS -- (RATE PER 100,000)

YEAR	MURDER ( )	MANSLTR ( )	HOMICIDE ( )	RAPE ( )	ASSAULT ( )	ROBBERY (1)	THEFT (2)	POP
1946	9 (0.95)			1 (0.11)		1171 (123.13)	2088 (219.56)	951
1947	2 (0.21)			3 (0.31)		1611 (168.51)	1525 (159.52)	956
1948	16 (1.66)					1086 (113.01)	1582 (164.62)	961
1949	9 (0.93)			3 (0.31)		846 (87.67)	1284 (133.06)	965
1950	6 (0.62)			9 (0.93)		1022 (105.36)	1094 (112.78)	970
1951	7 (0.72)			4 (0.41)		1248 (128.13)	1454 (149.28)	974
1952	2 (0.20)			9 (0.92)		837 (85.50)	1888 (192.85)	979
1953	6 (0.61)			2 (0.20)		953 (96.95)	1322 (134.49)	983
1954	1 (0.10)			3 (0.30)		998 (101.01)	1488 (150.61)	988
1955	3 (0.30)			7 (0.70)		858 (86.40)	1673 (168.48)	993
1956	1 (0.10)			8 (0.80)		750 (75.15)	1879 (188.28)	998
1957	4 (0.40)			8 (0.80)		866 (86.34)	1845 (183.95)	1003
1958	6 (0.60)			10 (0.99)		1133 (112.40)	3154 (312.90)	1008
1959	3 (0.30)			1 (0.10)		1115 (110.07)	1984 (195.85)	1013
1960	3 (0.29)			5 (0.49)		1283 (126.16)	2027 (199.31)	1017
1961	2 (0.20)			8 (0.78)		1834 (179.28)	2310 (225.81)	1023
1962								
1963	7 (0.67)			10 (0.96)		2014 (193.47)	1839 (176.66)	1041
1964	4 (0.38)			14 (1.32)		1936 (182.99)	2416 (228.36)	1058
1965	2 (0.19)			1 (0.09)		1757 (164.82)	2244 (210.51)	1066
1966	4 (0.37)					1791 (166.76)	2340 (217.88)	1074
1967	9 (0.83)			1 (0.09)		2537 (235.13)	2446 (226.69)	1079
1968	3 (0.28)			4 (0.37)	193 (17.99)	2599 (241.32)	2439 (226.46)	1077
1969	6 (0.56)			6 (0.56)		2401 (223.77)	2276 (212.12)	1073
1970	7 (0.65)			5 (0.47)	178 (16.56)	3201 (297.77)	2597 (241.58)	1075
1971	6 (0.56)			9 (0.84)	170 (15.81)	3273 (304.47)	2561 (238.23)	1075
1972	8 (0.75)			17 (1.59)	239 (22.36)	3506 (327.97)	2772 (259.31)	1069
1973	7 (0.66)			6 (0.56)	274 (25.78)	3297 (310.16)	3158 (297.08)	1063

FOOTNOTES:
* COMPUTED RATES BASED ON POPULATION ESTIMATES
  FOR "BRUSSELS AGGLOMERATION"
1. ROBBERY (VOLS QUALIFIES); INCLUDES ASSAULT, 1946-1968
2. THEFT (VOLS SIMPLES)

CALCUTTA, INDIA *

NUMBER OF OFFENSES REPORTED -- (RATE PER 100,000)

YEAR	MURDER ( )	MANSLTR ( )	HOMICIDE ( )	RAPE ( )	ASSAULT ( )	ROBBERY (1)	THEFT ( )	POP
1956	49 (1.79)					40 (1.47)	7004 (256.56)	2730
1957	49 (1.77)					36 (1.30)	6742 (243.57)	2768
1958	37 (1.32)					23 (0.82)	6714 (239.19)	2807
1959	34 (1.19)					32 (1.12)	7285 (255.97)	2846
1960	51 (1.77)					23 (0.80)	6879 (238.44)	2885
1961	39 (1.33)					18 (0.61)	5681 (193.96)	2929
1962	35 (1.19)					10 (0.34)	5676 (192.41)	2950
1963	31 (1.04)					7 (0.24)	4906 (165.13)	2971
1964	68 (2.27)					28 (0.94)	5000 (167.06)	2993
1965	26 (0.86)					14 (0.46)	4828 (160.19)	3014
1966	41 (1.35)					20 (0.66)	4853 (159.85)	3036
1967	57 (1.86)					38 (1.24)	5984 (195.63)	3058
1968	56 (1.82)					48 (1.56)	5818 (188.90)	3080
1969	68 (2.19)					66 (2.13)	5460 (176.02)	3102
1970	157 (5.03)					90 (2.88)	5169 (165.46)	3124
1971	285 (9.05)					152 (4.83)	4225 (134.17)	3149

FOOTNOTES:
* COMPUTED RATES BASED ON QUESTIONABLE POPULATION ESTIMATES
1. INCLUDES "DACOITY" (ROBBERY COMMITTED BY GROUPS)

CARACAS, VENEZUELA *   NUMBER OF OFFENSES REPORTED -- (RATE PER 100,000)

YEAR	MURDER (1)	MANSLTR ( )	HOMICIDE ( )	RAPE ( )	ASSAULT ( )	ROBBERY ( )	THEFT (2)	POP
1956	678 (63.60)						2012 (188.74)	1066
1957	777 (66.52)						1140 (97.60)	1168
1958	878 (56.03)						3108 (198.34)	1567
1959	890 (61.04)						2899 (198.83)	1458
1960	911 (67.18)						3008 (221.83)	1356
1961	939 (66.83)						3296 (234.59)	1405
1962	860 (59.11)						2002 (137.59)	1455
1963	561 (37.23)						1726 (114.53)	1507
1964	661 (41.62)						664 (41.81)	1588
1965	455 (27.18)						1121 (66.97)	1674
1966	429 (24.32)						1230 (69.73)	1764
1967	890 (47.88)						2922 (157.18)	1859
1968	1024 (52.30)						2033 (103.83)	1958
1969	1620 (78.49)						1235 (59.84)	2064
1970	1516 (69.70)						618 (28.41)	2175
1971	1349 (58.83)						558 (24.33)	2293
1972	815 (33.73)						356 (14.74)	2416
1973	669 (26.28)						420 (16.50)	2546

FOOTNOTES:
* DISTRITO FEDERAL; COMPUTED RATES BASED ON QUESTIONABLE
  POPULATION ESTIMATES
1. VIOLENT CRIMES
2. ROBBERY, STEALING

COLOMBO CITY, SRI LANKA (CEYLON)   NUMBER OF OFFENSES REPORTED -- (RATE PER 100,000)

YEAR	MURDER ( )	MANSLTR ( )	HOMICIDE (1)	RAPE ( )	ASSAULT (2)	ROBBERY ( )	THEFT (3)	POP
1900			7 (4.43)	3 (1.90)	95 (60.13)	18 (11.39)		158
1901			7 (4.32)	1 (0.62)	88 (54.32)	13 (8.02)		162
1902			7 (4.22)	0 (0.00)	83 (50.00)	9 (5.42)		166
1903			10 (5.88)	4 (2.35)	98 (57.65)	7 (4.12)		170
1904			4 (2.30)	2 (1.15)	89 (51.15)	3 (1.72)		174
1905			5 (2.81)	3 (1.69)	84 (47.19)	16 (8.99)		178
1906			8 (4.40)	4 (2.20)	98 (53.85)	13 (7.14)		182
1907			11 (5.91)	3 (1.61)	113 (60.75)	7 (3.76)		186
1908			5 (2.63)	0 (0.00)				190
1909			6 (3.09)	3 (1.55)	89 (45.88)	4 (2.06)		194
1910			13 (6.57)	2 (1.01)	166 (83.84)	4 (2.02)		198
1911			8 (3.96)	1 (0.50)	135 (66.83)	2 (0.99)		202
1912			9 (4.37)	2 (0.97)	127 (61.65)	3 (1.46)		206
1913			7 (3.33)	6 (2.86)	130 (61.90)	3 (1.43)		210
1914			8 (3.74)		159 (74.30)			214
1915			6 (2.75)		123 (56.42)			218
1916			6 (2.70)		148 (66.67)			222
1917			6 (2.65)		175 (77.43)			226
1918			7 (3.04)	3 (1.30)	212 (92.17)			230
1919			12 (5.11)	2 (0.85)	140 (59.57)			235
1920			11 (4.60)	1 (0.42)	162 (67.78)			239
1921			11 (4.51)		72 (29.51)			244
1922			9 (3.63)		132 (53.23)			248
1923			8 (3.17)		147 (58.33)			252
1924			16 (6.25)		177 (69.14)			256
1925			9 (3.46)		246 (94.62)			260
1926			15 (5.68)		225 (85.23)			264
1927			11 (4.10)		243 (90.67)			268
1928			9 (3.31)		238 (87.50)			272
1929			4 (1.45)		235 (85.14)			276
1930			26 (9.29)		239 (85.36)			280
1931			9 (3.17)		266 (93.66)			284
1932			17 (5.88)		297 (102.77)			289
1933			19 (6.44)		375 (127.12)			295
1934			12 (3.99)		275 (91.36)			301
1935			21 (6.89)		363 (119.02)			305
1936			11 (3.55)		387 (124.84)			310
1937			14 (4.44)		459 (145.71)			315
1938			14 (4.36)	1 (0.31)	546 (170.09)	120 (37.38)	795 (247.66)	321
1939			16 (4.91)		450 (138.04)	44 (13.50)	831 (254.91)	326
1940			23 (6.95)		535 (161.63)	62 (18.73)	902 (272.51)	331
1941			19 (5.65)		455 (135.42)	57 (16.96)	1045 (311.01)	336
1942			15 (4.40)		342 (100.29)	55 (16.13)	1410 (413.49)	341
1943			13 (3.76)		406 (117.34)	76 (21.97)	2277 (658.09)	346
1944			25 (7.10)		456 (129.55)	155 (44.03)	2849 (809.38)	352

COLOMBO CITY, SRI LANKA (CEYLON)   NUMBER OF OFFENSES REPORTED -- (RATE PER 100,000)   CONTINUED

YEAR	MURDER ( )	MANSLTR ( )	HOMICIDE (1)	RAPE ( )	ASSAULT (2)	ROBBERY ( )	THEFT (3)	POP
1945			31 (8.68)		401 (112.32)	190 (53.22)	2572 (720.45)	357
1946			24 (6.63)		446 (123.20)	288 (79.56)	2288 (632.04)	362
1947			24 (6.47)		461 (124.26)	330 (88.95)	2408 (649.06)	371
1948			8 (2.11)		409 (107.92)	213 (56.20)	1836 (484.43)	379
1949			10 (2.58)		434 (111.86)	145 (37.37)	1569 (404.38)	388
1950			10 (2.52)		363 (91.44)	126 (31.74)	1532 (385.89)	397
1951			17 (4.19)		446 (109.85)	88 (21.67)	1202 (296.06)	406
1952			12 (2.88)		453 (108.89)	66 (15.87)	1204 (289.42)	416
1953			8 (1.88)		513 (120.42)	113 (26.53)	1171 (274.88)	426
1954			18 (4.14)		490 (112.64)	134 (30.80)	1264 (290.57)	435
1955			21 (4.71)		525 (117.71)	113 (25.34)	1139 (255.38)	446
1956			20 (4.33)		586 (126.84)	132 (28.57)	1152 (249.35)	462
1957			16 (3.39)		615 (130.30)	107 (22.67)	1101 (233.26)	472
1958			14 (2.92)		564 (117.50)	173 (36.04)	961 (200.21)	480
1959			14 (2.88)		535 (110.08)	121 (24.90)	1020 (209.88)	486
1960			16 (3.25)		625 (127.03)	98 (19.92)	1019 (207.11)	492
1961			24 (4.82)		655 (131.53)	128 (25.70)	1035 (207.83)	498
1962			21 (4.17)		659 (130.75)	210 (41.67)	1270 (251.98)	504
1963			25 (4.89)		703 (137.57)	243 (47.55)	1547 (302.74)	511
1964			27 (5.22)		643 (124.37)	257 (49.71)	1492 (288.59)	517
1965			20 (3.82)		602 (115.11)	276 (52.77)	1720 (328.87)	523
1966			24 (4.54)	11 (2.08)	540 (102.08)	222 (41.97)	1894 (358.03)	529
1967			27 (5.04)	6 (1.12)		403 (75.19)	2468 (460.45)	536
1968			27 (4.98)	11 (2.03)	738 (136.16)	386 (71.22)	2067 (381.37)	542
1969			31 (5.65)	5 (0.91)	806 (146.81)	394 (71.77)	2091 (380.87)	549
1970			43 (7.75)	7 (1.26)	771 (138.92)	439 (79.10)	1989 (358.38)	555
1971			34 (6.05)	11 (1.96)	670 (119.22)	405 (72.06)	1862 (331.32)	562
1972			41 (7.22)	12 (2.11)	740 (130.28)	657 (115.67)	2990 (525.41)	568
1973			23 (4.00)	7 (1.22)	662 (115.13)	772 (134.26)	3652 (635.13)	575

FOOTNOTES:
1. HOMICIDE OR MURDER
2. INCLUDES ATTEMPTED MURDER FROM 1925
3. THEFT OF CATTLE AND PRAEDIAL PRODUCTS

DOHA CITY, QATAR *

NUMBER OF OFFENSES REPORTED -- (RATE PER 100,000)

YEAR	MURDER ( )	MANSLTR ( )	HOMICIDE ( )	RAPE ( )	ASSAULT ( )	ROBBERY ( )	THEFT ( )	POP
1956	0 (0.00)	0 (0.00)		4 (15.38)	21 (80.77)	0 (0.00)	52 (200.00)	26
1957	1 (3.85)	0 (0.00)		0 (0.00)	14 (53.85)	0 (0.00)	88 (338.46)	26
1958	1 (3.70)	2 (7.41)		8 (29.63)	38 (140.74)	2 (7.41)	84 (311.11)	27
1959	1 (3.57)	2 (7.14)		6 (21.43)	46 (164.29)	0 (0.00)	90 (321.43)	28
1960	0 (0.00)	2 (6.90)		8 (27.59)	43 (148.28)	0 (0.00)	83 (286.21)	29
1961	1 (3.33)	3 (10.00)		2 (6.67)	206 (686.67)	1 (3.33)	140 (466.67)	30
1962	1 (2.86)	2 (5.71)		1 (2.86)	104 (297.14)	0 (0.00)	146 (417.14)	35
1963	2 (4.44)	3 (6.67)		6 (13.33)	114 (253.33)	2 (4.44)	182 (404.44)	45
1964	0 (0.00)	2 (4.08)		6 (12.24)	140 (285.71)	4 (8.16)	130 (265.31)	49
1965	0 (0.00)	1 (1.85)		2 (3.70)	124 (229.63)	4 (7.41)	141 (261.11)	54
1966	1 (1.67)	2 (3.33)		6 (10.00)	94 (156.67)	2 (3.33)	142 (236.67)	60
1967	1 (1.54)	2 (3.08)		3 (4.62)	100 (153.85)	0 (0.00)	114 (175.38)	65
1968	0 (0.00)	5 (6.94)		1 (1.39)	20 (27.78)	0 (0.00)	45 (62.50)	72
1969	2 (2.53)	3 (3.80)		5 (6.33)	36 (45.57)	0 (0.00)	122 (154.43)	79
1970	0 (0.00)	3 (3.45)		1 (1.15)	48 (55.17)	1 (1.15)	152 (174.71)	87
1971	1 (1.05)	2 (2.11)		5 (5.26)	69 (72.63)	1 (1.05)	120 (126.32)	95
1972	2 (1.92)	2 (1.92)		4 (3.85)	102 (98.08)	0 (0.00)	432 (415.38)	104
1973	4 (3.48)	3 (2.61)		1 (0.87)	145 (126.09)	1 (0.87)	154 (133.91)	115
1974	1 (0.79)	2 (1.59)		2 (1.59)	54 (42.86)	0 (0.00)	25 (19.84)	126

FOOTNOTES:
* COMPUTED RATES BASED ON VERY QUESTIONABLE
  POPULATION ESTIMATES

NUMBER OF OFFENSES REPORTED -- (RATE PER 100,000)

DUBLIN, IRELAND *

YEAR	MURDER ( )	MANSLTR ( )	HOMICIDE ( )	RAPE ( )	ASSAULT ( )	ROBBERY ( )	THEFT (1)	POP
1927	8 (1.64)	27 (5.52)		4 (0.82)	694 (141.92)	10 (2.04)	1946 (397.95)	489
1928	1 (0.20)	3 (0.60)		1 (0.20)	778 (156.85)	17 (3.43)	1178 (237.50)	496
1929	3 (0.60)	6 (1.19)		2 (0.40)	791 (157.26)	9 (1.79)	1563 (310.74)	503
1930	0 (0.00)	10 (1.96)		1 (0.20)	700 (137.25)	4 (0.78)	1645 (322.55)	510
1931	3 (0.58)	10 (1.93)		1 (0.19)	555 (107.35)	5 (0.97)	1678 (324.56)	517
1932	0 (0.00)	7 (1.33)		0 (0.00)	554 (105.52)	13 (2.48)	1723 (328.19)	525
1933	5 (0.94)	6 (1.13)		2 (0.38)	598 (112.41)	8 (1.50)	1838 (345.49)	532
1934	1 (0.19)	9 (1.67)		1 (0.19)	656 (121.48)	4 (0.74)	1586 (293.70)	540
1935	3 (0.55)	0 (0.00)		3 (0.55)		6 (1.10)	1421 (259.78)	547
1936	4 (0.72)	0 (0.00)		1 (0.18)		8 (1.44)	1771 (319.10)	555
1937	5 (0.89)	1 (0.18)		6 (1.07)		12 (2.16)	1967 (349.38)	563
1938	7 (1.24)	0 (0.00)		3 (0.53)	480 (84.81)	13 (2.30)	2817 (497.70)	566
1939	2 (0.35)	2 (0.35)		0 (0.00)	471 (82.92)	14 (2.46)	3898 (686.27)	568
1940	5 (0.88)	1 (0.18)		0 (0.00)	291 (51.05)	14 (2.46)	4307 (755.61)	570
1941	1 (0.17)	6 (1.05)		1 (0.17)	266 (46.50)	34 (5.94)	6369 (1113.46)	572
1942	6 (1.05)	0 (0.00)		2 (0.35)	294 (51.22)	26 (4.53)	7742 (1348.78)	574
1943	1 (0.17)	2 (0.35)		2 (0.35)	260 (45.14)	49 (8.51)	7411 (1286.63)	576
1944	2 (0.35)	2 (0.35)		2 (0.35)	248 (42.83)	17 (2.94)	7079 (1222.63)	579
1945	4 (0.69)	3 (0.52)		0 (0.00)	382 (65.75)	21 (3.61)	7506 (1291.91)	581
1946	1 (0.17)	1 (0.17)		1 (0.17)	401 (68.78)	16 (2.74)	7219 (1238.25)	583
1947	0 (0.00)	1 (0.17)		2 (0.34)	293 (49.24)	12 (2.02)	7294 (1225.88)	595
1948	6 (0.99)	0 (0.00)		6 (0.99)		29 (4.78)	7105 (1170.51)	607
1949	1 (0.16)	2 (0.32)		4 (0.65)		14 (2.26)	5697 (920.36)	619
1950	1 (0.16)	2 (0.32)		4 (0.63)		22 (3.48)	5804 (918.35)	632
1951	0 (0.00)	1 (0.16)		0 (0.00)		16 (2.52)	6875 (1084.38)	634
1952	1 (0.16)	1 (0.16)		0 (0.00)		7 (1.10)	7589 (1191.37)	637
1953	2 (0.31)	2 (0.31)		2 (0.31)		19 (2.97)	8138 (1271.56)	640
1954	1 (0.16)	1 (0.16)		1 (0.16)		9 (1.40)	5638 (876.83)	643
1955	1 (0.15)	1 (0.15)		0 (0.00)		8 (1.24)	5407 (837.00)	646
1956	2 (0.31)	0 (0.00)		2 (0.31)		14 (2.16)	5880 (906.01)	649
1957	1 (0.15)	1 (0.15)		3 (0.46)	456 (69.62)	15 (2.30)	7122 (1092.33)	652
1958	1 (0.15)	0 (0.00)		1 (0.15)	454 (69.00)	30 (4.58)	9294 (1418.93)	655
1959	0 (0.00)	0 (0.00)		1 (0.15)		34 (5.17)	8446 (1283.59)	658
1960	1 (0.15)	0 (0.00)		1 (0.15)	487 (73.68)	33 (4.99)	7281 (1101.51)	661
1961	4 (0.60)	0 (0.00)		1 (0.15)	517 (76.93)	18 (2.68)	6198 (922.32)	672
1962	0 (0.00)	1 (0.15)		2 (0.29)	575 (84.31)	12 (1.76)	5931 (869.65)	682
1963	1 (0.14)	1 (0.14)		1 (0.14)	592 (85.43)	15 (2.16)	5954 (859.16)	693
1964	3 (0.43)	2 (0.28)		7 (0.99)	805 (114.35)	35 (4.97)	6331 (899.29)	704
1965	3 (0.42)	0 (0.00)		10 (1.40)	998 (139.39)	51 (7.12)	6160 (860.34)	716
1966	3 (0.41)	0 (0.00)		4 (0.55)	1136 (156.26)	47 (6.46)	7620 (1048.14)	727
1967	1 (0.14)	2 (0.27)		7 (0.95)	1107 (149.80)	58 (7.85)	8104 (1096.62)	739
1968	4 (0.53)	2 (0.27)		7 (0.93)	1117 (148.74)	69 (9.19)	9227 (1228.63)	751
1969	3 (0.39)	1 (0.13)		2 (0.26)	1191 (156.09)	85 (11.14)	9885 (1295.54)	763
1970	2 (0.26)	0 (0.00)		3 (0.39)	1316 (171.35)	138 (17.97)	12083 (1573.31)	768
1971	2 (0.26)	1 (0.13)		3 (0.39)	1576 (203.88)	207 (26.78)	15770 (2040.10)	773

DUBLIN, IRELAND * NUMBER OF OFFENSES REPORTED -- (RATE PER 100,000) CONTINUED

YEAR	MURDER ( )	MANSLTR ( )	HOMICIDE ( )	RAPE ( )	ASSAULT ( )	ROBBERY ( )	THEFT (1)	POP
1972	4 (0.51)	3 (0.39)		8 (1.03)	1785 (229.73)	401 (51.61)	15864 (2041.70)	777
1973	11 (1.41)	3 (0.38)		18 (2.31)	2553 (327.31)	423 (54.23)	13961 (1789.87)	780

FOOTNOTES:
* ALL FIGURES ARE FOR DUBLIN METROPOLITAN AREA
1. LARCENY

FREETOWN, SIERRA LEONE * NUMBER OF OFFENSES REPORTED -- (RATE PER 100,000)

YEAR	MURDER ( )	MANSLTR ( )	HOMICIDE ( )	RAPE ( )	ASSAULT ( )	ROBBERY ( )	THEFT ( )	POP
1962			6 (4.84)	44 (35.48)	586 (472.58)	51 (41.13)	2983 (2405.65)	124
1963			4 (3.13)	42 (32.81)	754 (589.06)	38 (29.69)	3772 (2946.88)	128
1964			2 (1.52)	60 (45.45)	559 (423.48)	41 (31.06)	4306 (3262.12)	132
1965			1 (0.73)	48 (35.04)	524 (382.48)	41 (29.93)	4257 (3107.30)	137
1966								
1967								
1968			3 (1.99)	23 (15.23)	192 (127.15)	48 (31.79)	2529 (1674.84)	151
1969			6 (3.85)	24 (15.38)	432 (276.92)	88 (56.41)	3414 (2188.46)	156
1970			20 (12.35)	46 (28.40)	491 (303.09)	93 (57.41)	3866 (2386.42)	162
1971			28 (16.77)	22 (13.17)	326 (195.21)	91 (54.49)	3879 (2322.76)	167
1972			67 (38.73)	30 (17.34)	450 (260.12)	81 (46.82)	4173 (2412.14)	173
1973			30 (16.76)	35 (19.55)	419 (234.08)	122 (68.16)	3926 (2193.30)	179
1974			37 (20.00)	53 (28.65)	363 (196.22)	70 (37.84)	4279 (2312.97)	185

FOOTNOTES:
* CITY OF FREETOWN AND ITS ENVIRONS; COMPUTED RATES BASED
ON VERY QUESTIONABLE POPULATION ESTIMATES

GEORGETOWN, GUYANA *

NUMBER OF OFFENSES REPORTED -- (RATE PER 100,000)

YEAR	MURDER ( )	MANSLTR ( )	HOMICIDE ( )	RAPE ( )	ASSAULT ( )	ROBBERY ( )	THEFT ( )	POP
1956	5 (4.17)			8 (6.67)	1023 (852.50)	10 (8.33)	3186 (2655.00)	120
1957	6 (4.72)			17 (13.39)	2012 (1584.25)	20 (15.75)	3202 (2521.26)	127
1958	5 (3.73)			14 (10.45)	1447 (1079.85)	27 (20.15)	2371 (1769.40)	134
1959	13 (9.22)			13 (9.22)	1374 (977.47)	32 (22.70)	2153 (1526.95)	141
1960	6 (4.05)			25 (16.89)	1184 (800.00)	35 (23.65)	3086 (2085.14)	148
1961	3 (1.99)			10 (6.62)	2013 (1333.11)	20 (13.25)	1210 (801.32)	151
1962	10 (6.54)			22 (14.38)	2586 (1690.20)	46 (30.07)	2596 (1696.73)	153
1963	3 (1.92)			47 (30.13)	2249 (1441.67)	96 (61.54)	2180 (1397.44)	156
1964	30 (18.87)			54 (33.96)	2877 (1809.43)	102 (64.15)	3010 (1893.08)	159
1965	12 (7.41)			52 (32.10)	4018 (2548.25)	109 (67.28)	3186 (1966.67)	162
1966	8 (4.79)			61 (36.53)	4163 (2492.82)	131 (78.44)	4110 (2461.08)	167
1967	6 (3.51)			55 (32.16)	3487 (2035.18)	88 (51.46)	3376 (1974.27)	171
1968	10 (5.71)			67 (38.29)	2186 (1249.14)	129 (73.71)	3214 (1836.57)	175
1969	9 (5.00)			52 (28.89)	3340 (1855.56)	146 (81.11)	3077 (1709.45)	180
1970	13 (7.03)			74 (40.00)	4010 (2167.57)	192 (103.78)	4347 (2349.73)	185
1971	16 (8.42)			84 (44.21)	4174 (2196.84)	207 (108.95)	4473 (2355.21)	190
1972	17 (8.72)			90 (46.15)	3678 (1886.15)	163 (83.59)	4510 (2312.82)	195
1973	18 (9.00)			77 (38.50)	3524 (1762.00)	159 (79.50)	4373 (2186.50)	200

FOOTNOTES:
  * COMPUTED RATES BASED ON QUESTIONABLE POPULATION
    ESTIMATES FOR GEORGETOWN METROPOLITAN AREA

GLASGOW, SCOTLAND

NUMBER OF OFFENSES REPORTED -- (RATE PER 100,000)

YEAR	MURDER (1)	MANSLTR ( )	HOMICIDE ( )	RAPE ( )	ASSAULT ( )	ROBBERY ( )	THEFT ( )	POP
1900			17 (2.19)	1 (0.13)	600 (77.32)	74 (9.54)	6267 (807.60)	776
1901	4 (0.49)		7 (0.88)	6 (0.75)	572 (71.86)	70 (8.79)	6768 (850.25)	796
1902	2 (0.24)		10 (1.23)	8 (0.98)	549 (67.28)	123 (15.07)	6811 (834.68)	816
1903	6 (0.70)		17 (2.03)	4 (0.48)	563 (67.26)	173 (20.67)	7153 (854.60)	837
1904	2 (0.23)		11 (1.28)	2 (0.23)	523 (60.88)	212 (24.68)	10061 (1171.25)	859
1905	2 (0.22)		10 (1.14)	3 (0.34)	551 (62.54)	230 (26.11)	10941 (1241.88)	881
1906	4 (0.43)		10 (1.11)	2 (0.22)	593 (65.67)	171 (18.94)	12023 (1331.45)	903
1907	1 (0.11)		12 (1.30)	2 (0.22)	629 (67.93)	143 (15.44)	12103 (1307.02)	926
1908	2 (0.21)		13 (1.37)	1 (0.11)	497 (52.32)	153 (16.11)	10954 (1153.05)	950
1909			6 (0.62)	0 (0.00)	326 (33.47)	112 (11.50)	10053 (1032.14)	974
1910	2 (0.20)		10 (1.00)	4 (0.40)	362 (36.20)	111 (11.10)	10328 (1032.80)	1000
1911	1 (0.10)		17 (1.69)	5 (0.50)	440 (43.78)	120 (11.94)	10255 (1020.40)	1005
1912	3 (0.30)		19 (1.88)	4 (0.40)	509 (50.40)	101 (10.00)	10219 (1011.78)	1010
1913	2 (0.20)		10 (0.99)	5 (0.49)	689 (67.88)	99 (9.75)	11660 (1148.77)	1015
1914	2 (0.20)		9 (0.88)	3 (0.29)	683 (66.96)	100 (9.80)	11595 (1136.76)	1020
1915	3 (0.29)		20 (1.95)	4 (0.39)	526 (51.32)		10355 (1010.24)	1025
1916	3 (0.29)		15 (1.46)	5 (0.49)	327 (31.75)	103 (10.00)	11366 (1103.50)	1030
1917	3 (0.29)		8 (0.77)	3 (0.29)	202 (19.50)	77 (7.43)	9860 (951.74)	1036
1918	1 (0.10)		8 (0.77)	3 (0.29)	167 (16.04)	40 (3.84)	9027 (867.15)	1041
1919	3 (0.29)		19 (1.82)	1 (0.10)	323 (30.88)	121 (11.57)	9503 (908.51)	1046
1920	7 (0.67)		17 (1.62)	8 (0.76)	609 (57.89)	141 (13.40)	12349 (1173.86)	1052
1921	7 (0.66)		15 (1.42)	3 (0.28)	446 (42.23)	99 (9.38)	11307 (1070.74)	1056
1922	4 (0.38)		14 (1.32)	5 (0.47)	329 (31.04)	62 (5.85)	11096 (1046.79)	1060
1923	3 (0.28)		10 (0.94)	6 (0.56)	362 (34.02)	32 (3.01)	11456 (1076.69)	1064
1924	5 (0.47)		7 (0.66)	4 (0.37)	361 (34.02)	27 (2.53)	8332 (780.15)	1068
1925	4 (0.37)		13 (1.21)	11 (1.03)	328 (30.60)	29 (2.71)	7776 (725.37)	1072
1926	2 (0.19)		9 (0.84)	5 (0.46)	284 (26.39)	61 (5.67)	6519 (605.85)	1076
1927	3 (0.28)		11 (1.02)	5 (0.46)	285 (26.39)	22 (2.04)	5022 (465.00)	1080
1928	8 (0.74)		14 (1.29)	4 (0.37)	321 (29.61)		5675 (523.52)	1084
1929	2 (0.18)		10 (0.92)	9 (0.83)	329 (30.21)		6813 (625.62)	1089
1930	1 (0.09)		13 (1.20)	6 (0.55)	367 (33.86)	13 (1.20)	6705 (618.54)	1084
1931	1 (0.09)		8 (0.74)	6 (0.55)	358 (32.90)	11 (1.01)	6751 (620.50)	1088
1932	2 (0.18)		8 (0.73)	8 (0.73)	326 (29.80)	92 (8.41)	12597 (1151.46)	1094
1933	5 (0.45)		3 (0.27)	5 (0.45)	331 (30.09)	130 (11.82)	12120 (1110.82)	1100
1934	5 (0.45)		7 (0.63)	2 (0.18)	365 (33.00)	90 (8.14)	12236 (1106.33)	1106
1935	8 (0.72)		8 (0.72)			85 (7.64)	14888 (1338.85)	1112
1936	5 (0.45)		7 (0.63)			129 (11.54)	12657 (1132.11)	1118
1937	6 (0.53)		2 (0.18)			93 (8.27)	12322 (1096.26)	1124
1938	7 (0.62)		6 (0.53)			79 (6.98)	12556 (1110.17)	1131
1939	1 (0.09)		4 (0.35)				12280 (1088.65)	1128
1940	2 (0.18)		6 (0.53)				13748 (1222.04)	1125
1941	1 (0.09)		5 (0.45)				15784 (1408.03)	1121
1942	5 (0.45)		6 (0.54)				15586 (1399.10)	1118
1943	1 (0.09)		6 (0.54)				15923 (1429.35)	1114
1944	4 (0.36)		3 (0.27)				14944 (1345.09)	1111

GLASGOW, SCOTLAND

NUMBER OF OFFENSES REPORTED -- (RATE PER 100,000)   CONTINUED

YEAR	MURDER (1)	MANSLTR ( )	HOMICIDE ( )	RAPE ( )	ASSAULT ( )	ROBBERY ( )	THEFT ( )	POP
1945	11 (0.99)		6 (0.54)				15949 (1439.44)	1108
1946	5 (0.45)		4 (0.36)				14019 (1268.69)	1105
1947	2 (0.18)		4 (0.36)			313 (28.40)	13115 (1190.11)	1102
1948	2 (0.18)		4 (0.36)			253 (22.98)	13490 (1225.25)	1101
1949	6 (0.55)		2 (0.18)			241 (21.97)	11608 (1058.16)	1097
1950	5 (0.46)		2 (0.18)	5 (0.46)		268 (24.50)	12179 (1113.25)	1094
1951	1 (0.09)		5 (0.46)	12 (1.10)	412 (37.83)	199 (18.27)	12994 (1193.20)	1089
1952	4 (0.37)		5 (0.46)	8 (0.74)	333 (30.61)	203 (18.66)	12593 (1157.44)	1088
1953	8 (0.74)		5 (0.46)	8 (0.74)	287 (26.40)	206 (18.95)	10817 (995.12)	1087
1954	6 (0.55)		5 (0.46)	7 (0.65)	297 (27.35)	177 (16.30)	9825 (904.70)	1086
1955	6 (0.55)		6 (0.55)	9 (0.83)	254 (23.41)	202 (18.62)	11040 (1017.51)	1085
1956	3 (0.28)		5 (0.46)	16 (1.48)	252 (23.25)	233 (21.49)	11197 (1032.93)	1084
1957	4 (0.37)		6 (0.55)	12 (1.11)	310 (28.62)	334 (30.84)	11509 (1062.70)	1083
1958	7 (0.65)		6 (0.55)		322 (29.76)	450 (41.59)	12891 (1191.40)	1082
1959	7 (0.65)		6 (0.56)		357 (33.06)	416 (38.52)	13024 (1205.93)	1080
1960	4 (0.37)		10 (0.93)	14 (1.30)	418 (38.74)	373 (34.57)	14003 (1297.78)	1079
1961	7 (0.66)		8 (0.76)	14 (1.33)	451 (42.75)	393 (37.25)	13326 (1263.13)	1055
1962	10 (0.96)		8 (0.77)	8 (0.77)		525 (50.29)	13109 (1255.65)	1044
1963	5 (0.48)		11 (1.06)		541 (52.37)	504 (48.79)	14485 (1402.23)	1033
1964	12 (1.17)		6 (0.59)	11 (1.08)	600 (58.65)	653 (63.83)	14645 (1431.57)	1023
1965	18 (1.79)		9 (0.90)	19 (1.89)	767 (76.39)	803 (79.98)	16229 (1616.43)	1004
1966	10 (1.01)		10 (1.01)	11 (1.11)	933 (94.24)	817 (82.53)	16789 (1695.86)	990
1967	15 (1.54)		9 (0.92)	30 (3.08)	1081 (110.87)	1081 (110.87)	16390 (1681.03)	975
1968	13 (1.35)		9 (0.94)	33 (3.43)	1349 (140.37)	1218 (126.74)	16146 (1680.12)	961
1969	13 (1.37)		16 (1.69)	38 (4.01)	1164 (122.78)	1094 (115.40)	15777 (1664.24)	948
1970	12 (1.29)		26 (2.79)	24 (2.57)	1054 (112.97)	1356 (145.34)	17279 (1851.98)	933
1971	13 (1.41)		11 (1.20)	42 (4.57)	1210 (131.52)	1483 (161.20)	17102 (1858.91)	920
1972	24 (2.65)		8 (0.88)	23 (2.54)	1240 (136.71)	1425 (157.11)	17110 (1886.44)	907
1973	18 (2.01)		11 (1.23)	31 (3.47)	1073 (120.02)	1215 (135.91)	16730 (1871.36)	894

FOOTNOTES:
  1. MURDER AND MANSLAUGHTER

HELSINKI, FINLAND

NUMBER OF OFFENSES REPORTED -- (RATE PER 100,000)

YEAR	MURDER ( )	MANSLTR ( )	HOMICIDE ( )	RAPE ( )	ASSAULT (1)	ROBBERY ( )	THEFT (2)	POP
1927	5 (2.26)	17 (7.69)		4 (1.81)	145 (65.61)	152 (68.78)	1779 (804.98)	221
1928	6 (2.63)	25 (10.96)		10 (4.39)	147 (64.47)	121 (53.07)	1459 (639.91)	228
1929	4 (1.70)	33 (14.04)		4 (1.70)	161 (68.51)	97 (41.28)	1859 (791.06)	235
1930	10 (4.13)	21 (8.68)		15 (6.20)	156 (64.46)	102 (42.15)	1967 (812.81)	242
1931	1 (0.40)	28 (11.24)		5 (2.01)	290 (116.47)	117 (46.99)	1873 (752.21)	249
1932	6 (2.34)	27 (10.55)		2 (0.78)	225 (87.89)	103 (40.23)	1999 (780.86)	256
1933	1 (0.38)	9 (3.41)		9 (3.41)	335 (126.89)	98 (37.12)	1979 (749.62)	264
1934	4 (1.48)	10 (3.69)		13 (4.80)	459 (169.37)	92 (33.95)	1816 (670.11)	271
1935	5 (1.79)	11 (3.94)		8 (2.87)	414 (148.39)	85 (30.47)	1649 (591.04)	279
1936	2 (0.70)	9 (3.15)		13 (4.55)	450 (157.34)	81 (28.32)	1583 (553.50)	286
1937	5 (1.71)	13 (4.44)		13 (4.44)	514 (175.43)	78 (26.62)	1618 (552.22)	293
1938	4 (1.34)	9 (3.02)		10 (3.36)	448 (150.34)	68 (22.82)	1318 (442.28)	298
1939	7 (2.27)	18 (5.84)		14 (4.55)	409 (132.79)	62 (20.13)	1413 (458.77)	308
1940	4 (1.26)	19 (5.99)		12 (3.79)	294 (92.74)	152 (47.95)	2283 (720.19)	317
1941	7 (2.18)	14 (4.36)		9 (2.80)	296 (92.21)	191 (59.50)	2463 (767.29)	321
1942	4 (1.23)	20 (6.13)		10 (3.07)	405 (124.23)	271 (83.13)	3751 (1150.61)	326
1943	9 (2.72)	24 (7.25)		11 (3.32)	325 (98.19)	332 (100.30)	3133 (946.53)	331
1944	7 (2.08)	20 (5.95)		18 (5.36)	230 (68.45)	434 (129.17)	4055 (1206.85)	336
1945	9 (2.63)	16 (4.68)		19 (5.56)	457 (133.63)	772 (225.73)	5867 (1715.50)	342
1946	4 (1.15)	16 (4.61)		25 (7.20)	620 (178.67)	520 (149.86)	4977 (1434.29)	347
1947	11 (3.11)	15 (4.24)		27 (7.63)	342 (96.61)	294 (83.05)	3504 (989.83)	354
1948	7 (1.96)	18 (5.03)		28 (7.82)	175 (48.88)	157 (43.85)	2220 (620.11)	358
1949	2 (0.55)	12 (3.31)		29 (7.99)	185 (50.96)	108 (29.75)	1736 (478.24)	363
1950	7 (1.90)	12 (3.25)		29 (7.86)	185 (50.14)	77 (20.87)	1335 (361.79)	369
1951	2 (0.53)	9 (2.39)		43 (11.41)	264 (70.03)	53 (14.06)	1267 (336.07)	377
1952	10 (2.60)	11 (2.86)		36 (9.38)	217 (56.51)	84 (21.88)	1386 (360.94)	384
1953	5 (1.28)	13 (3.32)		28 (7.14)	230 (58.67)	56 (14.29)	1414 (360.71)	392
1954	7 (1.75)	10 (2.50)		22 (5.50)	197 (49.25)	67 (16.75)	1242 (310.50)	400
1955	3 (0.73)	10 (2.44)		31 (7.58)	214 (52.32)	54 (13.20)	1174 (287.04)	409
1956	2 (0.48)	13 (3.10)		9 (2.14)	145 (34.52)	59 (14.05)	2013 (479.29)	420
1957	2 (0.46)	11 (2.52)		17 (3.89)	134 (30.66)	82 (18.76)	2246 (513.96)	437
1958	0 (0.00)	16 (3.60)		17 (3.82)	127 (28.54)	87 (19.55)	2327 (522.92)	445
1959	0 (0.00)	11 (2.45)		13 (2.90)	147 (32.74)	85 (18.93)	2061 (459.02)	449
1960	4 (0.88)	9 (1.99)		50 (11.04)	150 (33.11)	108 (23.84)	2092 (461.81)	453
1961	3 (0.65)	15 (3.25)		22 (4.77)	142 (30.80)	77 (16.70)	2086 (452.49)	461
1962	4 (0.85)	11 (2.34)		48 (10.21)	172 (36.60)	75 (15.96)	2343 (498.51)	470
1963	1 (0.21)	26 (5.47)		29 (6.11)	196 (41.26)	118 (24.84)	2859 (601.89)	475
1964	2 (0.42)	18 (3.74)		41 (8.52)	201 (41.79)	90 (18.71)	3297 (685.45)	481
1965	5 (1.03)	11 (2.26)		38 (7.82)	224 (46.09)	75 (15.43)	3543 (729.01)	486
1966	5 (1.02)	15 (3.05)		78 (15.85)	247 (50.20)	112 (22.76)	3618 (735.37)	492
1967	1 (0.20)	18 (3.62)		55 (11.07)	243 (48.89)	188 (37.83)	4430 (891.35)	497
1968								
1969	2 (0.40)	20 (4.00)		77 (15.40)	322 (64.40)	178 (35.60)	5479 (1095.80)	500
1970	3 (0.58)			40 (7.77)		252 (48.93)	5677 (1102.33)	515

FOOTNOTES:
1. FREQUENT MEASURE CHANGES, 1927-1946
2. FELONIOUS LARCENY

ISTANBUL, TURKEY

NUMBER OF OFFENSES REPORTED -- (RATE PER 100,000)

YEAR	MURDER ( )	MANSLTR ( )	HOMICIDE (1)	RAPE ( )	ASSAULT ( )	ROBBERY ( )	THEFT ( )	POP
1955			27 (2.25)	3 (0.25)		13 (1.09)		1198
1956			29 (2.33)	2 (0.16)		11 (0.88)		1246
1957			31 (2.39)	4 (0.31)		8 (0.62)		1296
1958			33 (2.45)	6 (0.45)		21 (1.56)		1348
1959			25 (1.78)	8 (0.57)		16 (1.14)		1402
1960			33 (2.26)	14 (0.96)		6 (0.41)		1460
1961			29 (1.92)	33 (2.18)		24 (1.59)		1513
1962			25 (1.60)			20 (1.28)		1567
1963			41 (2.53)			12 (0.74)		1623
1964			41 (2.44)			2 (0.12)		1682
1965			76 (4.36)			4 (0.23)		1743
1966			83 (4.53)	1 (0.05)		16 (0.87)		1834
1967			79 (4.09)	19 (0.98)		26 (1.35)		1930
1968			103 (5.07)	15 (0.74)		15 (0.74)		2030
1969			121 (5.66)	23 (1.08)		24 (1.12)		2136
1970			109 (4.85)	17 (0.76)		59 (2.62)		2248
1971			134 (5.73)	15 (0.64)		57 (2.44)		2340
1972			106 (4.36)	7 (0.29)		41 (1.69)		2430
1973			151 (5.97)			52 (2.06)		2530

FOOTNOTES:
1. MURDER AND MANSLAUGHTER

JERUSALEM, ISRAEL

CRIME STATISTICS -- (RATE PER 100,000)

YEAR	MURDER ( )	MANSLTR ( )	HOMICIDE (1)	RAPE ( )	ASSAULT ( )	ROBBERY ( )	THEFT ( )	POP
1968			7 (2.55)	10 (3.64)	50 (18.18)	14 (5.09)	2770 (1007.27)	275
1969			7 (2.47)	3 (1.06)	35 (12.37)	10 (3.53)	2670 (943.46)	283
1970			10 (3.44)	13 (4.47)	34 (11.68)	9 (3.09)	3256 (1118.90)	291
1971			6 (1.99)	16 (5.32)	58 (19.27)	14 (4.65)	3436 (1141.53)	301
1972			7 (2.23)	13 (4.24)	45 (14.33)	22 (7.01)	3765 (1199.04)	314
1973			5 (1.53)	10 (3.07)	54 (16.56)	13 (3.99)	3519 (1079.45)	326

FOOTNOTES:
1. HOMICIDE AND MURDER

JOHANNESBURG, SOUTH AFRICA *

CRIME STATISTICS -- (RATE PER 100,000)

YEAR	MURDER ( )	MANSLTR ( )	HOMICIDE ( )	RAPE ( )	ASSAULT ( )	ROBBERY (1)	THEFT ( )	POP
1963	953 (77.48)			813 (66.10)	8337 (677.80)	5007 (407.07)	27876 (2266.34)	1230
1964	1173 (93.32)			977 (77.72)	9636 (766.59)	5426 (431.66)	30661 (2439.22)	1257
1965	1305 (101.64)			989 (77.02)	7921 (616.90)	5763 (448.83)	30066 (2341.59)	1284
1966	1268 (96.57)			1092 (83.17)	7819 (595.51)	5743 (437.40)	31426 (2393.45)	1313
1967	1316 (98.06)			1051 (78.32)	7644 (569.60)	5502 (409.99)	34299 (2555.81)	1342
1968	1330 (97.01)			1152 (84.03)	8671 (632.46)	5302 (386.72)	34395 (2508.75)	1371
1969	1101 (78.59)			1129 (80.59)	8397 (599.36)	4919 (351.11)	34179 (2439.61)	1401
1970	1470 (102.65)			1101 (76.89)	10626 (742.04)	6374 (445.11)	39319 (2745.74)	1432
1971	1664 (115.74)			1638 (111.96)	11293 (771.91)	6643 (454.07)	41543 (2839.58)	1463
1972	1333 (89.16)			1804 (120.67)	10771 (720.47)	6619 (442.74)	42695 (2855.85)	1495

FOOTNOTES:
* ALL FIGURES FOR JOHANNESBURG URBAN COMPLEX; COMPUTED
  RATES BASED ON VERY QUESTIONABLE POPULATION ESTIMATES
1. ROBBERY AND AGGRAVATED ROBBERY

KHARTOUM, SUDAN *

NUMBER OF OFFENSES REPORTED -- (RATE PER 100,000)

YEAR	MURDER ( )	MANSLTR ( )	HOMICIDE ( )	RAPE ( )	ASSAULT ( )	ROBBERY ( )	THEFT ( )	POP
1960			30 (23.62)	32 (25.20)		27 (21.26)	2584 (2034.65)	127
1961			30 (21.90)	31 (22.63)		23 (16.79)	2583 (1885.40)	137
1962			36 (24.32)	25 (16.89)	221 (149.32)	45 (30.41)	3870 (2614.87)	148
1963			36 (22.50)	22 (13.75)	232 (145.00)	64 (40.00)	4308 (2692.50)	160
1964			78 (45.09)	41 (23.70)	202 (116.76)	84 (48.55)	6800 (3930.64)	173
1965			85 (46.20)	46 (25.00)	289 (157.07)	127 (69.02)	7944 (4317.39)	184
1966			60 (30.77)	54 (27.69)	367 (188.21)	167 (85.64)	7897 (4049.74)	195
1967			66 (31.88)	54 (26.09)	317 (153.14)	143 (69.08)	9644 (4658.94)	207
1968			82 (37.44)	52 (23.74)	308 (140.64)	175 (79.91)	10423 (4759.36)	219
1969			58 (24.89)	81 (34.76)	309 (132.62)	133 (57.08)	11247 (4827.04)	233
1970			57 (23.08)	71 (28.74)	335 (135.63)	79 (31.98)	11377 (4606.07)	247
1971			83 (31.68)	83 (31.68)	357 (136.26)	139 (53.05)	12462 (4756.49)	262
1972			81 (29.14)	91 (32.73)	443 (159.35)	183 (65.83)	15745 (5663.67)	278

FOOTNOTES:
* FIGURES ARE FOR FISCAL YEARS BEGINNING IN YEAR INDICATED;
  COMPUTED RATES BASED ON QUESTIONABLE POPULATION ESTIMATES

KUWAIT CITY, KUWAIT *

NUMBER OF OFFENSES REPORTED -- (RATE PER 100,000)

YEAR	MURDER ( )	MANSLTR ( )	HOMICIDE ( )	RAPE ( )	ASSAULT ( )	ROBBERY ( )	THEFT ( )	POP
1970	26 (32.50)			216 (270.00)	1034 (1292.50)	24 (30.00)	1010 (1262.50)	80
1971	28 (34.15)			208 (253.66)	1154 (1407.32)	29 (35.37)	1106 (1334.78)	82
1972	37 (44.05)			248 (295.24)	1121 (1333.52)	56 (66.67)	921 (1096.43)	84
1973	27 (31.40)			231 (268.60)	769 (894.19)	355 (412.79)	1028 (1195.35)	86
1974	54 (61.36)			228 (255.09)	958 (1088.64)	90 (102.27)	718 (815.91)	88

FOOTNOTES:
* COMPUTED RATES BASED ON VERY QUESTIONABLE
  POPULATION ESTIMATES

LAGOS CITY, NIGERIA * NUMBER OF OFFENSES REPORTED -- (RATE PER 100,000)

YEAR	MURDER ( )	MANSLTR ( )	HOMICIDE ( )	RAPE (1)	ASSAULT ( )	ROBBERY ( )	THEFT ( )	POP
1959	4 (1.02)	1 (0.25)		52 (13.20)	1204 (305.58)	55 (13.96)	5377 (1364.72)	394
1960	13 (3.10)	7 (1.67)		43 (10.24)	1323 (315.00)	89 (21.19)	6212 (1179.05)	420
1961	5 (1.12)	17 (3.79)		61 (13.62)	1006 (224.55)	104 (23.21)	7679 (1714.06)	448
1962	13 (2.72)	13 (2.72)		93 (19.46)	1303 (277.59)	150 (31.38)	7925 (1657.95)	478
1963	10 (1.96)	34 (6.68)		87 (17.09)	1440 (282.91)	234 (45.97)	7569 (1487.03)	509
1964	4 (0.74)	34 (6.26)		95 (17.50)	1733 (319.15)	217 (39.96)	7874 (1450.09)	543
1965	11 (1.90)	17 (2.93)		122 (21.03)	2001 (345.00)	323 (55.69)	10231 (1763.97)	580
1966	18 (2.91)			136 (22.01)	2027 (327.99)	379 (61.33)	9945 (1609.22)	618
1967	32 (2.19)	19 (1.30)		171 (11.71)	2679 (183.49)	311 (21.30)	8064 (552.33)	1460
1968	24 (1.64)	10 (0.68)		627 (42.83)	3244 (221.58)	74 (5.05)	7177 (490.23)	1464
1969	33 (2.25)	9 (0.61)		175 (11.92)	3691 (251.43)	25 (1.70)	8839 (602.11)	1468
1970	37 (2.51)	10 (0.68)		229 (15.55)	4588 (311.47)	81 (5.50)	11033 (749.02)	1473
1971	48 (3.25)	16 (1.08)		181 (12.25)	5949 (402.78)	107 (7.24)	12800 (866.62)	1477
1972	49 (3.31)	18 (1.22)		154 (10.40)	5722 (386.36)	48 (3.24)	11313 (763.88)	1481
1973	49 (3.30)	22 (1.48)		179 (12.05)	7222 (486.33)	43 (2.90)	14279 (961.55)	1485

FOOTNOTES:
 * COMPUTED RATES BASED ON VERY QUESTIONABLE POPULATION
   ESTIMATES; FROM 1967, ALL FIGURES ARE FOR "LAGOS STATE"
 1. RAPE AND INDECENT ASSAULT

MADRID, SPAIN CRIME STATISTICS -- (RATE PER 100,000)

YEAR	MURDER ( )	MANSLTR ( )	HOMICIDE ( )	RAPE ( )	ASSAULT ( )	ROBBERY ( )	THEFT ( )	POP
1953			22 (1.23)	6 (0.34)	137 (7.66)	464 (25.94)	705 (39.41)	1789
1954			12 (0.65)	3 (0.16)	141 (7.63)	574 (31.04)	832 (45.00)	1849
1955			16 (0.84)	2 (0.10)	156 (8.16)	469 (24.53)	631 (33.00)	1912
1956			18 (0.91)	0 (0.00)	137 (6.93)	386 (19.52)	610 (30.85)	1977
1957			25 (1.22)	1 (0.05)	150 (7.34)	360 (17.61)	618 (30.23)	2044
1958			24 (1.14)	1 (0.05)	151 (7.14)	360 (17.03)	738 (34.91)	2114
1959			6 (0.27)	2 (0.09)	136 (6.22)	240 (10.98)	643 (29.41)	2186
1960			22 (0.97)	0 (0.00)	127 (5.62)	428 (18.94)	945 (41.81)	2260
1961			17 (0.73)	2 (0.09)	119 (5.09)	528 (22.60)	1082 (46.32)	2336
1962			17 (0.70)	3 (0.12)	107 (4.43)	417 (17.27)	773 (32.01)	2415
1963			12 (0.48)	1 (0.04)	127 (5.09)	357 (14.30)	934 (37.42)	2496
1964			18 (0.70)	3 (0.12)	99 (3.84)	415 (16.09)	811 (31.43)	2580
1965			9 (0.34)	3 (0.11)	136 (5.10)	469 (17.59)	856 (32.11)	2666
1966			14 (0.51)	2 (0.07)	101 (3.66)	380 (13.79)	667 (24.20)	2756
1967			23 (0.81)	2 (0.07)	105 (3.69)	386 (13.55)	472 (16.57)	2849
1968			13 (0.44)	8 (0.27)	145 (4.92)		467 (15.86)	2945

MANILA, PHILIPPINES *   NUMBER OF OFFENSES REPORTED -- (RATE PER 100,000)

YEAR	MURDER ( )	MANSLTR ( )	HOMICIDE ( )	RAPE ( )	ASSAULT (1)	ROBBERY ( )	THEFT ( )	POP
1950	50 (4.96)		159 (15.77)	61 (6.05)	231 (22.92)	855 (84.82)	4807 (476.88)	1008
1951	43 (4.21)		185 (18.12)	66 (6.46)	310 (30.36)	922 (90.30)	3536 (346.33)	1021
1952	54 (5.23)		239 (23.14)	76 (7.36)	346 (33.49)	1472 (142.50)	6340 (613.75)	1033
1953	88 (8.41)		245 (23.42)	86 (8.22)	389 (37.19)	1349 (128.97)	6092 (582.41)	1046
1954	71 (6.70)		261 (24.65)	109 (10.29)	320 (30.22)	1305 (123.23)	6101 (576.11)	1059
1955	71 (6.62)		269 (25.09)	91 (8.49)	196 (18.28)	1294 (120.71)	6045 (563.90)	1072
1956	110 (10.14)		261 (24.06)	128 (11.80)	180 (16.59)	1314 (121.11)	6399 (589.77)	1085
1957	97 (8.83)		264 (24.04)	123 (11.20)	201 (18.31)	1441 (131.24)	6313 (574.95)	1098
1958	82 (7.37)		267 (24.01)	81 (7.28)	191 (17.18)	1300 (116.91)	6023 (541.64)	1112
1959	88 (7.82)		284 (25.24)	65 (5.78)	199 (17.69)	1467 (130.40)	5992 (532.62)	1125
1960	102 (8.96)		389 (34.15)	82 (7.20)	230 (20.19)	1745 (153.20)	5980 (525.02)	1139
1961	135 (11.67)		488 (42.18)	104 (8.99)	212 (18.32)	2240 (193.60)	6360 (549.70)	1157
1962	146 (12.43)		666 (56.68)	97 (8.26)	239 (20.34)	2684 (228.43)	6110 (520.00)	1175
1963	218 (18.27)		635 (53.23)	71 (5.95)	403 (33.78)	2303 (193.04)	4513 (378.29)	1193
1964	184 (15.18)		620 (51.16)	99 (8.17)	350 (28.88)	2325 (191.83)	4636 (382.51)	1212
1965	182 (14.78)		698 (56.70)	104 (8.45)	179 (14.54)	1625 (132.01)	4421 (359.14)	1231
1966	258 (20.64)		925 (74.00)	104 (8.32)	302 (24.16)	2402 (192.16)	4228 (338.24)	1250
1967	264 (20.80)		901 (71.00)	116 (9.14)	183 (14.42)	2833 (223.25)	4897 (385.89)	1269
1968	265 (20.56)		817 (63.38)	60 (4.65)	138 (10.71)	2569 (199.30)	3565 (276.57)	1289
1969	335 (25.59)		760 (58.06)	115 (8.79)	134 (10.24)	3160 (241.41)	3628 (277.16)	1309
1970	422 (31.73)		1000 (75.19)	112 (8.42)	115 (8.65)	3190 (239.85)	3555 (252.26)	1330
1971	644 (47.21)		920 (67.45)	102 (7.48)	137 (10.04)	4692 (343.99)	3836 (281.33)	1364
1972	333 (23.80)		437 (31.24)	105 (7.51)	177 (12.65)	4285 (306.29)	4377 (312.87)	1399

FOOTNOTES:
* DATA IN FISCAL YEARS BEGINNING IN YEAR INDICATED;
  COMPUTED RATES BASED ON QUESTIONABLE POPULATION ESTIMATES
1. PHYSICAL INJURY

MEXICO CITY, MEXICO *

NUMBER OF CONVICTIONS -- (RATE PER 100,000)

YEAR	MURDER ( )	MANSLTR ( )	HOMICIDE ( )	RAPE ( )	ASSAULT ( )	ROBBERY ( )	THEFT ( )	POP
1952	541 (22.29)			238 (9.81)	2909 (119.86)	3296 (135.81)		2427
1953	186 (7.52)			114 (4.61)	1327 (53.64)	1152 (46.56)		2474
1954								
1955	288 (11.20)			163 (6.34)	2325 (90.43)	1916 (74.52)		2571
1956	352 (13.42)			139 (5.30)	2461 (93.86)	1891 (72.12)		2622
1957								
1958	357 (13.10)			164 (6.02)	2269 (83.27)	1584 (58.13)		2725
1959	402 (14.47)			172 (6.19)	2485 (89.45)	1643 (59.14)		2778
1960	332 (11.72)			150 (5.30)	1953 (68.96)	1378 (48.66)		2832
1961	349 (12.24)			134 (4.70)	1916 (67.20)	1503 (52.72)		2851
1962	356 (12.40)			111 (3.87)	1939 (67.56)	1534 (53.45)		2870
1963								
1964								
1965								
1966	384 (13.03)			167 (5.77)	2410 (81.78)	1649 (55.96)		2947
1967	409 (13.79)			161 (5.43)	2314 (78.02)	1574 (53.07)		2966
1968								
GAP								
1972	433 (14.12)			215 (7.01)	2276 (74.23)	1890 (61.64)		3066

FOOTNOTES:
* COURT CASES

MONTEVIDEO, URUGUAY *

CRIME STATISTICS -- (RATE PER 100.000)

YEAR	MURDER ( )	MANSLTR ( )	HOMICIDE ( )	RAPE ( )	ASSAULT ( )	ROBBERY ( )	THEFT ( )	POP
1943	28 (6.35)			133 (30.16)		2895 (656.46)		441
1944	28 (6.06)			146 (31.60)		3043 (658.66)		462
1945	32 (6.61)			157 (32.44)		2733 (564.67)		484
1946	28 (5.52)			166 (32.74)		3410 (672.58)		507
1947	30 (5.66)			171 (32.26)		4752 (896.60)		530
1948	34 (6.13)			135 (24.32)		6554 (1180.90)		555
1949	35 (6.02)			145 (24.96)		5402 (929.78)		581
1950	41 (6.73)			104 (17.08)		7540 (1238.10)		609
1951	40 (6.28)			109 (17.11)		8103 (1272.06)		637
1952	40 (6.00)			108 (16.19)		8846 (1326.24)		667
1953	38 (5.44)			152 (21.78)		8935 (1280.09)		698
1954	31 (4.24)			95 (13.00)		7865 (1075.92)		731
1955	50 (6.54)			121 (15.82)		8327 (1088.50)		765
1956	54 (6.74)			138 (17.23)		8923 (1113.98)		801
1957	38 (4.53)			110 (13.11)		8752 (1043.15)		839
1958	56 (6.38)			122 (13.90)		10663 (1214.46)		878
1959	133 (14.47)			302 (32.86)		13196 (1435.91)		919
1960	141 (14.66)			306 (31.81)		12283 (1276.82)		962
1961	143 (13.95)			415 (40.49)		12856 (1254.24)		1025
1962	105 (9.62)			392 (35.90)		13626 (1247.80)		1092
1963	114 (9.80)			496 (42.65)		14153 (1216.94)		1163
1964	76 (6.29)			477 (39.45)		14141 (1169.64)		1209
1965	74 (5.88)			517 (41.10)		15453 (1228.38)		1258
1966	47 (3.59)			608 (46.48)		16180 (1237.00)		1308
1967	58 (4.26)			625 (45.96)		16231 (1193.46)		1360
1968	31 (2.19)			977 (69.05)		16949 (1197.81)		1415
1969	31 (2.11)			1491 (101.36)		14877 (1011.35)		1471
1970	31 (2.03)			2195 (143.46)		12719 (831.31)		1530
1971	18 (1.13)			2736 (171.97)		12646 (794.85)		1591
1972	22 (1.33)			3250 (196.37)		14543 (878.73)		1655
1973	50 (2.91)			2805 (162.99)		15702 (912.38)		1721

FOOTNOTES: * COMPUTED RATES BASED ON VERY QUESTIONABLE POPULATION ESTIMATES

MUNICH, GERMANY

NUMBER OF OFFENSES REPORTED -- (RATE PER 100,000)

YEAR	MURDER (1)	MANSLTR (2)	HOMICIDE ( )	RAPE ( )	ASSAULT ( )	ROBBERY ( )	THEFT (3)	POP
1946	144 (19.59)			115 (15.65)		1044 (142.04)	35172 (4785.30)	735
1947	71 (9.31)			144 (18.87)		711 (93.18)	37061 (4857.27)	763
1948	45 (5.70)			70 (8.87)		338 (42.84)	35028 (4439.54)	789
1949	28 (3.50)			87 (10.88)		416 (52.00)	26516 (3314.50)	800
1950	34 (4.10)			119 (14.35)		343 (41.38)	24782 (2989.38)	829
1951	45 (5.30)			175 (20.61)		257 (30.27)	26708 (3145.82)	849
1952	26 (3.00)			120 (13.84)		179 (20.65)	25588 (2720.65)	867
1953	32 (3.60)			178 (20.02)		152 (17.10)	20826 (2342.63)	889
1954	22 (2.40)			161 (17.56)		133 (14.50)	18358 (2001.96)	917
1955	38 (4.10)			177 (19.09)		138 (14.89)	20396 (2200.22)	927
1956	24 (2.50)			162 (16.88)		162 (16.88)	21513 (2240.94)	960
1957	25 (2.50)			142 (14.20)		167 (16.70)	24164 (2416.40)	1000
1958	32 (3.20)			173 (17.30)	744 (74.40)	149 (14.90)	25510 (2551.00)	1000
1959	21 (2.00)			186 (17.71)	758 (72.19)	227 (21.62)	25358 (2415.05)	1050
1960	20 (1.90)			170 (16.14)	716 (68.00)	228 (21.65)	26048 (2473.69)	1053
1961	25 (2.30)			242 (22.26)	682 (62.74)	267 (24.56)	27921 (2568.63)	1087
1962	32 (2.80)			179 (15.66)	605 (52.93)	149 (13.04)	27435 (2400.26)	1143
1963	38 (3.30)	10 (0.87)		227 (19.70)	710 (61.63)	304 (26.39)	31416 (2727.08)	1152
1964	36 (3.00)	9 (0.75)		161 (13.42)	696 (58.00)	265 (22.08)	32147 (2678.92)	1200
1965	52 (4.30)	11 (0.91)		114 (9.43)	743 (61.46)	263 (21.75)	34218 (2830.27)	1209
1966	71 (5.80)	20 (1.63)		148 (12.09)	874 (71.41)	396 (32.35)	35940 (2936.27)	1224
1967	60 (4.80)	11 (0.88)		134 (10.72)	799 (63.92)	385 (30.80)	42317 (3385.36)	1250
1968	56 (4.40)	10 (0.79)		169 (13.28)	885 (69.52)	507 (39.83)	46076 (3619.48)	1273
1969	44 (3.30)	17 (1.28)		166 (12.45)	974 (73.07)	493 (36.98)	47829 (3588.07)	1333
1970	67 (5.00)	23 (1.72)		167 (12.46)	1052 (78.51)	616 (45.97)	53215 (3971.27)	1340
1971	76 (5.70)	19 (1.43)		177 (13.28)	755 (56.64)	561 (42.09)	51956 (3897.67)	1333
1972	79 (5.90)	18 (1.34)		196 (14.64)	838 (62.58)	716 (53.47)	51931 (3878.34)	1339
1973	72 (5.40)	13 (0.98)		237 (17.78)	937 (70.29)	801 (60.09)	52971 (3973.82)	1333

FOOTNOTES:
1. MURDER AND SLAYING, INCLUDING ATTEMPTS
2. MANSLAUGHTER AND HOMICIDE
3. SERIOUS AND SIMPLE THEFT

NAIROBI CITY, KENYA *

NUMBER OF OFFENSES REPORTED -- (RATE PER 100,000)

YEAR	MURDER ( )	MANSLTR ( )	HOMICIDE ( )	RAPE ( )	ASSAULT ( )	ROBBERY ( )	THEFT ( )	POP
1953	202 (127.04)			9 (5.66)	185 (116.35)	1150 (723.27)	5967 (3752.83)	159
1954	139 (82.74)			19 (11.31)	179 (106.55)	614 (365.48)	4922 (2929.76)	168
1955	118 (66.29)			29 (16.29)	287 (161.24)	271 (152.25)	4186 (2351.69)	178
1956	11 (5.82)			17 (8.99)	228 (120.63)	268 (141.80)	6730 (3560.85)	189
1957	41 (20.50)			52 (26.00)	509 (254.50)	562 (281.00)	7852 (3926.00)	200
1958	15 (7.08)			14 (6.60)	231 (108.96)	557 (262.74)	5370 (2533.02)	212
1959	14 (6.22)			10 (4.44)	291 (129.33)	447 (198.67)	5982 (2658.67)	225
1960	23 (9.66)			25 (10.50)	455 (191.18)	820 (344.54)	7925 (3329.83)	238
1961	14 (5.56)			7 (2.78)	462 (183.33)	949 (376.59)	8306 (3296.03)	252
1962	15 (5.62)			5 (1.87)	602 (225.47)	1061 (397.38)	8910 (3337.08)	267
1963	18 (6.36)			4 (1.41)	583 (206.01)	882 (311.66)	9788 (3458.66)	283
1964	19 (6.31)			11 (3.65)	633 (210.30)	1003 (333.22)	11019 (3660.80)	301
1965	11 (3.45)			21 (6.58)	695 (217.87)	936 (293.42)	7985 (2503.14)	319
1966	18 (5.31)			41 (12.09)	799 (235.69)	1039 (306.49)	7567 (2232.15)	339
1967	17 (4.72)			32 (8.89)	782 (217.22)	1029 (285.83)	7486 (2079.44)	360
1968	25 (6.54)			20 (5.24)	966 (252.88)	1122 (293.72)	7282 (1906.28)	382
1969	22 (5.42)			28 (6.90)	940 (231.53)	704 (173.40)	6289 (1549.01)	406
1970	25 (5.80)			30 (6.96)	881 (204.41)	1177 (273.09)	6742 (1564.27)	431
1971	40 (8.75)			35 (7.66)	955 (208.97)	1736 (379.87)	9026 (1975.05)	457
1972	60 (12.37)			40 (8.25)	1151 (237.32)	2016 (415.67)	11323 (2334.64)	485
1973	52 (10.10)			43 (8.35)	738 (143.30)	1495 (290.29)	10361 (2011.84)	515

FOOTNOTES:
* COMPUTED RATES BASED ON VERY QUESTIONABLE
* POPULATION ESTIMATES

NEW YORK CITY, USA *

NUMBER OF OFFENSES REPORTED -- (RATE PER 100,000)

YEAR	MURDER (1)	MANSLTR ( )	HOMICIDE ( )	RAPE (2)	ASSAULT ( )	ROBBERY ( )	THEFT ( )	POP
1954	387 (4.94)			1148 (14.65)	9519 (121.49)	46670 (595.66)	47291 (603.59)	7835
1955	306 (3.91)			1165 (14.90)	8679 (110.98)	38746 (495.47)	38396 (491.00)	7820
1956	315 (4.04)			1267 (16.23)	9517 (121.92)	38768 (496.64)	35476 (454.47)	7806
1957	314 (4.03)			1170 (15.01)	10467 (134.28)	38946 (499.63)	34837 (446.91)	7795
1958	354 (4.54)			1115 (14.31)	10636 (136.52)	44231 (567.72)	33806 (433.91)	7791
1959	390 (5.01)			1247 (16.01)	11168 (143.42)	48821 (626.96)	32949 (423.13)	7787
1960	390 (5.01)			841 (10.81)	11021 (141.62)	53586 (688.59)	35236 (452.79)	7782
1961	483 (6.20)			788 (10.11)	11976 (153.68)	53896 (691.59)	37712 (483.92)	7793
1962	508 (6.51)			882 (11.30)	12418 (159.12)	58408 (748.44)	40568 (519.84)	7804
1963	549 (7.02)			823 (10.53)	13025 (166.67)	67525 (864.04)	41911 (536.29)	7815
1964	637 (8.14)			1054 (13.47)	14831 (189.51)	77029 (984.27)	44792 (572.35)	7826
1965	634 (8.09)			1154 (14.72)	16325 (208.28)	84206 (1074.33)	50106 (639.27)	7838
1966	653 (8.32)			1761 (22.44)	23204 (295.67)	140974 (1796.30)	149765 (1908.32)	7848
1967	746 (9.49)			1905 (24.24)	24827 (315.91)	171658 (2184.22)	119783 (1524.15)	7859
1968	986 (12.53)			1840 (23.38)	18061 (229.49)	196487 (2496.66)	173559 (2205.32)	7870
1969	1043 (13.23)			2120 (26.90)	17552 (222.71)	207877 (2637.70)	171393 (2174.76)	7881
1970	1118 (14.16)			2141 (27.12)	18410 (233.19)	236701 (2998.11)	181694 (2301.38)	7895
1971	1466 (18.54)			2415 (30.55)	20460 (258.79)	254098 (3213.99)	181331 (2293.59)	7906
1972	1691 (21.36)			3271 (41.32)	23357 (295.02)	198862 (2511.84)	148046 (1869.98)	7917
1973	1680 (21.19)			3735 (47.11)	24469 (308.60)	196610 (2475.63)	149311 (1883.10)	7929

FOOTNOTES:
* UNSPECIFIED MEASURE CHANGE FROM 1966
1. MURDER, NON NEGLIGENT MANSLAUGHTER
2. FORCIBLE RAPE FROM 1960

OSLO, NORWAY *

CRIME STATISTICS -- (RATE PER 100,000)

YEAR	MURDER ( )	MANSLTR ( )	HOMICIDE ( )	RAPE ( )	ASSAULT ( )	ROBBERY ( )	THEFT (1)	POP
1923	1 (0.39)	2 (0.78)		3 (1.16)	143 (55.43)		1335 (517.44)	258
1924	1 (0.39)	1 (0.39)		2 (0.78)	80 (31.13)		1382 (537.74)	257
1925	0 (0.00)	2 (0.78)		0 (0.00)	85 (33.20)		1262 (492.97)	256
1926	1 (0.40)	1 (0.40)		2 (0.79)	49 (19.37)		1283 (507.11)	253
1927								
1928								
1929								
1930	0 (0.00)	1 (0.39)		2 (0.78)	59 (23.14)		1207 (473.33)	255
1931	2 (0.77)	2 (0.77)		0 (0.00)	59 (22.78)		1116 (430.89)	259
1932	3 (1.15)	1 (0.38)		0 (0.00)	56 (21.37)		969 (369.85)	262
1933	0 (0.00)	0 (0.00)		1 (0.38)	55 (20.75)		1136 (428.68)	265
1934	1 (0.37)	0 (0.00)		0 (0.00)	82 (30.71)		1178 (441.20)	267
1935								
1936								
1937								
1938								
1939								
1940	1 (0.37)	1 (0.37)		0 (0.00)	52 (19.33)		1408 (523.42)	269
1941	2 (0.73)	1 (0.36)		1 (0.36)	65 (23.64)		1408 (512.00)	275
1942	0 (0.00)	3 (1.05)		2 (0.70)	63 (22.03)		1470 (513.99)	286
1943	2 (0.61)	0 (0.00)		1 (0.30)	111 (33.74)		1475 (448.33)	329
1944	0 (0.00)	0 (0.00)		1 (0.26)	103 (27.25)		1157 (306.08)	378
1945								
1946								
1947								
1948								
1949								
1950	2 (0.46)	1 (0.23)		1 (0.23)	43 (9.91)		559 (128.80)	434
1951	2 (0.46)	0 (0.00)		5 (1.15)	35 (8.05)		675 (155.17)	435
1952	0 (0.00)	4 (0.92)		3 (0.69)	50 (11.44)		627 (143.48)	437
1953	1 (0.23)	1 (0.23)		1 (0.23)	63 (14.55)		623 (141.91)	439
1954	2 (0.45)	0 (0.00)		0 (0.00)	56 (12.70)		563 (127.66)	441
1955	2 (0.44)	4 (0.89)		1 (0.22)	57 (12.67)		666 (148.00)	450
1956							730 (161.86)	451
1957							671 (145.55)	461
1958							751 (159.45)	471
1959								
1960							883 (185.50)	476
1961							1006 (211.34)	476
1962							1134 (237.74)	477
1963							1175 (246.33)	477
1964							1208 (254.32)	475
1965							1040 (215.77)	482
1966							1316 (272.46)	483
1967							1593 (329.13)	484
1968							1306 (269.28)	485

OSLO, NORWAY *

CRIME STATISTICS -- (RATE PER 100,000)   CONTINUED

YEAR	MURDER ( )	MANSLTR ( )	HOMICIDE ( )	RAPE ( )	ASSAULT ( )	ROBBERY ( )	THEFT (1)	POP
1969							1350 (277.78)	486
1970							1323 (271.66)	487
1971							1123 (230.12)	488

FOOTNOTES:
* PERSONS PROCEEDED AGAINST; TWO YEAR PERIODS 1923-50
1. THEFTS AND ROBBERY, 1923-1956

PANAMA CITY, PANAMA

CRIME STATISTICS -- (RATE PER 100,000)

YEAR	MURDER ( )	MANSLTR ( )	HOMICIDE ( )	RAPE ( )	ASSAULT ( )	ROBBERY ( )	THEFT ( )	POP
1963			20 (6.80)	18 (6.12)	16 (5.44)			294
1964			9 (2.99)	16 (5.32)	16 (5.32)			301
1965			17 (5.50)	33 (10.68)	20 (6.47)			309
1966			13 (4.11)	20 (6.33)	41 (12.97)			316
1967			5 (1.54)	15 (4.63)	58 (17.90)			324
1968			25 (7.53)	22 (6.63)	85 (25.60)			332
1969			21 (6.18)	32 (9.41)	117 (34.41)			340
1970			19 (5.44)	39 (11.17)	154 (44.13)			349
1971			27 (7.56)	31 (8.68)	101 (28.29)			357
1972			11 (3.01)	40 (10.93)	107 (29.23)			366
1973			49 (13.07)	60 (16.00)	133 (35.47)			375

PARIS, FRANCE *

CRIME STATISTICS -- (RATE PER 100,000)

YEAR	MURDER (1)	MANSLTR (2)	HOMICIDE ( )	RAPE (3)	ASSAULT ( )	ROBBERY ( )	THEFT ( )	POP
1931	72 (1.59)			5 (0.11)	6 (0.13)	57 (1.26)	2 (0.04)	4528
1932								
1933	54 (1.17)			4 (0.09)	9 (0.19)	58 (1.25)		4627
1934	51 (1.09)			4 (0.09)	27 (0.58)	34 (0.73)		4678
1935	49 (1.04)			1 (0.02)	6 (0.13)	23 (0.49)		4733
1936	62 (1.29)			5 (0.10)	34 (0.71)	15 (0.31)		4791
1937	67 (1.38)			4 (0.08)	26 (0.54)	42 (0.87)		4850
1938	44 (0.90)			17 (0.35)	10 (0.20)	14 (0.28)		4914
1939								
1940	35 (0.69)			2 (0.04)	7 (0.14)	21 (0.42)		5051
1941	25 (0.49)			6 (0.12)	5 (0.10)	15 (0.29)		5124
1942	12 (0.23)			5 (0.10)	5 (0.10)	6 (0.12)		5201
1943	13 (0.25)			6 (0.11)	5 (0.09)	18 (0.34)		5279
1944	8 (0.15)			5 (0.09)	0 (0.00)	29 (0.54)		5362
1945	17 (0.31)			2 (0.04)	5 (0.09)	37 (0.68)		5448
1946	47 (0.85)			3 (0.05)	10 (0.18)	15 (0.27)		5537
1947	68 (1.20)			7 (0.12)	13 (0.22)	85 (1.50)		5656
1948	65 (1.12)			7 (0.12)	20 (0.34)	127 (2.20)		5779
1949	94 (1.59)			4 (0.07)		264 (4.47)		5905
1950	62 (1.03)			26 (0.43)	12 (0.20)	197 (3.28)		5998
1951	58 (0.95)			14 (0.23)	5 (0.08)	183 (2.99)		6116
1952	47 (0.75)			14 (0.22)	17 (0.27)	123 (1.97)		6235
1953	19 (0.30)			19 (0.30)	21 (0.33)	133 (2.09)		6358
1954	13 (0.20)			19 (0.29)	21 (0.32)	101 (1.56)		6482
1955	24 (0.36)			15 (0.23)	23 (0.35)	82 (1.24)		6609
1956	19 (0.28)	185 (2.75)		6 (0.09)	31 (0.46)	72 (1.07)	4898 (72.68)	6739
1957	26 (0.38)	280 (4.08)		6 (0.09)	31 (0.45)	49 (0.71)	6723 (97.85)	6871
1958	29 (0.41)	296 (4.22)		10 (0.14)	23 (0.33)	50 (0.71)	6947 (99.16)	7006
1959	32 (0.45)	229 (3.21)		5 (0.07)	15 (0.21)	57 (0.80)	6935 (97.09)	7143
1960	42 (0.58)	140 (1.92)		17 (0.23)	9 (0.12)	42 (0.58)	7522 (103.22)	7287
1961	31 (0.42)	203 (2.77)		4 (0.05)	15 (0.20)	43 (0.59)	7518 (102.59)	7328
1962	51 (0.69)	225 (3.05)		5 (0.07)	11 (0.15)	55 (0.75)	7770 (105.44)	7369
1963	45 (0.60)	230 (3.07)		10 (0.13)	31 (0.41)	94 (1.25)	8820 (117.58)	7501
1964	42 (0.55)	263 (3.44)		15 (0.20)	19 (0.25)	115 (1.51)	8853 (115.95)	7635
1965	40 (0.51)	219 (2.82)		6 (0.08)	15 (0.19)	142 (1.83)	8570 (110.28)	7771
1966	59 (0.75)	333 (4.21)		12 (0.15)	32 (0.40)	167 (2.11)	10546 (133.31)	7911
1967	46 (0.57)	311 (3.86)		20 (0.25)	22 (0.27)	144 (1.79)	11571 (143.69)	8053
1968	50 (0.61)	360 (4.39)		14 (0.17)	30 (0.37)	89 (1.09)	13771 (168.00)	8197
1969	37 (0.44)	299 (3.58)		34 (0.41)	39 (0.47)	92 (1.10)	11404 (136.69)	8343
1970	56 (0.66)	248 (2.92)		19 (0.22)	40 (0.47)	67 (0.79)	14138 (166.47)	8493
1971	38 (0.44)			10 (0.12)	27 (0.31)	62 (0.72)		8645

FOOTNOTES:

* RAW CRIME FIGURES FOR "REGION PARISIENNE";
  COMPUTED RATES BASED ON QUESTIONABLE POPULATION ESTIMATES
  ESTIMATES FOR PARIS METROPOLITAN AREA

1. MURDER,HOMICIDE,PARRICIDE,POISONING,INFANTICIDE
2. MANSLAUGHTER IN ROAD ACCIDENTS AND OTHER MANSLAUGHTERS
3. FORCIBLE RAPE, MINORS AND ADULTS

PORT OF SPAIN, TRINIDAD AND TOBAGO * NUMBER OF OFFENSES REPORTED -- (RATE PER 100,000)

YEAR	MURDER ( )	MANSLTR ( )	HOMICIDE ( )	RAPE ( )	ASSAULT ( )	ROBBERY ( )	THEFT ( )	POP
1950	17 (16.50)	22 (21.36)	4 (3.88)	32 (31.07)		54 (52.43)	239 (232.04)	103
1951	3 (2.94)	3 (2.94)	21 (20.59)	38 (37.25)		36 (35.29)	209 (204.90)	102
1952	23 (22.77)	0 (0.00)	20 (19.80)	22 (21.78)		34 (33.66)	197 (195.05)	101
1953	16 (16.00)	1 (1.00)	23 (23.00)	34 (34.00)		24 (24.00)	173 (173.00)	100
1954	12 (12.24)	0 (0.00)	20 (20.41)	20 (20.41)		30 (30.61)	189 (192.86)	98
1955	5 (5.15)	0 (0.00)	14 (14.43)	11 (11.34)		20 (20.62)	193 (198.97)	97
1956	15 (15.79)	4 (4.26)	10 (10.53)	18 (18.95)		40 (42.11)	202 (212.63)	95
1957	15 (15.96)	7 (7.53)	22 (23.40)	22 (23.40)		45 (47.87)	190 (202.13)	94
1958	8 (8.60)	7 (7.53)	21 (22.58)	21 (22.58)		49 (52.69)	194 (208.60)	93
1959	12 (13.04)	3 (3.26)	18 (19.57)	33 (35.87)		50 (54.35)	214 (232.61)	92
1960	16 (17.20)	4 (4.30)	19 (20.43)	17 (18.28)		43 (46.24)	204 (219.35)	93
1961	12 (13.04)	2 (2.17)	12 (13.04)	15 (16.30)		24 (26.09)	303 (329.35)	92
1962	13 (14.44)	2 (2.22)	14 (15.56)	26 (28.89)		34 (37.78)	275 (305.56)	90
1963	18 (20.45)	5 (5.68)	15 (17.05)	38 (43.18)		71 (80.68)	327 (371.59)	88
1964	13 (14.94)	2 (2.30)	10 (11.49)	38 (43.68)		76 (87.36)	275 (316.09)	87
1965	13 (15.29)	4 (4.71)	11 (12.94)	50 (58.82)		100 (117.65)	435 (511.76)	85
1966	12 (14.46)	8 (9.64)	18 (21.69)	33 (39.76)		124 (149.40)	458 (551.81)	83
1967	18 (21.95)	0 (0.00)	9 (10.98)	45 (54.88)		106 (129.27)	510 (621.95)	82
1968	6 (7.41)	1 (1.23)	21 (25.93)	37 (45.68)		91 (112.35)	519 (640.74)	81
1969	11 (13.75)	1 (1.25)	11 (13.75)	27 (33.75)		70 (87.50)	611 (763.75)	80
1970	15 (18.99)	1 (1.27)	9 (11.39)	25 (31.65)		119 (150.63)	538 (681.01)	79
1971	8 (10.26)	4 (5.13)	7 (8.97)	47 (60.26)		131 (167.95)	774 (992.31)	78
1972	11 (14.47)	4 (5.26)	9 (11.84)	49 (64.47)		171 (225.00)	810 (1065.79)	76
1973	7 (9.33)	2 (2.67)	5 (6.67)	36 (48.00)		115 (153.33)	599 (798.67)	75
1974	11 (14.86)	2 (2.70)	5 (6.76)	21 (28.38)		108 (145.95)	699 (944.59)	74

FOOTNOTES:
* COMPUTED RATES BASED ON QUESTIONABLE POPULATION ESTIMATES

QUEZON CITY, PHILIPPINES *   NUMBER OF OFFENSES REPORTED -- (RATE PER 100,000)

YEAR	MURDER ( )	MANSLTR ( )	HOMICIDE ( )	RAPE (1)	ASSAULT ( )	ROBBERY ( )	THEFT ( )	POP
1962	4 (0.89)		25 (5.54)	3 (0.67)	6 (1.33)	32 (7.10)	21 (4.66)	451
1963			17 (3.53)	2 (0.42)	2 (0.42)	54 (11.23)	18 (3.74)	481
1964	6 (1.17)		22 (4.29)	3 (0.58)	1 (0.19)	42 (8.19)	23 (4.48)	513
1965	4 (0.73)		10 (1.83)	2 (0.37)		13 (2.38)	7 (1.28)	547
1966	2 (0.34)		12 (2.06)			25 (4.29)	5 (0.86)	583
1967	3 (0.48)		25 (4.02)	5 (0.80)	1 (0.17)	31 (4.98)	8 (1.29)	622
1968			19 (2.87)	1 (0.15)	2 (0.32)	32 (4.83)	9 (1.36)	663
1969	18 (2.55)		17 (2.40)	1 (0.14)	1 (0.14)	54 (7.64)	14 (1.98)	707
1970	11 (1.46)		67 (8.89)	6 (0.80)	3 (0.40)	84 (11.14)	34 (4.51)	754
1971	16 (1.99)		53 (6.59)	6 (0.75)		104 (12.94)	35 (4.35)	804
1972			28 (3.27)	4 (0.47)		45 (5.25)	6 (0.70)	857

FOOTNOTES:
* CRIMES GIVEN IN FISCAL YEARS BEGINNING IN YEAR INDICATED
1. RAPE AND OTHER SEX OFFENSES

SALISBURY, RHODESIA *

CRIME STATISTICS -- (RATE PER 100,000)

YEAR	MURDER ( )	MANSLTR ( )	HOMICIDE ( )	RAPE ( )	ASSAULT (1)	ROBBERY ( )	THEFT ( )	POP
1950	3 (2.78)		8 (7.41)	1 (0.93)	423 (391.67)	26 (24.07)	4698 (4350.00)	108
1951	6 (5.08)		3 (2.54)	1 (0.85)	462 (391.53)	17 (14.41)	5091 (4314.41)	118
1952	1 (0.78)		5 (3.88)	25 (19.38)	626 (485.27)	36 (27.91)	4948 (3835.66)	129
1953	3 (2.11)		8 (5.63)	28 (19.72)	566 (398.59)	31 (21.83)	5666 (3990.14)	142
1954	7 (4.52)		10 (6.45)	14 (9.03)	597 (385.16)	40 (25.81)	7080 (4567.74)	155
1955	10 (5.88)		3 (1.76)	14 (8.24)	649 (381.76)	27 (15.88)	6952 (4089.41)	170
1956	5 (2.69)		14 (7.53)	27 (14.52)	822 (441.94)	41 (22.04)	8127 (4369.36)	186
1957	14 (6.90)		10 (4.93)	6 (2.96)	836 (411.82)	59 (29.06)	10405 (5125.61)	203
1958	9 (4.04)		8 (3.59)	23 (10.31)	1276 (572.20)	103 (46.19)	10555 (4733.18)	223
1959	16 (6.56)		29 (11.89)	45 (18.44)	1432 (586.89)	172 (70.49)	11109 (4552.87)	244
1960	11 (4.12)		9 (3.37)	28 (10.49)	1289 (482.77)	156 (58.43)	11327 (4242.32)	267
1961	31 (11.15)		42 (15.11)	37 (13.31)	1334 (479.86)	269 (96.76)	11436 (4113.67)	278
1962	10 (3.46)		33 (11.42)	60 (20.76)	921 (318.69)	170 (58.82)	9551 (3304.84)	289
1963	11 (3.65)		9 (2.99)	29 (9.63)	808 (268.44)	241 (80.07)	10881 (3614.95)	301
1964	57 (18.15)		18 (5.73)	50 (15.92)	1630 (519.11)	265 (84.39)	13347 (4250.64)	314
1965	34 (10.40)		7 (2.14)	69 (21.10)	1039 (317.74)	66 (20.18)	10863 (3322.02)	327
1966	20 (5.88)		5 (1.47)	70 (20.59)	897 (263.82)	227 (66.76)	17345 (5101.47)	340
1967	26 (7.34)		13 (3.67)	48 (13.56)	794 (224.29)	176 (49.72)	10295 (2908.19)	354
1968	39 (10.57)		8 (2.17)	54 (14.63)	1164 (315.45)	241 (65.31)	10946 (2966.40)	369
1969	20 (5.21)		13 (3.39)	85 (22.14)	1397 (363.80)	295 (76.82)	9623 (2505.99)	384
1970	28 (7.00)		11 (2.75)	82 (20.50)	1840 (460.00)	501 (125.25)	10592 (2648.00)	400
1971	13 (3.13)		11 (2.64)	71 (17.07)	1842 (442.79)	668 (160.58)	11243 (2702.64)	416

FOOTNOTES:
* COMPUTED RATES BASED ON QUESTIONABLE POPULATION
  ESTIMATES FOR SALISBURY METROPOLITAN AREA
1. COMMON ASSAULT AND GRIEVIOUS BODILY HARM

SEOUL, KOREA *

CRIME STATISTICS -- (RATE PER 100,000)

YEAR	MURDER ( )	MANSLTR ( )	HOMICIDE ( )	RAPE ( )	ASSAULT ( )	ROBBERY ( )	THEFT ( )	POP
1965			80 (2.27)	123 (3.49)	4560 (129.40)	403 (11.44)		3524
1966			93 (2.44)	147 (3.86)	4929 (129.54)	304 (7.99)		3805
1967			79 (1.90)	223 (5.37)	4023 (96.96)	242 (5.83)		4149
1968			101 (2.23)	255 (5.62)	3970 (87.46)	293 (6.46)		4539
1969			136 (2.74)	256 (5.16)	3060 (61.64)	190 (3.83)		4964

FOOTNOTES:
* CASES ACCUSED

STOCKHOLM, SWEDEN

NUMBER OF OFFENSES REPORTED -- (RATE PER 100,000)

YEAR	MURDER (1)	MANSLTR ( )	HOMICIDE (2)	RAPE (3)	ASSAULT (4)	ROBBERY (5)	THEFT (6)	POP
1951	4 (0.54)		8 (1.08)	64 (8.60)	1546 (207.80)	70 (9.41)	30481 (4096.91)	744
1952	4 (0.53)		5 (0.66)	48 (6.38)	1462 (194.41)	59 (7.85)	26002 (3457.71)	752
1953	6 (0.79)		13 (1.71)	54 (7.09)	1505 (197.51)	97 (12.73)	25839 (3390.94)	762
1954	11 (1.43)		4 (0.52)	50 (6.49)	1552 (201.56)	99 (12.86)	27386 (3556.62)	770
1955	7 (0.90)		9 (1.16)	59 (7.59)	1887 (242.86)	99 (12.74)	35351 (4549.68)	777
1956	12 (1.53)		12 (1.53)	75 (9.54)	2005 (255.09)	138 (17.56)	37634 (4788.04)	786
1957	7 (0.88)		9 (1.13)	67 (8.44)	2015 (253.78)	166 (20.91)	44330 (5583.12)	794
1958	12 (1.50)		14 (1.75)	97 (12.14)	2061 (257.95)	181 (22.65)	50093 (6269.46)	799
1959	11 (1.37)		16 (1.99)	98 (12.17)	1936 (240.50)	163 (20.25)	46960 (5833.54)	805
1960	10 (1.24)		14 (1.73)	90 (11.14)	2055 (254.33)	162 (20.05)	44446 (5500.74)	808
1961	9 (1.11)		19 (2.35)	85 (10.52)	1935 (239.48)	168 (20.79)	46681 (5777.35)	808
1962	10 (1.24)		24 (2.97)	100 (12.39)	1752 (217.10)	213 (26.39)	47759 (5918.09)	807
1963	14 (1.75)		35 (4.36)	87 (10.85)	1900 (236.91)	246 (30.67)	50952 (6353.12)	802
1964	3 (0.38)		16 (2.01)	86 (10.80)	2081 (261.43)	226 (28.39)	54854 (6891.20)	796
1965	18 (2.27)		17 (2.14)	106 (13.35)	2445 (307.93)	352 (44.33)	60466 (7615.36)	794
1966	24 (3.09)		24 (3.09)	130 (16.73)	2598 (334.36)	426 (54.83)	59339 (7636.93)	777
1967	16 (2.08)		28 (3.65)	136 (17.71)	2526 (328.91)	400 (52.08)	66986 (8722.13)	768
1968	24 (3.17)		48 (6.34)	108 (14.27)	3169 (418.63)	501 (66.18)	75549 (9980.05)	757
1969	10 (1.35)		49 (6.62)	129 (17.43)	3442 (465.14)	558 (75.41)	69399 (9378.24)	740
1970	13 (1.76)		45 (6.08)	140 (18.92)	3221 (435.27)	614 (82.97)	81826 (********)	740
1971	16 (2.20)		45 (6.20)	125 (17.22)	2916 (401.65)	615 (84.71)	85809 (********)	726
1972	10 (1.41)		41 (5.77)	85 (11.95)	2848 (400.56)	712 (100.14)	74999 (********)	711
1973	15 (2.15)		43 (6.17)	101 (14.49)	2883 (413.63)	755 (108.32)	53436 (7666.57)	697

FOOTNOTES:

* NEW PENAL CODE INSTITUTED IN 1965
1. MURDER AND MANSLAUGHTER
2. MURDER AND MANSLAUGHTER ATTEMPTS
3. INCLUDES ATTEMPTS
4. ASSAULT AND BATTERY, INCLUDING AGGRAVATED CASES AND
   ATTEMPTS
5. INCLUDES ATTEMPTS
6. THEFT, ROBBERY, ARBITRARY CONDUCT AND ATTEMPTS UNTIL
   1965; THEFT, ROBBERY AND OTHER ACTS OF LARCENY FROM 1965

SYDNEY, AUSTRALIA *

NUMBER OF OFFENSES REPORTED -- (RATE PER 100,000)

YEAR	MURDER ( )	MANSLTR ( )	HOMICIDE ( )	RAPE ( )	ASSAULT ( )	ROBBERY ( )	THEFT (1)	POP
1931	16 (1.29)	14 (1.13)		6 (0.48)	111 (8.96)		12817 (1034.46)	1239
1932	19 (1.52)	11 (0.88)		5 (0.40)	119 (9.54)		12357 (990.94)	1247
1933	9 (0.72)	14 (1.12)		8 (0.64)	127 (10.12)		13013 (1036.89)	1255
1934	8 (0.63)	17 (1.35)		14 (1.11)	95 (7.52)		13211 (1046.00)	1263
1935	14 (1.10)	25 (1.97)		12 (0.94)	147 (11.57)		12025 (946.11)	1271
1936	14 (1.09)	32 (2.50)		7 (0.55)	134 (10.48)		12925 (1010.55)	1279
1937	14 (1.09)	19 (1.48)		16 (1.24)	111 (8.62)		12810 (995.34)	1287
1938	11 (0.85)	18 (1.39)		7 (0.54)	120 (9.27)		14550 (1123.55)	1295
1939	16 (1.23)	13 (1.00)		9 (0.69)	118 (9.06)		15139 (1116.86)	1303
1940	32 (2.42)	23 (1.74)		9 (0.68)	98 (7.42)		12635 (957.20)	1320
1941	14 (1.05)	20 (1.50)		11 (0.82)	115 (8.60)		11559 (864.55)	1337
1942	15 (1.10)	16 (1.18)		13 (0.96)	139 (10.21)		12104 (889.35)	1361
1943	18 (1.30)	32 (2.31)		4 (0.29)	166 (11.99)		12044 (869.60)	1385
1944	16 (1.14)	47 (3.34)		11 (0.78)	193 (13.70)		12038 (854.36)	1409
1945	18 (1.26)	40 (2.79)		13 (0.91)	199 (13.88)		13065 (911.09)	1434
1946	33 (2.26)	31 (2.13)		13 (0.89)	206 (14.14)		12784 (877.42)	1457
1947	27 (1.82)	41 (2.76)		8 (0.54)	199 (13.41)		12203 (822.30)	1484
1948	30 (1.93)	31 (2.00)		9 (0.58)	210 (13.52)		11447 (737.09)	1553
1949	25 (1.54)	29 (1.78)		9 (0.55)	193 (11.87)		12109 (744.71)	1626
1950	21 (1.23)	38 (2.23)		7 (0.41)	177 (10.40)		12583 (739.31)	1702
1951	16 (0.92)	56 (3.22)		12 (0.69)	211 (12.12)		13974 (802.64)	1741
1952	24 (1.35)	77 (4.33)		9 (0.51)	211 (11.85)		14904 (837.30)	1780
1953	25 (1.37)	72 (3.95)		14 (0.77)	299 (16.42)		14625 (803.13)	1821
1954	23 (1.23)	58 (3.11)		22 (1.18)	293 (15.73)		15304 (821.47)	1863
1955	34 (1.79)	65 (3.42)		22 (1.16)	269 (14.16)		16209 (853.11)	1900
1956	42 (2.17)	60 (3.10)		17 (0.88)	305 (15.75)		17800 (919.42)	1936
1957	31 (1.57)	58 (2.94)		20 (1.01)	260 (13.16)		18136 (918.28)	1975
1958	23 (1.14)	56 (2.78)		21 (1.04)	285 (14.13)		18165 (900.59)	2017
1959	33 (1.61)	38 (1.85)		35 (1.70)	334 (16.26)		20221 (984.47)	2054
1960	30 (1.41)	67 (3.14)		52 (2.44)	324 (15.18)		21645 (1014.29)	2134
1961	31 (1.42)	77 (3.53)		78 (3.57)	344 (15.76)		23662 (1083.92)	2183
1962	33 (1.48)	70 (3.13)		56 (2.51)	387 (17.33)		23234 (1040.48)	2233
1963	26 (1.14)	69 (3.02)		87 (3.81)	346 (15.15)		26751 (1171.23)	2284
1964	41 (1.76)	73 (3.13)		99 (4.24)	451 (19.31)		27849 (1192.17)	2336
1965	33 (1.38)	87 (3.64)		70 (2.93)	370 (15.48)		31929 (1335.94)	2390
1966	41 (1.68)	42 (1.72)		80 (3.27)	426 (17.42)		32835 (1342.94)	2445
1967	39 (1.55)	57 (2.27)		116 (4.62)	465 (18.53)		36215 (1443.40)	2509
1968	51 (1.98)	65 (2.53)		155 (6.02)	487 (18.92)		46004 (1787.26)	2574
1969	28 (1.07)	50 (1.90)		118 (4.49)	470 (17.90)		51608 (1965.27)	2626
1970	43 (1.59)	50 (1.84)		138 (5.09)	635 (23.41)		67256 (2479.94)	2712

FOOTNOTES: * ALL FIGURES ARE FOR SYDNEY METROPOLITAN AREA
1. MOTOR VEHICLE THEFT

TANANARIVE, MADAGASCAR CRIME STATISTICS -- (RATE PER 100,000)

YEAR	MURDER ( )	MANSLTR ( )	HOMICIDE ( )	RAPE ( )	ASSAULT ( )	ROBBERY ( )	THEFT ( )	POP
1966					1618 (490.30)		2857 (865.76)	330
1967					1202 (364.24)		4604 (1395.15)	330
1968					1513 (457.10)		4413 (1333.23)	331
1969					1436 (432.53)		3084 (928.92)	332
1970					1671 (501.80)		3472 (1042.64)	333
1971					1408 (422.82)		3633 (1090.99)	333

TOKYO, JAPAN *

NUMBER OF OFFENSES REPORTED -- (RATE PER 100,000)

YEAR	MURDER ( )	MANSLTR ( )	HOMICIDE ( )	RAPE (1)	ASSAULT ( )	ROBBERY ( )	THEFT ( )	POP
1900	27 (1.80)			35 (2.34)		170 (11.35)	23915 (1596.46)	1498
1901	33 (2.07)			55 (3.45)		125 (7.85)	25212 (1583.67)	1592
1902	29 (1.72)			50 (2.97)		153 (9.07)	27453 (1628.29)	1686
1903	29 (1.63)			79 (4.44)		186 (10.45)	33275 (1869.38)	1780
1904	34 (1.81)			57 (3.04)		190 (10.14)	36051 (1923.75)	1874
1905	31 (1.57)			73 (3.71)		145 (7.36)	33365 (1693.66)	1970
1906	46 (2.33)			64 (3.24)		150 (7.59)	38676 (1956.30)	1977
1907	75 (3.78)			67 (3.38)		111 (5.59)	37090 (1868.51)	1985
1908	71 (3.56)			216 (10.84)		131 (6.58)	33434 (1678.11)	1992
1909	113 (5.65)			159 (7.95)		185 (9.25)	27124 (1356.88)	1999
1910	79 (3.94)			154 (7.68)		203 (10.12)	18379 (916.20)	2006
1911	86 (4.27)			195 (9.69)		213 (10.58)	16601 (824.69)	2013
1912	89 (4.41)			144 (7.13)		226 (11.19)	18860 (933.66)	2020
1913	98 (4.83)			236 (11.64)		231 (11.40)	23397 (1154.27)	2027
1914	90 (4.43)			200 (9.84)		269 (13.23)	28515 (1402.61)	2033
1915	105 (5.11)			145 (7.05)		275 (13.38)	31167 (1515.90)	2056
1916	86 (4.14)			103 (4.95)		232 (11.16)	30316 (1458.20)	2079
1917	107 (5.09)			101 (4.81)		186 (8.85)	30821 (1466.97)	2101
1918	82 (3.86)			83 (3.91)		159 (7.48)	34666 (1631.34)	2125
1919	86 (4.00)			98 (4.56)		136 (6.33)	25083 (1166.65)	2150
1920	85 (3.91)			104 (4.79)		127 (5.84)	31824 (1464.52)	2173
1921	99 (4.53)			166 (7.60)		117 (5.35)	30389 (1390.80)	2185
1922	124 (5.64)			255 (11.61)		186 (8.47)	35368 (1609.83)	2197
1923	146 (6.61)			88 (3.98)		132 (5.98)	22657 (1025.67)	2209
1924	142 (6.39)			205 (9.23)		286 (12.88)	54087 (2435.26)	2221
1925	168 (7.52)			246 (11.02)		555 (24.85)	60010 (2687.42)	2233
1926	191 (8.51)			202 (9.00)		422 (18.80)	62917 (2802.54)	2245
1927	166 (7.35)			104 (4.61)		554 (24.55)	67994 (3010.37)	2257
1928	164 (7.23)			94 (4.14)		558 (24.59)	72770 (3207.14)	2269
1929	181 (7.93)			92 (4.03)		570 (24.98)	91184 (4026.47)	2282
1930	198 (8.63)			88 (3.83)		493 (21.48)	111456 (4856.47)	2295
1931	145 (5.15)			93 (3.30)		466 (16.55)	113666 (4037.87)	2815
1932	188 (5.64)			144 (4.32)		478 (14.33)	125872 (3774.27)	3335
1933	207 (5.37)			84 (2.18)		413 (10.71)	135053 (3503.32)	3855
1934	183 (4.18)			124 (2.83)		410 (9.37)	125732 (2877.87)	4375
1935	157 (3.21)			138 (2.82)		447 (9.13)	119057 (2432.22)	4895
1936	190 (3.51)			114 (2.11)		352 (6.50)	105513 (1948.53)	5415
1937	144 (2.43)			74 (1.25)		292 (4.92)	104297 (1757.32)	5935
1938	135 (2.09)			78 (1.21)		289 (4.48)	103769 (1606.83)	6458
1939	122 (1.71)			68 (0.96)		144 (2.02)	95042 (1335.23)	7118
1940	115 (1.56)			55 (0.75)		192 (2.61)	100211 (1362.67)	7354
1941	82 (1.29)			68 (1.07)		160 (2.53)	95552 (1508.32)	6335
1942	77 (1.41)			104 (1.91)		178 (3.26)	92400 (1693.24)	5457
1943	68 (1.45)			76 (1.62)		100 (2.13)	92603 (1970.28)	4700
1944	52 (1.28)			89 (2.20)		100 (2.47)	87976 (2172.78)	4049

TOKYO, JAPAN *

NUMBER OF OFFENSES REPORTED -- (RATE PER 100,000)   CONTINUED

YEAR	MURDER ( )	MANSLTR ( )	HOMICIDE ( )	RAPE (1)	ASSAULT ( )	ROBBERY ( )	THEFT ( )	POP
1945	44 (1.26)			26 (0.75)		167 (4.79)	49943 (1431.85)	3488
1946	83 (1.96)			24 (0.57)		1052 (24.78)	135270 (3186.57)	4245
1947	88 (1.76)			35 (0.70)		1086 (21.72)	133155 (2662.57)	5001
1948	106 (1.96)			91 (1.68)		1443 (26.62)	183297 (3381.86)	5420
1949	143 (2.44)			170 (2.91)		988 (16.89)	178703 (3054.75)	5850
1950	177 (2.82)			285 (4.54)		979 (15.60)	138333 (2203.81)	6277
1951	178 (2.71)			239 (3.64)		822 (12.52)	138250 (2105.54)	6566
1952	169 (2.46)			218 (3.17)		862 (12.55)	136582 (1988.38)	6869
1953	157 (2.18)			212 (2.95)		901 (12.54)	135693 (1888.30)	7186
1954	195 (2.59)			442 (5.88)		1158 (15.41)	148327 (1973.22)	7517
1955	179 (2.28)			392 (4.98)		1095 (13.92)	164295 (2088.41)	7867
1956	159 (1.94)			348 (4.24)		962 (11.71)	142215 (1730.95)	8216
1957	181 (2.11)			422 (4.93)		1108 (12.94)	156121 (1822.99)	8564
1958	187 (2.11)			602 (6.80)		1071 (12.10)	164224 (1855.85)	8849
1959	171 (1.87)			539 (5.90)		1141 (12.48)	173987 (1903.16)	9142
1960	228 (2.35)			619 (6.39)		1137 (11.74)	178370 (1841.90)	9684
1961	217 (2.19)			686 (6.92)		856 (8.64)	176405 (1780.25)	9909
1962	174 (1.72)			605 (5.97)		782 (7.71)	175470 (1730.47)	10140
1963	189 (1.82)			542 (5.22)		713 (6.87)	172104 (1658.51)	10377
1964	197 (1.86)			655 (6.17)		672 (6.33)	160110 (1507.77)	10619
1965	196 (1.80)			561 (5.16)		773 (7.11)	164587 (1514.14)	10870
1966	204 (1.86)			564 (5.14)		674 (6.14)	165314 (1506.96)	10970
1967	193 (1.74)			606 (5.47)		522 (4.72)	160274 (1447.82)	11070
1968	190 (1.70)			498 (4.46)		495 (4.43)	161563 (1446.40)	11170
1969	195 (1.73)			449 (3.98)		461 (4.09)	167866 (1489.36)	11271
1970	213 (1.87)			500 (4.40)		472 (4.15)	175533 (1543.28)	11374
1971	186 (1.62)			426 (3.71)		436 (3.80)	170545 (1485.97)	11477
1972	208 (1.80)			465 (4.01)		435 (3.76)	169894 (1466.88)	11582

FOOTNOTES:
  * COMPUTED RATES BASED ON POPULATION ESTIMATES FOR
    TOKYO METROPOLITAN AREA; ESTIMATES ARE QUESTIONABLE BEFORE 1940
  1.SUSPECTS BEFORE 1915. INCLUDES BIGAMY AND INDECENCY BEFORE 1927

VIENNA, AUSTRIA CRIME STATISTICS -- (RATE PER 100,000)

YEAR	MURDER ( )	MANSLTR ( )	HOMICIDE ( )	RAPE ( )	ASSAULT ( )	ROBBERY ( )	THEFT (1)	POP
1953	13 (0.75)	5 (0.29)		103 (5.93)	466 (26.83)	62 (3.57)	5827 (335.46)	1737
1954	12 (0.70)	8 (0.46)		96 (5.57)	519 (30.12)	70 (4.06)	6342 (368.08)	1723
1955	8 (0.47)	4 (0.23)		120 (7.02)	529 (30.95)	99 (5.79)	6756 (395.32)	1709
1956	12 (0.71)	5 (0.29)		105 (6.19)	491 (28.97)	151 (8.91)	8440 (497.94)	1695
1957	11 (0.65)	9 (0.54)		89 (5.29)	518 (30.81)	127 (7.56)	10599 (630.52)	1681
1958	13 (0.78)	3 (0.18)		117 (7.02)	428 (25.67)	205 (12.30)	10180 (610.68)	1667
1959	18 (1.09)	4 (0.24)		134 (8.10)	477 (28.84)	128 (7.74)	11619 (702.48)	1654
1960	15 (0.91)	4 (0.24)		183 (11.16)	514 (31.34)	187 (11.40)	12456 (759.51)	1640
1961	5 (0.31)	4 (0.25)		123 (7.56)	350 (21.51)	199 (12.23)	14529 (892.99)	1627
1962	8 (0.49)	3 (0.18)		165 (10.15)	490 (30.14)	190 (11.69)	17026 (1047.11)	1626
1963	13 (0.80)	5 (0.31)		131 (8.07)	607 (37.38)	190 (11.70)	18730 (1153.33)	1624
1964	7 (0.43)	6 (0.37)		130 (8.01)	500 (30.81)	191 (11.77)	19794 (1219.59)	1623
1965	12 (0.74)	10 (0.62)		88 (5.43)	479 (29.53)	240 (14.80)	23119 (1425.34)	1622
1966	6 (0.37)	3 (0.19)		88 (5.43)	475 (29.32)	208 (12.84)	25723 (1587.84)	1620
1967	15 (0.93)	7 (0.43)		88 (5.44)	652 (40.27)	300 (18.53)	28983 (1790.18)	1619
1968	15 (0.93)	3 (0.19)		96 (5.93)	627 (38.75)	281 (17.37)	33079 (2044.44)	1618
1969	15 (0.93)	9 (0.56)		116 (7.17)	636 (39.33)	266 (16.45)	35294 (2182.68)	1617
1970	21 (1.30)	11 (0.68)		117 (7.24)	734 (45.42)	275 (17.02)	37247 (2304.89)	1616
1971	20 (1.24)	19 (1.18)		102 (6.32)	690 (42.75)	333 (20.63)	29793 (1845.91)	1614
1972	24 (1.49)	14 (0.87)		114 (7.06)	610 (37.79)	386 (23.92)	41307 (2559.29)	1614
1973	22 (1.36)	8 (0.50)		104 (6.44)	576 (35.67)	412 (25.51)	33515 (2075.23)	1615

FOOTNOTES:
1. AGGRAVATED THEFT

WARSAW, POLAND

NUMBER OF CONVICTIONS -- (RATE PER 100,000)

YEAR	MURDER ( )	MANSLTR ( )	HOMICIDE ( )	RAPE ( )	ASSAULT (1)	ROBBERY ( )	THEFT (2)	POP
1946			9 (1.88)	1 (0.21)	24 (5.01)	40 (8.35)	1425 (297.49)	479
1947			11 (2.12)	3 (0.58)	16 (3.09)	45 (8.69)	1428 (275.68)	518
1948			10 (1.78)	4 (0.71)	39 (6.95)	49 (8.73)	1430 (254.90)	561
1949			6 (1.04)	0 (0.00)	49 (8.48)	21 (3.63)	1127 (194.98)	578
1950			14 (2.33)	3 (0.50)	84 (13.98)	36 (5.99)	1376 (228.95)	601
1951			25 (3.68)	6 (0.88)	76 (11.19)	40 (5.89)	874 (128.72)	679
1952			14 (1.82)	4 (0.52)	57 (7.42)	21 (2.73)	1210 (157.55)	768
1953			16 (1.84)	4 (0.46)	58 (6.68)	42 (4.84)	893 (102.88)	868
1954			15 (1.53)	2 (0.20)	69 (7.03)	47 (4.79)	1053 (107.34)	981
1955			11 (1.10)	6 (0.60)	90 (8.99)	78 (7.79)	1150 (114.89)	1001
1956			11 (1.08)	2 (0.20)	33 (3.23)	76 (7.43)	730 (71.36)	1023
1957			9 (0.84)	5 (0.47)	60 (5.61)	117 (10.94)	886 (82.88)	1069
1958			10 (0.92)	17 (1.56)	65 (5.97)	89 (8.18)	1019 (93.66)	1088
1959			14 (1.26)	9 (0.81)	86 (7.77)	85 (7.68)	1244 (112.38)	1107
1960			5 (0.44)	7 (0.61)	94 (8.25)	68 (5.97)	1183 (103.86)	1139
1961			10 (0.85)	19 (1.62)	123 (10.50)	100 (8.54)	1396 (119.21)	1171
1962			9 (0.76)	20 (1.68)	166 (13.95)	144 (12.10)	1132 (95.13)	1190
1963			20 (1.64)	17 (1.39)	89 (7.28)	184 (15.06)	764 (62.52)	1222
1964			2 (0.16)	25 (2.01)	65 (5.24)	125 (10.07)	1021 (82.27)	1241
1965			15 (1.20)	52 (4.16)	55 (4.40)	143 (11.43)	1021 (81.61)	1251
1966			17 (1.34)	82 (6.47)	55 (4.02)	192 (15.14)	1459 (115.06)	1268
1967			12 (0.94)	75 (5.85)	39 (3.04)	235 (18.32)	1228 (95.71)	1283
1968			13 (1.01)	66 (5.11)	60 (4.65)	244 (18.90)	1249 (96.75)	1291
1969			13 (1.00)	85 (6.54)	80 (6.16)	228 (17.55)	861 (66.28)	1299
1970			11 (0.84)	111 (8.49)	55 (4.20)	236 (18.04)	1254 (95.87)	1308
1971			4 (0.30)	55 (4.14)	64 (4.81)	141 (10.60)	1453 (109.25)	1330
1972			5 (0.37)	57 (4.21)	78 (5.76)	191 (14.11)	1295 (95.64)	1354
1973			19 (1.38)	71 (5.16)	104 (7.55)	293 (21.28)	1191 (86.49)	1377

FOOTNOTES:
1. ASSAULT AND BATTERY
2. BURGLARY

WELLINGTON, NEW ZEALAND *　　NUMBER OF OFFENSES REPORTED -- (RATE PER 100,000)

YEAR	MURDER (1)	MANSLTR ( )	HOMICIDE ( )	RAPE (2)	ASSAULT ( )	ROBBERY (3)	THEFT ( )	POP
1956	2 (1.41)	15 (10.56)		7 (4.93)	429 (302.11)	2 (1.41)	3100 (2185.10)	142
1957	1 (0.70)	4 (2.80)		11 (7.69)	462 (323.08)	10 (6.99)	3229 (2258.04)	143
1958	5 (3.45)	4 (2.76)		7 (4.83)	404 (277.62)	16 (11.03)	4028 (2777.93)	145
1959	5 (3.42)	2 (1.37)		10 (6.85)	498 (341.10)	12 (8.22)	3919 (2684.25)	146
1960								
1961	3 (1.99)	1 (0.66)		17 (11.26)	510 (337.75)	13 (8.61)	4028 (2667.55)	151
1962	0 (0.00)	0 (0.00)		6 (3.90)	499 (324.03)	21 (13.64)	4394 (2853.25)	154
1963	6 (3.82)	1 (0.64)		15 (9.55)	572 (364.33)	13 (8.28)	4772 (3039.49)	157
1964	5 (3.13)	2 (1.25)		9 (5.63)	563 (351.88)	15 (9.38)	4726 (2953.75)	160
1965	1 (0.61)	3 (1.84)		33 (20.25)	716 (439.26)	23 (14.11)	5386 (3304.30)	163
1966	8 (4.82)	0 (0.00)		18 (10.84)	391 (235.54)	9 (5.42)	3812 (2296.39)	166
1967	1 (0.59)	2 (1.18)		29 (17.06)	780 (458.82)	26 (15.29)	6271 (3688.82)	170
1968	1 (0.58)	0 (0.00)		27 (15.61)	768 (443.93)	31 (17.92)	6723 (3886.13)	173
1969	5 (2.84)	1 (0.57)		37 (21.02)	896 (509.09)	26 (14.77)	7401 (4205.11)	176
1970	5 (2.78)	2 (1.11)		22 (12.22)	1081 (600.56)	23 (12.78)	8237 (4576.11)	180
1971	9 (4.92)	1 (0.55)		13 (7.10)	1291 (705.46)	56 (30.60)	9486 (5183.61)	183
1972	3 (1.60)	1 (0.53)		25 (13.37)	1383 (739.57)	66 (35.29)	9812 (5247.06)	187
1973	5 (2.63)	1 (0.53)		36 (18.95)	1586 (834.74)	82 (43.16)	10456 (5503.16)	190

FOOTNOTES:
* RAW CRIME FIGURES FOR "WELLINGTON HEADQUARTERS DISTRICT";
  COMPUTED RATES BASED ON POPULATION ESTIMATES FOR
  WELLINGTON METROPOLITAN AREA
1. MURDER, ATTEMPTED MURDER AND INFANTICIDE
2. EXCLUDES ASSAULT WITH INTENT TO RAPE
3. EXCLUDES ASSAULT WITH INTENT TO ROB AND AGGRAVATED ROBBERY

ZURICH, SWITZERLAND

CRIME STATISTICS -- (RATE PER 100,000)

YEAR	MURDER ( )	MANSLTR ( )	HOMICIDE ( )	RAPE ( )	ASSAULT ( )	ROBBERY ( )	THEFT (1)	POP
1900			1 (0.60)					168
1901								
GAP								
1907								
1908								
1909			0 (0.00)				2671 (1335.50)	200
1910								
1911			0 (0.00)				3073 (1422.69)	216
GAP								
1920								
1921			1 (0.43)				4173 (1775.74)	235
GAP								
1925								
1926			2 (0.77)				4025 (1542.15)	261
GAP								
1930								
1931			7 (2.41)				5611 (1928.18)	291
GAP								
1940			3 (0.90)				6024 (1814.46)	332
1941			4 (1.18)		573 (168.53)		8917 (2622.65)	340
1942								
1943								
1944								
1945			1 (0.28)	3 (0.84)	803 (224.93)		11716 (3281.79)	357
1946								
GAP								
1950			1 (0.26)	4 (1.03)	1893 (485.38)		12379 (3174.10)	390
1951								
GAP								
1955			3 (0.72)	3 (0.72)	2371 (568.59)		14823 (3554.68)	417
1956								
GAP								
1960			2 (0.46)	19 (4.34)	406 (92.69)	17 (3.85)	18845 (4302.51)	438
1961			4 (0.90)	7 (1.58)	387 (87.56)		19020 (4303.17)	442
1962								
GAP								
1965			0 (0.00)	10 (2.28)	288 (65.60)	22 (5.01)	15049 (3428.02)	439
1966								
GAP								
1970			3 (0.70)	23 (5.39)	330 (77.28)	31 (7.26)	19457 (4556.67)	427
1971								
1972								

ZURICH, SWITZERLAND   CRIME STATISTICS -- (RATE PER 100,000)   CONTINUED

YEAR   MURDER ( ) MANSLTR ( ) HOMICIDE ( ) RAPE ( )   ASSAULT ( )   ROBBERY ( )   THEFT (1)   POP

1973   3 (0.73) 19 (4.63) 299 (72.93)   69 (16.83)   19716 (4808.78)   410

FOOTNOTES:
   1. OFFENSE AGAINST FORTUNE, INCLUDES SERIOUS AND MINOR
      THEFT, THEFT OF VEHICLES, SHOP THEFT, RECEIVING
      STOLEN GOODS, EMBEZZLEMENT, ETC.

References

Abbott, E. 1918. Crime and the war. *Journal of Criminal Law and Criminology* 9:32–45.

Abbott, E. 1927. The Civil War and the crime wave of 1865–1870. *Social Service Review* 1:212–34.

Archer, D. Social deviance. n.d. In *The Handbook of Social Psychology*, (3d ed., ed. G. Lindzey and E. Aronson. Reading, Mass.: Addison-Wesley. In press.

Archer, D. and Gartner, R. 1976a. The myth of the violent veteran. *Psychology Today*, December, 94–96, 110–11.

———. 1976 b. Violent acts and violent times: A comparative approach to post-war homicide rates. *American Sociological Review* 41: 937–62.

———. 1977. Homicide in 110 nations: The development of the Comparative Crime Data File (CCDF). *The Annals of the International Society of Criminology* (Special Issue) 16:109–39.

———. 1978. Legal homicide and its consequences. In *Violence: Perspectives on Murder and Aggression*, ed. I. L. Kutash, S. B. Kutash, and L. B. Schlesinger, 219–32.

———. 1980. Homicide in 110 nations: The development of the Comparative Crime Data File (CCDF). In *Criminology Review Yearbook*, vol. 2, ed. E. Bittner and S. L. Messinger, 433–64. Beverly Hills: Sage Publications.

———. 1981 a. Homicide in 110 nations: The development of the Comparative Crime Data File (CCDF). In *Readings in Comparative Criminology*, ed. L. I. Shelley, 78–99. Carbondale: Southern Illinois University Press.

———. 1981 b. Peacetime casualties: The effects of war on the violent behavior of noncombatants. In *Readings About the Social Animal*, ed. E. Aronson, 236–48. San Francisco: W. H. Freeman.

———. 1983. War and violent crime. In *The Encyclopedia of Crime and Justice*, ed. S. H. Kadish. New York: The Free Press.

Archer, D., Gartner, R., Akert, R., and Lockwood, T. 1977. Cities and homicide: A new look at an old paradox. *Comparative Studies in Sociology* (now called *Comparative Social Research*) 1: 73–95.

Bailey, W. C. 1975. Murder and the death penalty. *Journal of Criminal Law and Criminology* 65:416–23.

———. 1978 a. An analysis of the deterrent effect of the death penalty in North Carolina. *North Carolina Central Law Journal* (Fall): 29–49.

———. 1978 b. Deterrence and the death penalty for murder in Utah: A time series analysis. *Journal of Contemporary Law* 5:1–20.

———. 1979 a. Deterrence and the death penalty for murder in Oregon. *Willamette Law Review* (Winter): 67–85.

————. 1979 b. The deterrent effect of the death penalty for murder in California. *Southern California Law Review* (March): 743–64.

————. 1979 c. The deterrent effect of the death penalty for murder in Ohio: A time series analysis. *Cleveland State Law Review* 28:51–70.

Ball-Rokeach, S. 1980. Normative and deviant violence from a conflict perspective. *Social Problems* 28:45–62.

Bandura, A. 1973. *Aggression: A Social Learning Analysis*. Englewood Cliffs: Prentice-hall.

Bedau, H. and Pierce, C., eds. 1976. *Capital Punishment in the United States*. New York: AMS Press.

Bennett, J. V. 1953. The ex-G.I. in federal prisons. *Proceedings of the American Correctional Association*, 131–36.

Biderman, A. D. 1967. Surveys of population samples for estimating crime incidence. *Annals of the American Academy of Political and Social Science* 374: 16–33.

Biderman, A. D. and Reiss, A. J. 1967. On exploring the "dark figure" of crime. *Annals of the American Academy of Political and Social Science* 374:1–15.

Black, D. J. and Reiss, A. J. 1970. Police control of juveniles. *American Sociological Review* 35:63–77.

Blumenthal, M. D., Kahn, R. I., Andrews, F. M., and Head, K. B. 1972. *Justifying Violence*. Ann Arbor: University of Michigan Press.

Blumstein, A., Cohen, J., and Nagin, D., eds. 1978. *Deterrence and Incapacitation: Estimating the Effects of Criminal Sanctions on Crime Rates*. Washington, D.C.: National Academy of Sciences.

Boggs, S. 1966. Urban crime patterns. *American Sociological Review* 30:899–908.

Bohannon. P., ed. 1960. *African Homicide and Suicide*. Princeton: Princeton University Press.

Bonger, W. A. [1916] 1969. *Criminality and Economic Conditions*. Translated by H. P. Horton. Boston: Little, Brown, and Company, 1916: republished by Indiana University Press.

Borus, J. F. 1975. The re-entry transition of the Vietnam veteran. *Armed Forces and Society* 2:97–114.

Bowers, W. J. 1974. *Executions in America*. Lexington, Mass.: Lexington Books.

Bowers, W. J. and Pierce, G. L. 1975. The illusion of deterrence in Isaac Ehrlich's research on capital punishment. *Yale Law Journal* 85:187–208.

————. 1980. Deterrence or brutalization: What is the effect of executions? *Crime and Delinquency* 26:453–84.

Braithwaite, J. 1979. *Inequality, Crime and Public Policy*. London: Routledge and Kegan Paul.

Brenner, H. 1976 a. *Effects of the Economy on Criminal Behavior and the Administration of Criminal Justice in the United States, Canada, England, Wales and Scotland*. Rome: United Nations Social Defense Research Institute.

————. 1976 b. Time-series analysis: Effects of the economy on criminal behavior and the administration of criminal justice. In *Economic Crises and Crime*, 25–68. Rome: United Nations Social Defense Research Institute.

Brenner, M. H. 1973. *Mental Illness and the Economy*. Cambridge, Mass.: Harvard University Press.

Brier, S. S. and Fienberg, S. E. 1980. Recent econometric modeling of crime and punishment: Support for the deterrence hypothesis? In *Indicators of Crime and Criminal Justice: Quantitative Studies*, ed. S. E. Fienberg and A. J. Reiss, 82–97. Washington, D.C.: U.S. Government Printing Office.

British Royal Commission on Capital Punishment. 1953. *Royal Commission Final Report on Capital Punishment*. London: Her Majesty's Stationery Office.

Bromberg, W. 1943. The effects of war on crime. *American Sociological Review* 8:685–91.

Bye, R. 1919. *Capital Punishment in the United States*. Philadelphia: Committee on Philanthropic Labor of Philadelphia.

Calbairac, M. G. 1928. Les répercussions de la Grand Guerre sur la criminalité en France. *Études Criminologiques* 3:62–70.

Calvert, E. R. 1931. *The Death Penalty Enquiry: A Review of the Evidence Before the Select Committee on Capital Punishment*. London: Camelot Press.

Campbell, D. T. and Stanley J. C. 1966. *Experimental and Quasi-Experimental Designs for Research*. Chicago: Rand-McNally.

Christiansen, K. C. 1960. Industrialization and urbanization in relation to crime and delinquency. *International Review of Criminal Policy* 16:3–8.

Clinard, M. B. 1942. The process of urbanization and criminal behavior. *American Journal of Sociology* 68:202–13.

———. 1964. The relationship of urbanization and urbanism to criminal behavior. In *Contributions to Urban Sociology*, ed. E. Burgess and D. Bogue, 541–58. Chicago: University of Chicago Press.

———. 1974. *Sociology of Deviant Behavior*. New York: Holt, Rinehart and Winston.

Clinard, M. B. and Abbott, D. J. 1973. *Crime in Developing Countries: A Comparative Approach*. New York: John Wiley.

Cohen, J. 1977. *Statistical Power Analysis for the Behavioral Sciences*. New York: Academic Press.

Cohen, L. E. and Felson, M. 1979. Social change and crime rate trends: A routine activity approach. *American Sociological Review* 44:588–608.

Commission Internationale Pénale et Pénitentiaire. 1951. *Les Effets de la guerre sur la Criminalité*. Berne: Staempfli.

Cook, P. J., ed. 1981. *Gun Control*. A special issue (Vol. 455) of *The Annals of the American Academy of Political and Social Science*.

Cook, T. D. and Campbell, D. T. 1979. *Quasi-Experimentation: Design and Analysis Issues for Field Settings*. Chicago: Rand-McNally.

Couch, C. 1968. Collective behavior: An examination of stereotypes. *Social Problems* 15:310–21.

Dann, R. H. 1935. *The Deterrent Effect of Capital Punishment*. Philadelphia: The Committee of Philanthropic Labor of Philadelphia Yearly Meeting of Friends, Bulletin no. 29.

Darrow, C. 1922. *Crime: Its Causes and Treatment*. New York: Crowell.

Dhanagare, D. N. 1969. Urbanism and crime. *Economic and Political Weekly* (July): 1239–42.

Durkheim, E. 1933. *The Division of Labor in Society*. Translated by G. Simpson. New York: Free Press.

———. [1897] 1951. *Suicide*. Reprint. New York: The Free Press.

————. 1957. *Professional Ethics and Civil Morals.* Translated by C. Brookfield. London: Routledge and Kegan Paul.

Ehrlich, I. 1975. The deterrent effect of capital punishment: A question of life and death. *American Economic Review* 65:397–417.

Ellsworth, P. and Ross, L. 1976. Public opinion and judicial decision-making: An example from research on capital punishment. In *Capital Punishment in the United States,* ed. H. A. Bedau and C. Pierce. New York: AMS Press.

Engelbrecht, H. C. 1937. *Revolt Against War.* New York: Dodd, Mead.

Ennis, P. H. 1967. *Criminal Victimization in the United States: A Report of a National Survey.* U.S. President's Commission on Law Enforcement and the Administration of Justice, Field Survey II. Washington, D.C.: U.S. Government Printing Office.

Exner, F. 1927. *Krieq und Kriminalitat in Oesterreich.* Vienna: Holder-Pichler-Tempsky.

Ferdinand, T. 1967. The criminal patterns of Boston since 1849. *American Journal of Sociology* 73:84–99.

Frankel, E. 1939. One thousand murders. *Journal of Criminal Law and Criminology* 29:672–88.

Gamson, W. A. and McEvoy, J. 1972. Police violence and its public support. In *Collective Violence,* ed. J. F. Short and M. E. Wolfgang, 329–42. Chicago: Aldine.

Gelles, R. J. and Straus, M. A. 1975. Family experience and public support of the death penalty. *American Journal of Orthopsychiatry* 45:596–613.

Glaser, D. 1970. *Crime in the City.* New York: Harper and Row.

Glueck, E. T. 1942. Wartime delinquency. *Journal of Criminal Law and Criminology* 33:119–35.

Green, W. M. 1967. An ancient debate on capital punishment. In *Capital Punishment,* ed. T. Sellin, 46–54. New York: Harper and Row.

Gurr, T. R. 1976. *Rogues, Rebels, and Reformers.* Beverly Hills: Sage.

————. 1977. Crime trends in modern democracies since 1945. *International Annals of Criminology* 16:41–85.

————. 1979. On the history of violent crime in Europe and America. In *Violence in America: Historical and Comparative Perspectives,* ed. H. D. Graham and T. R. Gurr, 353–74. Beverly Hills: Sage.

————. 1981. Historical trends in violent crimes: A critical review of evidence. In *Crime and Justice: An Annual Review of Research,* Vol. 3, ed. N. Morris and M. Tonry. Chicago: University of Chicago Press.

Hagan, J. and Leon, J. 1978. Philosophy and sociology of crime control: Canadian-American comparisons. In *Social System and Legal Process,* ed. H. Johnson, 181–208. San Francisco: Jossey-Bass.

Hamon, A. 1918. *Lessons of the World War.* Translated by B. Mall. London: Fisher Unwin.

Hanawalt, B. A. 1979. *Crime and Conflict in English Communities, 1300–1348.* Cambridge, Mass.: Harvard University Press.

Harries, K. 1974. *The Geography of Crime and Justice.* New York: McGraw-Hill.

Henry, A. F. and Short, J. F. 1954. *Suicide and Homicide: Some Economic, Sociological, and Psychological Aspects of Aggression.* Glencoe: The Free Press.

Hindelang, M. J. 1974. The Uniform Crime Reports revisited. *Journal of Criminal Justice* (Spring): 1–17.

————. 1976. *Criminal Victimization in Eight American Cities: A Descriptive Analysis of Common Theft and Assault.* Cambridge, Mass.: Ballinger.

Hornum, F. 1967. Two debates: France, 1791; England, 1956. In *Capital Punishment,* ed. T. Sellin, 55–76. New York: Harper and Row.

Huggins, M. D. and Straus, M. A. 1975. Violence and the social structure as reflected in children's books from 1850 to 1970. Paper presented at the 45th annual meeting of the Eastern Sociological Society.

Humphries, D. and Wallace, D. 1980. Capitalist accumulation and urban crime. *Social Problems* 28:179–93.

Johnston, J. 1972. *Econometric Methods.* New York: McGraw-Hill.

Jouvenal, B. 1966. Société d'études et de documentation économiques, industrielles et sociales. *Analyse et Prévision* 2:755–58.

Joyce, J. A. 1961. *Capital Punishment: A World View.* New York: Grove Press.

Kahn, R. L. 1972. Violent man: Who buys bloodshed and why. *Psychology Today,* June, 46–48, 83.

Kelman, H. C. and Lawrence, L. H. 1972. American response to the trial of Lt. William L. Calley. *Psychology Today,* June, 41–45, 78–81.

Kendall, M. G. 1973. *Time-Series.* London: Griffin.

Kitsuse, J. I. and Cicourel, A. V. 1963. A note on the use of official statistics. *Social Problems* 11:131–39.

Klein, L. R., Forst, B., and Filatov, V. 1978. The deterrent effect of capital punishment: An assessment of the estimates. In *Deterrence and Incapacitation: Estimating the Effects of Criminal Sanctions on Crime Rates,* ed. A. Blumstein, J. Cohen, and D. Nagin, 336–59. Washington, D.C.: National Academy of Sciences.

Krohn, M. 1976. Inequality, unemployment and crime: A cross-national analysis. *The Sociological Quarterly* 17:303–13.

Lane, R. 1969. Urbanization and criminal violence in the 19th Century: Massachusetts as a test case. In *The History of Violence in America,* ed. H. D. Graham and T. R. Gurr, 468–84. Washington, D.C.: U.S. Government Printing Office.

————. 1979. *Violent Death in the City: Suicide, Accident, and Murder in Nineteenth Century Philadelphia.* Cambridge, Mass.: Harvard University Press.

Leipman, M. 1930. *Krieq und Kriminalitat in Deutschland.* Stuttgart: Deutsche-Verlagsanstalt.

Leonard, A. E. 1952. *Crime Records in Police Management.* New York: Institute of Public Administration.

Levi, N. 1929. Statistica criminale e riforma della legislazione penale. In *Scritti in Onore di Enrico Ferri,* 267ff.

Lieberson, S. and Hansen, L. K. 1974. National development, mother tongue diversity, and the comparative study of nations. *American Sociological Review* 39:523–41.

Lifton, R. J. 1970. The veterans return. *New York Times,* 8 Nov. 1970, p. 32.

Lodhi, A. Q. and Tilly, C. 1973. Urbanization, crime and collective violence in 19th Century France. *American Journal of Sociology* 79:296–318.

Loftin, C. 1980. Alternative estimates of the impact of certainty and severity of punishment on levels of homicide in American states. In *Indicators of Crime and Criminal Justice: Quantitative Studies*, ed. S. E. Fienberg and A. J. Reiss, 75–81. Washington, D.C.: U.S. Government Printing Office.

Lowell, A. L. 1926. *Public Opinion in War and Peace*. Cambridge, Mass.: Harvard University Press.

Lunden, W. A. 1963. *War and Delinquency*. Ames, Iowa: The Art Press.

———. 1967. *Crimes and Criminals*. Ames: Iowa State University Press.

Lundman, R. J., Sykes, R. E., and Clark, J. P. 1978. Police control of juveniles: A replication. *Journal of Research in Crime and Delinquency* 15:74–91.

Maltz, M. D. 1977. Crime statistics: A historical perspective. *Crime and Delinquency* 23:32–40. Mannheim, H. 1941. *War and Crime*. London: Watts.

———. 1955. *Group Problems in Crime and Punishment*. London: Routledge and Kegan Paul.

———. 1965. *Comparative Criminology*. London: Routledge and Kegan Paul.

Mantell, D. M. and Pilisuk, M., eds. 1975. *Soldiers in and After Vietnam*. A special issue (Vol. 31) of the *Journal of Social Issues*.

Marx, G. T. 1970. Civil disorder and the agents of social control. *Journal of Social Issues* 26:19–57.

McCord, W. and McCord, J. 1959. *Origins of Crime: A New Evaluation of the Cambridge-Somerville Youth Study*. New York: Columbia University Press.

McHale, V. E. and Johnson, E. A. 1976–77. Urbanization, industrialization, and crime in Imperial Germany. *Social Science History* 1976. 1:45–78 and 1977, 1:210–47.

McLennan, B. 1970. *Crime in Urban Society*. New York: Dunellen.

Miller, D., Rosenthal, A., Miller, D., and Ruzek, S. 1971. Public knowledge of criminal penalties: A research report. In *Theories of Punishment*, ed. S. S. Grupp, 205–26. Bloomington: Indiana University Press.

Miller, W. B. 1967. Theft behavior in city gangs. In *Juvenile Gangs in Context: Theory, Research and Action*, ed. M. W. Klein, 25–38. Englewood Cliffs: Prentice-Hall.

Mulvihill, D. J. and Tumin, M. M. 1969. *Crimes of Violence*. National Commission on the Causes and Prevention of Violence, vols. 11–13. Washington, D.C.: U.S. Government Printing Office.

Murphy, E. M., Shirley, M. M., and Witmer, H. L. 1946. The incidence of hidden criminality. *American Journal of Orthopsychiatry* 16:686–95.

Naroll, R. 1962. *Data Quality Control: A New Research Technique*. New York: Free Press.

Naroll, R. and Cohen, R., eds. 1970. *A Handbook of Methods in Cultural Anthropology*. New York: Natural History Press. (Reprinted, New York: Columbia University Press, 1973.)

Naroll, R., Michik, G. L., and Naroll, F. 1980. Holocultural research methods. In *Handbook of Cross-Cultural Psychology: Methodology* (Vol. 2), ed. H. C. Triandis and J. W. Berry, 479–521. Boston: Allyn and Bacon.

Nettler, G. 1974. *Explaining Crime*. New York: McGraw-Hill.

Nevins, A. 1924. *The American States During and After the Revolution*. New York: Macmillan.

Ogburn, W. F. 1935. Factors in variation in crime among cities. *Journal of the American Statistical Society* 30: 12–13.

Ogburn, W. F. and Thomas, D. S. 1922. The influence of the business cycle on certain social conditions. *Quarterly Publication of the American Statistical Association* 18:324–40.

Parsons, C. 1917. The influence of war on crime. *Proceedings of the American Correctional Association,* 266–68.

Passell, P. and Taylor, J. B. 1976. The deterrence controversy: A reconsideration of the time series evidence. In *Capital Punishment in the United States,* ed. H. A. Bedau and C. Pierce, 359–71. New York: AMS Press.

Phillipson, M. 1974. *Understanding Crime and Delinquency: A Sociological Introduction.* Chicago: Aldine.

Piliavin, I. and Briar, S. 1964. Police encounters with juveniles. *American Journal of Sociology* 70:206–14.

Powell, E. 1966. Crime as a function of anomie. *Journal of Criminal Law, Criminology, and Police Science* 57:161–71.

President's Commission on Law Enforcement and the Administration of Justice. 1967. *Task Force Report: Crime and Its Impact—An Assessment.* Washington, D.C.: U.S. Government Printing Office.

Radzinowicz, L. 1971. Economic pressures. In *Crime and Justice, Volume I: The Criminal in Society,* ed. L. Radzinowicz and M. E. Wolfgang, 420–42. New York: Basic Books.

Reckless, W. C. 1942. The impact of war on crime, delinquency, and prostitution. *American Journal of Sociology* 48:378–86.

———. 1969. The use of the death penalty. *Crime and Delinquency* 15:43–56.

Remarque. E. M. 1931. *The Road Back.* New York: Little Brown.

Ross, R. A. and Benson, G. C. S. 1979. Criminal justice from East to West. *Crime and Delinquency* 25:76–86.

Roux, J. A. 1917. Ce que sera la criminalité après la guerre? *Revue Politique et Parlementaire* 91:27–42.

Russett, B. M. Alker, H. R., Deutsch, K. W., and Lasswell, H. D. 1964. *World Handbook of Political and Social Indicators.* New Haven: Yale University Press.

Santarelli, D. E., Work, C. R., and Velde, R. W. 1974a. *Crime in Eight American Cities.* Washington, D.C.: U.S. Department of Justice, July, 1974.

———. 1974b. *Crime in the Nation's Five Largest Cities.* Washington, D.C.: U.S. Department of Justice, April, 1974.

Scherer, K. R., Abeles, R. P., and Fischer, C. S. 1975. *Human Aggression and Conflict.* Englewood Cliffs: Prentice-Hall.

Schuessler, K. 1952. The deterrent influence of the death penalty. *Annals of the American Academy of Political and Social Science* 284:54–62.

Sellin, T. 1926. Is murder increasing in Europe? *Annals of the American Academy of Political and Social Science* 126:29–34.

———. 1931. The basis of a crime index. *Journal of Criminal Law and Criminology* 22:335–56.

———. 1937. *Research Memorandum on Crime in the Depression.* New York: Social Science Research Council.

———. 1942. *War and Crime: A Research Memorandum.* New York: Social Science Research Council.

———, ed. 1959. *The Death Penalty.* Philadelphia, Pa.: American Law Institute.

———. 1961. Capital punishment. *Federal Probation* 25:3–11.

———, ed. 1967. *Capital Punishment.* New York: Harper and Row.

———. 1981. *The Penalty of Death.* Beverly Hills: Sage.

Shelley, L. I. 1981. *Crime and Modernization: The Impact of Industrialization and Urbanization on Crime.* Carbondale, Ill.: Southern Illinois University Press.

Short, J. F. 1975. The National Commission on the Causes and Prevention of Violence: Reflections on the contributions of sociology and sociologists. In *Sociology and Public Policy: The Case of Presidential Commissions,* ed. M. Komarovsky, 61–91. New York: Elsevier.

Singer, J. D. and Small, M. 1972. *The Wages of War, 1816–1965: A Statistical Handbook.* New York: Wiley.

Skogan, W. G. 1976. The victims of crime: Some national survey findings. In *Criminal Behavior Systems,* ed. A. L. Guenther, 131–48. Chicago: Rand-McNally.

———. 1977a. The changing distribution of big-city crime: A multi-city time series analysis. *Urban Affairs Quarterly* 13:33–48.

———. 1977b. Dimensions of the dark figure of unreported crime. *Crime and Delinquency* 23:41–50.

———. 1981. *Issues in the Measurement of Victimization.* Washington, D.C.: U.S. Department of Justice, Bureau of Justice Statistics, June, 1981.

Smelser, N. J. 1976. *Comparative Methods in the Social Sciences.* Englewood Cliffs: Prentice-Hall.

Solnar, V. 1929. La guerre mondiale et la criminalité en Tchéchoslovaquie. *Revue de Droit Pénale* 9:858–93.

Sorokin, P. 1925. *The Sociology of Revolution.* Philadelphia: Lippincott.

———. 1928. *Contemporary Sociological Theories.* New York: Harper.

Sparks, R. F. 1976. Crimes and victims in London. In *Sample Surveys of the Victims of Crime,* ed. W. G. Skogan, 43–71. Cambridge, Mass.: Ballinger.

Sparks, R. F., Genn, H. G., and Dodd, D. J. 1977. *Surveying Victims.* New York: John Wiley.

Sumner, W. G. 1906. *Folkways: A Study of the Sociological Importance of Usages, Manners, Customs, Mores, and Morals.* Boston: Ginn.

Sutherland, E. H. 1925. Murder and the death penalty. *Journal of Criminal Law and Criminology* 15:522–29.

———. 1943. Crime. In *American Society in Wartime,* ed. W. F. Ogburn, 185–206. Chicago: University of Chicago Press.

———. 1956. Wartime crime. In *The Sutherland Papers,* ed A. Cohen, A. Lindesmith, and K. Schuessler, 120–28. Bloomington: Indiana University Press.

Sutherland, E. and Cressey, D. 1960. *Principles of Criminology.* Chicago: Lippincott.

———. 1970. *Criminology.* Philadelphia: Lippincott.

Szabo, D. 1960. *Crimes et Villes.* Louvain: Université Catholique.

Tanter, R. 1969. International war and domestic turmoil: Some contemporary evidence. In *The History of Violence in America,* ed. H. D. Graham and T. R. Gurr, 550–69. New York: Praeger.

Tarde, G. 1912. *Penal Philosophy.* Boston: Little Brown.

Tarniquet, H. 1968. Crime in the rapidly industrializing urban environment. *Revue Internationale de Criminologie et de Police Technique* 22:49–58.

Taylor, C. and Hudson, M. 1972. *World Handbook of Political and Social Indicators,* 2d ed. New Haven: Yale University Press.

Thomas, D. S. 1927. *Social Aspects of the Business Cycle.* New York: Alfred A. Knopf.

Tobias, J. J. 1967. *Crime and Industrial Society in the 19th Century.* London: Batsford.

U.S. Bureau of the Census. 1974. *Current Population Reports,* Series P-25, no. 519. Estimates of the Population of the United States, by Age, Sex, and Race: April 1, 1960 to July 1, 1973. Washington, D.C.: U.S. Government Printing Office.

U.S. Department of Justice, Bureau of Justice Statistics. 1982. *Sourcebook of Criminal Justice Statistics—1981.* Washington, D.C.: U.S. Government Printing Office.

Van de Haag, E. 1969. On deterrence and the death penalty. *Ethics* 78:280–88.

Van Vechten, C. C. 1942. Differential criminal case mortality in selected jurisdictions. *American Sociological Review* 7:833–39.

Velde, R. W., McQuade, H. F., Wormeli, P. K., Bratt, H., and Renshaw, B. H. 1976. *Criminal Victimization in the United States: A Comparison of 1973 and 1974 Findings.* Washington, D.C.: U.S. Department of Justice, May, 1976.

Velde, R. W., Work, C. R., and Holtzman, W. P. 1975. *Criminal Victimization Surveys in the Nation's Five Largest Cities.* Washington, D.C.: U.S. Department of Justice, April, 1975.

Velde, R. W., Wormeli, P. K., Bratt, H., and Renshaw, B. H. 1977. *Criminal Victimization in the United States: A Comparison of 1974 and 1975 Findings.* Washington, D.C.: U.S. Department of Justice, February, 1977.

Venter, H. J. 1962. Urbanization and industrialization as criminogenic factors in the Republic of South Africa. *International Review of Criminology* 20:59–71.

Verkko, V. 1953. General theoretical viewpoints in criminal statistics regarding real crime. *Transactions of the Westermarck Society,* 47–75. Copenhagen: E. Munksgaard.

———. 1956. Survey of current practice in criminal statistics. *Transactions of the Westermarck Society,* 5–33. Copenhagen: E. Munksgaard.

Vigderhous, G. 1978. Methodological problems confronting cross-cultural criminological research using official data. *Human Relations* 31:229–47.

Vold, G. B. 1932. Can the death penalty prevent crime? *The Prison Journal* (October) 3–8.

———. 1941. Crime in city and country areas. *Annals of the American Academy of Political and Social Sciences* 217:38–45.

———. 1952. Extent and trend of capital crimes in the United States. *Annals of the American Academy of Political and Social Science* 284:1–7.

Von Hentig, H. 1947. *Crime: Causes and Conditions.* New York: McGraw-Hill.

Wasserstrom, R. 1982. Capital punishment as punishment: Some theoretical issues and objections. *Midwest Studies in Philosophy* 7:473–502. Minneapolis: University of Minnesota Press.

Webb, E. J., Campbell, D. T., Schwartz, R. D., Sechrest, L., and Grove, J. B. 1981. *Nonreactive Measures in the Social Sciences.* Boston: Houghton-Mifflin.

Wecter, D. 1944. *When Johnny Comes Marching Home.* Cambridge, Mass.: Houghton-Mifflin.

Wellford, C. F. 1974. Crime and dimensions of nations. *International Journal of Criminology and Penology* 2:1–10.

Wheeler, S. 1967. Criminal statistics: A reformulation of the problem. *Journal of Criminal Law and Criminology* 58:317–24.

Willbach, H. 1948. Recent crimes and the veterans. *Journal of Criminal Law and Criminology* 38:501–08.

Wirth, L. 1940. Urbanism as a way of life. *American Journal of Sociology* 47: 743–55.

Wolf, P. 1971. Crime and development: An international comparison of crime rates. *Scandinanvian Studies in Criminology* 3:107–21.

Wolfgang, M. E. 1963. Uniform Crime Reports: A critical appraisal. *University of Pennsylvania Law Review*, 111:708–38.

———. 1967. International crime statistics: A proposal. *Journal of Criminal Law and Criminology* 58:65–69.

———. 1968. Urban crime. In *The Metropolitan Enigma*, ed. J. Q. Wilson, 245–81. Cambridge, Mass.: Harvard University Press.

Wolfgang, M. E. and Ferracuti, F. 1967. *The Subculture of Violence*. New York: Tavistock.

Zehr. H. 1974. The modernization of crime in Germany and France, 1830–1913. *Journal of Social History* 8:117–41.

———. 1976. *Crime and the Development of Modern Society: Patterns of Criminality in Nineteenth Century Germany and France*. Totowa, N. J.: Rowan and Littlefield.

Index